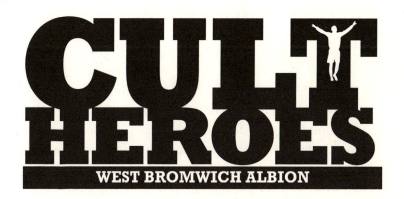

CULT HEROES

HEROES

WEST BROMWICH ALBION

Simon Wright

This edition first published by Pitch Publishing 2012

Pitch Publishing
A2 Yeoman Gate
Yeoman Way
Durrington
BN13 3QZ
www.pitchpublishing.co.uk

A CIP catalogue record is available for this book
from the British Library

ISBN 978-1-9080516-3-9

Typesetting and origination by Pitch Publishing.

Printed in India by Replika Press Pvt. Ltd.

CULT HEROES

WEST BROMWICH ALBION

Contents

Acknowledgements

SO MANY PEOPLE to thank. There are the Albion historians Colin Mackenzie, Steve Carr and Kevin Powell, without whom this volume would lack essential credibility.

Proofreading is a tedious, joyless process so I'm grateful to Amanda Hume for proofing this updated version, while not forgetting the proofers for the original also included Steve Carr and Glynis Wright.

Literally thanks for the memories. So many kind people volunteered thoughts or rummaged amongst their records and yet hardly any of them needing his or her arms twisted. Among the gallant band were: Andy Hyams, Colin Simpson, Tim Joyner, Jon Aroussi, Merv Scobie, Chris Pascoe, Steve Sant, Gary Brookes, Mike Harrison, Peter Whitehouse, Ian Thomson, Dave Watkin, Alex Chapman, David Worton, Dave Morgan, Shay Dunne, David L. Paget, John Goddard, Keith Cotter, Tony Jones, Neil and Charlie Reynolds, Dennis Brennan, Rick Janowski, John Clegg, Josie and Des Garbett, Wendy and the late John Maxfield, Laraine Astle, Martin Lewis, Carly Lewis, John Woodward, Brian Maydew, Stuart Basson, Gerald Frost, The Royal Regiment of Fusiliers Museum, the South Wales Borderers Museum archivists, Chris Flanagan, Cyril Randle, Ian Thomson, Harold Salt, Richard Brentnall, Robert Plant, Peter George, Ray Matthews, Terry Box, Keith Cotter, Ben Payne, Frank Summers, (Super) Bobby Taylor, John Groarke, Mark Hitcox, Mark Pumphrey, Mick Brown, Andy Jenkins, Pete Smith, Ray Wilson, John Habberley, Ally Robertson, Ed Vilade, Janette Carlucci, James Vilade, Alison Wheatley archivist for King Edwards School, Joe Mayo, Tam Bullimore, Dean Wood and Derek Kevan. Apologies and thanks to anyone who remains overlooked. Chris Lepkowski deserves a mention for just being himself.

And finally a big thank you to Adrian Goldberg for getting me the original gig and my latest publishers for not being too prescriptive.

Simon Wright

Foreword

by Laraine Astle

I SAW ALBION for the first time at Leicester on 30th September 1964. I didn't know I was going until my Jeff signed his contract three hours before, and I didn't know anything then about West Bromwich, other than somebody said they are called the Throstles.

I went into that tall, tall, stand at Filbert Street. I'd never seen anything like it. I thought I was going to fall off, but I reckoned I'd better get used to it, and do my bit so I shouted, *"Come on you Throstles"* over and over. Then somebody told me nobody ever uses that word! From then on, I thought, *"Right Laraine, I need to find out about West Bromwich."* I had to really quickly because me, Jeff and little Dorice were living there.

It didn't take me long to find out that supporters really love their centre-forwards. My Jeff, Tony Brown, of course, and before him came Ronnie Allen – they love their goalscorers, their heroes. Later still brought the talents of people like Cyrille Regis to the Hawthorns and supporters again appreciated their efforts, their goals. And always there was the rule that if players gave everything and didn't cheat them, the fans would always love them for it, and that applies to this very day. If one of them does something supporters like, even just by taking the time and trouble to talk with them before games, not coming the *"Great I Am"* all the time like some do, suddenly, in their eyes, they're not just players any more, they're respected, treasured, cherished, even, and for some, that love and respect lasts far longer than the time they finally hang up their boots; whatever the occasion, whenever they're seen turning up at The Hawthorns for some important game or other, so respected are they, they're literally mobbed, just as my Jeff was when he was alive.

And not just older supporters, either; the younger ones know all about the older players simply because their own dads and mums have wonderful memories, too, and want to share them with their own children and grandchildren as well. On top of looking at recent Albion men, this book is also a lovely way of making sure that the next generation of Albion supporters get to understand the past efforts of all those players long since gone, whose names, whose very souls, even, would otherwise remain buried in old newspapers.

After nearly 50 years, I reckon I know lots about the Baggies but I know even more about their wonderful, loyal, respectful and friendly supporters, and this book is mostly aimed at them. I once heard captain Graham Williams (he'll always be the captain to me and my Jeff) say: *"you're not supporters, you're friends."* I couldn't have put it better myself.

Introduction

The original 2005 criteria for this title was rigid but intriguing, namely to select 20 cult heroes to represent the full history of West Bromwich Albion. It's always worth underlining the incredible breath and richness of this unique Black Country social institution, which few other clubs can match.

About half the selection – The King, SuperBob, Willie, Ossie, Big Cyrille, The Bomber, Ronnie Allen, Billy Bassett and Jesse Pennington – picked themselves. The other ten were mainly chosen to cover the remaining decades. It was impossible to please all of the people all of the time and I was on the receiving end of much stick from certain individuals for not featuring their personal favourite. Most couldn't or wouldn't see the subtle distinction between 'best player' and cult hero. At the time of the original edition, the media made much of the "controversial" (their word) inclusion of Lee Hughes. The passing of time has since eased concerns.

The most exciting chapters for me to write then as now were those of Harold Bache and Tommy Magee, their stories previously sadly underplayed. I took much pleasure from rewriting their histories to bring these fine men back into the public arena. The profile of Bache in particular has increased in the last five years as a direct consequence of publication.

As a first-time author, I was highly gratified by the success of 'Cult Heroes'. With the entire print run sold out by 2011, there was an obvious opportunity for a reprint and to include new material and sources which have come to light during the intervening years. The publishers also encouraged me to add a more contemporary cult hero so I opted for Tony Mowbray – a decent and honest man in a cynical age.

Just as before I've leaned towards a "warts and all" approach for each cult hero. I remain convinced that this is the most inclusive and honest approach. There's only so much saccharine that readers can take!

Enjoy this updated version and if it's as successful as the first, who knows? Like a village bus service, there may be another one along in five years' time.

Simon Wright

Bob Roberts

1885-1890 & 1891-92: 400+ games, 2 goals

IN THE BEGINNING, there was Long Bob. And a very young club called West Bromwich Albion, who rose spectacularly from being just another team playing on the wide-open spaces of Dartmouth Park to FA Cup winners in just seven years. Here was pure synergy, with man and club feeding off each other.

Most sources concur that Robert John Roberts was born in April 1859 in West Bromwich. Thus at 20, he was in the prime of his youth when a completely new football team needed players in 1879. Robert had previously played for West Bromwich Strollers as early as November 1878, and prior to that may also have played for his school – Christ Church. As well as players, the new team needed funds and sensibly enough would-be players were asked to pay a subscription of sixpence (around 3p) to get the club going. Bob Roberts is said to have been the first to hand his money over. Such is the stuff that legends are made of.

The Albion team was new, the game was really still in its infancy, and local newspapers took very little notice of the sport. Despatching a reporter to a game was completely out of the question, and the only way a club might – and it was only 'might' – see any reference to their deeds in the local press was if a club official took the trouble to compile their own report and send it in.

Few players had a single position at that time, as not only team formations, but sometimes, even team numbers, varied. So it doesn't come as any great surprise that Bob played in different positions in different games – mainly full-back or half-back (midfield), or even up front, according to the reports that featured most of the 20 games that WBA participated in during that inaugural season. There's enough evidence to suggest he was probably not a regular performer. Neither is there any record of him playing in the famous friendly against Black Lake Victoria on 13th December 1879, a game, which for many years, was believed to be Albion's first ever game, but is now known to be their sixth.

Details are inevitably sketchy. Those match reports which did appear were limited to a very brief description of the play, a name drop for players who'd performed well, and occasionally, goalscorers might be listed. Roberts was never mentioned for any meritorious performances, but was noted as scoring for Albion in a 3-0 victory over Smethwick Holy Trinity on 28th February 1880.

Clumsy Big Bob just wasn't cutting the mustard. Someone summed up his outfield contribution thus: *"As a forward he was useless, and as a half-back, or back, he could stop a man, but invariably missed the ball."* It's entirely realistic to imagine him drifting away to try his luck elsewhere, had not persons unknown come up with the idea of giving him a go as a goalkeeper.

Curiously, this was the one position in the side that had a sitting tenant. Sam Biddleston always protected Albion's goal. And then one day he didn't. On 18th December 1880 against a team from Wednesbury is the earliest account of Bob Roberts appearing in goal for Albion for the first time. Quite what prompted the change for Biddleston is not completely clear. Certainly he never played for WBA again. At some point, Sam emigrated to North America, so perhaps the one factor prompted the other.

Beyond the classic schoolboy reason of going between the bare posts (no goal nets until 1891) – because he wasn't any good anywhere else – Bob's height and weight were distinct advantages. Barging the goalkeeper, whether he had the ball or not, was a legitimate tactic of the time. Bob was a very big lad. Depending on which source is trusted, he was between 6ft 1in & 6ft 4in tall; for a variety of reasons, people in the 1880s were far smaller than today, and such height made him a comparative giant. The few team pictures that survive show Bob standing several inches above his tallest team-mate. Even today, 6ft 4in would make him one of the Baggies' tallest-ever men. Add his weight (accounts vary between 12 and 14st) and you had a goalkeeper with the solidity of the proverbial brick outhouse. Yet despite his physique, he was remarkably agile, had a cool temperament, and a kindly good nature – all the attributes of a gentle giant.

His debut as a custodian was not a happy one. Albion suffered what may well have been their only defeat that season, going down 0-2 to Wednesbury Royal George. However, despite this setback, and possibly the odd mutter of, "*Can he actually play anywhere?*" the match reports that are available suggest he retained his position right to the season's end.

Other than his build, Roberts was unusual in his choice of occupation. In its early days, the team was comprised entirely of local men, many of them working for spring manufacturer George Salter & Co, one of the town's largest employers. The strong links between club and company were to be maintained for several decades to come, not just players, but stewards and gatekeepers, too. Roberts, however, was a journeyman plasterer, a trade learned from his widowed father James, with whom he lived at 31 Queen Street, virtually in West Bromwich's town centre. With five children to support, life could not have been easy for Roberts senior.

The rise of the fledgling club became noteworthy in their third season, when Albion battled their way into the Birmingham Cup semi-final. At this time, the Birmingham Cup was the biggest game in town. Reaching the last four equalled the achievement of West Bromwich Dartmouth, previously the town's biggest club, who were already on a downward slope. The Dartmouth decided to concentrate on cricket, leaving the town's footballing baton with Albion. Indeed, Dartmouth offered the newcomers the chance to use their enclosed ground during the football season.

WBA's upward momentum continued. Twelve months later, they set their cap at two competitions. In the Birmingham Cup, defeating Coseley, and Wolves (4-2) gave them a semi-final place against Wednesbury Old Athletic. Once again, they were bested in a closely-fought 2-1 defeat, "*exceptionally brilliant*" custodial work by Roberts keeping Albion in the fight. His reputation was building, and there were suggestions that he was worth a trial to play for the District. Most of all, he was noticed by his own supporters. The *West*

Bromwich Free Press recorded that *'Roberts received continued applause for the splendid defence he exhibited.' The Athlete* was impressed with both custodians that day: *'The feature was the excellence of the keeping of the goalkeepers of both sides. They were both kept busy, and both warded off some difficult shots, and both exhibited a skill, coolness and judgement rarely found.'*

MEANWHILE, IN THE Staffordshire Cup, the Albion would not be denied their first trophy, and in the second round, they knocked out Birmingham Cup holders Aston Villa. This was the first-ever meeting between the two clubs, prompting both sets of supporters to greet each other cordially with lumps of turf and stones. Once again, Roberts was catching the eye: *"The play of Roberts in goal was superb,"* commented *The Free Press*, following Albion's unexpected success in a replay. Two more such victories gave them a place in the Staffordshire Cup Final, at Stoke.

The Albion team travelled to the Potteries on 21st April 1883 by train, with team and supporters mixed together. However, nobody had thought of how the players would get from station to ground, so presumably, they walked. Not ideal preparation, and so it was no great surprise that the weary visitors were pressed back by a rampant Potteries side; Bob was kept busy – too busy – trying to shut Stoke out. As one correspondent from *The Athlete* had it, *"several rattling shots were sent spinning away by Roberts"* before Stoke inevitably took the lead. Stung by the goal, Albion fought back bravely to score twice, only for the home side to equalise by the interval. With 15 minutes remaining, George Bell put the Albion ahead again, and although City pressed in the closing stages, West Bromwich held on for a famous victory. *The Athlete's* correspondent chipped in, of course: *"Roberts may take a lot of credit for the win by his fine keeping,"'* was his post-match verdict.

Long Bob was soon creating firsts of his own: come October 1883, Bob became the first Albion player to take part in a representative fixture, turning out for Probables v Improbables, a trial match to select a Birmingham FA team for the then popular inter-association games. *"Roberts, in goal, was a veritable wonder, and I should think, at the present time, he is undoubtedly the best man for the position in the district,"* commented *The Athlete*.

Sure enough, Bob featured in Birmingham's 4-1 victory over Sheffield, in which *"the feature of the match was the grand goal keeping of Roberts,"* according to *The Athlete*, whilst the *Birmingham Gazette* added, *"had it not been for the magnificent form displayed by Roberts in goal, they* (Sheffield) *must have scored at least a couple more points."* His performance was so good that he received special congratulations from the president of the association.

The following year, such was the goalkeeper's cult status that dozens, possibly even hundreds, of Albion followers deserted their side's match against Walsall Swifts to give the popular custodian backing at the Aston Lower Grounds, where he was playing for Birmingham v Glasgow. A few weeks earlier, Bob had really endeared himself to the club's followers by declining an offer from Preston Zingari to sign for them (at a time when professionalism had not yet been legalised). Indeed, this was just one of several attempts by other clubs to lure away 'The Prince Of Goalkeepers'. This was the downside of West Bromwich Albion playing clubs further and further afield, notably in embryonic footballing-hotbed Lancashire, following their Staffordshire Cup triumph. Roberts was hot property, but his loyalty endeared him further to Albion fans.

Bob was to represent Birmingham several times in the years to come, against Sheffield, Glasgow, Nottinghamshire and London. In the latter game, the *Gazette* commented *"Roberts' services... were called into requisition... and by some judicious play, maintained his reputation as an accomplished goal keeper... each time the ball eluded the vigilance of the backs, Roberts, with a coolness seldom seen between the posts, averted the shots."*

He was also later selected for the annual Players v Gentlemen fixture, one of the top events of the social calendar, played at Kennington Oval in the presence of H.R.H. The Prince Of Wales. Reputedly, HRH was so struck by the feats of the big goalkeeper, he repeatedly cried, *"Well done, Bob."* Such was his reputation locally and nationally; the goalkeeper was much in demand over the years. He played a part in least two international trials (and had to turn down others due to injury), and even once played for his county, Staffordshire, against Lancashire.

IN BOB'S DAY, goal keepers occasionally wandered upfield when they were bored, generally when particularly hapless opponents were unable to mount any attacks worth mentioning. Not for Bob the rather mundane method of scoring via a freak long-range clearance (stories about him scoring from a long punt in the FA Cup v Derby Junction appear on close inspection to be incorrect). No, no – he wanted a real goal, and managed at least two, possibly three. The first came in a 15-0 Birmingham Cup victory over Bloxwich in November 1884, one source even suggesting he found the net twice.

His other 'proper' goal followed much later as part of a 23-0 massacre of Burton Wanderers in the Staffordshire Cup, Bob happily playing in midfield for much of the game. A Wanderers breakaway was highly unlikely because they only entered Albion's half to kick off after each goal. *The Free Press* reported, *"Considerable amusement was caused by Roberts heading the ball and running up amongst the spectators, some of whom called out and invited him to have a drink."* Just before he dribbled past a Burton player to register Albion's 19th goal, one warning shot from Bob hit a post. Burton clearly didn't heed the warning.

Content with his contribution, Bob then got back among the backs. Incidentally, an invitation to 'have a drink' was not such an outrageous one in that era: much like Victorian sailors with their daily rum issues, and Black Country chain-makers in nearby Netherton, Albion players had an official beer allowance. One newspaper described the scene: *"There is something very amusing in the way in which the allowance of beer to each thirsty Throstle is doled out by the trainer, any attempt at further amounts being sternly put down"*

Although club records for goalscoring are incomplete, it's likely that Bob remains the only WBA goalkeeper to score in open play. Penalty kicks were not introduced until Bob's day was nearly done, so there was little or no opportunity for the giant footballer to put his spectacular weight behind such a golden scoring opportunity.

Bob's club side continued to make progress, again putting Villa in their place in an FA Cup replay in 1885. During the course of their first meeting, *"…first half was noticeable for the remarkable fine goalkeeping of Roberts,"* as Albion escaped from enemy territory with a goalless draw. In the re-match, Bob had a rare rush of blood to the head. A Villa forward kicked him, so he kicked him back: the severity of the impact upon the opponent is not recorded, sadly. The visitors were given a free kick and the matter was forgotten. Cup holders Blackburn Rovers eventually ended Albion's run at the quarter-final stage: with home advantage, the

Staffordshire side fancying their chances until Roberts cried off with rheumatics. Rovers scored twice, and the feeling abounded that Big Bob would have stopped both goals.

Villa took a measure of revenge by inflicting heavy defeat in the Birmingham Charity Cup, though, as *The Athlete* reported, *"Roberts defended his charge in his best style, he saved many times in a most marvellous manner, and those shots that passed him were such that no (other) keeper could have stopped under the same circumstances."*

For a young club to reach the last eight of the national FA competition was impressive enough, but ever the pioneers, Albion wanted more and the following season, went all the way to the Cup Final, a first not just for them, but also for any Midlands side. Admittedly, five home draws and a bye aided their cause, but the path was not that straightforward. The Old Carthusians, for instance, were defeated by a single goal in Round Five, with no little thanks to West Brom's giant goalkeeper, as *The Athlete* noted: *"Roberts had not a lot to do. He kept out several beauties, but two called for special mention, so smartly did he act when the goal seemed lost."*

AND THE FA Cup run handed Roberts another opportunity to lay claim to being the first cult hero amongst Albion players. The Baggies beat Small Heath – latterly Birmingham City – 4-0 in the semi-final. During the game, a group of Birmingham youths invaded the pitch, surrounding and attacking the players. Unabashed, Long Bob laid out one hooligan caught sneaking up behind him, and presumably deterred anyone else from being so rash. As officials, supported by police, tried to clear the pitch, the hooligan gang made for the exit, but as they did, by way of a 'leaving present', they hurled every available missile at parked vehicles. Hooliganism, apparently, is nothing new.

West Bromwich were again up against their conquerors from the previous year, powerful Blackburn Rovers, at the Oval. The Lancashire side had won the cup in both the last two years, and were going for a hat-trick, with a side largely unchanged in those three years. This was a stiff task for the Staffordshire rookies, but they were well supported, and actually came close to an upset: *"Roberts had not a great deal to do in goal, but he played in his best style, and generally repelled all shots, and some were extremely difficult,"* wrote one correspondent as Albion's last line of defence gave them a secure base from which to attack. And attack they did, but their forwards froze in front of goal, and the game finished goalless, mighty Rovers subsequently feeling the need to make excuses about their players rushing their lunch in order to explain away their sudden, but perceptible lapse in form.

In the replay, at Derby: "*Roberts defended his charge in capital style and repelled three or four shots that would have undoubtedly beaten a less trustworthy custodian.*" But even with Bob giving everything, Rovers won 2-0. Albion's best chance had come and gone in London.

Albion at least lifted the Birmingham Cup Final for the first time, beating Walsall Swifts in a replay. In the re-match, a local correspondent enthused how Roberts: "*was in his best form, and as he was kept pretty busy all through, he had many opportunities of displaying his best form, and often he saved shots and repelled attacks few goalkeepers could have successfully met.*" Remarkably, big Bob turned provider, with a mighty long throw just before half time, from which George Woodhall scored. It was Albion's first shot on goal. Other than a short spell in the second half, the West Bromwich side needed to defend, often grimly, to hang onto their single goal lead. Albion also went on to secure the Staffordshire Cup, but that was an old challenge, previously conquered to death, almost. Albion now had bigger ambitions, they'd been so close to the FA Cup, and, having but briefly tasted the tempting fruit hanging on the vine, they wanted more.

And more they had next season. Four opponents were defeated before the Albion team travelled on a regular train service to Notts County in February 1887 for a quarter-final tie. Or rather most of the team did. Long Bob, not for the first time and as befits such an outstanding man, was doing things somewhat differently. Being a keeper, and therefore eccentric in nature – even in those early days they enjoyed a certain 'reputation' – he elected to travel on the excursion train instead, which then arrived an hour late. Remarkably, the Notts County captain, Cursham, agreed to delay the kick-off until Long Bob finally arrived on foot, after sprinting from the station in his white jersey, full-length white trousers and a pair of hob-nail boots, an unusual sight which must have prompted at least some of the locals to wonder whether or not the local asylum had just lost one of its patients. Sadly, the reaction of passers-by to this giant man pounding the streets in a tearing hurry is not recorded: more pertinently, neither are comments from his concerned team-mates. Cursham may well have bitterly regretted his generosity, Albion going 3-1 up before his side could build up any sort of attacking momentum. When they did, the tardy custodian blocked their way. *"Notts improved and again and again attacked, giving Roberts no end of chances to sustain his reputation. This he nobly did."*

If West Bromwich were to reach the final, they needed to overcome the might of Preston North End, that era's answer to modern-day Chelsea, in the semi-Final at Nottingham. But trains once again so nearly undid Bob. This time, he missed one completely, and was obliged to take a later one, so when the players took to the field, Roberts was nowhere to be seen. Then, with the game about to start, the crowd behind the goal dramatically parted, and there was the missing goalkeeper. Wearing his football gear, his modesty protected by a long overcoat, he leapt over the ropes and took his place in front of the goal as if his absence had never occurred. His dramatic late arrival didn't appear to disrupt his concentration unduly.

"Roberts' goal keeping was magnificent,' enthused *The Athlete, "and contributed largely to the victory of the Albion. Long Bob was kept busy, and did his work magnificently."* Albion equalised an early Preston goal, then added two more of their own while the Lancashire club were unable to find any way past Roberts. It was a magnificent display from the custodian, one that made his name nationally.

Their Cup Final opponents at the Oval were fierce rivals Aston Villa. On the day, in front of 15,000 spectators, Albion looked the better side – until their opponents changed their tactics and made better use of the wings. From then on, the Birmingham side were on top. Then came disaster: believing winger Dennis Hodgetts to be well offside, Long Bob made no attempt to stop his goalbound shot, even though he could have done so easily. The goal stood, much to his embarrassment. *The Athlete* offered scant consolation: *"No blame can be attached to Roberts, who had more to do than Warner* (the Villa keeper) *and did it right well – his reputation as a goal keeper was rather enhanced than damaged by his splendid goal keeping on Saturday."*

Once ahead, Villa increased the pressure and *"the goalkeeping of Roberts was now seen at its best; he saved several times miraculously."* Villa Captain Archie Hunter completed the scoring in the 88th minute when he ran at Roberts with the ball, the subsequent sickening collision leaving both men prostrate on the turf, but Hunter was just able (or conscious?) enough to poke the ball over the line with his foot. The defeat deeply shocked supporters far more used to winning: when the weary Albion party finally reached West Bromwich (admittedly at 4.00am on Sunday morning), there was absolutely no one there to meet them.

BOB ROBERTS HAD thus far been denied the kudos of being a cup-winner, but by way of compensation, he quickly found himself able to proudly describe himself as *Bob Roberts, England International*. In January, he'd taken part in an international trial (North v South) at Kennington Oval, in itself a milestone for any West Bromwich Albion man. Thanks to his astonishing display in the FA Cup semi-final against Preston, widely regarded as the finest of his career, his England call-up was sealed. The "Prince of Goal keepers" made his international debut against the Scots in March 1887, and was also reserve for the Wales game. Bob was the first Albion player to represent his country, and was so proud of his achievement; he wore his cap in every game he played thereafter. "*Roberts kept goal well and fairly earned his cap – some of his saves were really brilliant – he was not the cause of losing, and he was awfully hampered by the backs*" commented *The Athlete*. Two more caps were to follow in the next few years, both against Ireland.

In 1888, Albion reached the FA Cup Final for the third season in succession, a 2-0 third round victory over Wolves achieved after Roberts had kept Albion on level terms at half-time. In the semi-final versus Derby Junction, Roberts, along with full-backs Aldridge and Green, kept Albion level before West Brom could bang in three goals. There was high praise from the *Free Press* "....*two of the shots were the finest shots that ever a custodian had to manipulate, and few men but Roberts could have dealt with them as he did.*"

In the Final, Albion were predictably underdogs against proud Preston North End, as they had been when the two sides met in the semi-final a season earlier. But this was an Albion side victorious in over 80 per cent of their games that term, a team now boasting talented newcomers like Billy Bassett in their ranks. The meeting of two such fine teams created much interest, and for the first time ever in the competition's history, the gates were closed before kick-off, with 17,000 crammed inside the Oval.

Preston pressed early and *"for twenty minutes or so, Roberts & co had no end of work to do."* The Midlanders hit back strongly, though, and eventually took the lead. Stung, North End rallied, equalised, and then laid siege to the West Bromwich goal. The Midlanders defended stoutly, *"shots from their forwards were returned by Roberts, whose goal keeping was most remarkable,"* wrote the correspondent for the *Times*. The man from the *Standard* added, *"Roberts goal keeping was brilliant all through the game."* While Roberts was keeping Preston out at one end, Bassett was worrying the Lancastrians at the other end, his perfect cross setting up Woodhall to strike the decisive goal. Albion had won the FA Cup at last. Referee Major Marindin, who doubled up as trophy presenter, praised the *"indomitable pluck and perseverance"* of the Midlanders.

Albion also played in the Birmingham & Staffs Cup finals, making it the third year running they'd featured in the finals of all three of the main cup competitions entered. In this final pre-league season, such progress maintained the club's income, and arguably more importantly, acted as a powerful homing beacon for talented local players. The Birmingham Cup was lost 3-2 to Villa, but that game was also notable for some rare criticism of Albion's ever popular keeper. Harsh words for such an outstanding keeper were almost unknown, and stemmed from the big custodian's habit of frequently appealing to the referee rather than listening for the whistle. It's likely that this lack of concentration may have contributed to Villa's first goal.

The Staffs Cup proved something of a marathon for Albion. Stoke were despatched 1-0 in the semi-final, with no little thanks to their last line of defence, who were *"kept uncomfortably busy."* The final against Wolves needed three games: after a goalless first encounter, the *Free Press* reported: *"Roberts defended his charge admirably,"* in a 1-1 draw after extra time, whilst *"Roberts was not to be beaten, the spectators loudly applauding his brilliant and lightning-like save,"* in the third and final game. However, Bob's efforts weren't enough, and the Wanderers eventually won the day.

1888-89 BROUGHT WITH it the formation of the Football League: unsurprisingly, being such a powerful footballing force and current Cup holders, Albion were founder members. Although the League would quickly gain in importance, its initial impact was not great, with some clubs outside its auspices attracting larger attendances. Bob Roberts played in every league game that first season, despite some laments that his form was now deserting him and deputy Joe Reader deserved his chance to shine. The League was done and dusted by the end of February, with Preston the runaway champions, while West Bromwich finished in sixth spot. Come the draw for the last four of the FA Cup, the newly-crowned League Champions ended up facing Albion – the third such meeting of the two in the cup in consecutive seasons. Despite Roberts *"effecting brilliant saves"*, North End won by a single goal and went on to clinch the double.

In October 1889, the goal keeper displayed his rebellious streak when he participated in an unofficial match at Walsall; unsurprisingly, the FA were distinctly unamused. They suspended Roberts for four games, three of which were league fixtures against Villa, Bolton and Derby.

West Brom were now encountering something of a lean patch, a whole twelve months elapsing without winning any silverware. They came closest in the Staffordshire Senior Cup, reaching the final though they were fortunate to do so. It appears most likely that in April 1890, Bob had an accident at a hotel when he fell down a flight of stairs. His body was heavily bandaged into a rigid position that did not allow him to bend at all. This small handicap didn't prevent him playing against semi-final opponents Walsall Town Swifts, who were unaware of his difficulties until too late. With Long Bob displaying the kind of superhuman powers that all cult heroes are blessed, Albion won 2-1.

TO WIN NOTHING was disappointing in itself, but nowhere near as shocking as the news that Bob Roberts was leaving! In May 1890, instead of accepting club terms for the new season, Bob told Councillor Heckis, chairman of the Albion committee, that he'd had a better offer from Sunderland Albion.

Imitation Albion badly wanted to be top dog in the North-Eastern coastal town, and with rivals Sunderland freshly elected to the league elite, the other Sunderland side felt a need to push the boat out. Their formal offer to the big keeper was 50 shillings (£2.50) per match, plus a summer job that would guarantee him £2 per week. In addition, there was also the offer of a public house (Roberts was the licensee at The Three Horse Shoes Inn on High Street, West Bromwich, at the time).

These terms, highly generous for the period, were far in excess of what Albion could offer. Naturally, the money was tempting, but moving from the Black Country and leaving behind the club that he'd done so much to build, was a wrench. The clinching factor, though, proved to be his sisters' relocation to the North East.

West Bromwich Albion were furious, and set up a sub-committee to *"consider what action could be taken against Roberts for his infringement of contract"*. In practical terms, the answer was actually nothing at all. The keeper was out of contract, and had signed the deal with Sunderland before Councillor Heelis could even raise the matter with the full WBA Committee.

The Free Press summed up supporters' stunned reaction to the news: *"The history of Bob Roberts is the history of the Albion club and vice-versa, and most people regard his severance from the club as about the least likely event that could happen. Whether he has taken a wise step only time can show, but it is about the most formidable blow the Albion could have received. It is no easy thing for Roberts to leave the club he put the first sixpence in to form, and possibly he wishes now he could undo what has been done."*

No sooner had he signed the contract, Roberts was having doubts about the move. Once located in the North East, he quickly became homesick: worse, his wife was now unwell, and thus he was quickly exploring ways of getting back home. He tried to focus on his football instead, being an ever present in league fixtures, and his efforts helping Sunderland Albion finish runners-up in the Football Alliance, which later became adopted as the Second Division of the Football League. Bob even collected more representative honours, appearing in the Football Alliance v Football League fixture at Sheffield. However, Sunderland Albion received virtually no support in its bid to follow Sunderland into the Football League, and within a year had folded.

IN THE MEANTIME, on 2nd March 1891, Roberts returned to Stoney Lane to play in a benefit match for Charlie Perry, and made it very clear then that he wanted to return to West Bromwich. And indeed he did, returning to his native Black Country to play in the final of the West Bromwich Charity Cup for WBA v Wednesbury Old Athletic in May 1891. Probably to the disgruntlement of keeper Joe Reader, Bob Roberts was immediately given his place back in Albion's first team goal for the 1891-92 season. The new season started in fine style, Albion crushing the reigning champions, Everton, 4-0 at Stoney Lane, *The Free Press* commenting: *"Roberts was always on the alert, playing a specially meritorious game."*

Unfortunately, Albion's form then dipped, taking only two points from ten games in October and November, during a spell when Roberts and Reader shared the goal keeping duties. Initially Bob's form was good, but he was playing under the strain of knowing his wife was seriously ill, and his form quickly deteriorated. She died in October 1891, after just three years of marriage. Bob understandably missed games following his wife's death; he was then suspended for a week after failing to follow committee instructions in a game at Sunderland, before finally being dropped because his form was just not good enough. Such was his loss of heart and form that he even played badly for the reserves.

Reader was restored to the side permanently in late November, and league form recovered to some extent, though not enough for Albion to avoid the ignominy of having to apply for re-election. Despite this, Albion went on to win the FA Cup again, beating the Villa 3-0 in what proved to be the last final played at Kennington Oval. Roberts missed this and only earned a recall to the side when Reader was absent, playing for the Football League against the Scottish League.

Even then, Bob wasn't himself in the 2-2 draw with Stoke City (April 1892), and *The Free Press* admitted *"it was only due to the very poor display of Roberts between the uprights that The Throstles did not win, both the goals he let through being soft ones."*

At 33, his skills apparently deserting him, the end was imminent. Bob had played around 400 senior games with WBA all-told, and this was a wretched way for a genuine West Brom original to end a fine career. Even sadder was his decision to sign for Aston Villa the following term. He quickly realised this was no way to end his career and left after only turning out only four times for the Villains.

HE MOVED BACK to the North East, where he settled for the remainder of his life, working as a plasterer in Sunderland. He died at his home in Byker, Newcastle on 20th October 1929 at the age of 64. He never forgot his roots. Whenever Albion were in the North East, he always went to the match and was generally the guest of the club at dinner.

Even though surviving archives permit us no more than teasing hints about the personality of Albion's first significant goalkeeper, I like to perceive Bob as an 19th century Brian Jensen, a local version of the gentle Dane though lacking the dehabilitating effects of 'condor' moments which so blighted Jensen's career. Roberts was a giant-sized inspiration to a generation of Black Country folk, a living embodiment of a superb Albion side, much in the way that would-be young black players were inspired by Cyrille almost a century later. After Bob, size mattered in West Bromwich and with so many subsequent crowd favourites standing over 6ft tall, it still matters today.

Billy Bassett

1886-1899: 500+ games, 150+ goals

THE DARTMOUTH PARK Band played *See the Conquering Heroes Come* over and over again. The famous West Bromwich Albion team and the FA Cup were home, driving through the town in a four-horse carriage. The band played on and on until the early hours as thousands of supporters cheered their team. It was March 1888, and 19-year-old Billy Bassett had just made himself rather famous.

The Baggies had been rank outsiders to lift the cup, even though this was their third straight appearance in the final. Their opponents were Preston, "Proud Preston", who just a season later would combine an FA Cup win with the first ever League Championship. The mighty Preston, who, even before that first ever 'double' triumph, were genuinely thought to be invincible after 43 straight wins, who took their pick of the best Scottish footballers, who'd scored 50 goals just reaching the final... against 11 lads from in or around West Bromwich who each received ten shillings (50p) "expenses" a week.

Legend has it the Preston players were so confident of success they asked for permission to be photographed with the cup before the game. Referee Major Mandarin angrily denied the request. Mandarin was a traditionalist who had no truck with imported Scottish professionals.

Albion took a surprise lead in the final, thanks to Bassett's approach play. He pounced on a poor clearance from the PNE keeper, sprinting down the right flank and crossed perfectly for Jem Bayliss to score from close range. Another effort hit a post shortly after the interval. His speed off the mark, and astuteness in spotting an opening, often bewildered his adversaries, and although Preston equalised soon after the interval, it was Billy who again made his mark, creating an opening for Woodhall, whose shot was turned on to a post by Bayliss.

Perhaps inevitably, it was Bassett who provided the match-winning pass for Woodhall to score the goal that brought the cup to the Black Country for the first time. *The Free Press* reported *"....the little one, after the first ten minutes, played with a confidence and skill which was perfectly astonishing. The way at which he went at his big opponents was most laughable. Go where they would be, he was ever dodging round their heels and repeatedly foiled them.*

"Once, two of the giants went at him together and both he and they came to earth. With the nimbleness of a cricket, however, he was up and off with the ball before his big opponents could gather themselves together, much to the amusement of the spectators. He showed no vestige of fear, but went at his bulky opponents just as though they had been schoolboys and he a giant."

Had the young winger never played another game, his status and popularity was already permanently guaranteed. He was selected to represent England against Ireland in Belfast a fortnight later. Accompanied by Albion teammates Bob Roberts and Albert Aldridge, England won 5-1.

And there were more trophies to chase. Having won the 'English' Cup, Albion were invited to meet the Scottish Cup winners, Renton, for the Championship of the United Kingdom in May. With football yet to become established outside of the British Isles, this was also a play-off for the title of 'world champions'. Bassett and Woodhall came closest to giving Albion the lead before Renton went ahead against the run of play. An early second half goal put Albion on level terms before a three-goal burst on a bog of a pitch left the Scots clear winners. Never again would West Bromwich come so close to being the best team in the world!

FAR FROM BEING the meaningless competitions of today, the local cups were the be-all-and-end-all for football clubs in pre-league days. Thus West Bromwich badly wanted to win the Staffordshire Cup to go with the FA Cup. Unfortunately, so did Wolves who eventually won

2-1 in a second replay. In the first replay at Stoke, *"Bassett and Woodhall only rarely did anything worthy of their reputation."* In the first replay at Stoney Lane, Bassett and Woodhall *"put in occasional good shots, but they did not play at all well together and were not nearly as conspicuous or as effective as usual. Indeed there was much quarrelling between this wing and the centre."* Bassett had formed a formidable partnership with his inside-right, George "Spry" Woodhall, though not before Woodhall, in a 19th century example of dolly going out of pram, refused to pass to Bassett because he resented the youngster being considered a better player than him.

Bassett, at just 5ft 6in and weighing barely 10 stone, depended entirely upon speed and skill to defeat burly opponents in what was a far more physical game than today. A game lacking bodily or financial protection against injury. Not only was he a fast runner, but also he could run with the ball, knew exactly when to centre and could place the ball in the goalmouth with uncanny accuracy. One of his favourite ploys, where space permitted, was to flick the ball past his marker, keeping the ball in play whilst he ran outside the pitch. Another trick was to cut in diagonally towards goal, rather than the traditional heading for the corner flag. He was also adept at stopping suddenly when in full flight, and back-heeling the ball to a colleague.

Thus Billy was Albion's first ever flying winger, an idyllic genre that has fascinated Baggies fans ever since. The nearest modern Albion counterparts are perhaps Willie Johnston and Laurie Cunningham, though neither really matched the role filled by Bassett. In that period, the sole job of the winger was to get past the opposing half-back. Few got the better of Bassett. He was at his best on the big occasion, which was great news for his country, (for whom he supposedly never had a bad game) but not always so helpful for his club. Certainly the larger pitches at the Kennington Oval and Crystal Palace would have afforded him much more space than Albion's notoriously cramped Stoney Lane enclosure. In Billy's own words: *"I always disliked a narrow ground."*

WILLIAM BASSETT, OR Billy as he was universally known, was one of six children born to Charles and Rebecca Bassett. His father was a colliery agent and the family lived at 48 Overend Street, near West Bromwich town centre. The first recorded mention of young Billy came when he represented Christ Church school at the age of just nine, amongst lads a couple of years older. As Bassett admitted much later: *"I had the reputation of being rather a slippery youth, and continued to play in these school games until I left school."* The school adjoined the Four Acres ground used by the West Bromwich Dartmouth Cricket & Football Club (and later WBA), and Bassett would have been amongst the spectators at the games of the Dartmouth, then the town's top football club, a position usurped by the Albion as the 1880s progressed.

AT THE AGE of 14 *"and a little wisp of a chap"*, Billy featured prominently for another local club, Oak Villa, where the average age was 18. *"Finding enough pocket money to defray expenses for away matches"* was a continual problem for him. Conditions were basic, as the man himself explained. *"I remember walking to Hamstead Hall, four miles from West Bromwich in a blinding snowstorm, and then finding no dressing room accommodation whatsoever. We had to get under the biggest tree we could find. There we undressed and got into our football attire, leaving one of our faithful camp followers to mind our clothes. When we went for them at the end of the match, we found them frozen stiff."*

It was with another junior side, West Bromwich Strollers, that Bassett was spotted when playing in two local cup finals, and invited to join West Bromwich Albion, having appeared in a trial for the Albion earlier that season. Not that Billy needed much encouragement. *"It is difficult for anyone accurately to convey the idea of reverence which every Black Country lad had for 'The Throstles' in those days."* Bassett was just 17 when he joined the club in March 1886.

Initially, he played in the club's 3rd XI, but by the start of the following campaign he had already progressed to the reserve team. Once the 1887 FA Cup Final was out of the way, young Billy was given his chance in the first team challenge matches, making his debut against Third Lanark, one of the top Scottish clubs of those times. The crowd of 5,000 saw Albion win 3-1, Bassett featuring prominently with his crossing and shooting. A month later, he made the first of several appearances against Albion's biggest rivals, Aston Villa, whilst on 28th May he registered his first senior goal in a 2-0 win against Bolton Wanderers.

Billy began the 1887/88 season in the first XI. Even before the season started, he was described as *"a clever and fast player, and is destined to become a conspicuous figure in the football world. His only drawback is his height, but for that his activity will more than make up."* His early appearances for the first team were at inside-right (a support role to the centre-forward), as George Woodhall was already established on the wing, though these positions were ultimately reversed.

BACK THEN there were only cups, no league. Clubs could only make their name by competing in the various local knockout competitions, many of them organised by county football associations. Success in these competitions paved the way for meetings with successful clubs from other counties, as did the FA Cup that also became increasingly popular as the 1880s progressed. It was a risky existence, for just one defeat meant the end of the interest in that particular competition for another year, and paved the way for other clubs from within your town or neighbourhood to grab the public's attention. Consequently the success of West Bromwich Albion in reaching the final of all three major cup competitions (Birmingham, Staffordshire and FA Cup) in the 1885-86 season was a major achievement.

Although winning the Birmingham and Staffs Cup competitions was a cause for much celebration, the FA Cup Final was lost to Blackburn Rovers, who thus won the trophy for the third consecutive season, a feat never since matched. A year later, Albion again reached all three cup finals, this time winning just the Staffs Cup. It was a grand achievement for young Billy Bassett to break into the team and keep his place in such a famous side.

Concern was expressed in some quarters that Billy lacked the physical strength considered necessary to compete at this level, but the doubters were to be proven wrong. This he did to such effect that Albion reached all three cup finals yet again, and at the third attempt, won the FA Cup at last. But prior to that, Bassett's first cup final appearance for the Albion came in the 1888 Birmingham Senior Cup against the Villa before 12,000 spectators at the Aston Lower Grounds. He exhibited some superb passing, the Albion coming from behind twice, with Bassett's pass leading to the second equaliser, before losing to a late goal.

WBA were about as successful as any club could wish to be. There was never any doubt that any new league of football clubs must include such a well-known progressive outfit. And so it came to pass – Albion became one of the invited dozen founder members. Their league form was never great despite the little winger's best efforts. He was joint leading scorer for Albion, averaging a goal in every second league game, in that first season of league football. Bassett was a member of the historic team who played at Stoke in the first ever league fixture and indeed, his centre set up Woodhall for the clinching goal in a 2-0 win.

INEVITABLY, BASSETT BECAME a marked man in league, cup and friendlies that term. In the 1889 Staffs Cup Final against Leek, the *Leek Times* reported that *"Smethurst stuck to little Bassett, whose international cap didn't frighten him, like a leech."* Nevertheless, a Bassett shot was rushed through to give his side the lead, Albion eventually lifting the cup courtesy of a 2-0 victory.

The following season, with the league still just another competition, Albion were pleased to reach the final of the Birmingham Senior Cup, but this time the enormous silver trophy eluded them as Villa won 2-0. *The Free Press* reporter claimed that *"Bassett and Bayliss did not get on. Bassett made more effort than his colleague, but neither greatly exerted themselves."*

Albion put in a poor display. The *Birmingham Gazette* reporter saw things differently, claiming that *"the feature of the match was the really grand exhibition of Clarkson (the Villa half-back) whose display was a revelation. He had both Bassett and Bayliss against him, but time after time beat them both. It must have been a new experience to Bassett to be so persistently taken down."*

Bassett was Albion's highest paid player, albeit earning just £3 per week. Even that modest amount represented a spectacular increase compared to those 10 shillings expenses! Other clubs were always keen to sign him, as "Half Back", writing in *The Free Press* in March 1889 noted. *"Rumour is busy concerning Bassett and quite a multitude of stories, some possessed of quite a grain of truth, but most of them surrounded with bushels of its opposite, one being told as to the fine opportunities which he has been offered."* There was more. *"If I were in his place, it would require an offer surpassing fine to induce me to leave West Bromwich. To take a position elsewhere, purely for football, would be about the most absurd thing he could do, and he would not be the man I take him for if he did so. At present, he is among friends, and has a good berth with everything in his favour, and the wise course is to look very curiously before making any leap in the dark."*

Despite the reporter's exhortations, some offers must have tempted the footballer such as the £200 per season proffered by Everton. When rejecting these temptations, it's easy to imagine Bassett expecting at least some appreciation back from his club. But from his perspective, he didn't always get it.

In October 1891, Bassett had a disagreement with club officials. The Albion team were staying in the Shaftesbury Hotel in London. Billy was chatting to several friends who had called in to see him. At 10.30pm, a club official told him to go to bed. The little winger reacted angrily, refusing to leave his friends and considered the order to be insulting. Bassett was summoned before the board days later where he asked for a transfer. Rumours suggested Arsenal had made him a better offer. The board declined to release Bassett and the wide player had no choice other than to accept their decision as final.

This was not the attacker's first transfer request, according to the *Birmingham Post*, who reported Bassett wanted to move to Molineux in the summer of 1891, but once again Albion's rulers gave him the thumbs-down. Apparently, some sort of sweetener was offered to the player, either a testimonial or a non-playing position at the club.

Two years later, the directors apparently needed a reminder, for Billy refused to sign his contract unless their promise was honoured. He was dissatisfied with the offer of a Monday afternoon match, because of the small attendance, holding out for a Saturday afternoon benefit fixture. He didn't get it and so reluctantly put pen to paper on the Tuesday before the season started. Fortunately, his benefit match against Sheffield Wednesday on Monday 27th November pulled in one of the highest gates of the season.

After falling at the semi-final stage two years out of the previous three, West Bromwich reached the 1892 FA Cup final, after finally overcoming Nottingham Forest in a twice-replayed semi-final. Bassett scored in two of those ties. Their opposition in the last cup final at the Oval was once again Aston Villa, who were apparently as arrogant as Preston in their belief that they would triumph. According to their supporters, *"it was a sheer waste of time and money for Albion to travel down to London."*

BUT ALBION HAD Billy Bassett. The winger again rose to the big occasion, setting up Albion's first two goals, the first after just four minutes when his speed took him beyond the Villa defence, and Geddes turned in his cross. Inside half an hour, another Bassett run finished with Nicholls doubling Albion's lead. Though the then chocolate and blues dominated in terms of possession, they had no answer to Bassett's speed, and the accuracy of his crosses.

Less than a fortnight after winning the cup at the Oval, barely one thousand supporters turned up at Stoney Lane for the visit of hapless Darwen. With over 13 weeks since the last home league game, perhaps supporters might have forgotten about the competition. Albion were 5-0 up by half-time, with Bassett's goal the pick of the bunch as he dribbled past four opponents. So bad were Darwen that Albion's captain urged his defenders to come forward too and the goals feast continued. Bassett completed his hat-trick, and Sam Nicholls scored his side's twelfth goal in the last minute, when he thumped both ball and goalkeeper in the net. The 12-0 win still stands as the highest margin of victory in the top flight of English league football. Barely three weeks later, the return match finished 1-1. This was not a good league season for WBA. By finishing in the bottom four, Albion should have been obliged to apply for re-election, but were excused the inconvenience because they'd won the FA Cup!

Hat-tricks were rare for the winger during his playing days, even with his cutting-in technique, although both he and Roddy McLeod obliged in a then league record 8-0 away victory at Molineux in December 1893. *"It is doubtful whether he ever played a better game,"* reported *The Free Press*. Best of all was the six notched in one game a few years earlier, as Albion ran riot in a Staffordshire Cup game v Burton Wanderers, winning 23-0!

IN AN ERA long before the advent of blank weekends to accommodate international matches, cancellations to accommodate international call-ups, and international caps being handed out like sweeties, Albion fans could take great pride in Bassett's performances for England, even though these often deprived the club of his much needed services. Billy netted his first international goal in his first appearance against Scotland in 1889, opening the scoring from long range in the game at the Kennington Oval. However, despite leading 2-0 at one stage, England were beaten 3-2. There was some consolation as *"Bassett was the brightest particular star of the forward division, and if each of the*

English representatives had performed as brilliantly as he, Scotland would not have been in the majority at the finish!"

In the 1891 game against Ireland at Molineux, Billy notched England's fifth goal in a 6-1 victory and *"gave his best display of the season"*, whilst a month later against Scotland, Bassett did not disgrace himself, but was deprived of service on the right wing.

The legendary England centre-forward GO Smith said: *"Though rather on the small side, Bassett was no easy man to move, and the way in which he could travel over the ground was marvellous. Taking rather short strides, he was down the wing like a flash, and it took a very fast back to even keep up with him. His merits as a player were by no means confined to his speed, as you see in so many cases, he could pass well, and neatly, and was a delightful partner, but almost every requirement of his was, to my mind, overshadowed by his power of middling. He could centre the ball from every position, sometimes seemingly over his head, and rarely did the ball go where it was not intended... as a player in his position, then, Bassett stands first. Scotland must have had enough of him, as he gained innumerable caps against that country."*

A year later, he featured in a brilliant English display at Ibrox Park as England opened up a 4-0 lead inside 25 minutes; eventually winning 4-1, whilst in 1893 came probably his finest display in an England shirt. *"Bassett's runs were pretty generally considered to be the feature of the match"* said the *Chronicle*, reporting on Billy laying on a stream of accurate crosses as England won 5-2. Billy was one of three players to have featured in what was England's third consecutive victory over the Scots, and was awarded a special international cap in recognition of this. In the following year's fixture at Celtic Park before a crowd of 30,000, Bassett was England's saviour. Three minutes from time, Bassett went off on one of his well-known electric runs, and from his cross former Albion colleague Jack "Baldy" Reynolds equalised. *"Bassett worthily upheld his reputation in this game."*

In 1895/96, for the first time, Bassett appeared for England in all three of that season's internationals. These included a record 9-1 trouncing of Wales in Cardiff, with Bassett's partner, Derby County's Black Country-born Steve Bloomer, notching a record five goals. With football relatively unknown outside the British Isles, there were only three international games played each season, and with Ireland and Wales providing such weak opposition, it was not uncommon for fixtures against these two countries to be fulfilled on the same day, with two different XI's being selected. This would naturally reduce the total number of appearances Bassett could make for his country.

For the match against Ireland at Belfast, the England team sailed to Larne for a night's rest before the game, but Bassett had a particularly unpleasant trip and felt very ill on arrival in Ireland. A motherly old Irish woman took pity on him, saying: *"And shure it's only the cold I'll have to be taking out of ye."* She then put Billy's feet in hot mustard and hot water, gave him a mysterious concoction to drink, rolled him in blankets and vowed that if the cold had not gone by the morning she would *"eat her ould grandfather that's been dead these 40 years."* In the morning Billy, as promised, was revitalised, and he played a full part in his country's 2-0 victory.

The true measure of his worth is that this was the eighth consecutive season that Bassett had appeared in the annual fixture against Scotland. His international career ended with a total of 16 appearances and seven goals, but nowadays it is not unreasonable to suggest that he could have clocked anything in the region of 80 to 100 appearances for England.

What proved to be Bassett's final representative honours came when he played for the Football League against the Irish League in November 1896. He and his partner Steve Bloomer played, and the pair turned it on against the Irish. Once they ran half the length of the field, passing to each other, until an Irish full-back was heard to cry *"oh, let the beggars have the ball."* He was actually selected to represent England against Ireland the following February, but had to withdraw through injury, and lost his place to his great rival Charles Athersmith, whom Bassett had kept out of the England side for so long. With Villa on the verge of achieving the cup and league double, and Albion in decline, it was perhaps inevitable that Athersmith would get the chance to establish himself in the England team at Bassett's expense.

ALBION CONTINUED to chase silverware. Nothing less was expected from such a major club. There was a bizarre conclusion to the 1894 Birmingham Senior Cup Final against Wolves. On the pitch, Bassett was again prominent, breaking away down the wing and centring for Bastock to give Albion the lead after just eight minutes. Just before the interval, it was Bassett again, evading both Swift and

Kinsey, carrying the ball half the length of the field, and scoring himself to give Albion a 2-0 half-time lead. In between times, however, Albion had lost a player through injury and, in these days before the advent of substitutions, were consigned to play the rest of the game a man short. Wolves pulled a goal back, but with 15 minutes remaining Bassett again made his mark, sending Norman clear to set up a third goal scored by Geddes. However, the extra man eventually told for the Wolves and the game finished 3-3. In the confusion that followed, the players left the field, despite the fact that extra time should have been played. Albion were naturally reluctant to play another half hour with such an obvious handicap, whilst Wolves were reluctant to take up the suggestion of no less an authority than Charles Crump, the president of the Birmingham Football Association, that the rules should be bent to allow Albion to field a substitute. In the meantime, the Albion team had got changed and one of the players had even gone home! Eventually, the cup was shared for six months each.

There were two personal firsts for the West Bromwich winger that year. On 28th April, he was the first Albion player ever to be sent from the field of play for using *'unparliamentary'* language to the referee during a friendly with Millwall. Presumably his ability and loyalty saved him from severe punishment. At the end of the same year, he underlined his national popularity by winning the Silver Cup offered by the *"Answers"* journal, having been voted by its readers as being the best player in the country – the equivalent of the modern Player of the Year award. He romped home with nearly 2,000 votes more than the runner-up, Jimmy Crabtree, of Burnley.

Albion met Villa in the FA Cup Final again in 1895 for the third time in nine seasons (not until Arsenal met Newcastle in 1998 did any two other clubs meet in the Final for a third time). Possibly the fastest goal in cup final history ultimately won the cup for Villa, but Bassett played one of the greatest games of his life, taking advantage of the open spaces of the Crystal Palace ground. He seemed at times to be taking on the Villa defenders almost singlehandedly, but all too often, he was lacking in support and was crowded off the ball. Nevertheless, he created a host of openings for his colleagues, and came closest to equalising himself with a shot against the bar. A then world record attendance at a football match of 42,652 was present at this game.

TWO DAYS LATER, the club's future was in the balance, with Albion looking set to take part in the 'test matches' that then determined promotion and relegation. Bottom of the table, and needing victory by five clear goals to avoid the lottery, Albion rose to the occasion to thump Sheffield Wednesday 6-0, with Bassett creating the first five goals. Cometh the hour, cometh the man. The season then finished on a high note a week later, with victory at Villa's expense in the replayed Birmingham Cup Final, Bassett yet again proving to be a thorn in Villa's side by creating an opening early on for Hutchinson to score what proved to be the only goal of the game.

Little more success was to come Albion's way during Bassett's time as a player. The 1892 FA Cup winners were unable to add the Birmingham Cup to their list of honours, losing 2-5 to Wolves in the final, as if to emphasise the fact that one man can never make a team. Likewise, a below-par Bassett was unable to stop Albion losing to Second Division Port Vale in the 1898 Staffs Cup Final. This proved to be his last cup final appearance for the club, for in 1899 he retired.

By now cup success was starting to elude Albion, and the club were struggling in the league also. Bassett was no longer enjoying his football and, not wanting to live on his reputation, announced his retirement at the end of the season at the relatively young age of 30. Sadly, his last league appearance was a quite awful defeat; 1-7 to the Villa.

BILLY BASSETT'S retirement as a player didn't bring to an end his association with the club. Indeed, this was just the beginning. Bassett, whose playing performances alone merited cult hero status, went on to serve the club for over 50 years.

In 1900, Albion moved to its new home at The Hawthorns, but following Bassett's retirement as a player the club's fortunes declined further. Relegation followed in 1901, and although the Second Division championship was won at the first attempt, a second relegation followed in 1904 and there was no easy way back. In late 1906, the *Sports Argus* lamented mournfully: *"Since the days of Bassett, WBA have not had an outside-right whose occupation of the position has given complete satisfaction. A good many players have essayed to fill his shoes, but the fact has to be mournfully recorded that not a single one has succeeded to any memorable degree. The one and only William retains his unapproachable standard as far as the Albion are concerned. One is almost inclined to think that the international's wonderful wing play has, to some extent, rendered the followers of the club a little less appreciative of the merits of other outside-rights."*

Meanwhile, Bassett followed the traditional retired footballers' route by joining the licensing trade. He then took over at The Dartmouth Hotel in 1906 and stayed there until retiring in 1920 (It was perhaps not surprising that another ex-Albion player, Harry Clements, replaced Bassett as licensee!) In addition, he became a director of three companies, which included the Imperial Picture Palace in West Bromwich. He also took up golf, becoming captain of Sandwell Park, and acted as a Football League linesman. He became a member of the board of management of the West Bromwich & District General Hospital and in 1935 became a Justice of the Peace.

HIS BUSINESS ACUMEN came to the rescue of his former club when, in March 1905, with the club facing extinction, Bassett became part of a new board of directors and persuaded creditors to defer their claims for a period in two years. Being a particularly popular local figure, Bassett enjoyed huge credibility. In 1908, he became club chairman and rarely missed a board meeting between 1905 and 1932. In 1910, with Albion still in the Second Division, a directors meeting was called to decide whether or not the club should be wound up. These were difficult times. A bank official once felt it necessary to track the chairman down to a local golf course in order to sign a guarantee for the players' wages that week. Only Bassett of all the directors attended the meeting, but dismissed closure immediately and enlisted the help of like-minded individuals who, along with himself, gave personal guarantees to ensure the club's survival, and paved the way for promotion a year later. At the time, the Chairman admitted he *"had been connected with the club for 26 years, and this was one of the happiest days of his life."*

Every morning of the week, he could be found keeping a watchful eye on the players training and on match days his advice was often invaluable. His popularity with succeeding generations of players was enormous, being particularly kind and helpful to the club's youngsters.

Albion's greatest ever achievement, the winning of the League Championship, came about in 1920, whilst the runners-up spot was attained in 1925, and although another relegation followed in 1927, the unique double of FA Cup winners and promotion followed four years later. Indeed, Bassett led the team out at Wembley before the 1931 FA Cup Final victory, the club's first such success since Bassett's days as a player.

Bassett's health had not been good since August 1932 when, while travelling to Arsenal, he became so ill that he had to stop doing anything for six months. He recovered, but his heart was now much weaker. Since then he had recurrent attacks of increasing intensity. The players' well meaning gesture at the post-match dinner after defeat in the1935 FA Cup Final to hoist their popular chairman on their shoulders in the middle of the dance floor and sing "He's a jolly good fellow" probably wasn't a great idea. Billy had to resign from the committee of Sandwell Park golf club in early 1936 due to ill-health, but was well enough to receive a silver casket and an illuminated scroll at West Brom's AGM in 1936, in recognition of his 50 years' service to the club.

However, on 8th April 1937, Billy had a heart attack in bed and, despite receiving oxygen, passed away. His death came just two days before Albion met Preston in the FA Cup semi-final at Highbury. Bassett was a member of the FA Council, who insisted on a two minute silence with accompaniment from a full military band. The Albion players were thus not in the right frame of mind for such a vital game. The match kicked off before the scheduled start, and Albion were a goal down before 3 o'clock, then three down inside half-an-hour, eventually losing 4-1.

Thousands lined the streets for Bassett's funeral the following Monday, along the three-mile route from his home in Beeches Road, West Bromwich to the interment at All Saints church. Floral tributes, filling several cars and a lorry, were received from virtually every professional club in the land, whilst the list of mourners read like a *Who's Who* of past and present Albion players, football officials and other local organisations.

An obituary in the *Albion News* described Bassett as *"guide, philosopher and friend to the club"*, whilst another in the Midland Chronicle described him as *"the finest outside right the game had known."* Fred Howarth, secretary of the Football League, described him as *"the most popular man in the game"*. No man did more for West Bromwich Albion than William Isaiah Bassett.

Jesse Pennington

1903-1922: 495 games, 0 goals

AT THE AGE of 38 years and 256 days, Jesse Pennington captained the Albion side against Liverpool on 6 May 1922. He was Albion's oldest ever player and the normal rules of ageing just didn't seem to apply to him.

Only three months earlier, *"Linesman"*, writing in the *Sporting Mail* confessed *"last week, writing of Jesse Pennington, who by the way has no greater admirer, I suggested he should be rested more often because Anno Domini could not be forever denied. Pennington must have anticipated this suggestion, for the very day these lines appeared, he played one of the greatest games of his life, and Anno Domini seemed as far off as, say, ten years ago. Though the writer still holds to his opinion, Pennington, however, refuses to be rested when he can play, though he often played under conditions that could hardly help but be harmful to him. In a great game against Huddersfield, he was the outstanding figure. His kicking, tackling, judgement, and above all, his marvellous anticipation of what his opponents would do were simply amazing and until the end he maintained a remarkable speed. After Saturday, comments on Pennington's age seem out of place."*

Liverpool was Jesse's final competitive match. That evening, his doctor rang and asked him to visit. Although the medical man was an Albion supporter, he felt dutybound to tell Jesse that he believed he was now struggling. Jesse thought he had at least one more season. The club had retained his services and he'd even accepted the captaincy of the West Bromwich Dartmouth Cricket Club second XI. Before re-commencing football training, he was *"given a very stiff examination"* by a doctor who also took x-rays. The results were depressing. *"Jesse, you have an enlarged heart and a duodenal ulcer. No more football for you."* Medical science didn't find a cure for duodenal ulcers until 1970. Before then, advice to avoid said ulcer bursting was merely to avoid certain foods and crucially to avoid stress. A 19-year one-club career was at an end. *"I have had a wonderful time here"*, he reflected on his retirement. *"At the same time, I should have liked to stayed on a little longer, because I felt fit but couldn't in the face of what the doctor said, because, after all, I want to live."*

JESSE PENNINGTON WAS born at 45 Maria Street, West Bromwich on 23 August 1883, no more than a mile from Albion's eventual home. His father, William Henry Jesse, was a puddler, a heavy job in either the iron or steel industry. His mother was Mary Ann Pennington. In keeping with the fashion of the time, the family doctor delivered the new arrival at home. Jesse's practitioner in attendance was Dr Isaac Pitt. Next door lived Miss Clara Smith, sister of Albion secretary Eph Smith, later to be the bride of secretary Fred Everiss. As Jesse said himself, Albion was always going to be his destiny. Defending seemed to be the family's destiny with his brother also becoming a back, as an integral part of the all-conquering 4th Dragoon Guards football team in South Africa in 1907.

As a boy, Jesse supported the Baggies, walking the three miles from the now family residence in Pope Lane, Smethwick to Albion's home at Stoney Lane. A hole in the perimeter wall enabled him to get in without paying.

Playing, rather than watching, soon claimed the Black Country lad. At the age of 16, he was turning out for Smethwick Centaurs in the Birmingham Youth League. A year on, he represented the League against Small Heath (later Birmingham City), who were so impressed that they tried to sign him on the spot. But too late – he'd already signed amateur forms…for Aston Villa.

The history of both Albion and the Villains of Aston may have been so different had not the Birmingham club felt pressure to choose between Pennington and Aston lad Fred Miles, who effectively competed for the same position. The Villains chose Miles. *"He was an Aston boy, so that was that"* explained Pennington later in life with something of a sigh of relief. Jesse returned sadly to his native Black Country. He joined Dudley Town in the Birmingham and District League, the same League in which Albion reserves competed. At that time, Dudley had a fine side... or they did until Albion came a-knocking and "captured" four of their players, including Jesse, now 19. It was only later that the Baggies discovered that their new signing was already registered with Villa. Fortunately, the Aston outfit agreed to release him without fuss. The famous William McGregor later wryly noted *"It is sometimes stated that the Villa never does a neighbouring club a generous action. Pennington had a free transfer from Aston to West Bromwich."*

ALBION PAIRED JESSE with former Dudley full-back colleague Baverstock during their annual pre-season Whites v Stripes match on 15th August 1903. The defensive duo competed against their own club's first team forwards. Together, they were said to *"exhibit a strong defence"*. The Hawthorns friendly was the teenager's first appearance as an Albion professional. (Jesse had previously played as an Albion amateur at Molineux on 14th April 1903, in a benefit match for Wanderers centre-half Ted Pheasant.)

ALBION'S 1903/04 SEASON started badly with a series of defeats. Full-back Kifford was sent from the field during a 3-1 defeat by Aston Villa. *"He ran at Villa forward McLatchie, and kicked his legs from under him,"* explained the *Birmingham Gazette* in shocked tones. There was worse. *"This completely spoiled the closing stages for the spectators. He laughed and clapped his hands in response to the cries of disappointment that met him from the stands."* The dismissal was only the third in the club's history, with the fourth another 23 years distant. Kifford eventually received a six-week ban for his actions, during which he was not paid.

Meanwhile, his obvious replacement was up against Burton United in the Staffs Senior Cup. *"The Albion backs both made mistakes"* wrote the correspondent *"but Jesse Pennington seemed to warm to his work as the game progressed, and looks like developing into a useful back."*

Thus Jesse's debut came at Liverpool on 26th September 1903. Up to then, neither side had won. *"It will be a trying ordeal for Pennington, who makes his debut in the First Division, to figure in such a match away from home."* Thus read the concerned tones of the local Press reporter.

With Albion regularly beaten by the opposition that season, it was hard to imagine that the 20-year-old debutant could make matters much worse. In the event, with the Baggies recording their first victory, the same correspondent wrote three days later, *"Pennington played a very fine back game, being fearless and clever in tackling, while his kicking was vigorous enough for anything."* Albion director Dr Pitt was thrilled. *"Jesse, I am very proud. I brought you into the world. I have seen you play your first game for the Albion in the league, and we have won."*

Following his sound debut, Jesse retained his first team shirt for two decades of dedicated service which was to write his name large into the history of West Bromwich Albion Football Club, becoming a legend who is still considered amongst the top five players to appear for the club even 100 years later. That is the incredible impact he made, although the full story of Pennington's incredible career reveals there was far more to this Albion stalwart than usually first meets the eye.

IN 1903/04, PENNINGTON played in every game until mid-January, before injury intervened as it would regularly throughout his Albion career. With limited medical and fitness training knowledge, serious injuries and illness were regular occupational hazards, but one which spawned legends of Pennington's indestructibility. Consider these words from the man himself and read between the lines.

"Training was never a chore to me. I liked it, even though we only had a small shed where we did some skipping. Our main training was lapping, short sprints for the forwards, and practice matches." These factors, combined with international call-ups, meant that the full-back was to miss Albion games every season through finally submitting to a variety of serious injuries and ailments.

His worst injury and subsequent longest absence was courtesy of a shoulder dislocation in a league match against Stockport in September 1909. Rain fell heavily in the second half, so much so that the players were briefly taken off the pitch. When they resumed, the turf was very greasy and a serious injury was always a possibility.

The *Sporting Mail* described his misfortune. *"On Monday, Pennington fell heavily, and was compelled to retire from the contest. It was said at first that his collarbone had been broken, but a subsequent examination has shown that the injury is of a more serious nature. He has dislocated his left shoulder, and will be prevented from playing for at least two months. His services will be greatly missed, for his magnificent play at back has materially assisted the club in becoming prominent in the fight for promotion during the last two or three seasons. It is to be hoped that he will speedily recover from his injury, and will feel no after effects from it, for his clean and sound defence has endeared him to supporters of the club and football enthusiasts generally."* Jesse didn't return to first team action until a fortnight before Christmas.

Not surprisingly for one so dedicated to Albion's cause, worrying head injuries were not uncommon, such as the concussion he suffered in a cup match against Derby in 1907, and then again shortly afterwards in the annual England v Scotland battle. The defender *"sustained slight concussion of the brain through putting his head in the way of one of George Wilson's powerful shots. While at the hotel, the West Bromwich man became seriously ill, and needed medical attention. He was not able to set out for home until Tuesday."*

In the middle of the 1912/13 season, the full-back might be forgiven for thinking everyone was out to get him. At home to Derby on Boxing Day, *"he was off the field for a considerable amount of time due to injury."* Three days later at Notts County, he was "lame" for the last 30 minutes. His latest knock prevented him turning out at Middlesbrough on 4th January, but he returned three days later at Old Trafford. After 75 minutes of *"fine work"*, the hapless defender was off the field once more after receiving a kick on the leg when diverting a shot. The kick was so severe that he was out of action until March.

Injuries to team-mates also impacted upon the defender, most notably against Derby in October 1910. Both Betteley and Timmins retired hurt in the first 10 minutes. Jesse led out only nine men for the second half. Someone from the crowd called out: *"What are you going to do now?"*

Responded Jesse: *"The best I can."*

Timmins bravely returned later, but only as nuisance value. Derby were a goal up, but couldn't add to their tally, even against nine fit men marshalled into defensive security by Pennington. Albion played a one-back game (an offside trap) with Jesse as the solitary defender. The *Free Press* correspondent commented: *"Of Pennington's performance, it would be hard to speak too highly. He gave a really masterly display under most exceptionally difficult circumstances, and no back in England could have surpassed him."* With minutes to go and Derby still leading, *"Pennington was noticed to fall, and there were gloomy forebodings as to what was up but it fortunately proved but a trivial mishap and he was able to resume."* In the 87th minute, Pailor equalised for the Baggies and *"was almost overwhelmed by congratulations and handshaking from his comrades."*

The football club did what they could to keep the players fit with regular trips to Rhyl *"for sea airs"* and to the Droitwich salt baths. Once, intriguingly, after a midweek cup replay against Birmingham, the players were treated to a Turkish bath *"to remove the stiffness and soreness residential in the strenuous midweek contest in which they were engaged."*

Disease remained a constant worry in these unsophisticated times, even for the strongest. In February 1908, Jesse played poorly against Glossop. *"Pennington was the only weak spot in the defence, the international having a very disappointing display."* Within hours of the end of the game, he was diagnosed as suffering from influenza. The same month, he also endured land mal de mer (motion sickness) en route to Belfast to play for his country, a condition subsequently worsened by the vagaries of the Irish Channel. Thankfully, he recovered to play well in England's 3-1 victory.

In 1919, there were widely circulating rumours that JP was suffering from a fatal dose of influenza and pneumonia in the midst of the global epidemic. The tales were not far from the truth. Indeed, Jesse was confined to bed. He did have the same illness that was literally killing dozens of people in West Bromwich each week and millions world wide. But Jesse was stronger than most and made a full recovery. In early 1923, he fell seriously ill again. Such was his status, even in retirement; bulletins on his health were considered significant news in the local press. Once again, he battled through to win – as it seemed he had throughout his career.

JESSE'S DEBUT SEASON coincided with an Albion side en route for relegation. Still, for young would-be first team hopefuls, this was not necessarily such a disaster for their careers as such a downturn in club fortune always brings with it a need for fresh talent. Cynical supporters noted that despite the drop to Division Two, and investing £16 in a horse to pull heavy rollers across the turf, Albion still managed to record a £419 profit.

Those were the theories going into the new season. Unfortunately, the Baggies were selling players, not buying, as the financial position was genuinely grim. Results regularly matched the balance sheets, leading to attendant team reshuffles. The thoughts of one local journalist made familiar reading, "*The difficulty Albion find is with the style of the Second Division. Scientific football in many instances is out of the question.*" Attendances were quite awful, starting with barely 4,000 and dropping as low as 2,072 for the visit of Gainsborough Trinity. Even those who turned up did so apparently when they felt like it, with claims in the *Chronicle* that only 500 were present to see the kick-off against Barnsley in December.

The club's existence was at stake. The players agreed to accept half-wages in December, but it wasn't enough. The following month, the directors appealed for money to keep going. Although Aston Villa, Everton, Stafford Rangers and even Northwich Victoria made donations; there was little local support. Fans didn't want to prop up a regime they didn't believe in. In desperation, the directors declared that all donations would go to buy better players, and then sold another – Hadley to Aston Villa. The reaction was predictable. Even supportive local organs such as the *West Bromwich Free Press* bluntly declared, "*The club is going to the dogs.*"

At a shareholders meeting in March, the board resigned en-masse, and new men were voted in, to deal with the adverse balance sheet of £697. The new board quickly brought in new players, and reduced admission prices. Attendances rose and the club were safe – in the short term.

Jesse slowly became a favourite of the Hawthorns crowd, as he accumulated dozens of fine appearances. In the unglamorous position of full-back, there were only three ways to get noticed. Jesse's positive route of consistent top-notch performances was one way. Being dismissed from the field like his predecessor Kifford was another or finally to make numerous mistakes, which was ultimately self-defeating. Full-backs of the 1900s were the last line of defence, so bore far more resemblance to modern day central defenders than full-backs. There was no expectation of supporting the attack; their job was very simply to block out the opposition forwards, supported by the half-backs. They were expected to tackle forcibly and quickly, plus kick strongly. There didn't appear to be much expectation about finding a striped shirt, just kick that ball as hard and as quickly as possible in the direction of away. To do otherwise was to attract criticism. After defeat in Oldham

Athletic's first ever home League match, *Argus Junior* commented, *"Jesse Pennington seems to be getting into the habit of delaying his clearance and I hope he will remember that the best back is he who gets the ball away with the least amount of delay."* But his composure on the ball indicates the class of a player bound for greatness.

IN JESSE'S TIME, there was little merit in keeping clean sheets – not for them the Megson 1-0 approach. Outscoring the opposition was the sole requirement. Thus defenders had much in common with defensive midfielders today – they were simply workhorses, whose labours were largely unseen and unappreciated. Reporters of that era would normally describe the defenders' contribution in one short sentence if at all, normally offering more expansive comments on the opposition forwards.

Despite the meagre reporting, and Albion's Second Division status, the defender built a reputation. His performances in a three-match marathon against First Division Stoke City in the FA Cup helped greatly, as W. McGregor noted in the *Sports Argus* ("A Journal of all manly pursuits"), *"Above all others, one man on the Albion side has enhanced his reputation during the club's recent encounters with the Potteries representatives. I refer to Pennington – he is the ideal footballer, and looks an athlete all over. He has been of splendid service to the West Bromwich team, and I question if he has ever played three better games in his life. Certainly the selection committee would do well to keep this dashing back under observation."*

The England selection committee agreed, and chose Jesse to represent the English League against Scotland. Jesse gave a *"cool and skilful"* display. Chairman Harry Keys accompanied him to Glasgow, subsequently sending a telegram highlighting Jesse's *"grand showing"* to West Bromwich, where the Baggies were doing battle. The telegram was paraded around the pitch on a large board, and the spectators cheered enthusiastically. After such a showing, selection for England against Wales (becoming Albion's 13th England international in the process) wasn't a great surprise, though nonetheless enthusiastically received. Jesse received a special cheer from the Hawthorns crowd before the Blackpool game for his selection, and then earned *" a round of cheers for the clever way he robbed the Blackpool left-wing."* Now he was getting noticed!

The entire Albion team travelled to Craven Cottage to see Jesse make his England debut (before immediately setting off for Rhyl for a training camp). Another cap followed quickly against Scotland, where once again *"he distinguished himself"*. This was the start of a long international career; playing mainly as a defensive pair with the Blackburn Rovers legendary full-back Bob Crompton. The partnership was not without critics. In 1911, Bird's Eye, writing in the *Sports Argus* was quick to back the local man. *"Since 1907/08, when the Albion back first represented his country, there has not been a better defender in England and he well deserves the latest honour conferred upon him. According to some of the critics, Crompton and Pennington have had their day, but while the Blackburn back may not be the power he was a few years ago, the West Bromwich man has never played better than he has done this season."*

Even though England's results were impressive, Jesse was often more effective for club rather than country. *"Not at his best"* was an uncomfortably familiar comment on his international games. Criticism intensified by 1913 when the initials "PMG" were much bandied about as in *'Pennington Must Go'*. Even the local press had doubts, with one Free Press reporter commenting *"there seems too much of the 'old firm' idea about the defence."* The war diverted everyone's attention and Jesse continued to win more caps after the Armistice. Probably his most memorable England game was his last, the 1920 epic against Scotland at Hillsborough, Sheffield. Thirty seven year-old Jesse captained his country in an epic 5-4 victory in wind and rain, which gave his country the Home International Championship (a prestigious annual tournament played between the four Home counties).

With all that practice early in his career, Pennington had little trouble kicking the ball firmly as required, accurately too. But his best asset was always his positioning, often described as *"uncanny."* Instinctively, he knew where the ball was heading, faster than any opponent.

It became his trademark. Such was the case in Albion's 1-0 away victory at Oldham in October 1908, where the *Argus* noted, *"Pennington has never played with more brilliance. He always seemed able to divine the intentions of his opponents, and was as sharp and penetrating as a needle."* Similarly in a Cup match at Bristol City two years later, "Half-Back" of the *Free Press* enthused, *"The man who shone above all others on the field was Pennington, who has rarely if ever made a greater display. His work was marked by superb judgement and excellent resource."*

His consistency was remarkable. Even at 38, one reporter remarked on his contribution against Spurs, *"Pennington saw three moves ahead, and intervened in time."* JP rarely got physical, preferring to subtly nudge his opponent off the ball if he couldn't dispossess him with a fair tackle. This approach was quite unusual for its time and did much to suggest Jesse eschewed traditional values.

OPPOSITION SUPPORTERS WERE sometimes quicker to appreciate Albion's best player. "Half-Back", writing for the *West Bromwich Free Press* in January 1905, noted during a visit to Blundell Park, *"Jesse Pennington was in quite exceptionally fine form, and the Grimsby spectators could not refrain from cheering the splendid clearances he made."* Similarly, at Oldham, in what was the Latics first-ever home league match in September 1907, Jesse was *"deservedly applauded time after time for his fine work. He seemed almost infallible."* The reporter noted a comment from one millhand *"Yon Pennington is a stone-waller, not half."* The *West Bromwich Chronicle* noted *"among players, friends and opponents alike, he enjoyed a popularity which was almost unique, he was Jesse to everybody, and when Albion were visiting the grounds of other clubs, there was always a succession of players and enthusiasts of other clubs eager to shake hands with one of the outstanding personalities of the game."*

Often, only big FA Cup matches stirred Albion supporters into life. Such as the previously mentioned three-match slog against Stoke, or a pair of cup matches against Birmingham City in 1908. In the latter game, 'Peerless' was marking City's Eyre. The Blues man wasn't exactly the first player to be frustrated by Jesse, the forward was making no progress at all. The *Midland Chronicle* noted, *"Pennington was repeatedly cheered for his magnificent returns"* and such was the forwards' unease, *"Pennington and Eyre almost came to loggerheads"*. In one incident, Eyre jumped wildly at Pennington, but missed and sprawled over on the turf. *"The biter, thus bit, caused some laughter."*

NOT ONCE DID Jesse get his name on the Albion scoresheet, despite his length of service. This wasn't seen as particularly noteworthy in that period. Unless they were penalty takers, full-backs literally didn't have a chance. Jesse had one go from the spot himself, in a seriously under strength side playing at Leicester Fosse in December 1904. The experience was not a positive one as the *Midland Chronicle* described,

"Pennington missed a penalty, but it was not his fault. The ball was placed true enough, but Smith, the Leicester goalkeeper got at it in a marvellous fashion."

Jesse did find the net on several occasions, though it was inevitably his own. He managed a pair during 1909. Firstly, in the FA Cup against Bradford City when *"O'Rourke and Pennington made for the ball, the former rushing in such a manner that Pennington could not help heading the ball through his own goal, thus equalling the score."* The second came in a local derby against Birmingham City in December, after a misunderstanding with his goalkeeper Stringer. A third "oggie" followed in October 1910 at Burnley, when the defender, *"who was facing his own goal, endeavoured to hook the ball over his head, but he merely planted it over Pearson's head into the net, the goalkeeper being taken by surprise."*

PENNINGTON ACTUALLY TWICE took on the goalkeeping role himself. On Christmas Day 1906 Stringer, the goalkeeper, received a bad cut on his head and had to go off. Jesse pulled on the gloves and, according to the *Midland Free Press*, *"acquitted himself with considerable credit."* Only one shot got past him as ten-man Albion hammered Grimsby 6-1. The Baggies were in a rich vein of form at the time, scoring 17 goals in four home matches in eight days. Nevertheless, it's easy to imagine the 19,000 Hawthorns crowd, in benevolent Bank Holiday spirit, warming to the efforts of the emergency custodian. There was one other brief spell between the sticks, standing in for Pearson in the latter stages of the Lord Mayor of Birmingham's Charity Cup, which merited a virtual first team. The opponents, in September 1912, were Aston Villa, who were so far ahead when the Baggies required an emergency custodian, that the switch made no significant difference.

OF COURSE NO cult hero's story would be complete without tales of brushes with authority and Pennington's is no different. Jesse had an image of a gentleman. But he could only maintain such honourable intentions within the limitations of his social class. Having ideas *"above his station"*, led swiftly to instant and painful reminders of his lowly status.

In February 1909, he was suspended *"sine die"* by the directors. Jesse fell out with the club's great and good over his benefit match against Leeds City the previous October. At that time, players were rewarded for long service, not with an additional match, but with part of the proceeds from a league match. The directors agreed that Jesse should have half the proceeds against the Yorkshire side, with a guaranteed minimum of £150. The player considered his five-year contribution to the club meant he was deserving of at least £250, a significant difference in an era of a £5 maximum weekly wage. Only a big attendance would resolve the matter. Mavis of the *Argus* did his best to talk up Jesse's benefit. *"Albion has never had a better defender than Pennington, whose international distinctions are testimony to his playing abilities. He is scrupulously fair in his tactics, and always plays the game in the true spirit of sport, with the remit that there are few more popular footballers in the country today than Jesse Pennington."*

Sadly, the crowd was only 13,554, the lowest of the season so far, and Jesse would only receive the lower of the two figures. As the *Free Press* delicately put it, "*he made use of expressions that the directors found impossible to ignore. It is a great pity that a man who has done such excellent service and who has attained so excellent a reputation should have his career marred by such an incident.*"

This was dangerous territory for mere players to stray into. Two years earlier, Bruce Rankin, one of the Albion's best attackers at the time, was sent home in disgrace from a training break in Rhyl for "*insubordination*". Within days, he was transferred to Manchester City.

The *Argus* steamed in on Jesse's insolence, *"Public opinion supports the attitude of the directors. Players are only the servants of the club, not the masters."* Canvassing the opinion of mere spectators was not in the mandate of journalists in that era. Thus "public opinion" and the party line were probably identical. But in a more conciliatory tone, the reporter added, *"Pennington probably recognises that he let his feelings get the better of him."*

After backing down by "expressing his regret" to the board, Pennington was restored to the first team, after missing only one game. But the ill-feeling persisted and in the summer of 1910, the full back refused to sign his new contract. "*Has Jesse signed yet?*" was heard repeatedly throughout the Black Country during the close season. The dispute centred on money. Although chairman Billy Bassett claimed the club had offered the player the maximum wage, this was disingenuous, for additional under-the-counter payments were rife in the game. Jesse wouldn't be the only Albion player to represent his country and discover that his fellow stars were paid far better than he. If this was so, then

Jesse's timing was unusually poor, because club finances were very tight. Rumours abounded, and separating fact from fallacy is always difficult. One shareholder, a Mr Bastable, asked the club board to comment on reports that Pennington had been badly treated, but Bassett would not be drawn. Perhaps he was mindful that Jesse was an influential member of the fledgling Players' Union.

Alternatively, there was talk at the end of the previous season that Albion players were unhappy with their weak side, and considered reinforcements were urgently needed. The Baggies had picked up only one point in their last five games, including a 5-1 thrashing by Hull City.

EITHER WAY, TO not sign his contract was once more dangerous ground for the player. The club owned his registration, and Jesse could not choose to move to another English professional club without their consent. The contract rebel considered a move to Belfast Distillery, but he had much to lose – his international career, possibly most of his wages, his business, friends and family – so, instead, in the same week that Florence Nightingale was buried, he signed for Kidderminster Harriers of the Birmingham League, outside the influence of the Football League. The move was a massive drop in status. Was this just a protest or a general disillusionment with the slave-like status of the full-time footballer? His friends asserted that he was determined never to play for Albion again.

In addition to playing for Harriers, there was mention of him managing a "well-known" Kidderminster hotel. Furthermore, as a result of the defender's signature, *"many members had offered to pay weekly contributions towards the cost of running the team"*, according to the club secretary, thus implying that perhaps Jesse would not be financially worse off in the lower league.

Albion were unimpressed. Pennington was their asset. Understandably, there were several enquiries from other clubs. In public at least, chairman Bassett maintained, *"We wanted to sign him. Many clubs have asked our price. We have got no prices. We wanted to sign him."* However, one local newspaper claimed Albion sought a transfer fee of £1,500, a massive amount for the period.

FA committee member Mr W. McGregor sided with the club and quickly pronounced, *"Pennington must satisfy the Council of the FA that he has special grounds for his proposed change. If the association are not satisfied with his reason for a change, he must not come to terms, or Ireland will be the only "open port" for him. But wherever he may go, unless transferred with the Albion's consent, he will remain an Albion player."* Within days, Harriers were informed that the England international could not sign for them. The FA's influence was far wider than that of the League. Kidderminster secretary George Moulder said the letter *"was a great disappointment"*, adding that he thought the actions of Pennington was *"entirely justifiable"*.

In modern parlance, Jesse was stuffed. For a time, he remained defiant, turning out at left-back for the Harriers in a charity practice match on 27th August where *"there was a great crowd which gave him a very enthusiastic greeting as he appeared in Harriers colours"*. His options were to leave the game altogether, go to Belfast Distillery (much the same thing!) or sign a contract with WBA. He signed.

DESPITE THE SENSE of injustice, Jesse was quickly in top form. Barely a week after his reluctant signature, the *West Bromwich Free Press* commended his play against Fulham *"Pennington played a hard and persevering game, affecting many smart clearances and delighting the crowd by one particularly fine return as he lay upon the ground."*

Jesse stuck with his principles of fair play. To quote the *Midland Chronicle*, *"he set an example of personal conduct and dignity which left its impression upon the whole team."* His most famous example of being true to his beliefs came in the 1912 FA Cup Final replay against Barnsley. Two minutes from the end of extra time, there was no score. Then Barnsley's Tufnell ran on to a long ball with Pennington virtually alongside him for ten yards. Jesse could have brought the striker down well outside the penalty box, but chose not to, unlike their opponents who'd been kicking wildly all night. Tufnell continued his run and scored off the post. The *Free Press* offered a consolation. *"It ought to be mentioned that Pennington has rarely played a greater game. He hardly made a slip or a mistake during the whole match."*

Jesse was never to get that close to the FA Cup again. His previous best was reaching the semi-final in 1907. Albion faced an all-star Everton outfit. Sadly, Jesse's own mistake let Sharp of Everton in for the winner in a close 2-1 defeat. The FA Cup was a huge competition in this era, yet the international refused to take advantage of his status.

In later life, he revealed, *"I have been offered money many times for FA Cup tickets. But not once in my life have I accepted a penny more than the price on the ticket. I don't believe in it."*

Ample compensation came in the form of a League Championship medal. The Baggies were unstoppable in the 1919-1920 season, racking up over 100 goals.

In their crucial home game in March against eventual runners-up Burnley, the *Midland Chronicle* highlighted the midfield and defence's mastery of the Lancashire club. They commented, *"Pennington's display fully justified the assumption that he is England's greatest full-back today. He was invincible."* The Baggies won 4-1.

Albion made certain of the title with four games still remaining, by beating Bradford Park Avenue 3-1 at the Hawthorns, in front of 30,000. There was even a poem celebrating the event, albeit perfectly awful.

The Albion team were presented with their trophy after the last home match against Chelsea. The main interest in the game was the contest between Pennington and Chelsea's forward, Jack Cock. Although the Londoners' best player, Cock repeatedly came off second-best to "Peerless", prompting ironic cries of *"Let Cock have a kick"* from the jubilant faithful. By special request of the chairman, league president John McKenna presented Albion's only championship trophy, not to Bassett as per the custom of the day, but to club captain Jesse. McKenna claimed, *"Never has the championship been won by a more brilliant team."*

Said chairman Bassett of the championship team, *"They were good, clean, honest–living men and there was never any trouble with them."* The captain agreed; *"I've been pleased to have played for West Bromwich Albion for 17 years, and in that time, I cannot think of an instance when the referee has been justified in speaking to any Albion player for having done anything against the rules of the Football Association."*

The late Bill "Popeye" Martin was a legendary Albion supporter. Born in 1913, Bill saw his first game just seven years later. Even by the early 1980s, Bill's claim to have seen Jesse in action as part of the Baggies' Championship team was probably unique. Pennington later became a family friend, initially through his sports and cycle shop in Smethwick, which the footballer first opened in 1908. *"He an' me Dad were great mates. The first time I ever met him was when I was five. Me*

Dad went in the shop with me and got talkin' to him. Me Dad said 'it's my lad's birthday today.' And Jesse said "ave a look in the winder, see if you like anything.' 'He'd got all these little Hornby railway carriages in the winda. I had my eye on a little mini one in red, green and black. So I says 'Yes, that little carriage.' 'Great!' he says, patting me on the head. 'I'll wrap it up and you can have it as your birthday present. And then you must come to tea.' I was chufftest."

FOR MUCH OF Jesse's career, just playing in the top division seemed elusive, never mind any pipe dreams of actually winning the League Championship. Year after year in the Second Division passed, most with hard luck stories of coming so close to promotion. With the maximum wage firmly in place, Albion's captain wasn't losing out financially by not being in the top flight, more the experience of regularly competing against the best in the country. The full-back had seven years of the second tier before Albion finally lifted the *"coffin lid"* (as the Second Division championship was nicknamed due to its odd shape) in 1911.

Defeating Huddersfield 1-0 in the final match was just sufficient to secure the Championship. Jesse even had a shot on the opposition goal during this game, but presumably with his nose streaming blood, he missed the target. The *Argus* described the after-match scenes of the tumult of promotion celebration. *"Like a wave, the crowd swept round the grandstand, and, amid an almost indescribable scene of enthusiasm and hilarious joy, the Albion players were fetched from the dressing room to mount the stand and face volley after volley of cheers. It was a scene the like of which had never been witnessed at the ground before."* To loud cheers, captain Jesse said it was the proudest day of his life. Nearly 90 years would elapse before another Albion captain would lift a league trophy.

With Jesse being such an upright citizen, he made an unlikely target for bribery yet one foolish individual did try in 1913. A well-dressed gentleman visited his shop, claiming to be a Mr Johnstone, an Everton director (Albion were at home to the Merseyside club the following day). He offered £5 (just over a week's wages at that time) to each of the Albion players if they failed to win. JP invited the visitor to make the offer in writing on one of his business memoes and later, he reported the incident to chairman Billy Bassett. Bassett called the police. The game was, by coincidence, drawn 1-1. Afterwards Pennington stood under the Hawthorns' stand wearing a coat over his strip. Johnstone met him and handed over the cash. The defender gave the money to his chairman, while Johnstone was arrested. The "Everton director" was later revealed as Frederick Pater from Birmingham. He received six months in jail and the cash was divided between local charities.

SUCH WAS HIS status in society, Jesse once ran for election to the Council, standing as an independent against Councillor George Betts in the Spon Lane ward. In 1919, Labour man Betts was a clothier and draper, living in Oldbury Road and with an impressive council record. Jesse was described as an "athletic outfitter". On polling day, he travelled with the team to Notts County rather than be at the polling station. He emphasised throughout his battle that he didn't wish to take advantage of his football status; he merely sought to stand as a citizen.

A local cartoonist sought to link the Baggies' rout of Notts County with the election campaign. A Throstle was pictured; telephone in hand, with the message *"Eight nothing". "M'yes, not a bad majority, but Pennington says it's nothing to what he'll have at Smethwick."* In the event, Betts was re-elected, securing 1,436 votes to the Albion man's 760 (50 per cent turnout). Jesse was gracious in defeat, acknowledging the strengths of his opponent. He made such a positive impression that he was invited to stand again, though he declined. The Spon Lane residents put on a public dinner the following month, and Jesse was invited as their special guest.

In fact, in an era 60 years before the advent of the sporting dinner, Pennington was regularly asked to attend dinners or speaking engagements. For instance, in early 1922, he spoke at West Brom Town Hall on the snappy subject of *"The value of outdoor recreation in its relation to the education of the child."* A medical expert was the other main guest before a small but enthusiastic audience. All the first team players were present to take a collection on behalf of the Mayor's Boot Fund. Jesse did his best, and in between eulogising on the benefits of an outdoor life, he revealed, *"at the extreme end of a football career, I enjoy the game as much as I did in my younger days."*

Presumably the international didn't manage to work into his speech the full details of his epic trips to Bradford in 1920, but on other occasions, it was surely too fine a story to resist. The Baggies side travelled to Bradford City by train on a very foggy day. They were disappointed, if not surprised, to find the game postponed. Hastily, the two sides agreed a re-match on Monday night with the visitors spending the weekend in the woollen city. Due to a family bereavement, Jesse was obliged to return home that night. On Monday morning, he travelled north once again; arriving just in time for the referee to decide that play was impossible. The Albion party took the 3.20pm train to Stockport. The service was scheduled to arrive just five minutes before a connection from Manchester, which would take them speedily home. Due to foggy weather, the four-hour journey to Stockport took seven hours. The weary party managed to catch a later connection, arriving back at Dudley Port in the Black Country at 1.00am. Then there was just the small matter of walking home…

Poor Jesse spent 16 hours travelling that day. The match was re-arranged for December. Once more the team travelled, and once more the match was postponed. It eventually took place in February.

AFTER SETTING A new appearance record for an Albion player only broken by Tony Brown's extraordinary devotion and longevity over 50 years later, Jesse Pennington's legacy still reverberates around the Hawthorns. His sense of fair play and solid stoicism in defence are the stuff of legend.

JESSE WAS TOO important to be allowed to just fade away after his extraordinary playing career.

His services were retained at the Hawthorns as a trainer. The *Midland Chronicle* in December 1922 opined that "*Pennington's compulsory retirement was not a great disaster because he's a great judge of a young player, has been spotting talent and encouraging the young, and has found for Albion a host of young men of exceptional merit. Albion's young men are certainly the talk of the football world, winning the reserve championship two years in succession.*"

EVEN AFTER HIS retirement from full-time work, Jesse was persuaded to scout for the club between 1950 and 1960. He was treated with reverence. Fan Chris Flanagan recalled meeting the great man in Halfords Lane in 1952.

"*I was standing with my Dad and Uncle and Dad had just snubbed out a fag when Uncle nudged him.*

'Jesse!' said Uncle Bert to a man in a belted mac and grey hat who had just stepped up onto the pavement. They exchanged words and then looked down at me. Jesse Pennington smiled and touched my shoulder. Jesse Pennington! I had him in my scrapbook ... a photo clipped from the Argus ... captained Albion and England ... played way back when full backs had centre-partings and lump hammers in their boots. But he didn't look like any of them then. He was upright, alert, old world. I'm not sure what he said to me, but that matters little now. I'd met him."

SUPPORTER HAROLD SALT had a similar referential experience. *"When I played for my school team, we had the opportunity to listen to Jesse Pennington on several occasions. Advice and demonstrations that he gave us never failed to help me especially in my later years when I was relegated to defence. I can still hear him now: 'Remember it is the ball that you play with; never lose sight of it and make sure you don't give it away, once you've won it.' His simple wisdom haunted me for decades."* Such is the enduring power of genuine cult heroes.

THE GREAT WAR
1914–1919
R.I.P.

FRANK.ASTON	L.LAWTON
FRED.ASTON	W.TOY
H.C.BACHE	E.VAUGHAN
J.BAINES	

THE WORLD WAR   1939–1945
I.CHADWICK   H.COTTERILL

Harold Bache

1914-15: 14 games, 4 goals

THERE'S A SMALL village in Worcestershire called Churchill. It's not far from Kidderminster; just turn right off the A456 to Kiddy when you see the signpost for the village – go right through the place, keeping to the main drag, and about a mile beyond that, you'll see a war memorial on the left-hand side, set some way back from Stakenbridge Lane. This commemorates that village's war dead, and those who served. On it are the names of four members of the Bache family, including one Lieutenant Harold Bache of the Lancashire Fusiliers, and West Bromwich Albion FC.

HAROLD GODFREY BACHE was born in Churchill, near Kidderminster, on 20th August 1889, probably within the confines of the family home, Stakenbridge House. He was the youngest of eight sons born to William Bache. The legal profession and sport were always prominent in the well-to-do Bache household. Dad was well known in West Bromwich legal circles (he founded Bache Solicitors, which still exists today, though without any resident Baches). *"Legal Bache"* (as he was commonly known) was a fine cricketer with both West Bromwich Dartmouth and Salters. He also turned out for West Bromwich (Dartmouth) FC during the mid-1870s to early 1880s. So occasionally did six other members of the family, including several of Harold's older brothers.

In 1891, when Harold was just two, William became a director of West Bromwich Albion, although commitments elsewhere meant he only served for a year. Sadly, William died in 1899, aged 54, when Harold was only ten. He would not lack for male guidance though, with seven older brothers, and numerous uncles.

Significantly, since John Salter married Ann Bache (William's great aunt) in 1827, the fortunes of the Salters and the Baches became intertwined. William's second son Ernest (commonly known as Bill), became an engineer at Salters, where he came into daily contact with his relative, the famous George Salter, who played such a prominent role in the fledgling years of the Baggies.

Harold was educated privately in West Bromwich, and then at King Edward's Grammar School, Birmingham, where his remarkable all-round sporting talents first came to the fore. He then became captain of the first cricket eleven, for whom he'd already played for four years. In his final season of 13 matches, he averaged over 41 per innings as a left–hander and took 31 wickets. His remarkable haul of three fifties in one week, including one against the Masters, even made the pages of the *Sports Argus*. At 16, he'd captained the Rugby Second XI through an unbeaten season, before moving on to the first team. There was still time to play outside-left for West Bromwich Hockey Club but not the beautiful game. The *Argus* observed, *"He has not yet found time for association football."*

One of his many impressed school mates was George Alabaster, who had many memories to share via the Old Edwardian (school magazine). *"Harold always looked rather pale with deep set blue eyes beneath dark brows and light build that suited a tireless runner. I played half-back with him in the School first, second and third teams. He was the flyest of fly-halves and I learned one thing quickly – get the ball to Bache. I have never seen a better rugby dribbler – though he was largely soccer trained."* Alabaster went on to describe other talents of young Bache such as his skilfully training his terrier to catch rats at the family farm and his talent for fishing and concluded his letter with *"he was a very principled boy, who at bedtime for us all, always saw to it there was no cutting of prayers for anyone or their guests. His character was the best possible; his writing was the worst."*

From King Edward's, he was accepted by Caius College, Cambridge in 1908. In addition to studying for what appears to be a teaching degree, with history elements, Harold played rugby union, tennis at university level, and also in the Wimbledon singles where he was acknowledged to have invented the double handed backhand. Then there was hockey for Staffordshire and first class cricket for Worcestershire and his university, some twenty matches in all between 1907 and 1910. Running was fun, too, for Harold, who excelled at 440 yards and half-mile events (400 and 800 metres respectively)

Harold finally found time for the Beautiful Game, typically rising to the challenge so well that he became captain of the university football team. He was the first ever from the rugby-loving King Edward's School to hold that honour. The *Athletic News* featured Bache in October 1910, describing him in terms that were to become familiar. "*He is a magnificent dribbler, and for a man of his small avoirdupois [weight], possesses abnormal pluck and dash*". At the time, Harold stood 5ft 8in high and weighed 10st.

In addition, he played for England amateurs seven times (remarkably scoring seven goals in a 20-0 rout of France in 1910) while regularly turning out for famous amateur side Corinthians over a five-year period. The vast majority of this club's players came from Oxford or Cambridge, and regularly beat the best professional sides in the land. He averaged two goals per game for the Corinthians, the highest average of any Corinthian. *The Times* in 1911 compared him to the great G.O. Smith, who played for England 21 times in the 1880s and 1890s. "*Like G.O., he possessed that wonderful faculty of slipping his opponent, and to the wonderful dribbling ability, he added the priceless gift of being a most dangerous shot in any position.*"

Bache joined the unpaid side's tours to Spain, France and Canada. One Canadian newspaper admitted, "*Bache was in his most dangerous scoring mood, and one knows what that means*", while another one ran with, "*Bache was the shining star of the field, being prominent in attack and defence...he was known to shoot and break the crossbar.*" The latter claim was later refuted as an exaggeration, but with the Cambridge striker scoring 19 goals in five games, it was easy to get carried away. The happy amateur team returned home on the liner *Lusitania*.

THE FIRST LINKS between WBA and the Caius man date back to 1910, with the *County Express* noting, "*Last season, there was some talk of him turning out with the Albion.*" Such a link-up wasn't possible at the time; as the feature went on to explain, although the tone remained hopeful. *"Someday, we may see him leading the Albion attack."* In the short-term, Bache's goals were benefiting the university team. In 17 matches between the start of the season and February 1911, Cambridge scored 85 goals. Of that number, 42 were in Bache's name. The *Standard* described H.G. as simply *"the finest amateur forward playing today."*

Harold relocated to Cumbria in early 1911, probably to conclude his teaching degree with hands-on experience. Both Kendal Rugby Club and Kendal Cricket Club were very pleased with both his arrival and his prowess. In the school holidays, Harold *"occasionally assisted"* the short-lived West Bromwich Springfield Football Club, or West Bromwich Dartmouth Cricket Club, depending on the time of year. A *Midland Chronicle* reporter was on hand for one such match for Springfield. *"We recollect during a game versus Hagley, what a delightful exhibition he gave on the extreme left wing. He was that day faced with a rough, heavy and somewhat clumsy full-back, but he waltzed merrily around him, and although being on the small side the easy and clever way he can beat opponents is oftentimes very tantalising to them."*

Once his degree was secured in August 1912, the all-rounder moved again to St Andrews College *"to engage in scholastic coaching in Eastbourne."* This time, the lucky beneficiaries were the ailing Eastbourne FC. Harold missed the kick-off against Addiscombe Park, but didn't miss the net, scoring the first seven goals in a 10-0 slaughter.

Meanwhile in West Bromwich, WBA couldn't manage ten goals in a month, let alone one game. Although the Baggies were more than holding their own in the top division in 1913, they relied overly on Jesse Pennington and his defensive colleagues shutting out the opposition. Their current forward line was goal-shy; West Bromwich amassed only 46 goals in 38 matches, six and nine goals less respectively than the bottom two sides, Preston and Derby. Only two clubs in the First Division scored fewer goals, yet Albion did finish in an impressive looking fifth spot, just a point shy of Villa in the runners-up position. If only the Hawthorns outfit could acquire a goalscorer, then who could stop them?

It's easy to imagine that with so many of Harold's relatives based in West Bromwich, at least three of his brothers Foley, Charles Sidney, and Eric all being articled in the family legal firm, plus Bill Bache and the now ageing George Salter at the scale manufacturers, the subject of *"little brother being just right for the Albion"* was a familiar topic. Previously, a dispute between the Football Association and the Amateur Football Association made such a move impossible, but by 1913, reconciliation cleared the way.

By now, Harold was teaching English at the Ecole de l'Isle de France in Liamcourt, vaguely near Amiens in the north of the country. Physically getting to him would not be easy. Inevitably secretary –cum-jack-of-all-trades Fred Everiss was dispatched. This was a difficult and arduous journey in this period, made even more difficult for Fred as he had only just returned from Ireland. The weary official managed to travel as far as Amiens before darkness beat him. Unable to secure accommodation overnight, possibly because of the language barrier, he spent an uncomfortable, and no doubt cold, night at the railway station. The following morning, Fred continued his epic journey by walking for eight miles before getting a lift for the remaining 30 miles on a farm wagon. Harold Bache was in class but an enthusiastic colleague Mr King (enthusiastic after initially cursing loudly having been got out of bed) agreed to take his class. Bache himself was a strange sight, sporting two black eyes after an accident playing hockey the previous day. Despite his surprise and mauled state, Bache needed very little persuasion to join his local club for the big Cup match against Villa and *"as often as possible afterwards"*, signing on the dotted line in just ten minutes. On his long way back home, Everiss was obliged to divert to the FA offices in London to hand in the completed registration document.

HAROLD RETAINED HIS amateur status; a great curiosity in what was now an all-professional game. The only other amateur to turn out for the Baggies during that era was the Reverend W.C. Jordan, also a centre-forward. To play, purely for the love of the game, must have intrigued the hard-working Black Country audience.

The *Midland Chronicle* was mightily impressed with the signing. *"Bache is a regular box of tricks on the football field. He has heaps of pluck, yet he is a brainy player and he knows how to avoid the bumps."* The *Free Press* were a little more restrained: *"As from past records, it would seem that Mr Bache will supply a need long felt, namely that of a first-class goal getter"* while as the *Daily News* pointed out *"good Corinthian forwards know how to pass: in fact, you cannot teach him very much about football."*

The new signing was pencilled in for his first game against Middlesbrough – but a late dose of influenza meant that Fred Everiss had an apologetic telegram rather than a new striker – *"much to the regret of the crowd"* according to the *Sports Argus*.

Harold made his Albion debut in a rather important match a week later – in the FA Cup at Villa Park in February 1914. The *"slim, black-haired, slightly stooping youth"* was completely undaunted by the occasion or by the 58,000 in attendance, according to the correspondent at the *Midland Chronicle*.

"By his clever cool and plucky exhibition, H.G. Bache left a great impression. He was a marked man throughout, and the attentions (of several Villa players) were closely bestowed upon the amateur, who was watched as a cat watches a mouse. But despite this, he shone, and was, in my opinion, the cleverest footballer on the field. He was nippy and fast, and his touches to his colleagues were beautiful, and should have been utilised, only there seemed a lack of understanding between them which lost many good chances. But the way he eluded his opponents who showed him no consideration, was marvellous, and he was as slippery as an eel, as most of the Villa defenders… found out to their sorrow. Once, one of the Villa men sent the amateur yards, and it was thought he was hurt, but he got up smiling and being such a fine athlete, it got him a big advantage, and the philosophical way he took things made him a big favourite with the crowd." However, a physical Villa team battered their way to a 2-1 win. The *Argus* added *"Bache went straight through and beat the goalkeeper with a delightful shot"* but the reporter was alluding to Villa's Joe Bache (no relation) rather than Harold Bache.

So tough was the cup-tie that even normally mild-mannered Jesse Pennington got "stuck in" with a vicious tackle that winded his opponent for several minutes. Days later, rumour spread quickly around the Black Country that Albion forward Sheerman had been badly injured in a collision with Villa's Lyons, and subsequently died. Albion moved quickly to deny the stories, admitting he was staying at Jesse Pennington's house in Smethwick and confined to bed. Sheerman was alive – if not very well.

The Albion directors were criticised for choosing an amateur. Wrote 'Brum' in the *Birmingham Gazette: "I see that some contemporaries have suggested that Harold Bache was a complete failure. I cannot conform to that opinion, but I do think, on reflection that it was a mistake to put him into the team for the first time in a match in which science was likely to be at a big discount."* Other journalists disagreed, such as Argus Junior. *"The faults Harold Bache displayed were those of one not accustomed to the work of the men alongside him. He kept the ball on the floor, was smart in his passes, nippy in his movements, and quick to seize his chances. The cause of the defeat did not rest upon his shoulders."*

For reasons that are not totally clear, Harold didn't play again that season. He was said, *"to be unavailable"* for the next league fixture against Derby. Most likely, he returned to his French teaching duties for in April 1914 he led a party of Liamcourt boys to England to play football against his old school from Folkestone. Harold couldn't resist turning out himself – at centre-half – with the Eastbourne press describing him *"as a towering presence"*. Subsequently, the French party played in a hockey tournament in nearby Folkestone.

In May, the Baggies entertained Corinthians with H.G. lining up for the visitors. The amateurs beat the professionals 4-0 (not uncommon at the time for the Corinthians were a brilliant side) with Harold setting up the first goal with *"one of the most brilliant forward passes it is possible to conceive."* Harold added the second goal himself in an exhibition fixture that didn't have a single foul in 90 minutes, implying Albion, sans Pennington due to a family bereavement, weren't exactly going all out.

THE CHURCHILL MAN stood out in Hawthorns pre-season training for the 1914/15 season. *"He created such a great impression"* exulted one writer. In the traditional final warm-up match (Stripes v Whites – basically the Albion squad forming two teams, with all proceeds to local charity), there was no doubt who attracted the attention of the near 7,000 crowd. *"The most prominent figure was H.G. Bache, whose cleverness in dribbling and placing often brought him the highest appreciation of the crowd. He had hard lines twice before he was successful in putting a goal to his credit after some pretty play."* Another correspondent added, *"The crowd often applauded his brilliant work."*

The new season opened on a Tuesday afternoon with a 2-1 victory at Newcastle. Bache lined up as an inside forward. At five and a half foot high and weighing less than 11st, he was never going to outmuscle the opposition. Harold was a man of many talents, however. As the *Sports Argus* had it, *"he is undoubtedly a clever player, and the best tactician among all the Albion forwards."* The Geordie victory was followed by a bashing at 'Boro. Still, the commentators again singled out the Albion amateur as *"far and away the best forward on display."*

Bache's home debut followed a week later. In normal times, the first opportunity to see such an exciting (and unpaid) attacker in the Albion ranks guaranteed a healthy gate. These were not normal times. Would-be attendees were learning to fight or indeed were already on their way overseas. In addition, the September weather was particularly unkind, with heavy rain throughout the day. Thus only 6,481 turned up for Sheffield United (1-1), 10,000 below the final home game of last season. Many of those attending felt guilty that they were indulging in such frivolous pursuits, even though everyone believed the war would be over by Christmas. A common newspaper quote of the times described supporters as *"loitering louts who have neither love nor loyalty for their country."* As a further reminder of their duty, a military band paraded during the interval with attendant loud appeals for more recruits. In such an atmosphere, no one present could fairly appreciate the dash and élan of Harold Bache. Time after time, his probing passes set up his rather lumbering centre-forward Poulton. *"Bache was wonderful,"* exclaimed the local press, despite him having to accurately move a greasy ball on slippery turf.

Chairman Billy Bassett and his Albion board offered their help to form a new battalion – the 10th South Staffs on the lines of a Pals battalion (where men from a single town or industry enlisted and served together). The Army were given unfettered access to club offices while Albion players would attempt to persuade their counterparts from other clubs to sign up. The Baggies were understood to be supplying a company of footballers (as companies consisted of 200 plus men in those days, the players must have come from other clubs also). The plan met with the approval of the Mayor of West Bromwich, Councillor Charles Sidney Bache, Harold's older brother No 3.

The recruiters were never far away. A small army of them moved among supporters during the derby match at Villa Park. Bache was again at inside-forward, backing up Swift as the main striker. Although Swift did score, generally he was no improvement on Poulton. Once more, the amateur stole the show with his drive, vision and shooting ability, even though the home side won 2-1. *"The star artist of the Albion attack." "The brainiest forward on display"* were just the pick of numerous accolades.

The recruitment drive bought results. Harold was the first Albion player to volunteer for the war. With his income secure, and no dependents requiring his attentions being other considerations, it was no doubt instilled into Harold from an early age that his privileged position came with a responsibility to respond when his country needed him. Several of the younger Bache clan had already joined up. Eric and Kenneth received their enlistment instructions on 24 September. (His two oldest brothers were above the recruitment limit). Most likely, he considered Army life to be just another adventure, or to use the vernacular of the day, *"a gay lark"*. Initially, he enlisted as a private in the new 10th Battalion. In the short term, he was able to continue playing.

AS A SERVING soldier *"doing his bit"*, Bache could be fairly exempted from criticism aimed at football players and supporters. His name and his deeds could be mentioned in the pub or the workplace without rebuttal. 18,000 left their troubles in their old kit bag and travelled to the Hawthorns to see Albion demolish Liverpool 4-0. Harold was now a centre-forward and loving the role, and using his speed and eye for a pass to fine effect. He might have scored, but passed unselfishly to Morris, who was better placed and duly netted the Baggies' third goal. The correspondent from the *Midland Chronicle* wrote, *"Bache was repeatedly applauded for his brilliance. This is probably Bache's last game with the Albion for a time, and it is a pity when he is doing so splendidly, he should have to say goodbye to the football field to commence a course of training for the battlefield."* The *Birmingham Gazette* was quick to add their approval. *"Bache has the innate talent for grasping the possibilities of a situation before they have begun to dawn upon his opponents and largely accounts for his effectiveness."*

Harold had secured the No 9 shirt ... as long as the Army would let him have it.

There was one other lasting memory of this splendid victory. In a very rare example of impromptu collective voices, sections of the Hawthorns crowd bellowed *"FIVE"* (modern day chanting, as we know it, can trace its roots no earlier than the 1960s). Harold had played a very full role in creating such unity. A recruitment rally was staged in the main stand immediately after the game, and 14 men volunteered to join the Comrades Battalion (part of the new 10th Battalion).

Harold missed the Baggies' next game (lost 2-0 against Spurs), as he was obliged to travel to Lichfield with two of his brothers for military duties that day. Fortunately, he was granted leave the next weekend to travel to Bradford PA. With his leading of the line in his usual unselfish manner, the Baggies were unstoppable. The 4-1 win included Harold's first Albion goal, as described by "Mavis." *"Like a flash, Bache slipped behind Blackburn, and on the instant made a great drive and beat Drabble all the way. It was such a goal as drew a roar of appreciation from the [Bradford] supporters."* In the last minute, he and Morris broke through the PA ranks, and once again Bache stood back for Morris to score. "Mavis" again: *"H.G. Bache worked a revolution in the efficiency of the forward line."* The *Albion News* was equally enthusiastic: *"the home defenders could do nothing with him. He continually sent them running one way, while he passed the ball in the other.* His artistry was superb, and roused the admiration even of the home supporters. Another critic opined: *"Bradford were, in popular parlance, big enough to eat them, but when it comes to playing football there was no comparison possible. "*

Even the Football League had noted Bache's impact, and selected him for the Football League v Irish League fixture in October at the Hawthorns after just a remarkable seven appearances. The *West Bromwich Press* approved. *"He thoroughly deserves the honour bestowed upon him."* "His selection was significant as he was the first amateur to receive this honour since professional football became the norm, and was perceived as an encouragement to other amateurs, hopeful of joining the "big League". Sad to say for the League's ambitions, Harold was "all at sea" that afternoon, with a rare poor game, according to Birmingham newspapers. The West Bromwich Press chose to dwell on the positives: *"His pretty footwork was admired by all."* The Football League triumphed 2-1 in front of 10,000 spectators.

Three days later, he was *"unexpectedly delayed at his military quarters"* and shorn of his services, the Baggies forwards were like sheep without a shepherd. After the 0-0 with Oldham came a 0-0 with Manchester United with Bache all at sea. Literally. He'd transferred from the South Staffs to the Lincolnshire Regiment, then in training with the Chums Battalion at Grimsby, an obscure location in the 21st century, but the back of beyond in 1914. His leadership qualities were quickly identified as he was promoted to corporal. Typically, he set up a charity football match between the Chums and the 5th Lincolnshires, with the £34 profit donated to Grimsby and District Hospital.

AFTER THIS POINT, his Army postings become confusing. Local reports were clear that Harold had been offered a commission with the South Staffs. This was an easy assumption to make as Harold had undergone Officer Cadet training at University (how he found time for this additional activity on top of all his sporting activities and tuition isn't clear). In fact, one of Harold's brothers, Eric, had been offered a commission. Harold had also applied for officer status, but was awaiting a response. Nevertheless, Harold was apparently returning home to assist in recruiting for a new West Bromwich company. "Argus Junior" was impressed. *"This is the best bit of news heard for many a day in Throstledom."* But these reports may also have been incorrect for other sources have him still in Grimsby in early November.

With their number one striker available again, WBA's forward line went from ridiculous to sublime. Bolton were brushed aside 3-0 with brilliant skill from Bache. Keepers dived, opponents tackled…all to no avail. Two minutes from time, Sheerman raced away and centred for Bache to score at close range.

Bache was clearly the difference between below par and effervescence, mediocrity and goals. *"What a wonderful difference the appearance of H. G. Bache makes to the Albion attack"* enthused the *Midland Chronicle*. *"Apart from his own individual work, which is always par excellence, the amateur's inclusion seems to give confidence to the rest of his colleagues, and his beautiful dribbling and accurate passes are indeed a great help to the side. When he came on to the field, he received quite an ovation from the Hawthorns crowd."* With an attendance of 7,817, 'crowd' seems almost an exaggeration. Admittedly, the weather again played a part in the small attendance. The press, located in the Smethwick End, were unable to see who scored Albion's second and third goal, such was the gloom. The Football League remained under great pressure from the national press to abandon their competition. It was considered both unseemly and an unnecessary distraction. Indeed, Bache himself, with his upright Cambridge upbringing, would feel the dilemma acutely. Who really needed him most?

BOTH THE BIRMINGHAM and West Bromwich press were unanimous. With Bache at centre-forward, the Baggies would inevitably win and win well. Without him, they were really not very good. Unfortunately, nobody had told Blackburn Rovers. They beat the Baggies 2-1 despite the presence of the Albion's talisman, Morris netting the visitors' solitary goal. In a re-run of the Bradford PA match, he and Bache were clear on goal and H.G. stood aside for his fellow forward. In the very last minute the Blackburn keeper made a brilliant save from Bache to preserve the points for his team. The crowd included a number of injured Belgian soldiers.

The status quo was restored against the 'Pies' from Nottingham. Bache's clever footwork, in the best traditions of the Albion passing game, raised the enthusiasm of the 10,000 crowd. Fresh from a "*few days leave*", the Baggies centre-forward was rampant. His two successive shots at the County goal set up Morris for an easy strike. H.G. set up the second goal before adding the finale, dancing his way around three defenders before defeating Albert Iremonger with a side-footed shot. The supporters were "*unbounded in their enthusiasm*" as they metaphorically saluted their favourite. Harold was a one-man reason to escape from the devilment of the war for a few hours, the entertainer, the source of excitement, the reason to be at the Hawthorns, a breath of normality in an abnormal world. This, more than ever, was the forward's time. Revered although defender Jesse Pennington remained, Bache was the player to provide memories to take to France or Belgium – which was where inevitably many of the spectators were headed.

This same theme was picked up by Harold's niece, Mary Bache, who wrote in the 1960s: "*Harold's neat stylish action and clever dribbling is still recalled with enthusiasm by all who saw him play.*" Mary went on to boldly claim, "*it was due to Harold's influence that WBA developed a style closely resembling the Corinthians, with low short kicking and short quick passing.*" There is precious little evidence to support this assertion, and it appears unlikely given Harold's few games with their attendant erratic pattern. More likely is that his team-mates would give him ample possession, and fit in around him because they quickly realised his was the best route to winning matches.

Bache even made the leader column in the *Sports Argus*, traditionally a Villa preserve. Argus Junior felt a need to damp down the excitement. "*Generally the notion is that Harold G. Bache, with his sinuous and Corinthian ways, has brought about the wonderful improvement [in Albion's form]. Well, I am not going to deny it and belittle the Cantab's enormous influence, but as one soldier does not make an army, one man, even a Bache, cannot make a team. Bache has improved the forwards, but in addition to getting goals, you have to stop goals to win.*"

HAROLD'S COMMISSION FINALLY came through in early November, and with it, another transfer. He was now part of the 11th Battalion of the Kings Royal Rifles at Aldershot. On the 14th, West Brom completed their trio of North East slogs with a journey to Roker Park. They returned with all the points too, the Mackems unable to cope with Bache's *"brilliant dribbles"* and his usual unselfish nature. If Sunderland couldn't cope, the Baggies' next opponents Sheffield Wednesday certainly could. Wednesday detailed both Parkes and Spoors to take care of Bache, and take care of him they did. The *"running fire of adverse comment"* from the Baggie faithful didn't detract from the marking job. The West Bromwich cult hero's opportunities were severely limited *"but when he did get in a shot, it was always on the mark, and he certainly deserved to score on at least one occasion."* The match finished without goals.

The Wednesday match was almost the end of Bache's Albion career. The ever-mobile demands of the Army (he was now with the 10th Lancashire Fusiliers, stationed in Dorset) prevented him from playing any matches in December. The Baggies just had to get along as best they could. Harold played his final league match, at home to Middlesbrough on 2nd January 1915. That he was available for selection was excitedly noted in a prominent sub-heading in the major Birmingham paper. *"H.G. Bache may play."*

The following Monday, "Brum" in the *Athletic News* described how *"the occupants of the stand literally sprang from their seats and gave the military footballer an ovation"* after Harold scored the only goal. *"It was indeed a startling effort. The Corinthian had been baulked time after time. Once he hit the post with a very fine shot, and he had several other accurately delivered volleys charged down. It was late in the second half when he pounced on the ball, and tried, apparently in vain, to shake off his wasteful opponents. Then, while running at right angles to the posts, he suddenly checked the ball, and although apparently the opening he sought was as remote as ever, he shot with electrifying vigour and the ball flashed in the net, far out of Williamson's reach. It was one of the most brilliant goals the writer has ever seen."*

The fervour with which supporters greeted Bache's play was very rare in those days both because it was not a common occurrence anyway, but also as, with the war settling in for a long winter the country was in the grip of a huge depression. Bache's footballing genius allowed that gloom to be lifted for those lucky few at the Hawthorns for a brief hour and a half on a Saturday afternoon. He inspired through what Pelé would later call the Beautiful Game at a time when the public needed him most. But in those uncertain times, Bache's last visit to the Hawthorns went unheralded. There was a war on, and everyone had his or her own worries.

A week later, Albion lost 1-0 in the FA Cup at Hull, despite Bache's presence. City had realised the Albion threat and *"marked Bache with particular keenness."* "Stop Bache and you stop WBA' seemed to be the familiar message. But Harold was never to threaten an opposing football defence again. Qualifying as a Bombing Officer took priority, him being pretty handy with a cricket ball – bombs were thrown in similar fashion – Bache would have stuck out a mile as an obvious candidate for the job. Incidentally, despite the name, Harold's role involved the use of what would be called hand-grenades these days; versions approximating those in use today had only just been invented in 1915. More likely, Harold was initially trained on the variety whose fuse had to be ignited before throwing, and which were deemed pretty unreliable at best and downright dangerous at worst! The colloquial name for bomb-throwers at the time was *"The Suicide Club."*

BEFORE LEAVING THE country, Harold lined up twice for a 'Corinthian Under Arms' side against an Aldershot Command XI at Aldershot. In the first game on 27 February, Harold predictably found the net as he *"beat the backs, and steadying himself, scored with a smashing right footer."* In the return fixture on 20 March, he scored four times. But such footballing heroism paled into total insignificance for us when we uncovered the bravery of this talented man in the face of enemy action as he brought the ethos with which he played the game for the Baggies on to the fields of France.

According to the official history of the 10th Battalion, when it embarked at Folkestone for France, Harold, then a Second Lieutenant was with 'A' Company, as Bombing Officer. Harold, his 80 bomb throwers, and the rest of the Fusiliers were in for long and hard times on the front line.

By September, the regiment were based at an undisclosed location, presumably near Ypres. Half the company were billeted in an empty barn, and the others at a little cow house at the end. A working party on the road gave away the location, and quickly drew shellfire. One shell came through the barn roof, killing 20 soldiers and wounding 27 more. The officers rushed out to help. Captain Roberts spotted Harold dashing forward, with two sergeants, as even more shells landed around them. Roberts ordered his fellow soldiers to take cover behind a building but Bache refused, shouting back: *"I can't leave the wounded in danger!"*

In another incident, there was a breach in the parapets (front defensive wall of trench) and with enemy machine guns pouring bullets into the gaps, Lieutenant Bache was *"walking about the trenches, pulling the wounded out of danger, encouraging his men and binding up wounds, every moment in peril of his life."* Added Captain Roberts with considerable understatement *"it is difficult to explain to those who have not been in the trenches, what this means..."*

On the 6th February 1916, the Flanders-based Fusiliers moved into a piece of Ypres real estate called "The Bluff", which was partly bisected by a canal. After a major attack, the Germans seized The Bluff and also took around 600 yards of front-line as well. Because he realised that he must attack before dawn if he was to have any chance of recapturing the position, Major G.L. Torrens did precisely that at 4.15 am on 15 February. The attacking force was in three parts; the York and Lancaster troops on the right, Harold Bache's Lancashire Fusiliers in the middle, and a bombing party on the left. The right party met with stiff resistance, which held them up, Torrens leading forwards any reinforcements he could find, while the remainder worked their way on; the Regimental Diary refers to this as *'fighting hard'*, presumably a mastery of understatement. The three parties eventually reached the top of The Bluff and bombed the enemy in New Year Trench. Some even succeeded in getting into the trench proper, and hand-to-hand fighting continued for at least 45 minutes. Sadly, the numbers were insufficient to carry the day, and the attackers were compelled to fall back, pursued by bombs and machine-gun fire, and it was around this time that Harold Bache was killed.

THE COMMON EXPLANATION that a sniper took Harold's life is probably a fallacy despite his commanding officer Major Torrens claiming in a letter to Harold's mother that her son was shot by a sniper and *"died very happily and instantaneously"*. Putting aside the notion of "*dying happily*", snipers would simply not be operating in the early hours of a February morning. Regimental records do not mention any snipers so it's highly likely this "kinder" version was aimed at ameliorating his mother's grief somewhat.

Partial confirmation can be found in a separate letter to Mrs Bache from Lieutenant Geoffrey Barratt, who repeated the soothing "*death was instantaneous*", but added *"I will not worry you with the details of his last doings."* Significantly, the regimental journal made reference to *'hand to hand fighting'* and it was pretty common for both British and German solders to have what might be termed 'blunt instruments' to hand for such an eventuality. Whatever did happen, the end must have come pretty suddenly; just as well, really, as medical assistance for a severely wounded man was pretty rudimentary at that time. Harold's body was never recovered. His name is recorded alongside that of eight other Second Lieutenants on the 1927 memorial to those who have no marked grave at Menin Gate, Ypres.

It's also interesting to note that the severity of the action in which Harold was killed was later recognised by the powers-that-be; for gallantry shown during that operation, Major Torrens was awarded the Distinguished Service Order, two captains were mentioned in dispatches, and Military Medals were awarded to four of the NCOs and men taking part. Harold's name wasn't included in that list, but as the award of gallantry medals during that war was largely down to luck, or being in the right place at the right time – cynical squaddies used to refer to such decorations as *'coming up with the rations'* – it's perfectly possible that Harold, too, laid down his life for his country in equally inspiring circumstances without official recognition for his bravery.

BACK IN WEST Bromwich, the local press were fulsome in their tributes. *"One of the cleverest footballers of his day, an ideal centre-forward and his brilliant exhibitions with the Albion at the Hawthorns will not be easily forgotten by Midlands sportsmen. "*

Councillor Kendrick, at the West Bromwich Council meeting in March proposed a condolence motion. During his lengthy tributes, he described Harold as *"a worker, a hard worker and a good man when the time for play came, too. He was a gentleman in the largest sense, an English gentleman, and a sportsman."*

Billy Bassett added his own tribute. *"Bache is the greatest forward I have seen since the old days when the game produced men of individual skill. "*

Harold Bache was just one death among millions during the supposed 'war to end all wars'. Yet his loss particularly stands out because of the waste of talent, the unrealised potential lost forever. He was the only senior WBA player to lose his life while contracted to the club. We'll never know just how much further his Albion adventure could have gone. The addition of his skills to the Baggies' already devastating attack in their post-war championship-winning side might have pushed their success beyond a single season. Bache played for the Football League just prior to the conflict, and commentators of the period were convinced that an England cap was inevitable. And from there? New club records and a dynasty of success? Who can say with certainty? It's perfectly possibly that had he survived, the Worcestershire Wonder may have chosen another path, another sport or another go at teaching.

HAROLD'S PREMATURE DEMISE bears comparison with another footballer born close to the Hawthorns. Another young man with Black Country roots who, unlike Harold, he'd already played and scored for his country, but there was so much to come, so many new audiences to enthuse, records to break, cups to win. Until the day a plane crashed on take off in Munich… and Manchester United's Duncan Edwards was fatally injured. Edwards' death is marked by a grave in Dudley Cemetery.

Although Harold had gone, his contribution is remembered in several local places. His name, together will all the other Churchill men who did not return home, are remembered in a memorial window in the local church. The new window was marked by a dedication service on Christmas Day 1919. H.G. Bache is also among the 115 West Bromwich casualties immortalised in new reredos (panelling) and a mural tablet in Holy Trinity Church. Brother Eric Bache (who'd won a Military Cross) gave the dedication address in late January 1920. Further afield, he's mentioned on the Gonville and Caius College war memorial. The Bache Memorial Fund set up in 1919 by Captain J.E.K. Bache (also an Old Edwardian) in memory of his brother at their old Kings Edward's school. Subsequently, the Bache Memorial Cup to this day is awarded annually to the outstanding school sportsman every year, following a vote by the pupils.

In February 1922, Colonel J.V. Campbell VC of the Staffordshire Regiment unveiled a mural to all the Albion people (players, and deputy secretary) who had served or given their life during the war. (Lieutenant W.H. Jackson of the West Yorkshire Regiment was the other fatality). Each name was engraved on a brass tablet, surmounted by a portrait of Harold Bache in his football attire. The picture and the metal scroll remain on display at the Hawthorns to this day, located near to the boardroom.

The impression he made in those 14 brief appearances in a blue and white shirt should never be forgotten.

Years later, Albion players paid their own rather less permanent tribute to Harold and others who didn't return. The day before the 1931 Cup Final, the "*team of boys*", as they became known, placed a wreath adorned with club colours on the Cenotaph in London in memory of their counterparts who fell during the war. The inscription read: *"From the West Bromwich Albion Football Club to those great sportsmen who never returned."*

Tommy Magee

1919-1934: 434 games, 18 goals

FOR LITTLE TOMMY, this was the best afternoon in his best season in his long Albion career. The *Birmingham Gazette* correspondent opined: *"When considering the man of the match award, nearly everybody plumped for Magee"* – a sterling tribute to a man in his 13th season, and facetiously called the veteran, because in a team of players in their twenties, 'thirty plus' ranks as an old man.

"Where is Curtis?" a Birmingham supporter pondered. *"He was in Magee's pocket. The way in which Magee positioned himself for the pass, intercepted it, pivoted and despatched the ball to a well-positioned colleague, was beyond reproach, and, in the early stages, he had the temerity to introduce the ball to goalkeeper Hibbs by dropping it on top of the bar."*

Two goals from W.G. Richardson added to an ever-increasing volume of rain and the Baggies' defensive strength was too much for the Blues to match. 'The team of boys' – the WBA side had the lowest average age of any team to play in the final – had won the FA Cup. City did score, though Tommy considered the goal unfair. *"Gregg was a yard offside – he was in front of me and I was the last Albion defender, apart from the goalkeeper."*

As the soggy Albion team climbed the steps to the Royal Box to collect the FA Cup from the Duke of Gloucester, the blackest of black footballers was heard to ask, *'Has it been raining?'*

AS A GENERAL RULE, Albion supporters don't do defensive midfielders. Destructive spoiling players sit uncomfortably with the club's pure football traditions. That every team needs one is accepted, but collectively, we don't have to like it. And generally we don't!

Tommy "Mighty Atom" Magee was a rare exception. He was the best of his genre – a genre which fulfils an unglamorous, functional and often dull role. In this job, participants run themselves into the ground and are then subsequently dropped.

Modern day supporters will immediately make mental comparisons with Youssuf Mulumbu and there are similarities. Both were full internationals, had pace, competed against the best players in the country, could pass well and on occasions score goals. It's a commendable list but Magee was a direct marker rather than a channel blocker. He could also play as a winger, lived very locally and socialised with supporters and perhaps most significantly he wore the famous shirt for one and a half decades. Truthfully over the decades, only a handful of Albion men have fulfilled similar roles to Magee, and none so effectively.

Club secretary and de facto manager Everiss was fulsome in his praise of his right-half: *"He knew that football was a manly game, calling for qualities of pluck, grit and endurance. When he got hurt – as all men do – he never whined or grumbled. Tommy played football for the sheer love of the sport. He was fain to measure his strength and skill against the best pros in the game. Like his pals, Jimmy Edwards and Teddy Sandford, he dearly loved to rough it in a manly charge with the best and cleverest exponents of that period. Tommy was one of the midgets of the association game, and it was never known for him to play really badly for Albion or England."*

The late Harold Salt saw his first game in 1929. *"Little Tommy was the darling of the Brummie Road End, and indeed, of the entire crowd. 'The little bantam cock' my Dad called him and every youngster identified with him; they all wanted to play like Tommy Magee. What a character."*

Harold is adamant that the first Baggies middle section he saw are still the best he'd ever seen. *"Magee, together with Billy Richardson and Jimmy "Iron" Edwards comprised what I consider to be the most dependable, strong and capable half back line I ever saw in what I call 'logical' team arrangements."*

When the trio properly came together in September 1930, they meshed perfectly. They were able to build on the confidence that winning the first four games of the season brings. Tommy was no longer simply a hard working and highly popular individual, he was part of a powerful threesome who knew each other's game and instinctively covered for each other. The three men first made the same teamsheet for the final eight games of 1929/30, though "Iron" Edwards was turning out as a forward. In a remarkable surge of form, the Baggies won their last seven games. Using the adage of never changing a winning team, Tommy retained his No. 4 shirt, much to his relief after a long exile with the stiffs. The Baggies rattled in 23 goals in those final eight fixtures. The new improved midfield set-up was the driving force behind the Baggies 30-31 season, one of the best in the club's history.

BY THE END of September, WBA were top of the Second Division and sniffing promotion. The Baggies were full of confidence and full of goals, partly due to the introduction of a young and exciting talent in the form of a certain W.G. Richardson. Cardiff were beaten 6-3, Forest 6-1, Barnsley 5-0 and Stoke 4-0. The Widnes man was supporting the attack more often, in addition to his famed defensive qualities. Tommy scored during the aforementioned demolition of Stoke in December, in what turned out to be his last-ever goal.

Despite all the distractions of a cup run, Albion kept on track for promotion – just about. The team were wobbling with mistakes creeping in, such as during a 2-1 home defeat by Southampton in February when Tommy gave away the first goal. *"Instead of kicking into touch when he had the opportunity, the Albion half-back indulged in fancy deceptive work with the ball near to the corner flag and left winger Arnold refused to 'take the bait', with the result that the winger sent across a disconcerting square service, which eventually went into the net off an Albion defender."* Thankfully, promotion rivals Spurs had their own serious attack of jitters.

By May, Everton had won the Second Division championship comfortably, but if Albion could win their remaining two games, they'd join the Scousers in the First Division. With Albion travelling from their Buxton base (to escape the wake of their FA Cup success), Stoke were beaten 1-0 at the Victoria Ground. Magee charged out of the back line to set up W.G. Richardson for the vital winning goal.

And so on to Charlton. Over 52,000 packed into the Hawthorns to see Albion do battle with the Londoners for the fifth time that season. Athletic would not go quietly. Twice Horton beat Magee and twice Charlton scored. Twice Albion came back to level before snatching the lead twenty minutes from the end. They would not give anything away again. Finally, Charlton were beaten, and Albion were promoted. The final whistle was greeted with a massive pitch invasion. No one would leave until proper homage had been paid to a remarkable side.

To properly mark their achievements, players received a replica FA Cup – about 18in high. For many years, Tommy's replica took pride of place in the Cross Keys pub in West Bromwich. The Keys was run by Tommy's youngest daughter June and her husband Ken. It was one of Ken's weekly jobs to polish the trophy every Sunday. Indeed, the whole pub became a shrine to Tommy with around 50 pictures adorning the walls.

In 12 years, Tommy had moved on from his debut as a raw 20 year-old to the very top of his professional tree. The name of T. Magee, *"a dashing young inside-forward who shows such promise"*, featured for the first time on an Albion team list for the home match against Oldham Athletic on 30th August 1919. The day was special, for it marked the resumption of league football after the horrors of the First World War. The Baggies won 3-1 in front of 19,084 spectators. Magee turned out at inside-forward, one of the usual quintet of forwards in a standard 2-3-5 formation. The *Midland Chronicle* commented: "He was by no means prominent and acquitted himself with no outstanding display, but nevertheless he is a promising addition to the team." In his first appearance, Tommy, at 5ft 3in, set a new record as the smallest-ever Albion first teamer, a feat that held until the early 1990s, when the one-inch smaller Stewart Bowen played a handful of matches. That Tommy was able to start his football days with such a big name club is quite remarkable. His story is unique in Albion history.

THOMAS PATRICK MAGEE was born in Widnes on 12th May 1899, to James and Agnes, their first child. Twenty-three-year-old James worked as a chemical labourer in the town. Like most Magees in that area, their family had Irish ancestry. As a child, Tommy attended St Mary's School. He quickly became interested in sport, playing football for Widnes Athletic, and rugby league for Appleton

Hornets and St Helen's Recreation. He actually signed pro forms for St Helens, but was injured in his second match and decided rugby was not for him.

Following so many other starry-eyed teenagers, young Magee lied about his age to enlist and was accepted as a drummer boy in a labour battalion, thought to be the Royal Fusilieres. This was a nominal title, offering no concessions for his age. He may or may not have had a drum to lug about – either way he was just as exposed to German shells as any adult.

Despite his lack of height, Tommy was picked to play as a centre-forward for inter-unit matches. He was a natural, despite his rugger background. By happy coincidence, one of the many onlookers for these service battles was Tom Brewer, an Albion supporter.

Quickly, Brewer wrote to Albion secretary Fred Everiss recommending, *"the wizard playing for us out here. I think he could do great things for your club."* The story goes that Everiss wrote to Magee's commanding officer, one Lieutenant Hill – whose home just happened to be in Smethwick – enclosing amateur forms, which Tommy duly signed in the trenches. It's a common myth that the youngster effectively joined the Baggies during active service, with attendant images of a brave young soldier crouching in a trench with shells raining down, attempting to keep the precious paper dry. The reality is much more mundane. Tommy's autograph is dated 27th January 1919; two months after a ceasefire had been agreed. The conflict existed only in a technical sense until the treaty of Versailles was agreed.

The Widnes teenager was highly fortunate to be released from his Army duties a few weeks later. Little thought had been given to demobilisation. The whole process was frankly botched, creating much bitterness in the ranks and back in England. Many soldiers waited as long as a year to return home.

Signing a contract to play for First Division West Bromwich quickly brought a reward. Magee ran out at centre-forward against Aston Villa in a Colts (third team) match on 22nd March. This was his first appearance in an Albion jersey, indeed his first properly organised football match of any kind. A most successful introduction it was, too, with the ex-drummer boy troubling the opposition from Birmingham B6. He scored twice in a 5-0 victory. Five weeks later, after scoring regularly in the Midlands Victory League (a four club match practice exercise set up by WBA), Magee signed professional forms. *"I had no option, he was brilliant,"* explained Albion secretary Fred Everiss.

YOUNG TOMMY WAS excited as he turned up for his first day at work with one of the country's biggest football clubs, alongside some of the most famous players in the country like Jesse Pennington. He stood out immediately, with observers convinced that Magee, along with Howard Gregory, were the pick of the seniors' team.

These were troubled times for the area, and indeed, a frustrated and war-weary nation. In the dark days of mud and bullets in France, Black Country men mentally built up West Bromwich as a peaceful utopia. The reality fell well short of their dreams. Work was hard to find, with over 4,500 unemployed men in Oldbury, Wednesbury, and West Bromwich combined. Dozens died every week across West Bromwich from a new fatal strain of flu, which swept across the globe. Four other Albion men – Bentley, Reid, Sterman and Vardy returned home from active service at the end of January 1919. A month on, Crisp and Hatton, who'd won a Military Medal during his service, rejoined their teammates.

The gloomy picture was reflected nationwide. Rationing remained in force. Coal, the sole source of heating, was desperately short. Coal theft was a thriving industry. The continued absence of loved ones was a burden for everyone. Worse, over 800,000 males were maimed by the war. Most were found work of a kind, but by the autumn of 1919, 50,000 still sought employment, while a similar number remained in hospital. Football as a panacea was an unrecognised concept in that era, unlike it proved after the 1939-45 war. Few could put into words the beneficial effects of such a distraction. They just went to the match and felt better for doing so.

Following a decent debut against the Latics, Tommy retained his first team place and his first goal came at Newcastle just days later. Crisp set him up from a corner, and Tommy's powerful shot beat the keeper. He missed a good chance to double his tally *"because of an indiscriminate kick which went wide."* More accolades were slow to follow for the newcomer. In fairness, the Baggies were not short of goalscorers or headline grabbers. During Albion's 5-2 September win at Goodison Park, a victory appreciated by the home crowd; a correspondent noted, *"Only the impulsiveness of Magee prevented a larger score."*

In February, Magee dropped out of the first team, and did not play again that season. Thus he was a mere spectator, as the Baggies became comfortable league champions by nine points. However, as the baby of the team at 21-years-old in his first season, 24 games with seven goals was a grand start. He remains, to this day, the youngest Albion player ever to win a top division championship medal. The directors employed only 18 players in the first team, and with three of those only making four appearances between them, the remaining fifteen showed remarkable resilience and stamina.

Players turned out while injured, either through ignorance, or through fear of losing their place. Furthermore, any trip outside the Midlands took on epic proportions, travelling overnight and arriving home in the wee small hours.

As well as a medal, Tommy also had a wife, marrying Elizabeth Fanny Yates in West Bromwich. His new wife also originally hailed from Cheshire and, highly significantly for the time, was pregnant with their first child. The pressure was immediately on to "do the decent thing" and do it quickly. So, an April Sunday would suffice. A summer wedding was out of the question. Among the witnesses was Tommy's teammate Sammy Richardson. Presumably too, Elizabeth subsequently moved out of her accommodation in Mitchell Road to join her new husband at 119 Burlington Road, West Bromwich (near to the Vine pub). Such proximity to the Hawthorns was commonplace, and perfectly normal at the time. In those pre-car times, players and their families all lived locally.

With a wife and child to support, Magee needed all the appearance money he could get. Unfortunately for family finances, he didn't return regularly to the Baggies first XI until October 1921, by which time he was a proud Dad to daughter Irene. Tommy was now considered to be a right-winger.

This was not a good period to be overly concerned about preferred playing position, or, frankly, even being in the first team. Having a job at all in a recession was important – having a job receiving decent and guaranteed money was as good as it got. Unemployment was mounting by the week, virtually doubling in West Bromwich in just three months.

Tommy couldn't even claim to be a regular reserve player in these difficult social times. Reports were rarely positive about his contribution, with frequent mentions of *"weak shooting"* or *"sent outside"*. Magee had most of the assets needed to be a professional footballer, but perhaps inside or centre-forward was not his best position. So the next logical choice would be to play on the wing. Speed was more important than size out wide, and he began to get noticed, notably at Villa Park, where his contribution was described as "exceptional".

A COMBINATION OF illness, FA call-ups and lack of form from his team-mates (the Baggies' first home goal of the season didn't arrive until late October) gave Magee his big break in the number 7 shirt. In September, England international Claude Jephcott came a cropper at Middlesbrough with an injury which put him out of action until the following April. Magee did his best to impress the Board of Directors, then the team selectors. Finding the net at Bolton helped his cause, scoring from "a very oblique" angle after another new face, Blagden, set him up. Albion's form slowly picked up with Magee frequently combining cleverly with Blagden. He even scored a few goals himself, though one cup effort at Liverpool was ruled illegal when he knocked both keeper and ball into the net. Tommy may have been vertically challenged, but he was a tough cookie.

An example of just how tough came at Goodison. Tommy *"was laid out. Despite shouts of the spectators, neither the referee, linesman nor players took any notice, and a spectator jumped over the barrier, took off his overcoat, and laid it over the prone half-back until the arrival of the trainer. He soon resumed and was again in the thick of the fray."* Crosses from Tommy set up goals at Preston, both at home and away at Chelsea, at home against Barnsley, and at Burnley, as the Widnes man built a name for himself. He positively starred at Bradford. Magee was alone in approaching the usual brilliance of the line. His centres were always at the psychologically-correct moment, and were characterised with neatness and precision.

His good sense, however, only served to show the frequent ineptitude of the front men. Rarely in peacetime has football been so irrelevant to the Black Country. Local miners were striking, destitution was rife, while at West Bromwich Law court in early 1922, 300 police baton-charged an unhappy crowd of several thousands. Potentially deadly flu was everywhere with West Bromwich doctors now seeing over 20,000 cases in just one month. Perversely, rarely have Albion's remaining supporters needed the Beautiful Game more and, as they flocked to the Hawthorns, they took to the determined little bloke on the wing. He was like them, up against the odds all the time, but getting through by trickery, strength and perseverance. Perhaps they saw a reflection of their own lives in "wee Tummy" as he was sometimes known.

And yet still the football club were not satisfied. Jephcott was the preferred choice on the right-wing, and the Widnes man considered no more than a reserve. *"Not a finished player, but a useful man in an emergency."* To underline these sentiments, Jephcott had a run-out against Newcastle in April, a move announced weeks in advance. Tommy didn't play that day, but returned the following match – away to just-crowned champions Liverpool. Regular right half-back (the midfield of the time whose role was to "get the ball and part with it.") Sammy Richardson was hurt in a collision with a Liverpool player, and had to leave the field. A bad cut over his left eye required four stitches. In a career-changing move, Magee was asked to fill in for the stricken destroyer. He made an immediate impact in a marvellous personal triumph. Enthused the *West Bromwich Free Press*: *"He effectively blocked the way of [Liverpool forwards] Hopkin and Beadles, and kicked strongly in defence."* Buoyed up by their inspirational right-half, ten man WBA went on to beat the new champions 2-1 on their own ground.

Liverpool had immediate opportunity for revenge in the return fixture a week later, the final league game of the season. Albion selected a young reserve, Watson, at right-half in what transpired to be his only first team game. Watson was unable to prevent his Red opponent from charging past him and the game was virtually up by half-time. Captain Jesse Pennington, remembering Anfield, swapped Watson and Magee during the break, and once more Tommy made an impact. *"Magee certainly shaped better than Watson against the clever Liverpool left wing,"* opined the *Chronicle*'s reporter. Albion had a new option at right-half, and Tommy had a new career in front of him.

With Claude Jephcott available once more on the right wing, Tommy started the 1922/23 season in his second new position. At first, being the link between defence and attack didn't come easy, and enthusiasm alone wouldn't get him through 90 minutes. Being *"an animated bundle of concentrated energy and industry with unlimited pluck,"* according to the *Argus*, wasn't sufficient in itself.

After a few matches, doubts arose that he was the man for the job. In the fifth fixture, a 2-0 defeat at Villa Park, Claude Jephcott broke a leg and was carted off to a nursing home, never to play again. The right-wing berth was thus available, but Magee retained his No 4 shirt for the re-match.

Before a 40,000 crowd at the Hawthorns in September, Tommy made his name and his reputation. Villa's forwards found a diminutive snapping tiger in front of them who would not let them pass. His hustle and energy, his "unfaltering stability" and being "a terror for his size", provided a platform for a glorious 3-0 victory. The *Midland Chronicle* gleefully outlined *"giving the Villa the severest trouncing they have had in these local derbies for eleven years."* A sound piece of advice for any aspiring Baggies cult hero, if you want to get noticed, do it before the biggest gate of the season against your local rivals.

IN AN ERA when all players had the same coloured skin, wore the same boots and sported identical, short haircuts, any distinguishing features were sub-consciously well received. Good visibility in the 1920s heavily industrialised Black Country was a bonus, not a guarantee. Pollution was a normal social hazard. Smoke poured out of factory and colliery chimneys, and all too often knitted together to block out the sun. Fog or the potential for fog was often blamed for low attendances in winter. The infamous pea-souper could prove fatal. For instance, Sarah Barnsley of Tipton drowned when she fell into the local canal, having lost her way. *"As usual, it bought tragedy,"* reported the local press wearily. The absence of a roof for many spectators at the Hawthorns also hampered identification, as did poor eyesight, two decades before the start of the NHS. Size really did matter for Albion supporters. Particularly tall players (6ft was about as big as they came then) or rather small ones literally stood out. Add skill and dash to a non-standard sized body, and crowd favourite status was always a strong possibility.

Post-Villa, the diminutive right-half was suddenly a name, a player worthy of watching in action. All Albion's subsequent opposition such as Everton, Bolton and Sunderland found the "animated bundle" a great obstacle. He was here, there and everywhere, and heartily cheered by the Albion support. In the Baggies' 5-1 rout of Spurs, Tommy was even mentioned favourably in the London press (traditionally considered to be ignorant of the Midlands), a news story in its own right in the Black

Country. The only concern for supporters was the inclusion of Magee meant no place for the fine Sammy Richardson. It was a dilemma: Sammy did get a chance at Blackburn, but did his cause no good at all with a limp performance in a 5-1 defeat. This was awkward for Tommy too because he and Sammy were great pals.

THE ARRIVAL OF Sunderland for an FA Cup match broke the Hawthorns attendance record. Over 56,000 crammed in, with numerous journalists also in attendance for the big "English Cup" match. Tommy and his fellow half-backs dominated in an Albion victory, and once again, his name shone from national titles. The FA Cup enjoyed remarkable status and prestige in that era: supporters from the away team would be in attendance, a novelty otherwise reserved only for local derbies. This was the season which would result in the first ever Wembley final, white horse and overcrowded pitch, beginning a legend which prevails to this day. That around 200,000 people would wish to watch a mere football match gave as good an indication as anything that this game had taken a grip of the nation's imagination and passion in these grim times.

Albion home supporters were generally a laid-back bunch. Though they would prefer their side to win, applauding or even cheering opposition players or moves was commonplace. If Tommy could "turn it on" away from home, the opposition supporters would willingly show their appreciation – and it made his name all the more. For instance, at Burnley, *"Magee, who is Lancashire born, always has a fine reception, and on Saturday, the Burnley crowd fully appreciated the wonderful play of this little half-back. He bottled up Cross and Waterfield, and the spectators recognised it by giving him rounds of applause. On his form this year, Magee stands an excellent chance of earning a much sought-after international cap."*

SUCH WAS TOMMY'S rising reputation, he was selected for England trial matches against the South. Once more, the London press were impressed. *"Magee was a distinct success,"* admitted a *Daily Mail* reporter. His battles against the two opposition forwards made the whole match interesting. Tommy had another trial, this time against the North. His contribution to that match at Leeds was far more modest, however he was subsequently picked to represent his country against Wales in the

Home Internationals (a popular annual League competition between the four home nations).

Tommy, according to the *Birmingham Mail*, was "one of the most popular of all the Albion players, both among his colleagues and the club's supporters." More recognition followed when the midfielder played in the second of two matches against Sweden in Stockholm in May. Three more caps eventually arrived – against Belgium at the Hawthorns, Scotland at Hampden, and France in Paris. Being a local resident made good served to deepen Tommy's popularity according to the *Chronicle*. *"He received a capital reception when it was made known he had received another cap."*

Much was made of Tommy's small frame, but in his era, he was probably just below average weight at 10st 7lb. Nine of Albion's registered players were lighter, with a few below 10st. Neither was his lack of inches quite so distinctive at that time. Goalkeeper Pearson stood just over 6ft tall, but none of the other double winners were over 5ft 10in. Eight inches difference was certainly enough to be noticeable, but not an impossible shortfall to overcome.

His two most often used nicknames of "Mighty Atom" and "Pocket Hercules" were not original titles. It is likely that they were 'borrowed' from other great players in much the same way, in later decades, that any player called Robson was automatically dubbed "Pop", after the West Ham man who bore the original sobriquet. Patsy Gallacher of Celtic was known as the 'Mighty Atom', while Everton's Jack Sharp was dubbed 'Pocket Hercules' as far back as 1899.

Tommy was invited to join the FA XI on their epic voyage to Canada in 1926. For invited, read, "you're going". What the FA said, the FA got. For a man with such a modest background, this was a glorious extended opportunity to travel abroad without anyone shelling him – to visit such exotic locations like Toronto, Vancouver and Calgary, and other places he'd never heard of. The tour was a wearisome 18-game slog. The games stretched through May, June and July, involving numerous uncomfortable days rattling across the vast acreage of Canada by train. Tommy played in 15 of the 18 fixtures, all of which were won. His young wife Elizabeth gave birth to their second daughter, June, during his absence.

This tour was literally not the trip of a lifetime because five years later, Tommy went again. Magee, together with double-winning colleagues Cookson and Shaw were all selected to represent the FA. There were only 11 games this time, over two months. Fortunately, someone made the sensible decision that the players would not train between matches. The party travelled out on the Canadian Pacific liner *Duchess of Atholl* on the 15th May 1931, and didn't return until late July, just in time for pre-season training. Once more, every game was won with some ease, Cookson alone amassing 26 goals. The FA expressed their contentment with the efforts of the touring party, awarding each player an international cap and £10 additional personal expenses, a decent boost to Tommy's £7 weekly wage. Every player was also invited to a banquet in London.

Tommy's hopes of more international fayre were damaged between these two trips by the not insignificant problem of relegation. A deadly combination of leaky defence and the forwards' inability to find the net led to the drop in 1927. Only 15 goals each for top scorers Carter and Davies was not good enough for such a big club. *"Singularly unimpressive"* as one irate fan described their contribution. To quote the nursery rhyme, when they were bad, they were horrid. At West Ham, for instance, the correspondent for the *Birmingham Gazette* noted: *"When Albion caught the infection, and emulated the example of the United in a display of wild and aimless kicking, the crowd indulged in a form of communal hilarity which one has never heard equalled."*

IN GRIM TIMES, supporters feel a need to grasp what positives they can. In 1986, Steve Hunt, seemingly taking on the opposition by himself, caught the eye. In 1991, Don Goodman's pace and goals offered ultimately false hope. In 1927, it was little Tommy, refusing to let his opponent get past him and supporting his front men where possible, which captured the attention of supporters and reporters alike. The *Gazette* reported typically on a defeat at Old Trafford: *"... the magnificent display given by Magee. He smothered Thomas out of the picture altogether and repeatedly made forward thrusts that ended in a perfect pass to Davies or Carter. The crowd were highly appreciative of the little man's performance."* Filling in for injuries, Tommy made a few effective appearances on the wing, though without his defensive skills, the defence sagged. Albion needed two Tommy Magees – at least. However, even Tommy's enthusiasm and form waned as relegation became inevitable.

Like many other top-line players, Magee found adjusting to the different style of the Second Division most difficult. He was below his best for months on end, chided for making forward runs at the wrong moment, or not tackling his opponent quickly enough. Lamented the *Post* correspondent following a home defeat against Nottingham Forest *"Magee certainly played a long way below the form which in the past has won him international fame."* After this low point, his timing and all round game improved somewhat, if still rather up and down. The consistency of another Richardson (Bill) at half-back only served to highlight the contrast. Returning from whence he came, though, remained elusive. As Albion have traditionally found throughout their history, returning to the top Division after relegation is both hard work and highly frustrating.

Still, there were the occasional high points, such as a victory at Clapton Orient, as the *Chronicle* correspondent recorded: *"One saw admirable work from Magee, who took a new leave of skill from the occasion and proved himself a very able defender and a half-back, who, when the opportunity presented itself, was not only aggressive, but skilfully aggressive. That is to say he made of his right wing a smartly working trio in which Glidden, Carter and he were conspicuously useful."*

Tommy managed only to score two goals in four seasons in the lower Division, curiously both against the same opposition – Stoke City. The first was a fluke, when his long punt so startled the City keeper (albeit he did have Albion striker Cookson "in attendance"), that the ball skidded off his hand into the net. The second, in December 1930, surprisingly was his last ever goal.

Poor health didn't help. Wee Tummy turned out for a crucial cup quarter-final replay at Huddersfield. *"Magee took a resolute hand in the spoiling process, considering that he had just left bed after an attack of influenza, he summoned up his strength to equal his zeal with rare pluck, and in the first half, particularly kept Smith establishing anything like a perfect liaison with the centre and right wing."*

After such an effort, he presumably suffered a relapse and was rested for the next league game at Vale. Or that was the idea, until Carter was taken ill en-route. A wire was sent to 'Get Magee'. Arriving by "special car", he was asked to play on the right wing. Sadly, he wasn't fully fit, and could do no more than lay the ball off when it came to him. Albion were wretched, losing 8-1 and Tommy felt wretched too.

He played very little part in the rest of the season, even after he was restored to full health. Neither did he make much of an impression on the next as the trio of Richardson, Evans and Darnall were playing so well together. "The Mighty Atom" was a second team regular, and still not in the best of form.

He made one of his most public appearances of this time in August 1931, not on the football pitch, but as a pallbearer at the funeral of Albion director Harry Keys, the six most senior players carrying the coffin. The future looked grim until a happy coming together of a dynamic midfield and a goalscoring machine were united, and a promotion charge was suddenly on.

MANY ALBION SUPPORTERS thought that the 1931/32 season would prove to be a farewell one for the diminutive midfielder. He'd given them good service, they'd loved him, but now he was obviously coming to the end. Not so, the directors including the name of Tommy Magee on the retained list. (At that time, players were either retained – effectively a one-year contract – or released or transfer listed). The local press were taken aback, but quickly rallied. *"It is a great tribute to Tommy Magee, the 'veteran' of the side, that he should be retained after 13 years service with the club. That there is 'life in the old dog yet' has been amply demonstrated by his wonderful performances during the latter half of the season. His experience of First Division football as a member of the Albion side before relegation should be an asset to the younger members next season."* However, despite his extra time, football life again became more problematic for Tommy. Following on from such triumphs would be admittedly difficult for anybody.

Still, the first season back in the top flight began superbly for the club's senior professional. Tommy's tackling was an integral part of an excellent team, who had the temerity, as a promoted side, to challenge strongly for the title. The Baggies had the toughest opener possible – at Highbury, against league champions Arsenal. Remarkably, Albion won 1-0 with the Widnes man highly prominent. One commentator said: *"It was gratifying to see how well Magee acquitted himself against the James-Bastin wing. His Canadian tour has given him new vigour."* By this point, the England international had played football continually for twelve months, without any substantial rest, due to his inclusion on that FA tour. Eric Brook, the famous Manchester City and

England forward said Magee, together with Edwards of Leeds, were the hardest right-halves he had ever played against. *"They play so much on top of you that it is difficult to go ahead, and I usually have to make a back pass."*

At Christmas, life became much tougher for the right-half. He injured his knee in the Christmas Day battle with Birmingham City, and couldn't play in the return fixture the following day. It was the end of his run of 61 successive first team games. At first, doctors feared a displaced cartilage, for which an operation was required. Thankfully, the final diagnosis was a torn ligament and (long overdue) rest was the only cure. Without him and other key personnel, the Baggies slipped from second position in the League to finish sixth. *"Magee's absence has been severely felt"* lamented the *Albion News*.

Tommy was a day short of his comeback game against Wolves reserves in late February when domestic tragedy struck at their new home at 34 Westbourne Road, West Bromwich. His wife went to the bathroom on Friday night to take a bath. Tommy heard a noise, and hastened to the bathroom, where he found his wife dying, struck down by a brain haemorrhage. It's impossible to comprehend the anguish he must have endured at that moment, and since. His other half was just 33-years-old, and they had two young daughters to care for. Elizabeth Magee was buried at St. Peter's Church, Whitehall Road, West Bromwich. It is at such times of crisis when personal popularity is tested. Tommy didn't want in this respect. People lined the streets the entire distance (around one and a half miles) between the family home and the church and St. Peter's was full to capacity with family, friends, supporters, players plus two club directors.

His parents made the trip down, and a saddened Tommy returned with them to spend a few days back in his home town of Widnes. He returned to piles of sympathetic letters from his team-mates and supporters, to which he responded with a "thank you" small ad in the local press. By mid-March, he was playing football again, cheered heartily on and off the pitch against Manchester United's second string. After all, he knew nothing else, and had to provide. But life would be difficult for a widower with two children, even with support from his in-laws. Fortunately, Elizabeth's grandparents ran the nearby Dunkirk Inn at neighbouring Greets Green and Tommy and his children moved in with them. The arrangement was ideal in several ways. Tommy always loved a drink, even on a matchday. His idea of relaxation was simply to have a good time with team-mates like W.G. Richardson and Harold Pearson, friends or later on his son-in-law. Attending race meetings or the dogs were both particular favourites (later in his life, he ran a chain of bookmakers in Widnes).

Another regular haunt was Ted Sandford's café. He was naturally outgoing with always a joke or two to share. Tommy regularly referred to the Black Country as "crow country" as in "caw do this" or "caw do that".

Some kind of temporary relief from Tommy's loss came in April, when the Baggies ventured northwards to turn out for a benefit match against a Widnes Select XI in order to raise funds for the local Widnes rugby club to buy their ground. As a Widnes lad, Tommy was named captain for the night. It was an uplifting return home. The West Bromwich side was met by a jazz band, which escorted them through crowded streets to meet the Mayor at the town hall.

The visitors won their match 4-1 (£200 raised) and then were welcome guests at a banquet. Tommy returned to the first team for the opening games of the new 1932/33 season, reunited with Bill Richardson and "Iron" Edwards. Then, after a run of four matches without a win, changes were made. Jimmy 'Spud' Murphy seized his chance, performing so well in the No 4 shirt he eventually played for his country. Tommy was to play only five more games at the top level in the following eighteen months. His regular absence from the second team further emphasised the writing on the wall.

His first team farewell came at the Hawthorns against Huddersfield in March 1934 in a 3-2 defeat, and a brief farewell it was, a leg injury causing him to retire hurt after just half an hour. His low-key departure (no benefit game) from the club he'd served for a decade and a half, followed on the 5th May, marked only by small sub-headings in the local press. The only Baggies player to win both cup winners and championship medals was never seen again in league football.

CONSIDER TOMMY AS a miniature midfield Jeff Astle, a man who contributed as much off the field as on it. He broke a mould that was hastily re-pieced together after his departure, by breaking up opposition attacks and being genuinely appreciated by supporters and England selectors for doing so. Of course, there was more to him than endless running and tackling. Thanks to his son-in-law Ken Taylor, we can now also appreciate Tommy the man – down to earth, modest; always ready to share a pint (or pull one in the Dunkirk). His gregarious nature was so well received in such a basic hard working area like the Black Country. Despite those Cheshire tones, he was one of us.

ALTHOUGH A RATHER elderly Tommy Magee was a special guest of the club at Wembley in 1968, subsequent generations of supporters and indeed his own family needed a reminder just how immense his contribution was to West Bromwich Albion. Directly as a result of publication of the first edition of Cult Heroes, Tommy's descendants, now scattered around the globe, were linked together by grandson Ed Vilade. Ed is well known across the USA in his own right as a journalist, author and speechwriter to several US Presidents. Ed was born locally but taken to the States at an early age. In October 2007, and enjoying the full red carpet treatment, he and his wife Alice visited the Hawthorns for the first time to watch in his grandfather's 'Throstles' in action. Tommy would have been proud.

W.G. Richardson

1929-1945: 444 games, 328 goals

ON 29 MARCH 1959, an unremarkable charity match was staged at the BSA Recreation Ground in Small Heath, Birmingham. The Midland All-Stars were doing leisurely battle with the combined might of the TV All Stars XI. Before kick-off, the captain of the Midland All-Star side was photographed next to the TV Stars' captain, one Bernie Winters.

After 20 minutes of the second half, the captain of the Midland All-Stars chased the ball down the right wing, but collapsed near the corner flag. He was carried from the pitch, but was dead on arrival at Birmingham Accident Hospital. William Richardson, West Bromwich Albion's most prolific goalscorer was gone. *"I'm sure this is the way he would have wanted it – wearing a No 9 shirt,"* offered his widow bravely. "W.G.", as he will be forever known, was two months short of his 50th birthday.

YOUNG WILLIAM WAS born in 1909 in Framwellgate Moor, a tiny mining village in close proximity to Durham. Not surprisingly, his father supported his family by working underground in a pit. His favourite pastime was supporting Sunderland and his son was carefully taught that there was really only one football club worthy of his time. And, as he was making a name for himself as both Durham County schoolboy and an England Schools international trialist, Richardson senior went right to the top to get advice about his son's talent, seeking out the Mackems' best-known player, Charlie Buchan. The footballer was precise with his thoughts. *"Don't let him play for three years when he leaves school. His muscles will adjust themselves to his physical growth by then, and he will be all the better."* Charlie's advice was sound: in those days, boys literally played against men because there were no age-limit matches.

So William left school at 14, and joined the United Bus Company in West Hartlepool working shifts on Saturday afternoons: football was well and truly off the agenda until he reached 17. His frame now suitably broadened by that time, he joined a local club, quickly turning a famine into a feast by scoring regularly. Hartlepool spotted him before too long, and signed the then-bus conductor as a part-time professional.

In the summer of 1929, Jesse Pennington happened to be holidaying in Hartlepool with former Albion team-mate Bob Pailor. Noting his host was particularly enthusiastic about a young footballer with 19 goals to his name, Jesse was quick to contact the Albion. As a result, Fred Everiss and director Lou Nurse travelled, and persuaded Hartlepool manager Will Norman to sell William Richardson for £1,250. As Bill recalled: *"The three of them were waiting for me when I got off the bus to go home for my dinner; I was a bus inspector then. We all trooped into my house where Mother was getting my meal out of the oven, and I signed on in the front parlour, aspidistra and all."*

The Framwellgate forward made an instant impact at his new Midlands club, as noted in the *West Bromwich Chronicle*: "*Those most successful in the first practice game included Richardson. In the second half [of the traditional Whites v Stripes public match] W.G. gave a rousing display which changed the whole aspect of the game and enabled the Whites to win. Scoring one goal himself, and providing Short with the chance to add another, Richardson proved himself to be a capable leader and a force to be reckoned with.*"

There was a practical difficulty. Albion already had a William or Billy Richardson in their squad. The other Richardson was a local-born centre-half, one of a host of intelligent signings in 1929, including Ted Sandford, Jimmy Edwards, and Bert Trentham, all of whom would play a part in Albion's renaissance. To distinguish between the two Richardsons, the North-East newcomer was called Ginger, because of the colour of his hair, or more commonly W.G. In the official football documents of the club, however, the centre-half was always W. Richardson No.1 and the centre-forward W. Richardson No. 2.

Naturally, the newly dubbed "W.G." started in the Central League, making his debut against Huddersfield. According to the *Albion News*: *"Richardson gave an impressive display – confirming the high opinion formed of him in the practice games."* He didn't score that day, but his first goal wasn't all that far away, nor his second and third… Two in a game were commonplace, such as the brace against Derby in a 12-2 win; there were several hat-tricks, too, even the odd four or five, over 50 goals in all. Such prowess could not be ignored. W.G. made his first team debut against Millwall on Boxing Day in 1929, replacing the injured Cookson. He scored in a 6-2 win, and went on to play in five out of the next six matches, finding the net against Barnsley, before Cookson returned. The Baggies were not short of goalscorers at the time, with their main three forwards managing 72 between them that season.

A series of injuries put young W.G. back in the first team in November 1930. Playing at inside-forward, rather than as the main striker didn't help his cause, but once switched to No. 9, he found the net eight times in eight games, meaning he was now in the team to stay, missing only a handful of games between then and September 1937 and every year he was the club's top league scorer.

Goals always make for popularity among the supporting hordes, but W.G. was so enthusiastic and wholehearted that even without his goals, he was destined to be popular. For instance, in a match against Burnley in December 1930, he'd needed the magic sponge after colliding with the Clarets goalkeeper. Within 15 seconds of re-entering the pitch, he'd made the most of a pass from Carter to score the winning goal. Curiously, for such an instinctive goalscorer, he proved to be wonderfully unselfish, dutifully passing to better-placed colleagues rather than shoot himself. Sometimes too unselfish, as in one game against Man City, when he effectively had a one-on-one with the City goalkeeper *"but to the amazement of the crowd, he flicked the ball in the direction of Robbins, who had little hope of using it."*

BUT ALL THAT was in the future, in the short-term there was a little grumbling among the Hawthorns faithful: bringing in a youngster was all very well, but why at the expense of Jimmy Cookson? Cookson was himself highly regarded with over 100 goals to his name. He did have one final chance to redeem himself in February 1931, though, when "W.G." moved to inside-forward to allow Cookson the No. 9 shirt. In two games, Cookson didn't score, but Richardson bagged three. With promotion to chase, this was not a time for further experiments: the old King was dethroned, his Albion playing days virtually finished. A new King of the Hawthorns was to be crowned.

And just not promotion: West Bromwich also fancied the FA Cup, despite their Second Division status. W.G.'s goal knocked out Charlton in a third round second replay, and Spurs bit the dust in round four. In the next tie at Fratton Park, W.G.'s solitary effort knocked out First Division Pompey. Not that he knew too much about it, mind: as W.G. made contact with a loose ball in the goalmouth, he fell flat on his face. *"No one was more amazed than me when I realised it had gone in."*

There was more to come. The ginger-haired striker found the net in the quarter-final at home to Wolves, where he was described as being *"Albion's most virile and dangerous forward."* No doubt excited by such a description, W.G. scored the winner in the Molineux replay. Nothing like crucial goals in cup matches against local opposition to raise your popularity! The *Chronicle* reported on the replay: *"W.G.'s leadership was inspiring enough to make his colleagues feel he was worth supporting."* When asked what he remembered best about the victory, W.G. modestly overlooked his own contribution. *"My abiding memory of that game was Harold Pearson saving a lob from Jimmy Deacon, who was clean through in the second minute. It was the sort of shot you don't expect a goalkeeper to save."*

The semi-final was against Everton, runaway Second Division leaders, at an absolutely crammed Old Trafford. Hardly a neutral location for such an important match, but nevertheless, special trains transported 3,000 Albion supporters, with more travelling by coach, Evertonians heavily outnumbering them.

On the pitch, the Midlanders probably felt outnumbered as well, as the Scousers battered away at the West Bromwich defence, missing chance after chance. As W.G. remembered: *"From the first minute, every Albion supporter must have had his heart in his mouth, There it must have stayed for the first half an hour. Every Everton forward missed more easy chances than you could count. I was at centre-forward – the spectator with the best view, for I couldn't have touched the ball more than half a dozen times in that half hour."*

The Baggies hung on, hoping desperately for a break. In the second half, they got one. Glidden crossed into the Everton goalmouth, hoping that W.G. might get a piece of it. The Everton custodian, Coggins, was so disconcerted by the sight of the onrushing W.G. that he hadn't noticed the ball's trajectory had been diverted by the wind. By the time he did, it was past him and in the net. W.G. again: *"The goal was like a whole season's luck rolled into one... Coggins had his eye on me, and before he knew what was happening, the ball had bounced over his head into the net."* The Baggies hung on to their slender lead to the end when: *"hundreds swarmed across the playing surface,"* according to the *Chronicle*, *"and before the players had time to get to the dressing room, they were caught and slapped and patted in a most affectionate, if somewhat brusque, manner."*

ALBION WERE AT Wembley for the first time in their history, and so too were neighbours Birmingham City. All West Midlands trains would leave for London that day, pouring into Paddington station every 12 minutes over a seven-hour period. The *Argus* claimed 48 special trains left Snow Hill and New Street stations alone by 11am, this on top of the scheduled service. Albion received 80,000 applications for a pathetic 7,500 tickets. A radio "beam-back" to Dartmouth Park, West Bromwich, was offered as a consolation to the tens of thousands of disappointed spectators – there being no big TV screens back then.

Cup Final Saturday was wet and miserable. On a soggy pitch in the rain, the two sides slogged away manfully. In the first half, Carter spotted W.G. making a run, and found him with an accurate pass. Richardson's shot wasn't the best, but it was sufficient to deceive the Blues keeper. W.G. had now added scoring at Wembley in the Cup Final to his list of achievements.

No cup final side, up to then, had ever recovered from being a goal down, but Birmingham hadn't read the script and hit back, equalising in the 59th minute. From the kick-off, a trio of Albion forwards charged forward against still-celebrating opponents. Supporter W.J. O'Reilly will never forget that moment. *"To see the Albion players passing and re-passing the ball, drawing nearer and nearer, bigger and bigger until Hibbs dashed out to dive at Richardson's feet, only for Billy to trick him and walk the ball into goal, was my greatest thrill in watching football for 65 years."* Pathe News footage underlines just how rooted to the mud the Blues players really were and also that the winning goal was very close to being an own goal.

City were bereft. Their heads went down and, bar a panic in the last five minutes; it was a comparatively easy task for the soggy Baggies to see out the rest of the game. Less than two years after turning professional, W.G. had scored two goals in an FA Cup final – immortality guaranteed!

The *Birmingham Gazette* summed up the achievement: *"It is safe to say there is no prouder man in the whole of England than W.G., West Brom's centre-forward. To score one goal in a cup final is an achievement of note: to get two, each time giving your side the lead, is an achievement. Fame has come early to Richardson comparatively early in his career, for he is only in his second season with Albion."*

The leg-weary Baggies accepted the trophy from the Duke of Gloucester, who offered his own appreciation: *Your boys have been wonderful"*. The cup winners rested overnight at Eastbourne before taking the silver pot home to West Bromwich the following day . Over 200,000 people turned out to greet both victorious team and trophy, its first appearance in the town for nearly four decades.

BUT TIME FOR celebrations was limited, as the Baggies were still chasing promotion. Truth to tell, the FA Cup had badly affected their league form, with only one win recorded in both February and March. Luck was with them – their nearest rivals Spurs had caught a crab of their own. Five precious strikes from W.G. in mid-April secured four points out of six. A nervous 1-1 draw at home to Bradford, though, meant West Brom had to put their Cup triumph aside, and win both their last two games to go up.

On a tense Thursday night at the Victoria Ground in Stoke, Albion did just enough to get the result they needed. Inevitably, it was that man again, W.G. Richardson, putting away a half-chance, just enough so that a missed penalty by West Brom's George Shaw didn't matter.

One game left… Charlton Athletic at the Hawthorns, in front of 52,000 people. Albion officials might fairly inquire where all these supporters came from: with the predictable exception of the derby with Wolves (40,000), the final match drew a gate double that of the previous highest league attendance that season.

The match itself was a dramatic one, with Athletic seemingly determined to spoil the party. Twice they led, and twice the weary

Baggies determinedly drew level – then, with only 20 minutes left, Glidden's cross was headed home by... it just had to be W.G., didn't it? The Londoners finally got the message, and didn't trouble Albion's defence any more. After the last whistle, the crowd poured onto the pitch until a sea of flat caps, mufflers, and dark coats replaced every bit of green. It must have been much like our own flooding of the Hawthorns turf to celebrate various promotions to the Premier League, except with silverware to cheer. Just like us, Albion's new-found 1931 army of supporters weren't going anywhere until the players made an appearance.

With irritating understatement, when responding to a question about his favourite time at the club, W.G. would only modestly say: *"The best week for both myself and the club was the last week of the 30/31 season, when I scored two goals on the Saturday at Wembley to win the FA Cup from Birmingham; the only goal of the match at Stoke on the Thursday afternoon; and the winning goal against Charlton Athletic at the Hawthorns on the following Saturday."*

A civic banquet was subsequently held to mark the achievement of the "double winners" which included a new song, specially written for the footballers of West Bromwich:

> Welcome the victors
> Youthful, faithful, true.
> Who at Wembley conquered
> As they meant to do.
> Football so inspiring
> Won the Cup and fame
> Sing the Albion's praises
> Join in this refrain"

Secretary Eph Smith worked at the Hawthorns for 54 years. When asked about his favourite goal, he didn't hesitate – for him it was W.G.'s winner in the '31 Cup Final. *"Whether it was that Birmingham had just scored, and had not got over it, we shall never know, but not one of their side touched the ball until Harry Hibbs picked it out of the net. To see a goal like that at any time is a thrill – but to see it in a cup final, scored by one of our own side, is something that will remain with me to my dying day."*

For West Bromwich Albion, traditionally more of a cup team, a good run in the FA Cup was an expectation. In the following three years, the team only managed to win a single cup match, so by 1935; a certain cynicism was creeping in. Add frustration to cynicism in round three against Port Vale, as only a very late goal from W.G. secured a 2-1 win. Sheffield United came and were conquered 7-1 with remarkable ease, a classic W.G. hat-trick blunting the Blades. Said the *Chronicle* correspondent: *"It did me good to see W.G. make a comeback as a marksman."* This was more like it – a Cup run. Nearly 25,000 packed into Stockport's ground to see the First Division side put the locals in their place, 5-0. The match was played in *"appalling conditions"*, with two more goals from the ace marksman. *"W.G. Richardson proved a good leader, and the others backed him up enthusiastically."*

In excess of 56,000 crammed in for the quarter-final at home to Preston, to see those old cup foes defeated by a single goal, set up by a W.G. free kick. Excitement was mounting. With eight of the 1931 Cup Final team still in the current line-up, could the Baggies win the cup again? Second Division Bolton were eventually defeated in the semi-final, which went to a replay; inevitably, that man again, W.G. Richardson, was on the scoresheet in both matches, including the key first goal (a *"rising shot"*) in a 2-0 victory in the re-match. Wembley again on the back of Richardson's goals.

It may be fairly said that Albion's Cup Final team selection proved crucial. Should they go with established players Carter and Glidden, who were not 100 per cent fit, or should they stick with their less experienced – but fit – understudies? Rightly or wrongly, Carter and Glidden got the nod. The gamble failed: Carter got a knock on his injured knee after 33 minutes, and become a hobbling passenger, leaving a mighty big ask against a Sheffield Wednesday side rated among the best in the country. The ten men battled bravely, and somehow scored twice against the Yorkshiremen.

At 2-2, and with only five minutes remaining, W.G. was put clear through Sheffield's defence. This was such a familiar scenario, with normally only one ending, that secretary Fred Everiss whispered to chairman Bassett: *"Here comes the Cup again"*.

Richardson ran forward into the penalty box, against a goalkeeper John Brown, who looked like a rabbit caught in headlights, yet he was a full England international. He froze and didn't move off his line:

W.G. could have dribbled the ball right into the goal past the immobile Brown, but tried to place the ball – and missed the goal completely. The hero of 1931 had just cost his club the Cup: Wednesday then scored two late goals to win 4-2.

W.G. would never visit the Twin Towers again as a player, although he was to accompany the 1954 team in the capacity of trainer. His best hope came two years later, when straightforward victories against three lower-division opponents (and five goals for the striker), presented Albion with a home quarter-final tie against the mighty Arsenal, the team of the thirties. A new (and still unbeaten) club record attendance of 64,815 crammed into the Hawthorns. W.G. set the Baggies on the way in the 10th minute, when he pounced on a goalkeeping error. So strong was his shot that the ball rebounded off the taut netting, and landed outside the penalty area. When Mahon added a second, it was all too much for the Londoners, who eventually lost 3-1. Cheering crowds invaded the pitch at the end, and wouldn't go home until secretary Fred Everiss had made a 'thank you' speech.

PRESTON WERE THE semi-final opponents, but it was not to be West Brom's year. Albion's hugely popular chairman, Billy Bassett, died just two days before the big game. No one felt like taking the field, a feeling heightened by the FA's insistence on a two-minute silence. West Bromwich were a goal down in minutes, three behind in half an hour, but it just didn't seem important any more.

W.G. RICHARDSON WAS an all-round talent. He could head, pass both accurately and cleverly, shoot, and was exceptionally fast in a short dash. Such was his ball control that later on in his career, he took all the corner kicks for the team. As the *Albion News* pointed out: *"The facility and accuracy with which W.G. takes corner kicks with either foot is a valuable asset."* There were long-range goals (a 25-yarder against Stoke in December 1930), not to mention bursts of skill, such as against Sheffield Wednesday, when he beat two opponents, then ran between the Sheffield backs before defeating the keeper. Charging goalkeepers was an accepted part of the game at that time: Gilfinnan of Portsmouth and Turner of Huddersfield were amongst those made to look very silly by W.G. knocking the ball out of their hands and tapping it over the line.

Sometimes, he could be lucky and unlucky in the same match, as the club programme illustrated. *"In March 1932, Albion beat West Ham 3-1 in a fine demonstration of how good fortune can swing in just one match. All Richardson needed to do was to tap the ball over the line. Somehow with the side of his foot, he managed to scoop the ball over the crossbar. By contrast, when the opposition keeper attempted to clear the ball, it struck W.G.'s head, then hit the post before rebounding to the grateful forward. This time, the ball crossed the line in perfect safety."*

IT'S HARD TO know how anybody can top scoring five goals to secure two honours in barely a week, but W.G. tried his best. Getting one over Albion's oldest rivals was always one of his best routes. In November 1931, Albion played Villa for the first time in five years. There were almost 60,000 in attendance, Albion's biggest gate of the season by a whopping 33 per cent. As the game wore on, the visitors from Birmingham were almost literally run off their feet by opponents who were yards faster and more thrustful. W.G.'s rare header was the middle of three goals without any reply. *"Richardson was invariably too good for Villa defender Talbot, and was a veritable thorn in the flesh for the Villa defence,"* wrote the *Chronicle* correspondent.

Several thousand happy Baggies invaded the pitch at the end of the game. But those who live by the boot …A month later, at home to Birmingham City, the striker was guilty of missing an easy chance from two yards out (City won 1-0) and a fortnight after that, in a painful 2-1 home defeat in the FA Cup by Villa, W.G. shot wide from three yards out. The popular marksman was a sure bet to find the net against local opposition, scoring against Wolves and Blues in five consecutive seasons, and in four straight against Aston Villa, who presumably then chose relegation to avoid any more punishment. Their last Villa Park derby ended in a 7-0 rout for the Baggies, with W.G. scoring four times, as well as missing two further excellent chances near the end. The victory was a triumph for speed, method and accuracy from the Albion men as they kept the ball on the ground, even managing four first half goals against a howling gale. At the time, it was Villa's worst ever defeat at home, and manager McMullan resigned shortly afterwards. Now that's the kind of thing that makes you a hero in these parts!

Perhaps there was just something about claret and blue that galvanised William "G" into a higher gear. In November 1931, the

Baggies were playing at Upton Park. After five minutes, W.G. collected a long clearance and scored at the second attempt. On seven minutes, an inviting centre fell nicely for W.G. – 2-0. With the Londoners having just kicked off, the excited striker burst between two defenders to net his hat-trick. Less than sixty seconds later, W.G. did it again, knocking in a cross from Woods. He'd scored four goals in five minutes. *"During 30 years experience of football reporting, I have never seen anything so wonderful as the way in which West Ham were swept off their feet by the Albion"* wrote 'Wanderer' in the *Sunday Express*. To their credit, the home supporters rose as a man to their executioner, cheering W.G. every time he touched the ball.

The *Albion News* added: *"W.G. Richardson deserves every credit for the brilliant way in which he took his chances, but he was the spearhead of an attack which for a time operated like clockwork."* Meanwhile, back at the Hawthorns, the reserves were putting ten past Liverpool, with Cookson netting seven of them. Both first and second teams led 4-0 at half time. The news from London was greeted *"with tumultuous cheering"* by supporters at the Hawthorns.

IF GOALS MAKE heroes then W.G. was your man. Other feats of scoring included a five-minute hat trick and four goals in total against Derby at the Hawthorns in September 1933. The foursome included a rare penalty. As the *Free Press* had it: *"There can be no two opinions about the value of W.G. Richardson. Without him occupying the berth, the team is never the same potent force."*

Barely three months later, W.G. netted a hat-trick at Everton in a 7-2 spectacular. He'd amassed 17 goals in total, but clearly that was deemed insufficient, as he was dropped three weeks later! Without a win in four fixtures, losing 0-1 to Blackburn at the Hawthorns was the final straw, as the *Chronicle* explained. *"Throughout the game, they [Albion] did most of the attacking, but they missed opportunities with exasperating frequency, and their finishing generally was nothing less than wretched... As though to crown everything, W.G. Richardson failed with a penalty kick.... His shot went straight to the goalkeeper and rebounded off his knees... What blame there is to be attached lies with the forwards. Constructive methods seem to be unknown to them."* W.G. missed two matches before being recalled against Derby.

Clearly Albion standards were very high in this era, as the striker had been dropped the season before due to *"loss of form"*, according to the *Free Press*. The centre-forward hadn't scored for three whole games. His absence didn't help, West Bromwich lost 3-1 at home to Sheffield Wednesday, so back came W.G. against the Wolves – and promptly scored twice. Two months later, there were back-to-back hat-tricks against Leicester and Portsmouth, and later that same season; "Ginger" found the net in nine consecutive league games. Only three men in Albion's history have equalled or bettered that feat.

In the 1935/36 season, W.G. scored 39 League goals – a club record that remains unbeaten to this day. The *Albion News* commented on the Boxing Day 5-2 win over Middlesbrough that featured four goals for W.G. in the second half: *"A brilliant individual achievement. The first of the four rewarded a magnificent dash between the backs, and a lightning shot. The second followed a tussle with Brown in which the latter had his knickers torn, and while he was on the sidelines donning another pair, our centre-forward was completing his quartet of goals. His low swift shots were completed with such precision, that Gibson had no chance to save."* W.G. was quite unstoppable in the next six weeks, regardless of the state of their opponents' knickers.

Two more followed in the next match against Manchester City (won 5-1), singles against Middlesbrough in the return fixture and Stoke, followed immediately by back-to-back hat-tricks in an 8-1 slaughter of Blackburn, and 6-1 demolition of Liverpool. W.G. remains to this day the only Albion man to score a treble against the Reds. However although the Baggies scored 89 goals that season, they also conceded 88. Their 39-point tally gave them safety by a 3-point margin.

And being a genuine goalscoring, W.G. benefited from the odd lucky goal. In a friendly against the Corinthians in January 1932, W.G. accidentally scored. Carter's hopeful cross was heading well wide of the goal until it hit the centre-forward on his head and the rebound flew into the net. As the cliché has it, you have to be in the right place to be a goalscorer. So regularly did his name appear on the Albion scoresheet that W.G. was also credited with some goals which he clearly didn't score. In December 1939, he was reported as a goalscorer for the Albion, but this came as something as a shock to the striker who was laid up in bed that day with a heavy cold.

Like anglers, every goalscorer has hard luck stories about the one that got away. In April 1933, in a 4-0 defeat of Man City, the game was noticeable "because of a refereeing decision to disallow a Richardson goal for offside when there was no possibility whatsoever that Albion were." Even the City players were amazed by the decision. Apparently, Robbins and W.G. had got past their defenders, they drew the keeper out then Robbins squared to W.G. to score. The writer called it *"a staggering decision"*. By remarkable coincidence, twelve months later Albion again beat City 4-0 and again Richardson had a legitimate goal chalked off. His shot went into the roof of the net then bounced straight back into play, but the referee refused to allow the goal.

BEING THE FIRST Division top scorer would normally lead to international recognition. Richardson was hopeful of adding to his solitary cap, earned against Holland in 1935, when England's regular centre-forward, Ted Drake of Arsenal, was unavailable. Albion's top striker was thrilled to wear the heavy, woollen cream shirt of his country.

In May 1936, in recognition of his leading scorer status, W.G. was selected for *Probables* against the *Possibles* in an international trial match, which included several Second Division players, and even two from the Third Division. Albion's top striker did everything possible asked of him by scoring all the goals in a 3-0 win: *"He became a great menace every time he touched the ball"* said one spectator. And yet W.G. wasn't picked for the England v Scotland match, Arsenal's Drake being preferred again. As ever, playing for Albion was a big drawback for international hopefuls. A year on, he was relegated to the *Possibles* team, and predictably, scoring didn't bring any reward.

In 1937, Albion agreed a fee of £7,000 to sell W.G. to Manchester United [the then transfer record was the £11,000 paid by Aston Villa for J. Allen in 1934], but the two clubs had overlooked something – W.G. refused to go. Albion didn't force the issue, so their top goalscorer stayed. The old stager – he was now all of 28 – was playing fewer matches now, as injury caught up with him. His goals, too, were fewer in number, with only 15 recorded in 1937-38. He had a rival too in raw -boned Harry Jones, who was sometimes preferred as centre-forward. An unfortunate set of circumstances, including a highly leaky defence, saw Albion relegated that season.

As war in Europe approached, W.G. was now Albion's shortest forward at just 5ft 7in tall; indeed he was almost the smallest player at the club. He spent much of the 1938-39 season with the second team. Meanwhile, four young players all made debuts in September. At 29, did W.G. already feel old and past it? Maybe he was best out of first-team action, as the fixtures didn't always consider the strains on the players.

Early on, there was a Thursday afternoon fixture at Norwich, the team staying overnight and then catching a train the following morning… for Plymouth! After that Saturday afternoon affair, there was no train back until 8pm, meaning a 3.00am return to West Bromwich. One of the new men, Harry "Popeye" Jones, now had W.G.'s No. 9 shirt full time, and continued to find the net rapidly. His goals continued after war was declared, and indeed he missed only one game up to March 1940, before injury and military service ended his career.

After a number of decent showings with the "seconds", W.G. reclaimed his first team shirt. A remarkable display at Old Trafford in a third round cup replay cemented his status with one goal scored, and three more set up in a 5-1 win, subsequently receiving more compliments for his football prowess

In February 1939, with the Baggies reduced to ten men through injury, they still managed to beat Southampton 2-0 in some style. *"W.G. dashed down the left with Affleck in pursuit. His pursuer overbalanced and slipped. Richardson ran to the touchline, and slipped across a head-height centre, which Elliott turned into the net."*

Albion's hopes of a return to the top flight were dashed in April when dramatically, their goals dried up completely. One goal in seven matches was out of character for a forward line who regularly found the net three or more times per match. The goals returned in the final fixture, a 4-2 victory over Norwich, in what turned out to be the last full League game until 1947. Thus, Richardson scored his last real league goals for Albion in this game. One might have hoped for a spectacular ending, but it was not to be. The second of his brace was a header which the Norwich keeper dropped, and the ball apologetically rolling over the line. Only 3,000 turned up to watch. War was horribly imminent while in addition W.G. was about to become a Dad to Brian.

SET IN CONTEXT, the wartime leagues were a brave, defiant morale-raiser, an attempt at preserving an oasis of normality in desperate times. But with an often-unrecognisable team, playing in an unrecognisable strip, and sometimes in unfamiliar locations, hostilities footie was hardly momma's home cooking. Locally, Aston Villa sat out some of the competitions, while bomb damage-improvements to St. Andrew's had the Bluenoses playing away from home, often at Villa Park. Games were regularly cancelled because of travel difficulties; both teams were sometimes stuffed with guests, or needed to borrow opposition players to make up their numbers. Notts County once turned up without a goalkeeper, while a weary Swansea team arrived three hours late (and predictably were 5-0 down after 25 minutes, losing 8-2 with W.G. scoring five). Even when playing at home, secretary Fred Everiss once went into the crowd to recruit two hopefuls to make up Albion's team against Walsall.

Little wonder that historians normally list W.G.'s 100 wartime league goals separately, lending them the afterthought nature of the Zenith Data Cup. Frankly, W.G. was past his best (a few months past his 30th birthday when war was declared), sometimes playing in the absence of younger men.

That said, scoring all six in a 6-1 victory over the RAF, five against Swansea and Villa, six past Luton and several hat-tricks must merit at least a nod of acknowledgement. Who can *ever* ignore an Albion man putting five in Villa's net? The *Midland Chronicle* and *Free Press* in May 1943 could not. *"The shining star of this 6-2 victory was centre-forward Billy Richardson. After 14 seasons with the club, he is still a power as leader of Albion's attack. His five goals were all opportunist: that gave the 6,000 crowd something to remember in the close season. Had it not been for the hard defensive grist of Callaghan, and smart saves by Waterman, he might have had two or three more."* This was a purple patch for W.G. with hat-tricks in three of his previous four games.

Albion were more fortunate than most, with access to their own players in the early years of the war. In March 1940, Minister Ernest Brown was questioned in the House of Commons by MP William Robinson if he would enquire into the circumstances in which 12-18 players of West Bromwich Albion, with no previous knowledge of the work, had been given jobs with a firm of munitions manufacturers, where experienced staff had to meet their military obligations. The Baggies felt horribly exposed, and subsequently didn't miss any opportunity to point out their players' contribution to the war effort: "*We now have 15 members of our squad in the Forces*" was a not untypical early justification, and the numbers mounted throughout the conflict. Initially, W.G. "did his bit" with the local Police Reserve, a commitment which varied enormously from season to season, at his lowest point he was able to play only twice in 1939/40.

Youngster Peter George described some of the sights and sounds of a home match during the war. *"Before joining the queue for the "boys" entrance in Halfords Lane (admission 6d) it was my solemn duty to walk to the players' entrance, clutching our autograph books. Nearly every player arriving wore some sort of services uniform – Army, RAF, Royal Navy, Merchant Navy, Police, Fire Service – and although we didn't see any Land Army girls (more's the pity) we often did see Italian prisoners-of-war in their brown uniforms, and a huge orange disc sewn into the back of their tunics. The P.O.W. camp was just opposite, behind the Co-op laundry in Camp Lane. Conversations between us teenagers tended to be like this: –*

"Who's that RAF Sergeant?"

"Who's the Army bloke?"

"That's Stan Cullis. He's England's centre-half!"

"He looks as if he's going bald!"

"Watch out, here comes a copper!"

"That's W.G. Richardson of the Albion, he's a Special."

"There's another one up there on traffic duty!" "Who's that then?"

" That's Don Dearson of Birmingham and Wales."

"Think he'd sign?" "We could try!"

"That's Jim Sanders – he's a fighter pilot. He's with Charlton, but he's playing as a guest today for us."

"Is he a real fighter pilot?"

"Oh yes, they say he's shot down 10 Jerries!"

POST WAR, THE Albion veteran refused to hang up his boots. At the age of 36, West Bromwich asked for – and got – a fee of £250 from Shrewsbury Town, a fifth of the original cheque that they'd given Hartlepool all those years ago. Any grumbles from the Shropshire folk were quickly stifled as their new signing scored 55 goals in just one season. But time was running out, even for W.G., as a footballer. He needed a new career, something longer-term.

The Albion goal record-holder took advantage of the FA coaching scheme to qualify as an instructor or coach. By happy coincidence, Albion needed a coach, and were delighted to recruit a man with both pedigree and qualifications: *"This is just the sort of job I wanted." rejoiced W.G.* The prolific forward was a popular coach, and was perfectly capable of practising what he preached.

Pete George was briefly an Albion footballer after the war: *"My father took me to my first Albion match in 1937 to see W.G. From that day, he was my hero, so I followed him throughout the war. When I reported back to the Hawthorns in 1949 after my National Service, I was delighted to see W.G. had been taken on the training staff, coaching the Central League and Midland Midweek teams. Bill was a practical joker of the highest standard, but as my own father had died in 1937, shortly after that first game, I looked upon W.G. as a second father. "*

Derek Kevan, who knew a little about shooting himself, admired his coach. *"Billy used to like a joke, and was a nice chap. Even in those days, when he used to hit a ball in training – along with Ronnie Allen, who was on a par, Billy was one of the finest players for hitting a moving ball that I've ever seen."*

Midfielder Ray Barlow agreed: *"W.G. joined in our forwards' shooting practice, and he really showed them how it should be done. He still packed a tremendous shot, and he was so consistent. The lads were rolling the balls to him, and he was cracking them home like a machine."* W.G. loved the involvement, and continued to play whenever he had the chance. And then one day, he played his last game.

W.G.'s funeral was held at Holy Trinity Church, West Bromwich, before cremation at Perry Barr. Six members of the 1930-31 Cup-winning side carried the coffin. He was also remembered with a minute's silence at a home match against Manchester City.

The last word goes to another Albion crowd favourite, Ray Barlow: *"Always ready with a grin and a leg-pull, Bill was a real 'player's man', a likeable figure who had hundreds of friends."*

Ray Barlow

1944-1960: 482 games, 48 goals

DURING WORLD WAR Two, Albion played in all blue shirts. Indeed, they were grateful to get those obviously wrong objects because of the strictures of rationing. Replacements were hard to come by with the football club appealing regularly and hopefully to their supporters to donate their clothing coupons. The temporary Regional League structure was rather a hit and miss effort, with each club attempting to fulfil as many scheduled fixtures as possible, with their final position based on average points per game. The ball, for which a permit was required, was made out of stitched panels of leather with a huge lace-up opening into which was placed an inflatable rubber bladder. Heading said ball when it was wet risked injury. All this fun was available for a flat match fee of 30 shillings (£1.50) each.

The entire West Bromwich squad either served His Majesty in the forces or were employed in factory work, normally munitions. Naturally, the team members varied from match to match, with guest players or trialists regularly called upon to make up the numbers.

Into this strange scenario within an even stranger world came a young player from Swindon. Raymond John Barlow made his debut for Albion's first team versus Walsall in a War League Cup match on 3rd February 1945, which Albion lost 2-0. By contrast, another cult hero, W.G. Richardson, was playing in his final fixture. Little did anyone present know that the banner of cult status was passing so neatly between these two Albion legends, nor how it would transfer from a goalscoring legend to a more prosaically talented but imperiously vital half-back.

RAY WAS BORN in Swindon on 17th August 1926, the only child of Thomas and May Barlow. *"Just ordinary"* was Ray's simple description of his childhood. He didn't begin to grow until he was 16 and then couldn't stop – something of a problem for his mother with rationing in force.

He was spotted playing for the Garrard's works side by former Albion centre-forward, Jimmy Cookson. Apprentice toolmaker and Arsenal lover Ray was completely two-footed and was comfortable either at inside-left or inside-right (best compared to a modern day striker's role). Cookson put together a Select side, made up from all the club sides around Swindon. Garrard's managed a 3-3 draw with this elite team, with Ray scoring all three. By happy coincidence, Ray's father was an occasional drinker in Cookson's pub and Jimmy asked him one day: *"Do you think Ray would like to go for a trial?"* Subsequently, Ray was happy to sign amateur forms for Albion on 20th June 1944.

Months passed without any news. Only in October, when the local Villa scout was sniffing, did the Baggies formally invite him for a trial at the Hawthorns. Just one game with the reserves was sufficient for Secretary Eph Smith to say, *"Bring your Dad next week. We'll want you to sign as a professional."*

Despite a decent showing against the Saddlers, inside-forward Barlow did not play for the firsts again until the following season, when he scored 12 goals in 32 Football League South games, most noticeably his first goal (at Newport in a 7-2 thrashing) and his first hat-trick against Spurs. Ray already boasted his first nickname – "Boy Barlow" – and comparisons were already being made with the great Charlie Buchan.

Many more alternative names followed, such was his popularity, mainly connected to his height. "Lofty", "Tiny", "Legs", "Daddy Long Legs" or "Skyscraper" were the most commonly used. Conversely, "Sugar Ray" Barlow was an obvious link to famous boxer Sugar Ray Robinson, though the title was ironic. One less flattering monicker was "First-Half" Barlow, a sarcastic reference to his inability to pace himself through the whole game. The accusation stuck, with a varying degree of justification, throughout his entire career. *"He had a good first half, with through passes constantly spelling danger. Then he slowed up,"* wrote local reporter Dick Knight about a match at Fratton Park in January 1951. Over eight years later, during a home defeat by Spurs, the *Birmingham Mail* correspondent noted, *"Barlow started off like a bomb, but faded a little towards the end. If he was to conserve his energy a little more...."*

SUPPORTER COLIN SIMPSON recalled Barlow's post-war debut in the new transitional league. He had, for those days, particularly among professional footballers, very long hair, which kept dropping over his eyes, causing much sardonic Black Country humour. When he appeared at the next home fixture, his hair was appreciably trimmed, and more in line with the short back and sides style of the era.

Team-mate Peter George remembered the new arrival. *"We trained with him and he was a smashing chap. A few of us nicknamed him "Zummerzet Zider" because of his lovely West Country accent, although I believe he hailed from Wiltshire.* "One of Ray's party tricks was already evident. *"With his long legs, he could bring a ball down from seven feet, and then execute a perfect pass."* Talk to any supporter of a certain vintage about Ray Barlow, and sooner rather than later, they'll mention how he was famed for not getting his shorts dirty. Ray thought nothing of trapping a heavy leather ball at shoulder height and directing it accurately to a colleague, all in one sweet movement. Think of John Cleese ('Boy' Barlow was just over 6ft tall) with football skills for a crude approximation.

BEING BORN IN 1926 meant that the Swindonian was too young to fight in the war, but the Army were determined to see him in uniform, and he was duly summoned for national service. He did his best to continue his football career, slipping out of camp whenever he could. Sadly, he chanced his arm once too often in March 1947 and the Army exacted retribution on Private Barlow by posting him to the Tank Regiment in Palestine as a Gunner. Playing for the Palestine Army team wasn't quite the same, particularly for a teetotal non-smoker.

Overseas service unsettled Ray (Charles Matheson of the *Argus* claimed *"he looked something like a scraggy end"* upon his return) and he was painfully out of form at the Hawthorns. He even missed games due to *"sore feet"*, a condition thought to be a legacy of ill-fitting Army boots. (In the early fifties, he was unimpressed to be called for his Z-reserve training, basically a two-week refresher event. Resisting the urge to scrawl *"Bollocks"* all over the form and return it as so many national servicemen did especially around the rise of Suez, he spent two weeks in a tank during the summer of 1951).

Much had changed at the Hawthorns in his absence. For the first time ever, the stars in stripes had a manager, Jack Smith, who took over from retiring jack-of-all-trades Fred Everiss. The new man added 13 new players to the club, much needed for once again, West Bromwich were attempting to get back into the top tier of the league, having been relegated in 1938 in painful circumstances. The Baggies had lost their last three matches and finished two points short of survival, despite having registered 14 wins.

THE LONG-LEGGED recruit did score some excellent goals as a forward, notably a spectacular 30-yard drive at Bury in August 1948. But his passing ability was more akin to that of a midfielder, or wing-half, to use the jargon of the period. Jack Smith chose to use his skills in the midfield and turned him into a half-back. Such a switch was curiously part of Albion traditions – it was a well-trodden path including two members of the 1931 double team in Teddy Sandford and Tommy Magee. After an eye-catching spell with the Albion reserves playing in the middle of the pitch, Barlow made the first team in the same position, and was just as impressive.

Argus Junior was among his admirers. *"Ray Barlow, at half-back, is addressing the ball differently. One day, maybe, this long-legged Swindonian of skyscraper altitude will develop a spring in his heels. When that happens he will be able to get up for high balls which others might require stilts. Barlow does not use his head a lot in the strictly heading sense. Does not have to with such strength of body and leg. Ray seems to have glue on the end of his boots as he fetches the ball down from shoulder height by sending either foot on an airborne mission. His control is exceptional and, oh boy, how he uses that long pass."*

Supporter Paul Collins was typical of Ray's admirers. *"Strong in the tackle and after getting the ball, Ray always had or made time to do what he wanted. He would ease past an opponent or two and then that ground-eating stride took him clear. A further strength was the weight and direction of his passes, particularly the one inside the full-back for the winger."*

But injuries elsewhere meant another stint at inside-forward supporting big forward Dave Walsh as West Bromwich chased another promotion and FA Cup double. Fulham, Spurs and Southampton provided the competition in a four-way scrap for two promotion places.

IN MARCH, RAY and two other players missed the train to an away game at Cardiff City. Hasty arrangements had to be made to drive them to the Principality and much to the relief of the manager the trio reached Ninian Park half an hour before kick-off. Not that Ray was perturbed as he set up both goals in a 2-2 draw. Albion's second goal is worthy of particular mention: Barlow hooked the ball over his head to Williams, the striker repeated the feat and it fell beautifully for Walsh to score.

Progress in the FA Cup was halted by a single goal defeat by eventual winners Wolves in the quarter-final stage, but promotion was still on. Barlow's efforts were to prove crucial in the run-in, thanks to his vision and accurate passes. With four games to go, a 1-1 draw at Southampton, where the "*long legged Swindonian*" battled on despite a leg injury, was just enough for Albion to keep their noses in front. Ultimately, the Baggies needed two wins from the last three – Ray scored in a 2-0 victory over Barnsley, and not just any goal, according to the *Argus*. "*Albion's outstanding personality was Barlow. His craft and accurate passing were a treat to see, and he scored a grand goal following a solo run from 30 yards out.*"

And so victory at Filbert Street would suffice. Although Leicester were good enough to reach the Cup Final, they still needed a point to avoid relegation to the Third Division. The official gate was just under 35,000, although many more scrambled in over the walls, and estimates suggested another 30,000 outside. The home side had all the play, but the visitors had all the goals – three of them with the last one from Barlow, hooking home from an acute angle. At the end, the 5,000 travelling Albion supporters invaded the pitch, and carried the entire promotion-winning team around the pitch on their shoulders.

A "*MILD FORM of polio*" put Ray out of action for most of the next season back in the top flight. He'd lost weight. As Barlow was one of only three unmarried men in the senior ranks, in the words of the time, 'he had no wife to fatten him up'. So the football club asked the Dyce family, who ran the Hawthorns Hotel, to take the player in and feed him as lavishly as restrictions allowed. Meat was still rationed, as were petrol and sweets. Houses were in short supply and new-fangled TV only accessible to the wealthy. These were difficult times. Still, Ray quickly got his feet under the table, indeed he was almost a member of the Dyce family. They quickly adapted to his keenness for a morning newspaper and weather forecast with his breakfast while as far as possible indulging his love of chocolate and steak.

It wasn't until November when Ray returned to first team football – playing up front again. Ray could simply play anywhere, and was initially happy to do so without complaint, a trait that endeared him to management and supporters alike, although he probably wasn't expecting his next opportunity to shine in an unusual position. In March 1954, goalkeeper Norman Heath was injured at Roker Park. Barlow volunteered to stand in, not such a surprise, as local reporter Charles Matheson explained. *"Ray really can keep. I've seen him do quite spectacular things between the sticks in training. He has the build and the reach and the grip to be a success there."* Ray won a standing ovation from the Roker faithful for his makeshift performance in the Albion goal, finally beaten only four minutes from time. Sad to say, the unfortunate Heath, with 169 games behind him, never played again. Ray's versatility did indeed seem endless, his long throw-ins becoming an Albion staple decades before Rory Delap made his name. He'd take penalties, too but with only a moderate degree of success.

One of Barlow's most endearing qualities was his desire. Its normal manifestation came merely in his zest, vigour and playing style, but Ray wasn't above taking advantage of weather conditions in order to improve his team's chances, as supporter Ben Payne remembers: *"We were playing Aston Villa on a very foggy day, so foggy that a modern game would be abandoned. Suddenly, Billy Goffin, a nippy Villa left-winger came sprinting out of the gloom with an Albion player on his tail. The lanky figure of Ray Barlow could just be seen over in the centre. As clear as a bell, I heard him shout 'here, Bill'. Without lifting his head, Goffin whipped the ball over whereupon Ray Barlow lifted his leg, brought the ball under control and went trotting up the field with it. We were left with the amusing sight of an exasperated Goffin standing with hands on hips."*

THE PROMOTED TEAM did enough to maintain their top division status for a couple of seasons. Goalscoring was a problem, a source of frustration for Barlow, who, now a fixture in the starting line-up, match after match would set up opportunities for his front men only to see them wasted. The *West Bromwich Chronicle and Free Press* noted in a 1-2 defeat at home to Spurs *"When promising moves initiated by Barlow and Kennedy broke down, they must have had a feeling akin to despair. So much so that towards the end, both were taking the ball upfield themselves in an effort to achieve something their forwards could not. Barlow's consolation goal two minutes from time was just reward for a grand wholehearted game."* One supporter, R. Williams, summed up the universal frustration in rhyme

> *"Half-backs, full-backs, goalie too are seldom slacking…*
> *But in this forward line, there must be something lacking."*

Manager Smith admitted he'd attempted to purchase twenty different centre-forwards. Each time, he had either been refused outright or the other manager would counter with *"Give us Barlow or Kennedy in an exchange deal and we'll talk.* "In the absence of new talent, existing squad members were tried up front, including Barlow again. Requests from Albion managers became quite frequent enough for Ray to be regularly quoted as saying, *"I know what you're going to ask me, and the answer is yes. I'll play anywhere for you, Boss."* The team came first in that era, and Ray gallantly played the role of the loyal club man. While it worked in his favour in terms of his dedication and adaptability being appreciated, supporters and press alike were unimpressed that such a great midfield talent should be misused in this way.

Fortunately, the arrival of new talented attacking players such as Ronnie Allen (who would eventually fill the troublesome central striking role), winger George Lee, and innovative managers like Jesse Carver and Vic Buckingham, eventually saw the team blossom into one of the most attractive sides in the country. Good times to be a Baggie, but these pleasures were typically celebrated in a mute manner as antique supporter Terry Wills recalled.

"At five to three, the players would run out for the first time to loud cheers. This being very much the era of the 'stiff upper lip', it was perfectly reasonable for them to expect to cheer when scoring a goal, AND for good

play, of course. Otherwise, the crowd spent the rest of the game being quietly appreciative of the fare served up for them on the playing surface. Swearing was frowned upon. If anyone temporarily forgot their manners, terrace etiquette demanded somebody yelled, 'Hey, there's a lady here' and the reply was invariably the standard apologetic Black Country response, 'Sorry, chap'. Nevertheless, the match was always the big pressure relief-valve for what was for many, a dull and dreary working week consisting of nothing but unstinting manual labour."

THE FAMOUS DUDLEY – Kennedy – Barlow classic half-back line played as a trio for the first time in April 1952 at Maine Road, Manchester where they were described as *"the mainstay of the side".* Once together, they were formidable, providing a stable platform to build an exciting Albion team around. That season finished with 13 points gathered out of the last available 16.

Jimmy Dudley was a former goalkeeper and winger (versatility seemed essential in that era!) who amassed over 300 games for the Albion. Joe Kennedy was a giant of a centre-half. Although the pair were jointly the tallest members of the side, Barlow broke up attacks with his feet at any height, leaving Kennedy to deal with aerial balls.

But sad to relate, the much-quoted trio were more often myth than reality. After their initial spell together up to February the following year, injuries and filling in gaps elsewhere meant the threesome averaged barely 10 games per season together right to the end of the decade.

As is common with such players who can play anywhere, Barlow's versatility often meant his personal good was subjugated to the needs of the team. As he became older, Ray considered himself solely a half-back. He was not best pleased when injuries to the regular strikers saw him again pressed into service up front midway through the 1955-56 season. After 13 reluctant games, he made his position very clear to the local press. *"I am not a centre-forward. And, try as they might, West Bromwich Albion will never make me one. That is why I am unhappy at the moment"* opened his 500-word plea. *"If things start to go wrong and we start to slide backwards, I hope the fans will not blame me."* Such a breast-beating statement must have been difficult for this most gentle and modest man. The return to fitness of striker Johnny Nicholls a fortnight later spared his discomfort.

In February 1953, the Baggies chose another manager in Vic Buckingham, who replaced the short-lived Jesse Carver, unable to resist a lucrative offer from Italy, *"a fee no English club could pay."* Buckingham was a man with a plan. He wanted Albion to emulate Spurs' "push and run" tactics (Buckingham was a former Tottenham man) utilising long passes rather than short ones. Barlow would provide the passes, 40 yarders were, after all, his speciality, while the forward pairing of Ronnie Allen and regular scorer Johnny *"on the spot"* Nicholls would do the rest. The whole team, from back to front, were encouraged to pass the ball and then defend when they didn't have possession. The plan was radical for its time, but worked because Albion had the right blend of players. After finishing fourth in 1953, they just missed out on the double twelve months later.

THE BAGGIES STARTED 1953/54 in magnificent style. Newcastle were defeated 7-3 on their own ground (*"the crowd simply rose to us… and we were 3-0 up"* gaped defender Stan Rickaby) as the stars in stripes lost only one of their first fifteen games. The first six away games were all straight wins. Chelsea were crushed 5-2, Manchester United beaten home and away, all unable to cope with the Baggies' first time, quick-passing game. WBA now stood for "*We'll Beat Anybody.*"

Providing the bullets for the deadly forwards was Ray Barlow, although sometimes he cut out the middle man. For instance, against Sunderland, he let fly from fully 40 yards and his wind-assisted shot found the gap below the crossbar and above the goalkeeper's fingers. Later, he hit the bar before setting up George Lee for the second and final goal. Just a normal day at the office…

A small squad, combined with injuries and international call-ups at the wrong moment, cost Albion the title, their season turning on a crucial match against championship rivals Wolves in April. With ace goal men Allen and Nicholls (55 goals between them) both selected for their country, good ol' Ray was asked to fill in up front. As Ray explained, their absence was crucial. *"I got injured early on in the match. Bill Shorthouse clogged me after ten minutes, but I had to carry on because there were no substitutes then. We lost a silly goal and ended up losing 1-0 and the league pretty much went with it, because the confidence went out of the side. We knew we could have finished them off and we hadn't done it."* The Baggies painfully slipped out of top spot after that local derby.

With Albion recording only one win and one draw in the last five games, the championship went instead to Wolverhampton by the margin of two victories.

BUT THERE WAS still the '54 Cup Final looming. Cup holders Newcastle were beaten in a classic fifth round match. Barlow scored one of the three goals as Spurs were dismissed in a rather comfortable quarter-final before Third Division Port Vale made life very awkward in the semi-final, having the temerity to take the lead before the Baggies just squeaked home 2-1 to meet old cup foes Preston at the Twin Towers.

Many years later, Ray revealed his Wembley memories to the *Albion News*: *"It was a big thrill to walk out in front of 100,000 people. You have butterflies for an hour before the game, and then it's nice to get out on the pitch and get on with it, but there was a real tingle from walking out in front of all those people and then walking up the steps to collect the medal after the game... It was a typical cup final really, a lot of nerves, a lot of mistakes, and it was one of those matches where it didn't really get going, which sounds funny if you think there were five goals in it."*

Barlow gave his usual 'laid back' display. An outrageously offside goal by Preston's Wayman was partly responsible for Albion trailing 2-1 with only 25 minutes left. Could West Bromwich miss out on both prizes? Ray got his infamously long legs moving. He dodged one tackle, and then evaded another before Tommy Docherty brought him down with a high lunge and the referee gave a penalty. *"It was obstruction at most,"* said Ray, honestly. *"Just an indirect free-kick, but the ref had made such a boob with Wayman..."* Ronnie Allen scored amid incredible tension with Albion keeper Jimmy Sanders unable to watch and the momentum was now with the Midlanders. Frank Griffin completed the job three minutes from the end. *"Frank Griffin always said it was down to my pass that we scored so that's nice of him."*

ALBION'S CHANCES OF returning to Wembley again that decade were thwarted, by defeat in the 1957 FA Cup semi-final replay to Villa in wretched circumstances. Albion supporters of mature years still rage about this cup exit. The first game finished 2-2, with Villa equalising through Peter McParland five minutes from the end. As John Thompson wrote in the *Express*, *"So often it would seem Villa would be outclassed. So often the tall commanding figure of Ray Barlow broke their attacks and their hearts. Barlow was uncanny in his positional movements."* Ray was understandably a little peeved. *"I thought we should have had the game won in the first half. But we faded after that."*

In the replay, Albion were again the better side, but a cynical foul by former Albion man Dugdale on Ronnie Allen took out the ace goalscorer. Albion's ten men, with Barlow outstanding all over the pitch, hit everything but the net, while the Villains pinched the game 1-0. Ray Barlow was never to get that close to Wembley again.

Testimony to the character of our 'Leggy' hero was confirmed when he was the first Albion player to walk into the Villa dressing room and say to Johnny Dixon, Villa captain, *"Well done! We have had our turn at Wembley. Now it's yours – and we hope you bring the cup back"*

Dick Knight in the *Evening Mail* was one among many to offer what succour they could. *"No team has ever been so great in defeat. A giant above all players rose to stamp his class and personality, upon this never to be forgotten game. Ray Barlow spurred his depleted team on with his burning enthusiasm and his own classic play. When they were reduced to ten men, he was a forward and a defender in one, and came within inches of launching Albion into the lead."*

A year later, the Albion side battled against the odds to defeat both Nottingham Forest and Sheffield United in the cup, with just ten men. Yet the emotion of the post-Munich nation was just too much to compete with against Manchester United in the FA Cup quarter-final. The Albion skipper explained: *"The crowd was fantastic for the replay at Old Trafford. I've never seen anything like it. The coach was completely blocked in by supporters, who mostly couldn't even get into the ground. It took us ages to get into the dressing rooms. I can remember in the last minute, Bobby Charlton picking the ball up on the right wing, ghosting down, a young lad, jinking past two or three, coming up to the line, pulling it over, a perfect ball for Colin Webster to put it in. And curtains for us."* The Baggies, good though they were, could not take on seemingly the whole world and a referee intimidated by the 60,000 inside the stadium and half as many outside.

The two sides met at the same venue in a league match just three days later and, in the absence of the Cup hysteria, the Baggies showed their real class by winning 4-0. But this was scant consolation.

BARLOW HAD CLASS, but was also prepared to put his body on the line. On top of a black eye at Sunderland in August 1954, a year later Barlow broke his jaw against Cardiff. Despite having his jaw wired up, to allow just the minimum chin movement which permitted a liquid-only diet, Ray missed only three games before returning to the Baggies line-up.

In terms of footballing ability in midfield, the nearest modern day counterparts for Ray can only be England stars Stephen Gerrard or Scott Parker. The Albion man really was that good. Consider this glowing review from a correspondent in the *Liverpool Echo*, who witnessed league leaders Everton being outplayed by the Baggies at Goodison. *"One man stood out. Ray Barlow, the tall West Bromwich left-half, strode through this game as like a professor of the Soccer arts. He was terrific. At times, I thought his legs were telescopic as he snipped off the intended through pass, and surged though the fluid Albion front line into devastating action. What a man and a half Barlow proved himself in defence as in his majestic first-half attacking role."* Like "Legs" Barlow, Gerrard and Parker make the game look easy, wherever they are on the pitch. They can score, pass, tackle – attack or defend. The most lamented Duncan Edwards bears comparison, too. All, like Ray, are great favourites.

Albion supporter Peter Whitehouse, had his own thoughts: *"What made him stand out was his outstanding ability to bring the ball from the penalty area to the opponents' defence and lay off a pass that was a scoring opportunity. He had long legs that with his long stride made him appear to be strolling between the two penalty areas. It was only when you saw opposing players running hard trying to stop him that you realised how fast he was moving. He was a player before his time, most wing halves were expected to be good tacklers and then hoof the ball hopefully up to their forwards."*

Despite his numerous admirers, Ray was called up for his country only once. Invariably, Portsmouth's more defensively-minded Jimmy Dickinson was preferred. Ray was regularly the team reserve; in those pre-substitute days, it was a highly frustrating position. His first non-appearance as spare was as early as 1951 against Portugal. One journalist came up with yet another nickname for the Albion star – Ray *"Bench"* Barlow. Still the £50 he received, equivalent to a month's wage, must have eased his irritation. His solitary cap was earned against Northern Ireland in October 1954. As Ray himself said: *"I was surprised when I got my cap because I thought I'd missed the boat, I'd been consistent and never got in, so to finally get a call-up was one of the highlights of my career, there's nothing like playing for your country."*

STILL, RAY DIDN'T completely miss out on foreign travel just because he was an Albion player and therefore not worthy. He was part of the FA party that toured *"the Americas"* in 1953. When visiting Buenos Aires, he was given a pair of light, leather continental-type shoes. To these boots, he added curved rubber bars and used the then revolutionary combination in a muddy FA Cup tie against Rotherham the following year.

IN JUNE 1957, the Baggies were the first British professional club to tour Russia, playing three games over 15 days. The players needed to make a rather large cultural adjustment, including feigning interest in a full day's tour of the 16 halls of Moscow's Agricultural and Industrial Exhibition.

"We had a good tour," said Ray, recalling the visit many years later. *"We were the first team to beat a Russian side, but foodwise – it was a bit of a disaster! I lost half a stone on tour. The first meal we had there was this macaroni soup at Riga airport, with all grease on the top, with a boiled egg floating in there somewhere. It wasn't all bad, but it wasn't to our liking. Certainly, half a dozen were trotting to the toilet all the time!"*

More foreign travel followed when Albion were invited to Spain to play in a special benefit match against Athletico Bilbao to recognise the achievements of one of their great stars, outside-left, Agustin Gainza, who had served Bilbao for 18 years. 35,000 people turned out expecting the home side to win in temperatures close to 90 degrees. But a weakened Albion side shocked them by winning 1-0. The Spaniards were quick to appreciate the visitors and one man in particular, as reporter Charles Harrold described, *"Barlow gave the crowd everything. That was why he was the hero. Whenever he had the ball, murmurs of anticipation swept round the ground."*

A year later, the squad were breaking new ground again, with a four-week visit to the USA and Canada. There's an often-seen tour picture, taken in Halfords Lane, with the squad resplendent in suits and ties. Ray is on the extreme right of the picture, holding the hand of his two-year-old daughter Lesley, busily stealing the entire scene.

AS WITH ANY player in the era of the maximum wage, Barlow had to make the most of any other talents to earn some extra pennies and plan for his future after football. Ray went into business with team-mate Stan Rickaby, setting up the Albion Cabinet Company in 1953, with offices in Pitt Street, West Bromwich. The pair designed a compact gramophone record cabinet with a built-in storage system and their plan was to sell them by mail order at six guineas each (£6.30p). But, as if to illustrate the fragility of a footballer's career, Rickaby was injured the following year and never played for Albion again. With his partner departed for Poole Town, Ray needed to re-think his plans, not least because his days as a single man were no more, having married singer Beryl Austin in late summer 1955. Around the same time, Barlow received £750 benefit money, equivalent to a year's salary. Benefit money was a kind of bonus for loyalty – £500 after five years' service or £750 after ten years. The money was taxable and was an alternative to a benefit game. In practice, many smaller clubs ignored the rules and paid the player what they could afford or what they could get away with. West Bromwich Albion were a big club and could easily afford these sums.

Ray and his new wife opened a newsagency in Bull Street, West Bromwich and moved into the flat above, thus finally tearing himself away from the Hawthorns Hotel, where he'd lived for over six years! Ray was particularly known for his sweet tooth, so a newsagency held certain dangers. An expanding waistline would not help him on the pitch.

IN 1957, LEN Millard asked the manager to transfer his club captaincy to Ray Barlow. Ray had deputised while veteran Millard was injured and felt the new man should carry on. *"I'm good at winning the toss, if that's any help!"* responded Ray in his usual modest way when asked about his new responsibility. Another change was to quickly follow. Stalwart centre-half Joe Kennedy was injured, so Ray filled in and played so well he now became a fixture in the No. 5 shirt. Bolton manager Bill Ridding was among his admirers. *"He's fantastic, incredible, brilliant, the best in the game. There can't be a finer centre-half in the country"* he gushed after Albion, who played with ten men for 85 minutes, earned a 1-1 draw in August 1958 against the Wanderers, then a power in the land. Barlow was cleverly marking Nat Lofthouse.

But did Albion need Barlow's passing skills to support the front men more than they needed him to bolster the defence? The debate raged for months in the local press. But age was a factor for the 32 year-old captain and the less mobile defensive position could prolong his playing career. In theory.

During the opening fixtures of the 1959/60 season, the debate arose again – was Barlow or the fit-again Kennedy a better choice as centre-half? The decision initially at least, was that Barlow, ever versatile, should try out at left-half (midfield) once more. But as journalist Charles Harrold warned *"Barlow cannot cope with 90 minutes of going backwards and forwards all the time from wing half."* In the end, the question was academic. "Tiny" was injured.

BARLOW HAD RARELY been injured or unavailable throughout his career. Admittedly he'd been obliged to sit out five fixtures around Easter 1959 for a most unusual reason. The Birmingham and England full-back Jeff Hall stood next to Ray during a five-a-side match, but the following day was rushed to hospital with polio. The killer disease was much feared at that time, as it was highly contagious. Ray himself had suffered mildly from it as we have already seen. Anyone who had been in contact with a sufferer was obliged to wait for 12 nervous days before doctors could be sure one way or the other. During that period, exercise was not recommended because it could potentially make the disease worse. Ray didn't catch polio, but tragically, Jeff Hall did not recover, and died shortly afterwards.

Fast forward to late 1959 and Ray was enduring fluid on the knee. Hopes of recovery were dashed in his comeback game at St James' Park, when stretching for a ball damaged his knee once more. *"Now, it looks as though I will have to have a good rest,"* observed Ray. Little did he know just how long that rest would be. Or that his next appearance seven weeks later at home to Manchester City would be his final one of his Albion career, typically filling in at centre-half for the absent Kennedy.

He looked slow, although ironically for "First Half Barlow", he improved as the game went on. His knee remained a problem. One specialist considered he had arthritis. Concerned supporters from all over the country wrote to Ray, suggesting their favourite cure. Ray read all the letters and was so impressed with one suggestion that he even met the writer. A second expert opinion muddied the water, suggesting that the Swindonian needed a cartilage operation.

Meanwhile, the Baggies were managing perfectly well without him. Record signing Bobby Robson took over at left-half and made a splendid job of the unfamiliar position. Full international Bobby also took over as captain and worse… took over Barlow's column in the *Sports Argus*. A string of youngsters had made their debuts, such as 16-year-old Bobby Hope, a very young pretender to Barlow's midfield crown. The club was evolving and it was time to go. The latest medical opinion advised him to retire, but Ray wasn't ready. *"My heart is in football and I have been a first team man for 14 years and I don't intend to give up easily."* In the summer of 1960, he moved to that well-known rest home for Albion veterans – St Andrew's.

The last word goes to modest Ray. *"I enjoyed playing football and all that went with it. I had a happy life in the game. What more could you ask for?"*

RAY BARLOW PASSED away in March 2012 at the age of 85. The last survivor of the 1954 Cup-winning team was gone.

Ronnie Allen

1950-1961: 458 games, 234 goals

CULT HERO STATUS at the Hawthorns tends to be earned over a period of time, or conferred on an already well admired player for the act of scoring a vital winning goal in a promotion campaign or in a vital FA Cup tie or even the final. But for one of our heroes his legendary status began the very first day he set foot inside West Bromwich Albion Football Club.

RONNIE ALLEN WAS born in Fenton, Stoke-on-Trent on 15 January 1929, the first born of George Henry Allen and his wife Elsie. A younger sister, Barbara, was to follow six years later. Ronnie's Dad was a builder and had dreams for his son. Ronnie had dreams too.

"Even during my schoolboy days, I dreamed of football fame, since I lived in Stan Matthews' home town. But never once was I fortunate enough to attend a school which had an association football team. At Hanley High school in the Potteries, Rugby Union was the only game played, and although I enjoyed handling the ball at scrum-half, soccer and a round ball was what I wanted" explained Ronnie, through the medium of his 1955 autobiography *It's Goals that Count.* Rather like the player himself, the publication was breaking new ground. *"Goals..."* was one of the first autobiographies written by a footballer.

PORT VALE SIGNED Ronnie on amateur forms in March 1944 at the age of 15. He made his first team debut in the wartime league at 16, even though he weighed 7st and wasn't even 5ft tall. In addition to football, he worked as a laboratory assistant for a porcelain company owned by one of the Vale directors.

Within a year, the lad from Fenton was holding down a regular first Port Vale team place on the wing. Even better, two hat-tricks enabled him to finish top scorer with 13 goals to his name. However, playing for a Potteries football club wasn't sufficient reason to escape National Service, so the Fenton teenager reluctantly began "doing his bit" in January 1947. Fortunately, footballers had an easy life in the forces. Indeed, many were still able to turn out for their club most Saturdays.

Vale supporter Stephen Gabb recalls: *"My late father served in the RAF at the same time as Ronnie Allen. They played together in a game in which Ronnie scored ten before half-time. He was banned from entering the opposition half during the second period, yet he still managed to score from within his own!"* Turning out for the RAF representative team put the Vale teenager in the shop window for several First Division clubs. All were sniffing, but none were biting, so Ronnie continued to find the net in the Third Division North.

Even the best players make mistakes. During one match, Vale were awarded a corner, and Ronnie went to take the kick. He moved away from the corner flag, preparing for his kick and fell backwards over the dog-track fence surrounding the pitch. Fortunately Ronnie was uninjured by his fall and climbed back to join in the laughter.

SHORTLY AFTER HIS 21st birthday, the Vale hotshot had a busy Saturday. He married 19-year-old Constance Brewer in the morning (the Stoke press didn't consider the new Mrs Allen worthy of naming; she was described only as an "Etruria resident" – Etruria being one of the small towns that make up the Potteries). Most of his team-mates were present, though none managed any more than a sip of champagne because Vale had a match that afternoon against Watford. Ronnie went straight from reception to ground to lead his team (he was named captain for the day) and scored the first goal in a 2-0 win. The goal was one of 40 he managed for the Potteries' less famous club. Port Vale remained a modest side. Even with the Fenton teenager contributing mightily from the flank, during his spell, their highest finishing league position in the basement Division was eighth.

Allen's all-round talent deserved a bigger stage, and it was the Albion who gave the newly-wed his chance two months later. A Vale club record £20,000 transfer was negotiated in 30 minutes. With a maximum wage in force and players basically owned by clubs, Ronnie didn't have any say in the deal.

REPORTING TO HIS new workplace was not a straightforward business for a young man unfamiliar with geography outside Stoke-on-Trent. He travelled by train from Stoke to Birmingham as instructed, alighted at Dudley Port and caught a number 74 bus to the Hawthorns, where he was to meet up with his team-mates. Ronnie was fearful of missing his stop, and nervously asked the driver several times not to forget to tell him where to get off.

In March 1950, Pete George was a young forward at the Hawthorns. His chances of playing in the senior side were suddenly boosted by first-team forward Billy Elliott tearing a tendon and Cyril Williams breaking a leg.

"This meant I was first choice for the first- team. Imagine my frustration when I dashed into the dressing room to see the team sheet had A.N. Other at number 7. 'Who on earth was he?' I asked Bill Richardson, our trainer, what was going on, and he replied, 'There's a transfer on.' I asked him who but he couldn't tell me. We all went to Ted Sandford's café, had tea and toast, and played the one armed tic-tac bandit with the odd sixpence. At 5pm, I bought my Evening Despatch. 'Albion signs ALLEN from Port Vale' was the headline. Allen was the AN Other."

The new signing went straight into the WBA first team on the wing, a newly promoted side struggling for goals. Propitiously the opposition on 4 March 1950 just happened to be Wolves.

His first day at the office started badly. The Potteries youngster knocked on the door of the Players' Entrance upon which the doorman asked him whom or what he wanted.

"I want to come in, please"
"Have you got a ticket?"
"No, I haven't got a ticket."
"Then bugger off!"

In high dudgeon, the new boy approached a policeman.

"Excuse me, officer; I'm trying to get into the ground"

Again, *"Have you got a ticket?"*

"No, I'm a player."

"Now come on sunshine, you're not a player, you're not big enough."

"Well do me a favour, will you go to the secretary's office, and ask him to come out, and tell him who I am?"

Off went the obliging constable to track down secretary Eph Smith.

"There's a young man outside who claims to be Ronnie Allen "

"Never seen him before in my life" was the discouraging reply.

Eventually, and thankfully, manager Jack Smith popped his head round the door saying, *"Where have you been? Come on in."*

It was five to three, and as the new boy said later: *"I've never changed so quick in my life!"*

Not surprisingly after such an unsettling introduction, the Fenton forward found getting into the game very difficult. Furthermore, playing in front of the Hawthorns' biggest-ever League crowd (60,945 – with an estimated 10,000 more locked outside) probably needed much mental adjustment for one used to Vale-sized crowds of 5,000 or less.

Wolves went one up. With only a single goal to the Baggies' name in the previous six matches, just where would an equaliser come from? And then… A cross from George Lee soared over the heads of the old gold and black defenders, and there, at the far post, was the debutant, meeting the ball on the volley with his left foot to crash it home. Note the left foot – Allen was a right winger. Spectacular debut goal, against Wolves, with his wrong foot… cult hero status started right here.

"GOT TO GET the ball in the old onion bag" was Ronnie's regularly used expression, and he did. He became club top scorer six years in a row, a remarkable record of consistency topped only by W.G. Richardson in the club's history to date. His 27 strikes in 1954/55 made him the top marksman in the First Division, and in three other seasons, he ran the top scorer very close indeed.

All these goals despite the keenest attentions of numerous defenders, as this typical match report below illustrates:

"One, two, three…. one, two, three…. Ronnie Allen flickered through the Wolves defence with the verge of a Bolshoi ballerina. Then whump! For the third time, Allen hit the turf after describing a not-so-graceful, but very spectacular arc. And once again, the Allen worshippers called on the referee to denounce (Wolves defender) Stuart".

DESPITE HIS REMARKABLE consistency, Ronnie was to win only five England caps. Partly because of the usual Midlands backwater prejudice (Astle, Bomber Brown, Barlow, Kennedy, Regis and many others could feel equally hard done by) and partly, as astute commentators of the time considered, he was so far ahead of his time that the tramline-tracked selectors simply didn't understand him. Ronnie himself provided an example. He was paired with Sunderland's Len Shackleton for a trial match – England against Charlton at the Valley. Both "Shack" and Allen scored hat-tricks in a 7-1 win yet England manager Winterbottom berated them after the game for not passing the ball as he'd instructed.

An England side played Albion in a trial game at the Hawthorns before tackling World Champions Germany at Wembley in 1954. England won 6-3, with Ronnie enhancing his chances of winning another cap by netting a hat-trick against his own club defence. Prior to the Wembley clash, German manager Sepp Herberger admitted he was perturbed about the speed and mobility of Allen and demonstrated on a diagram, the vast area in which he expected the West Bromwich player to operate. His fears were realised. The 'Genie' scored in a comfortable 4-2 victory.

Still, in an era when internationals were staged at the same time as league matches, his country's loss was his club's gain – and Baggies fans knew Allen's worth. The only debate about his inclusion in the line-up was which position he should play in? Ideally they'd like Allen to cross from the wing for Allen to convert in the centre.

Stratton Smith in the *Daily Sketch* agreed: "*Soccerwise, Albion manager Vic Buckingham has a stick of gold in England cast-off Ronnie Allen. The skimpy, devastating little man with the looks of a Latin lover, and the eternal motion of a whole–hearted soccer brilliant. Where to play him? 'Oh brother!' sighs Mr Buckingham. If they (being the lumped mass of supporters and press) had their way, Ronnie would be played in all five forward positions at once! Accept first that Allen IS the Albion attack. That no other player has his sense of positioning; nor his gift of pulling a ball out of trouble; nor his split-second decisiveness in knowing when to stop and when to go. Frankly, he's 80 per cent of Albion's fund of ideas – and I deplore deeply that he should ever have escaped the England set."*

Ronnie Allen and penalties seemed to go hand in hand. Whenever a referee pointed to the spot, the Baggies top scorer was quite deadly. His team-mate Frank Griffin in later years described the maestro's technique. *"He was fantastic – truly fantastic. He hit the ball so hard once he burst the ball. Left foot or right foot, it didn't matter to him. He'd keep a mental note of which keeper he'd sent the wrong way, and next time he faced them, he'd use the other foot and put it in the opposite corner."* Actually even Ronnie missed occasionally, but so occasionally that it made big news. After missing one against of all teams, Aston Villa, he was surrounded by a posse of reporters at the end of the game, asking what had gone wrong.

IN ALL, ALLEN found the net 234 times for the Baggies. This in itself is full justification for cult hero status. Albion supporters instinctively love a goalscorer, but then who doesn't? Almost every consistent finisher for the Baggies has had appreciation showered upon them, but Ronnie was more than just a goalscorer. He could use both feet, giving the advantage of being able to pass a ball instantly. Albion goalkeeper Jimmy Sanders was quite clear. The Potteries man was *"the best two footed player I've ever seen. At Bolton, he hit the bar with his right foot and smacked the rebound in with his left."*

Allen's shooting power couldn't be bettered, while his mental agility to envisage a potential goal-scoring situation was a joy to behold. And he was versatile too, able to perform well in any of the five forward positions. Any weaknesses were hard to identify. There was the physical one of not being very tall, but height is nature's doing. He scored only a few goals with his head. Numerous publications feature a photograph of Ronnie throwing himself full length to get on the end of a cross in a 1950s game at the Hawthorns. It looks spectacular and one imagines that the ball flew into the bottom corner of the opponents' net with bullet-like accuracy. Not so, as fan Terry Wills recalls: *"The fact is that Ronnie completely missed that cross. I had a perfect view of the action and he was at least a yard away from making contact."* But that photo is now used as something of an iconic image with which Allen is remembered for his goalscoring feats – an example of how rose-tinted spectacles can be applied when a player's status is unimpeachable.

Writing for the *FA Book for Boys*, Ronnie concluded that *"being on the short side, I came to the conclusion that I must make the utmost of my ability to move more quickly than the big fellows and devise my own special methods of getting within shooting range of that goal."*

Ronnie always played with a smile on his face, illustrated in a match at Filbert Street against Leicester City. It was one of those days. Albion as a team weren't playing well, Ronnie's shooting followed suit. A cross from the right, his marker eluded and the fans were already celebrating. Ronnie somehow managed to not only miss the target, but the stadium as well, ballooning the ball briefly into orbit. Ronnie simply grinned and joked with his colleagues.

EVEN WITH THE exciting new forward on board, scoring goals continued to be a problem at the Hawthorns. So too was the league position by October 1951, after only a solitary win was recorded in the first eight matches. Various players had been tried at centre-forward without a great deal of success. Manager Smith asked Ronnie if he fancied a shot at the job. He didn't. *"My first reaction to the idea was that it was a stupid one. Insofar as I could not expect to out-jump those big centre-halves, or bore my way through the middle on my own. I told Mr Smith, although I didn't fancy my chances, I would have a go, and do as he told me."*

The first two attempts weren't particularly encouraging, but on the journey to London to meet Chelsea, Albion's centre-half and captain, Jack Vernon, suggested to Ronnie that it might be useful to know the tactics he most disliked centre-forwards using against him, and offered a few tricks he could try out. Ronnie was immediately inspired and encouraged. The 'Pensioners' (as Chelsea were unflatteringly nicknamed at the time) were beaten 3-1, with Ronnie scoring twice and from then on, 'Mr Versatile' decided he'd adopt a pioneering new role. A roving commission, his strategy being that whenever possible, he'd position himself to always be available for a pass. This was tactically groundbreaking stuff in an era of rigid formations. Centre-forwards were always the central pivot on which all attacks were based. They kept basically to one small area of the pitch, where they would be marked by a centre-half. Centre-forwards did not wander off doing their own thing!

So add in the phrase "tactical intelligence" to the Allen CV. In the following games, the roving striker took full advantage of a succession of confused centre-halves, scoring in nine of the ten matches. And Ronnie carried on finding the net, finishing the season with 35 goals from league and cup, and in the following season, another 21 goals saw Albion finish fourth, their highest league position since 1933. He was also selected to represent England against Switzerland. The later but more famous "Revie Plan" from Manchester City, which relied on forwards dropping deeper to pick up the ball, thereby confusing their one-dimensional markers, owed a debt of gratitude to Allen. Laughably, the Revie Plan was later described as "revolutionary".

The Baggies' main man described the centre-forward's position as the "hardest role, but I love it."

Even the best forwards can end up frustrated as reporter Bill David described: *"Little Ronnie Allen versus big Ron Reynolds in the Spurs goal, that was the vital duel. The giant in the green jersey came out on top. But magnificent as Reynolds was, my heart went out to the non-stop Allen. If ever a man did enough, and some more, the wee Albion centre –forward did in this match. Allen shot from all angles and often from only half chances. When it wasn't Reynolds pushing aside his power drives, some other Spurs defender was in the way. All this one-man bad luck for Allen seemed to take the steam out of Albion for a time. But back again came Albion and it was the spring-heeled Reynolds who kept them at bay. On 84 minutes, Allen hit a low volley only to see Reynolds stretch his full length. This time Allen could not restrain from beating his hands into the mud in disappointment."* Those final words were a fair summary of the man. He focused completely on success, and if it wasn't forthcoming, he felt even more downtrodden than the supporters – another connection which intrinsically linked Ronnie to his fans.

IT WASN'T ONLY Ronnie's goals and imaginative tactical play that led to him securing a permanent place in the fans' hearts. He was a genuine 'nice guy', who always appreciated the support the Black Country worshippers bestowed upon him and the team, and he was ever considerate of supporters. The "Nice Guy" test remains a prerequisite for any Albion crowd favourite in the last half century, though less important for successful forwards. Fortunately, all the best Baggies goalscorers possess off-field charm (or perhaps more allowances are made, it being hard to judge character during star struck moments).

Ronnie wasn't the only crowd favourite. In a successful era of so many stars in stripes, he was merely one of a gang. Nicholls, Barlow, Kennedy and others were all magnificent players and all deserved cult hero status.

Quite why this 'pleasant personality' criterion only appears to apply from the 1950s is hard to easily quantify. Significantly, the cult hero as an entity hit new heights as a result of the propaganda era of the Second World War and its cult of celebrity associated with the RAF and film stars of the time. Post-war, newspapers gradually deepened their sporting coverage, and so did radio. Sporting heroes took over from military ones. Gradually, footballers escaped from their one-dimensional confines to become individuals who could speak, think, and even write for themselves. Another factor is footballers' wages. An insignificant issue in the 1950s, but certainly after the maximum wage was scrapped in the following decade, top line sportsmen slowly pulled ahead of average wages, with the "Nice Guy" factor becoming both an accolade and a justification.

It was commonplace in the Fifties for team and supporters to meet on the train travelling to away matches. Hundreds of Albion followers would gather at New Street Station in Birmingham, resplendent in an array of blue and white scarves and outsize rosettes. The Baggies were playing at Blackpool one day and to reach Bloomfield Road, passengers had to disembark at South Shore Station and then walk a goodly distance. Fan Terry Wills recalls: *"Together with all the rest of our support, we started down the road whirring rattles above our heads bellowing 'Albion, Albion'. To my astonishment, Ronnie joined in. He took my rattle and whirled it around his head and ran down the road joining in a chorus of 'Albion, Albion'. The respect and admiration he gained from that one moment couldn't be measured."*

But there was more. Albion had played badly at St James' Park in August 1954, losing 3-0. At that time, a one-way trip from Newcastle to Birmingham took seven hours and the glum, silent supporters knew they wouldn't arrive back at New Street until 2am on Sunday morning. Fan Terry Wills again, *"The door of our compartment slid open, and Ronnie*

Allen said, 'I'd just like to apologise for our performance today lads. We know we let you down. Sorry about that, but thanks for your support. We'll try and do better next time.'" Ronnie had recognised the travelling faithful and made a conscious effort to offer those consoling sentiments. On such a (train) platform is a hero constructed.

Indeed Ronnie always found time to chat to fans, whether at supporters club meetings, outside the ground, on a train to an away ground, or as recalled by supporter Gary Brookes, on a golf course. *"On return to the club house one evening, we enjoyed a few drinks and a meal, with Ronnie recounting a host of entertaining footballing memories. We were the last people to leave the club in the early hours after what was for me a truly memorable day."* Allen was a fine raconteur, and once in story telling mode was fascinating company. Supporters Club Secretary Alan Cleverley remembers chauffeuring the striker to and from a supporters club meeting in Kidderminster, *"Ronnie was telling so many tales on the way back that I wanted to make the evening last as long as possible. I was driving more and more slowly 'til literally we were moving only at five miles an hour."*

GOLF WAS ALWAYS important to Ronnie. He was awfully good at the sport, regularly beating the professional at his local course. Indeed at his peak, he played off a handicap of four, twice winning the Professional Footballers' Golfing Championship and twice finishing second. Graham Williams, the captain of the 1968 Albion Cup-winning team recalled his early days at the Hawthorns. *"We youngsters had so much respect for the '54 team that we used to call them Mr Allen, Mr Barlow and Mr Dugdale. I used to caddy for Ronnie when he played golf at Sandwell Park or Handsworth on a day-off and I hated it. I took up squash instead."*

Ronnie had film star looks, and immaculate dress sense. In a reference to the golden age of the cinema, local reporter Charles Harold once described him as *"the black haired idol of the Hawthorns crowd"*. Most of Hollywood's leading lights were 'blessed' with black hair including the swarthy, handsome legends Clark Gable, Robert Taylor, Errol Flynn, Howard Keel, Victor Mature, and numerous others. Add together the goals, the clever play, the off-field charm and good looks and Stanley Matthews' often repeated observation about Ronnie Allen – *"he was the complete footballer"* – makes perfect sense. Think a young Robin Van

Persie with a telepathic partner to get something close to the Baggies roving centre-forward.

BEFORE THE ERA of solitary strikers, goalscorers were always at their most effective as a partnership. Ronnie's record was decent without being outstanding, until he found his on-field partner. When Allen received an eye injury before a FA Cup match at Blackburn in February 1952, young Johnny Nicholls played instead, and did remarkably well, even though he lacked Allen's ball skills. On Allen's return, Nicholls kept his place and that was the start of a fine and lucrative partnership. Johnny shared the same attitude to the game as his forward partner. In just two seasons, the partnership netted 111 goals.

The understanding between Ronnie and Johnny really was something to behold. If Ronnie had the ball, he knew instinctively where his poaching partner would be to receive a pass likely to cause most damage. Conversely, if it was the 'poacher' in possession, he instinctively knew where Ronnie would prefer the ball to be played to him. The pair bore topical comparison to Lesley and Sydney Piddington, a 'second sight' radio act that astounded the nation courtesy of their amazing radio broadcasts. Once Lesley was ensconced in the Tower of London with her husband sat inside Broadcasting House. The challenge was to pass on a paragraph from a book chosen by a third party, by telepathy. And they did it! Albion's deadly pairing used their own understanding to take the Baggies to new heights in the 1953/54 season.

For the first time ever, the two top teams in the land were the Black Country's finest West Bromwich and Staffordshire's Wolverhampton Wanderers. As a result, a new, keener rivalry built up which exists to this day. Albion made a flying start ahead of their rivals, with a series of outstanding results taking them to the top of the table, and it was inevitably the 'terrible twins' of Allen and Nicholls who plundered the goals. It was as if they'd heard they were going out of fashion and wanted to stock up before the shelves were cleared. As the New Year came in, hopes were rising that Vic Buckingham's team could become the first team since Aston Villa in 1897 to achieve the Holy Grail status of double winners – league champions and FA Cup winners.

Allen believed the narrow FA Cup fifth round win over cup giants Newcastle was the best game he'd ever played in. Two first half strikes from the little maestro rocked the Geordies back, but a battling show of defiance led by Jackie Milburn reduced the arrears.

In Ronnie's own words: *"Then came the turning point of the match. We forced a corner-kick on our left wing. As our winger George Lee came to take the kick, I started to run along the 18-yard line towards him. He drove the ball towards me at a great pace, and I timed the run-in just right to volley the ball goalwards with my left foot on the half-turn. This was a shot I had practised many, many, times in training, and now my efforts were rewarded. The ball rocketed into the top left hand corner of the net. I can't describe my personal joy over this goal, and I didn't have time to think about it before my colleagues were shaking my hand."*

The Baggies went on to reach Wembley for the first time since 1935 by despatching Port Vale in an uncomfortable semi-final. The late winner came from a contentious penalty, scored by Ronnie against his old side. It was an agonising moment all round. Many Albion supporters turned their heads away. Others shut their eyes. But for the rest, they had to see the outcome, and as his ferocious shot hit the net, unrestrained joy was the order of the day. Naturally Vale fans were far from happy. One wrote to Ronnie asking: *"Why didn't you shoot wide, as you know only too well it wasn't a penalty? After all, the Vale gave you your chance and it was your duty to miss this in return."*

INJURIES AND INTERNATIONAL call-ups eventually did for the Baggies' league hopes. The England selectors had barely shown interest in Albion's top scorer to this point, yet selected both Allen and Nicholls to play for England and Scotland on the same day Albion met Wolves. The "terrible twins" sunk the "auld enemy" between them, but meanwhile, in their absence, West Bromwich were losing to theirs. The final straw was a particularly painful 6-1 defeat at Villa Park. The great man felt *"slightly down in the dumps. We had let the League championship slip through our fingers, having managed only half a dozen points out of the last twenty."*

The Cup Final provided much compensation. Albion beat Preston 3-2, with the peerless Allen notching twice. He scored the opening goal, and then after Preston had taken a 2-1 lead, Albion's fate depended on their top striker's ability to score from the penalty spot.

But there was a problem to overcome. As Ronnie put the ball on the spot, it rolled away. Twice.

"Referee, can I put the ball behind the spot?"

"No," came the reply, *"Put it on the spot."*

Ronnie did as he was told. Consequently the spot-kick lacked his usual panâche. As he confessed after the match: *"The ball seemed to take an hour to reach the net."*

In what is probably the best known of all FA Cup Final illustrations, Albion goalkeeper Jimmy Sanders is in the foreground, holding on to his goalpost, his back deliberately turned. He just couldn't bear to watch Ronnie Allen hurtling towards the penalty spot. Time was running away, and this spot-kick had to go in... it did, squeezing under the goalkeeper.

Yet, as Allen turned to go back to the halfway line, the referee wanted the final word.

"If he'd saved that shot, I'd have made you take it again, because the keeper wasn't standing on his line."

"Well if you had," responded Ronnie, *"you could have taken it!"*

SCORING A LATE penalty in an FA Cup semi-final and finding the net twice in the Final are the Allen goals that remain most cherished in supporters' memories. But there was one more at least on a par with those history-making strikes. On 29 April 1959, Villa visited the Hawthorns. The Villains had to win to stay up. With just two minutes remaining, a solitary one-goal lead gave them a top division future – until Ronnie Allen intervened. He picked up the ball just inside the 'D' with his back to goal; a typical swivel to lose his marker, a thunderbolt strike and the ball was in the net. Villa were down. Joy unconfined!

"These things happen in football, and someone has to go down" said Ronnie. *"Unfortunately, a late goal scored in the rain flew into the back of the net and poor old Villa were in the Second Division. I did feel bad in a way. Joe Mercer, their manager, was a good friend of mine. He was the first person to come for a chat and say, 'well done Ronnie'. I was more sorry for Joe than the Villa."*

But there was more, words to be shared only with close friends. *"I didn't really mean to score. I just swung my boot and it flew into the net. I always felt that having as many Midland teams in the First Division was best for the area. We always had enjoyed great games and full houses, and I wanted them to continue. But as it turned out, it was a perfect strike, and no one was more surprised than me when it flew into the net."*

Even almost half a century ago, these were dangerous sentiments, public thoughts not to be shared with the Albion faithful, still hurting from an unjust cup semi-final exit at Villa's hand two years earlier. Privately, the directors, with an eye on club finances, agreed with their top striker. A straight split of huge home and away gates were denied to the bank account.

HOWEVER MUCH RONNIE Allen achieved, his wage packet continued to reflect the strictures of the maximum wage. £12 was the limit at the end of the 1940s, an amount that rose slowly through the Fifties to £20 at decade's end, with deductions in the close season. Many players, if not all, chose to take a second job, partly to boost their income and partly to ensure they had alternative skills to earn a living after their sporting career came to an end. Ronnie acted as a representative for Repton Engineering, selling small fasteners. Frequently, Bobby Robson joined him. Baggies fan Steve Gregory remembered the excitement in his father's voice when he *"would tell of the times Ronnie called at the factory where he worked, promoting screws and bolts."*

In the end, Allen never needed to seek work outside the game. His Albion farewell came in a 3-2 win on 25 February 1961 at home against Bolton Wanderers. Appropriately he found the net. With Derek Kevan now in charge of scoring goals, it was time to move on. Ronnie re-located to London where he added 37 more to his overall tally from the wing for Crystal Palace before hanging up his boots at the age of 36.

Subsequently he managed Wolves, Athletico Bilbao, Sporting Lisbon and Walsall. He also married again, to Cynthia Mary Henn in Birmingham Registry Office. And then? He came home.

INITIALLY IN 1977, Ronnie became a scouting adviser, and famously not only found Cyrille Regis at Hayes, but also overcame the board's reluctance to pay all of £5,000 for his signature by threatening to buy him with his own money. Albion's decision-makers were not particularly adept at making crucial decisions in this period. Huge favourite player-manager Johnny Giles was allowed to leave rather than concede power to him. The job went to Ronnie Allen, but without a contract. Result? They lost him as well!

Ronnie himself *"The first time I became manager, it went very well. I joined Albion in August, and on Christmas Day 1977, West Bromwich*

Albion were top of the First Division. And the then directors did not believe in giving me a contract so I said, 'I'm sorry, I can't go any higher. It's either now or never for a contract.' Then they said, 'Wait till the end of the season' – which I didn't agree with. I left and that was that."

Albion winger Willie Johnston remembered the manager's abrupt departure. *"We had this game fixed in Saudi. We didn't want to go unless we got paid. Management said we'd get £200. Fair enough. So we flew in to Dubai and Ronnie Allen said he had to go and see Prince 'so and so' to get the money. So we waited. One hour went by, then two, three, four, and five hours. Still no money and then Ronnie comes bursting in to apologise for taking so long. He hands out the money, and tells the players to take the money to the nearby gold shop to convert it into gold. Then he told us he's just signed a two-year contract in Saudi, and he wouldn't be coming back with us."*

RONNIE ALLEN DID return through the Albion manager's revolving door in the early Eighties. It wasn't a particularly happy time for him, and he was diplomatically moved upstairs the following term. Now in his fifties, he found the modern game difficult. Bryan Robson had left the club in one of the first examples of transfer by newspaper, and Allen had not invested the club record transfer fee wisely.

Popular player Martyn Bennett didn't consider his manager as inspirational: *"One team talk consisted solely of the gaffer saying we need to win today because I need the bonus to buy new curtains."* Neither did team-mate Derek Monaghan, who remembered team-talks consisting of the manager describing the goals he'd scored against that particular opposition. And yet, although supporters look upon those nine months ending in May '82 with much frustration, a limited, unbalanced team did reach the semi-finals of both the League Cup and the FA Cup. In the subsequent three decades, Albion can note only one cup semi-final to their name.

Bobby Gould invited Allen back as an unpaid adviser and he stayed with the club under the next three managers until 1996. Forwards in particular benefited from his skills. *"Everything Ronnie said made sense,"* said Bob Taylor *"and he was always there for me if I wanted to practise to improve my technique."* In addition, the immense respect from older supporters remained.

Long-standing fan Cyril Randle relives a moment when Ronnie was a coach under Ardiles, *"One day, I was up at the ground, and ended chatting with two oldish traffic wardens about yesteryear. Just then, Ronnie came shuffling down towards us, concerned he might be nicked for parking and, thinking I was their well-dressed boss, he asked if he was OK to park. I said to Ron, 'If it was left to me, you could park on the centre circle of the pitch, mate.' Both wardens added 'too bloody true, mate'. He was amazed and delighted that we remembered him."*

In May 1995, Allen played the last seven minutes of a friendly at Cheltenham. This was a pointless end-of-season affair with both manager Alan Buckley and his assistant Arthur Mann starting the game. The pitch was bone hard and no place for a frail looking 66 year-old. Thankfully, the opposition kept a respectful distance allowing left-winger Ronnie to find an Albion player with each of his three touches during his final appearance.

Ronnie didn't enjoy good health during his later years when both Alzheimer's and Parkinson's gripped him. Former Youth team coach Richard O'Kelly recalled how Ronnie still strove to maintain his standards, even as a pensioner: *"One day Ronnie came in, but the first team were off, and it was a horrible day. Back then, if the weather was very bad, we'd take the boys to the gym, so he came with us. By then he couldn't walk so well, it was like a shuffle, but we were warming up in the corner and Ronnie got hold of a ball, and he was kicking it against the wall left foot, right foot, left foot, right foot it was brilliant to watch. I had to stop the lads, just so they could watch him. He actually joined in a couple of games and obviously the lads took it easy on the challenges, but he was still brilliant. It didn't matter how the ball came to him, he'd strike it first time. He scored a few goals, the quality of his striking of the ball at that age, and he must have been 68, it was incredible, a great example for the youngsters."*

His health continued to falter. In August 1997, he had a benefit match against Aston Villa. Older supporters had tears in their eyes to see Ronnie being wheeled around the pitch on a golf trolley, wearing his 1954 Cup Final-winning shirt. Supporter, Colin Simpson: *"I cried to see so great a sportsman bought low by the cruel twist of fate. This is the only time I've shed tears at the Hawthorns."* Younger fans couldn't be expected to understand the poignancy of this moment. Some just sat in their seats. Others stood, clapping politely. The old codgers, including some Villa fans among the crowd of 16,855, joined in to show their appreciation.

Ronnie required 24-hour care at the Hardwick Court nursing home, Great Wyrley. He could talk lucidly on his good days. He even chalked a No. 9 on the door of his room. Friends took him to the Hawthorns for matches, but his memory was failing badly. After one home match, he asked, *"What time is the kick-off?"* On his bad days? No, it's best not to dwell on his bad days. It was best to remember him in his prime, a goalscorer supreme.

A POISONOUS FRONT-page exposé by a regional Sunday newspaper painted a terribly negative picture of Ronnie's condition. Furthermore, they claimed the football club were doing nothing to help. The accusations created unnecessary additional distress, reopening old wounds in a very public arena. The conveniently overlooked testimonial match had garnered a six-figure sum, which covered nursing fees. There was nothing more to be done, but wait for the end.

Ronnie Allen died on 2 June 2001. Respected club secretary for many years, Dr John Evans said: *"Ronnie was my first hero when I was a youngster. I had many years of pleasure watching him play, and then several more privileged years after I joined the club in 1989 when I came to know him personally. One of the first things I did when I met him was to ask him to autograph a copy of his autobiography, 'Goals That Count', which I'd had as a Christmas present about 35 years earlier! His death is very sad for the club and our supporters."*

AMONG THE MANY other tributes was one from a sportsman who had no involvement in the beautiful game – golfer Seve Ballesteros. *"Ronnie was a wonderful person. I am lucky to have shared his friendship. When I first played for the Ryder Cup team at the Belfry, the place I headed for at the end of the day was Ronnie's home. He had a unique passion for golf, football, and sport in general. When I heard of his death, it was very upsetting. I count myself lucky to have shared the friendship of such a wonderful person."*

Joe Kennedy

1948-1961: 397 games, 4 goals

"JOE KENNEDY IS the highest paid footballer in the country." So deduced the *Birmingham Mail* in 1952. Their logic was simple – Joe received maximum club wages and regular win bonuses. Those, added to an involvement in every representative game (England, Football League and FA XI), meant top-earner status. Joe was reserve for three full internationals that year, plus reserve for the Football League, finally seeing action as captain of the FA XI. Reserves received the same pay as participants: second-string, left out, hard luck story, this was a typical cameo of one of Albion's most effective defenders of all time. Still, at least his 12th man status for his country meant he could visit Wembley for the first time ever. Joe certainly made sure of securing a souvenir – *"I've got a piece!"* he brightly announced in the dressing room afterwards, as he waved around a section of Wembley turf. *"It cannot be long until he gets his full cap"* opined the *Albion News* hopefully.

CUMBERLAND-BORN JOE had come a long way in three years, as indeed had Albion. He'd had something of a difficult baptism – but then Joe's career and legendary status was based on battling against the odds. That's why Albion folk loved him. Like them Joe suffered adversity and came through it, more often than not on top. He was an inspiration to them in prosaic times and his hero status began to develop from his very first appearance in a striped shirt.

In April 1949, the Baggies were chasing promotion to the old First Division, and needed a hole filled in the right side of their midfield at Kenilworth Road. Twenty-three year-old Kennedy was chosen for his first match, a notable step up for a novice who'd only made his reserve team debut less than two months earlier. But he didn't let anyone down. *"Kennedy showed up well in his unaccustomed role,"* commented the S*ports Argus* afterwards.

Joe kept his place in the next game – a spectacular 7-1 thrashing of Bradford, and also at promotion rivals Southampton, where *"he worked like a Trojan"*. The Albion had been eight points behind the Saints at the end of March, but the south coast team had imploded. The Baggies caught them up; with just three games remaining, they had their nose in front, and rather liked the notion of keeping it there. The Saints battered frantically at Albion's door for the first 45 minutes with Kennedy playing his part in the rearguard action, then the visitors caught them on the break and Southampton only managed an equaliser in the last minute of the game. It was a major result. Promotion was in Albion's hands, and two wins from their trio of remaining fixtures would do nicely.

Manager Jack Smith then made a brave decision. Young Kennedy would remain in the first team, but up front, at the expense of a woefully out-of-form Jack Haines. Joe was a big lad, quite superb in the air, but so inexperienced for such a big occasion.

Barnsley were defeated 2-0 easily enough, and with Southampton having completed their fixtures already, a win at Leicester would mean promotion. Joe didn't let his manager down. While City battered away gamely, it was his intervention that gave Albion the lead. Argus Junior described the moment in the *Sports Argus*: *"The tall, dark young man has a striking gift of making himself airborne. There's a spring in his heel, apparently. At Leicester, Joe was so quick in going up for a free-kick that he beat goalkeeper Major in the air and nodded down for Dave Walsh to score the first goal."* Joe followed that up with a goal of his own, his first for the club, when he finished off an Albion corner. Two goals to the good after 25 minutes, the visitors could sit on their lead, and eventually won 3-0. The Baggies had their promotion, and young Joe had his nickname – *"Spring-heeled Joe"* (or Jack – supporters memories vary on this point).

The newcomer had permanently made his mark on club history. Supporters never forget the men who secure promotion: think Bomber

Brown in 1976, "Big Dave" Darren Moore plus "Super Bob" in 2002, Jason Koumas's *"all but wrapped up"* finish at Sunderland (2004), Chris Brunt (2008) and Roman Bednar (2010). Joe Kennedy stands equal with any of them.

JOSEPH PETER KENNEDY was born in Cleator Moor in November 1925; a small town in Cumberland, known locally as "Little Ireland". The community owed its origins to mass immigration from the Emerald Isle during the early 19th century potato famine.

Football and defending in particular was in young Joe's blood. Centre-half was his father's preferred position, resulting in more than one offer to turn professional, but he steadfastly refused them all. Sadly, he died while Joe was still studying and playing football at St. Patrick's school, the Kennedy family subsequently moving to Manchester at the outbreak of war, when Joe was 14. The youngster had a troublesome appendix, which required an operation; for three years, he played no football at all, instead working on the railways as a fireman.

When he was 16, young Kennedy returned to his Cumberland roots, where his interest in football revived. His first club was Cleator Moor Celtic, a long established amateur side with strong Irish ancestry, who play in green and white hoops. To this day, Celtic maintains their tradition of developing young players, the most recent of which is one Scott Carson. Joe progressed to Workington before moving back to Manchester, and two years in the south of England followed, serving as a gunner in the Royal Artillery, while turning out for the Army football side as well. Then he went back to Manchester again, working in a local factory as a turner, playing football for their works side.

Joe played regularly for Altrincham reserves at centre-half, and could boast of a solitary outing with their first team. Many clubs watched him but were concerned that he appeared one-footed; something at that time not acceptable for a defender, apparently. What his critics didn't know was that he was having intense training to improve his kicking; Arthur Gale, a former Albion man, who resumed his teaching career after his footballing days was, in 1948, head-teacher of a school in Altrincham. While happy to give his time as an honorary trainer-coach at his local football club, then in the obscurity of the mid-Cheshire League, naturally, Arthur recommended the young defender to the Albion.

A month after he came of age (21, in those days), Joe was allowed to choose from his suitors, and without hesitation chose West Bromwich, although he'd probably never been there in his entire life. As he advised his mother only to pack a few clothes for him, his destination was to him irrelevant, as he feared wherever he was heading he'd be home within a week. Not so, it would seem: Albion's original £500 bid was matched by Manchester City, Preston, Bury, Crewe, Everton and Manchester United, who had collectively thought they had him lined up before the Baggies pinched him from (literally) their own backyard. Kennedy was eventually Hawthorns-bound in December 1948, in exchange for a measly £750.

PHYSICALLY, JOE WAS pale faced and lean, but blessed with heavy eyebrows and dark, curly hair. His interests were fishing, racing pigeons, table tennis and bowls. (He once won a pork pie in a fishing competition, and was unwise enough to tell his team-mates. Cue endless mickey-taking, of course). Joe was sometimes described as 'taciturn', or in more kindly terms, as 'quiet and modest'. Certainly, he didn't go in for smiling as a hobby, but then what centre-half of mean reputation do? As one reporter pointed out: "*Kennedy's facial expression would surely remain the same even if an earthquake split the Hawthorns turf beneath him.*"

In this era, such a personality was no barrier to genuine crowd-favourite status. New-fangled 'television' had yet to gain mass appeal, radio coverage was very limited, and unlike today, the press were both polite and deferential. Joe had to communicate only at the odd supporters club function, or more normally, on a one-to-one basis in the street, or on the bus to and from games. Occasionally, a pressman would painfully extract a sentence from him. Quite who at the *Birmingham Mail* came up with the idea of firing 20 questions at Joe for a sports feature clearly didn't know him very well. Perhaps they were happy for a series of minimal responses, as it superficially covered a lot of ground. Hopefully, they were, because that was all they got!

Only in his later days did the Cumberland man open up somewhat. Being a senior professional made a difference. Or becoming a husband or father: whatever was behind his later mellowing, his comparative outburst after his 10 men side had held out for a replay against the might of Blackpool in the cup came as a distinct surprise. Joe described his feelings as the Seasiders had a chance in the last few seconds. *"In the few seconds it took, I thought, 'This is it. We'll be beaten.' There were 15 players in the goal area, and the ball was teed up for a shot. Jim Sanders'll never see it, I thought. It looked a winner. I turned to watch Jim, and suddenly he dived to his right. He had the ball. I thought 'he'll never hold it.' But he did. He hung on that slippery ball as though it was as dry as on a summer day. It was a great save."*

JOE ALWAYS WANTED to play as a central defender; initially though, with Irish international Jack Vernon resident as the club's first choice stopper, he had to be content with playing slightly further forward and wider. But this wasn't easy for him, as the *Argus* noted: *"When he should be on the flank, Joe finds it hard to keep away from the middle. And it's such a waste of effort and good material with Jack Vernon already covering."* A year later, when 'Spring-heeled Joe' was pressed into service up front; once more he was *"prone to lie too far back."* Still, when together, the trio of Vernon, Kennedy and Barlow were a formidable midfield line, and Joe was quick to learn. For instance, after a 4-1 win over Fulham, journalist Jack Littlewood declared Kennedy as man of the match because: *"He has been improving steadily but on Saturday he had the hallmark of the class wing-half, and despite two injuries carried on unswervingly in making the ball do the work."*

Through most of the 1950/51 season, Joe continued to make his name in midfield. With the Baggies unable to find the right blend up front, the two wing-halves, Barlow and Kennedy, tried to be everywhere at once. Every single game, they both defended and supported the attack. Sometimes they *were* the attack... But the pair couldn't always do everything for their moribund colleagues. Even former Villa manager Alex Massie had sympathy for the job the duo were trying to do: *"I say Kennedy and Barlow are overworked owing to the fact they are very often facing three forwards when the centre-forward plays deep..."* The following season was only a little better, with one *Argus* reporter lamenting: *"Albion matches are stereotyped. Their strong defence controls the game, and their attack hammers away, hoping that enthusiasm and bursts of wing skill will produce a goal. "*

Joe made his debut in his favoured central defensive position at the Baseball Ground in October 1950 (1-1 draw), deputising for Vernon. He took to it as naturally as a salmon might leap a weir. The

Birmingham Mail correspondent was suitably impressed: *"Kennedy so effectively dominated the field wherever he was operating that neither Parry nor Stamps had any hope of exploiting a central spearhead policy. There was just never a gap or a loophole through which they could get more than a sight of goal."*

Despite this fine showing, Irish international Vernon understandably remained the main man at centre-half. Eleven months passed before Joe had another go in what is still largely known as the 'No.5 shirt'. Talk about last minute! With all the apparent organisation of a Sunday League team, he'd been told he would play at centre-forward (another unfamiliar position), but at the last minute, Vernon was unable to play, so he was now playing centre-half instead. Joe was rusty, not having played for the first team that season, and needed time to adjust.

Unfortunately, Newcastle didn't give him that time as the defender later admitted: *"I was lost for the first fifteen minutes."* The game finished 3-3 with Kennedy enjoying a wonderful second half. Former Albion man Sandy McNab was impressed, declaring, *"We've seen England's centre half here tonight."* Handily, England supremo Walter Winterbottom was at the Hawthorns that day.

Veteran Vernon's days were numbered: extended injury problems were followed by news of his father's ill-health back in his native Belfast. The big defender felt obliged to end his footballing days there and then, and return to take over the family butchers. This was Joe's chance.

JOE QUICKLY BECAME popular both at home, where *"his cleverness in attack and defence had the crowd cheering"*, and in these less-partisan times on the road as well, such as at Roker Park in October 1952. *"Several times Kennedy won the praise of the crowd"* for subduing the Mackem's star striker, Ford.

Talking to the *Albion News*, Ray Barlow recalled how he left the high balls to Joe. *"I never used to head the ball if it was coming in, I'd just shout, 'Your ball, Joe,' and he would come and get it. He was pretty near unbeatable in the air – if he ever missed one, you'd stop for a split second and think, 'What happened there?' I don't think Joe liked kicking the ball very much! He'd just roll the ball out to the wing-halves, and let us get on with it. Great reader of the game, timing was perfect. He used the ball well; it all came naturally to him. "*

But veteran fan Peter Whitehouse believes Barlow's assessment doesn't do Kennedy justice. *"What made him such a crowd favourite was his sheer artistry on the ball. Jackie Vernon, who played before him, and Jimmy Dugdale were stoppers; in other words they won the ball and got rid of it – anywhere. Joe had all the skills of an attacking midfielder. He could win the ball in a crowded penalty area right off the toes of a forward. He'd then quite calmly push it round said opponent and give it to an unmarked team-mate. Many were the choruses of "Good ol' Joe" as he converted defence into attack. "*

Of course, every player has a bad game. One of Joe's came in a 6-1 drubbing at Turf Moor. A misunderstanding between Kennedy and goalkeeper Sanders handed the Clarets their first goal – but worse followed, Kennedy and Sanders literally banging heads in classic *Keystone Kops* style. A heavy defeat and a headache! In fact pain and discomfort were to dog Joe all through his Albion years.

In his Albion youth, he once injured his ankle at Chelsea, but continued as a hobbling passenger on the wing. Once, he forgot his disability, picking up a loose ball then running into the middle, but shooting over. After that Kennedy was out for nearly a month, and typical of Joe's ill-fortune, he suffered a head injury in his comeback game.

In a 2-0 defeat at Sheffield Wednesday years later, Joe played despite suffering from flu. As a role-model in a struggling team, he must have felt pressure to continue playing. He somehow mustered an outstanding performance, even in his enfeebled state. With Maurice Setters sent off, and Ronnie Allen carried off, losing by only two goals seemed a decent trade-off. Don Howe remembered the post-match dressing room scene. *"We couldn't step into the bath because it was too hot. Joe went straight in and sat there – still shivering, and covered in goose pimples."*

There was something about the Hillsborough club, as Joe was also rendered *hors de combat* in the return fixture. During the second half, he collided with Wednesdayite Keith Ellis. Suffering concussion and double vision, Joe wandered up and down the right wing like a punch-drunk boxer, with team-mates encouraging him by shouting *"the pigeons are coming in, Joe!" (racing pigeons were his passion)*. After Albion scored their third and clinching goal, the trainer helped the stricken defender off the pitch. The sympathetic cheers ringing all around the Hawthorns barely registered. Neither had Albion's third goal. And yet there was even tougher to come. The following season, Don Howe thought he'd help out his team-mate in a difficult defensive situation, but only succeeded in elbowing Kennedy in the face. Joe was knocked unconscious, completely oblivious to the stimulant effect of the trainer's ammonia capsule.

In one week in September 1956 – Joe had a cyst removed on Monday, Thursday he gashed his leg after falling off a low wall and on Friday he had an unpleasant visit to the dentist.

But whatever the ailment Joe simply soldiered on. In 1957, at Wolverhampton, second-placed Albion visited the league leaders. Following a collision, Kennedy's eye swelled to the size of a duck egg, but Joe played on bravely, with that eye completely closed, albeit accepting a stop-gap role as emergency striker. *"Even with one eye, Kennedy made an astonishingly effective forward,"* penned one reporter from the nationals. Even with their main stopper out of position, the Baggies continued to play the better football, but a really harsh penalty, given against his deputy, Ray Barlow, meant Albion settled for one point instead.

Joe always seemed to be battling back from one kind of injury or another. He endured a painful and worrying double-cartilage removal operation in February 1953. Would he recover? Many others had not. Although initial signs were good, he broke down in training two months later. Inevitably, the hacks failed to get much comment from Joe. They settled for his economical *"tough, but it's the luck of the game."* Then, so characteristic of his ill-fortune, Joe broke his nose playing for the reserves, very early into the following term. He finally returned to the team in November against Sunderland; as the *Argus* observed, it was if he'd never been away. *"The ease with which he went through the game was the hallmark of a class player."* But quickly, his form deserted him, and he was dropped, Jimmy Dugdale getting the nod as stopper instead.

ALBION WERE PURSUING the elusive 'double' at that time, so watching from the sidelines must have been painful. Big Joe was recalled for three games in the crucial run-in to the 1953/54 season, firstly at right-back, and then in midfield; sadly, Albion lost all three games. Even worse, the league championship was heading straight to Wolverhampton, and Joe was heading straight back to the reserves.

But injuries continued to plague the undersized squad. Albion's first choice keeper, Norman Heath, was out of action, and so too was regular right-back Stan Rickaby. Who would fill this shirt at Wembley for the Cup Final? Joe Kennedy, of course. It was his first cup match for 15 months, but the unlikely full-back grew into the role magnificently as the match unfolded. Famously, Albion came from behind with Ronnie Allen's second goal, this one from the penalty spot, levelling the game. Joe's through ball put the Albion striker in for a hat-trick chance, but the shot just eluded the post. Joe would not be denied, though; his pass to Reg Ryan allowed the winger to set up Frank Griffin for the 87th minute decider.

Albion had won the cup, their first trophy since 1931. Even the upright figure of chairman Major Keys temporarily forgot his military dignity; he was spotted standing, up, cheering with the rest.

Joe had finally got one over Tom Finney, a regular opponent over the years, who, contrary to popular belief, didn't always play by the rules. In later times, Joe recalled playing against Finney, and being pushed and barged by the forward while waiting for a corner to be taken. Despite his appealing to the referee, it was obvious that no one believed that Gentleman Tom could do things like that.

By the mid Fifties, the man from Cleator Moor was once again master of the middle. His rival for the shirt, Jimmy Dugdale, gave up the fight and left *saying: "I could never hope to replace Joe Kennedy, so I put my future first."* Joe was a hardened professional by then, playing his 200th match at Bloomfield Road, Blackpool. Not only could he defend, he was additionally supplementing the forward line. There was even a rare goal (against Charlton), one of only four for the Baggies in his entire career. With five forwards, it was rarely considered necessary in this era for centre-halves to go up the field for corners and free kicks, their priority being to mark at least one of the players the opposition would leave up front.

SEASON 1955/56 DREW parallels with those at the start of the decade. Goalscoring was a constant problem, particularly away (Albion lost seven straight on the road), and the contributions of Kennedy and Barlow were vital to keep the Baggies in the game. The pressure was on – being only mid-table in the top league just wasn't good enough. This was West Bromwich Albion, after all.

Albion broke the losing run with a 1-0 win at Preston in October. Wrote one correspondent: *Joe Kennedy was in England form in anticipation and interception. One lost count of the number of attacks that broke down through his intervention.*

A win at championship-chasing Wolverhampton in the FA Cup gave an adrenalin rush, a moment to be treasured, and Joe was at the heart of the 2-1 victory. Reporter Edwin Buckley: *Kennedy stood out against this mass Molineux attack. He coolly headed away centres and took control of the penalty box to such an extent that Wolves attacks were blunted.* On such signal victories are reputations secured.

Joe's talents were now being recognised at a higher level. In October 1955, he played for the FA XI at Bristol, Albion at Sunderland and England 'B' in Manchester, before travelling to join training with the full England side at Porthcawl. In 12 days, he'd covered 1,000 miles, all by train. Months later, he was in top form for England 'B' against Scotland 'B'. A full England cap was surely imminent. ...and then he broke his collarbone. Albion's No. 5 collided with Bolton's Nat Lofthouse, and came off worse. For five weeks, Joe wore his left arm in a sling, struggling to do even basic tasks like tie his own shoelaces. He would not play again until mid-September. Meanwhile, Ray Barlow was picking up rave reviews as his deputy, a situation that would return to haunt Joe later in his career.

Joe's injuries, illnesses (such as shingles – out for a month), the occasional being left out of the side after disputes with the manager, plus being an Albion man, all conspired to ensure he never won that elusive full England cap. Joe didn't always help himself: not making the most of playing for the FA XI at Stamford Bridge in late 1952 (effectively an England B game) for example. Even the benevolent local press considered his contribution as *only average* adding, *he didn't seem comfortable.* Sheer bad timing, such as captaining an FA XI thrashed 7-1 by France, also played a leading role. However valid his personal contribution, certain fingers would always point at the team captain in that particular situation.

Then there was Billy Wright. The man from Wolverhampton always barred his way to a full England cap. Joe regularly drew praise for his games at 'B' level, but it was never quite sufficient to satisfy the full team selectors, even at his mid-fifties peak. The nearest he would get was as 12th man in the famous thrashing by Hungary in 1953. He did make an appearance for 60 seconds, though – helping the trainer carry his magic sponges on to the pitch. And yet Charles Matheson of the *Argus*, a regular watcher of both men, considered Joe to be stronger than Billy Wright. *"There's so little on which Joe can be faulted, even by the purists. He has the mobility to venture forward now and again. His tackling is Grade One, he is tops in the air, and although he has skill in ball play, he does not fiddle needlessly."* There were suggestions that Billy Wright could fill in as a defensive midfielder to give the Cleator Moor man a game, but this never happened. Joe's angst was greatly increased with so many of his team-mates getting the nod instead: just think Allen, Kevan, Howe, Robson and Barlow.

JOE BECAME GREAT friends with Albion winger Billy Elliott, who also originated from an obscure part of Cumberland. When Elliott retired from full-time football, he took over the Great Western Arms in West Bromwich town centre, a hostelry where there was ample living accommodation included with the pub. By coincidence, Kennedy and fellow Baggie Frank Griffin needed to find somewhere new to live, as the current landlords wished to end their arrangement, and so Billy invited them to become his tenants. There were obvious temptations involved, but officially at least, Joe's interest in the pub was no greater than politely helping out mine host to move the empties. He preferred table tennis in the local club than supping in his "own" house, so we're led to believe. Joe lived with the Elliotts for three years, then married West Bromwich girl Angela Thomas, and set up home together.

JOE DIDN'T ALWAYS have a smooth relationship with Albion managers. Early in his career, he wanted a wage level guarantee. When the club turned him down, he didn't sign his new one-year contract, the season kicking off with the Cumberland man literally refusing to play ball. He didn't get back in the first team until mid-September as a result.

When Joe read a newspaper story in January 1956 claiming he would be swapped for Fulham's Bobby Robson, he probably felt another disagreement coming on. Nothing whatsoever had been said to him about a move. His wife Angela was expecting baby Michael, so any potential upheaval was terribly unwelcome: even in these comparatively modern times, mere players didn't have much say in transfers. Fortunately, chairman Major Keys himself hastened to seek out big Joe on the training ground to assure him that the story was quite untrue. Albion did eventually sign Robson, but in exchange for a cheque, not a defender.

It was vital that Kennedy stayed as he was in the form of his life. In November 1956, a 1-1 draw with Manchester City moved one *Birmingham Post* correspondent to comment, *"Albion's dominating figure was again Joe Kennedy – rarely at fault with head or feet and revealing an uncanny power of anticipation. His wonderful consistency has been a big factor in wielding together Albion's defence into one of the most dependable in the country."*

Against Forest at home in the FA Cup in February 1958 which finished 3-3, Kennedy marked his 300th game with another domineering performance. Yet, although *"he ruled the centre of the field like a miniature John Charles,"* his mistake led to a goal for the visitors. Kennedy left the ball to Sanders who didn't come out and Simcoe scored.

Joe's normal ill-luck continued when in the same week he failed his driving test, probably in an Austin 7. *"It was a halt sign that got me down. And the funny thing was that I had successfully negotiated about eight or nine before this one and had only about five minutes to go before the end of his test."* His team mates were typical footballers, so they fell about laughing. Son Michael John Kennedy was two years old by this point. It wasn't the only time he was on the receiving end of footballers' "wit". After a night match at Highbury, the team returned to a hotel for the night whereupon the big defender received a phone call. *"I picked up the phone and someone said, 'Mr Kennedy, your plane for America will leave in two hours time. All arrangements have been made.' I didn't think I played that badly at Highbury."*

LATER THAT YEAR, Joe endured a stomach problem. Having had a medical during pre-season, he wanted to wait for the results before playing again. Manager Vic Buckingham didn't agree, so, highly reluctantly, the centre-half turned out in a practice match. His disinclination was obvious, quickly leading to an argument where Joe was told to leave the field, and was dropped from the first team. The player accepted his fate: *"I'm not going to ask for a transfer or do anything silly. My roots are in the Midlands now. I'm happy here."*

The concern for Joe was that Ray Barlow was now playing in his centre-half position. The manager considered Ray his first choice, feeling that the leaky defence from the previous season needed improving. It was certainly a dilemma. The Albion front men were missing Barlow's craft from midfield, and similarly, Barlow couldn't hope to match 'Spring-heeled Joe's' remarkable aerial ability. Neither did Joe give away penalties (only one on record), whereas Ray gave four to the opposition the previous season (and would go on to allow four more by December). But Ray was getting on a bit, and the argument went that the stresses and strains of midfield were a bit much for him. Albion started the term in modest fashion but … four wins in the next five matches eased the unrest, as did briefly going top of the league that December, despite Joe's long-term confinement to the stiffs.

At the time, the supporters' view was clear. They wanted *"one of the best and cleanest players Albion have ever had"* back in the No. 5 shirt, and Barlow back in midfield. *"We Want Joe"* chanted supporters during a 3-2 home defeat by Everton in October, rebellious stuff indeed for the time. They also made use of the only channel of protest open to them by writing to the local newspaper. A letter from Yvonne Hill neatly summed up the views of several correspondents. *"Kennedy's skill in the air and his distributional play are unrivalled by anyone West Bromwich could hope to play at centre-half."*

Joe's chance eventually came in January 1959, at Deepdale, as Barlow was injured. Albion won 4-2; their eighth away win of the season. Naturally, he spent the first half adjusting, but the second 45 was a glimpse of the old Joe. But it wasn't enough for him to keep his place as he battled with his fellow cult hero, Barlow, for a place in the side.

When 'Spring-heeled Joe' returned to the first team a month later for a decent run of matches in Division One, his coolness under pressure enabled the Baggies to end a run of eight games without a win. As one player confessed at the time: *"we were almost afraid to touch the ball."* Albion came from behind to beat Blackpool, Joe holding the back line together largely single-handledly, allowing Bobby Robson to play as a sixth forward as the Baggies won 3-1. Only now did Kennedy feel able to talk, as expansively as he ever managed, about his period in the cold. *"I was a bit upset when I was left out of the League team, but, after a bit, I began to enjoy my football with the youngsters."*

JOE WAS BACK, and back to stay, as Barlow's knee troubles would eventually finish his career. It is debatable whether Kennedy's imperious form in this period, which truly secured his cult status at the Hawthorns, would have ended Barlow's career at West Brom anyway. Reporter Jeff Hollinshurst observed at Preston: *"Ambling Joe Kennedy was the complete master in the middle, leaving not even the eye of a needle through which Tom Finney could find a way."* This, for a player basically overlooked the previous season. He was in exceptional form at the time, arguably the side's best player in what was perceived then as difficult times – being mid-table at the top level of the game.

As usual, not everything went to plan. Joe Kennedy ran on to the turf at Craven Cottage with kick off imminent – then the bottom eyelet on his right boot burst. The first kick sent his boot flying, so Joe hastened to the touchline to get his boot repaired. Fulham kicked off while he was on the sidelines, and some 45 seconds later, they were a goal up, the Londoners going on to win 4-2. Inevitably, another injury took yet another month out of his career – six stitches in a cut scalp after being carried off against Newcastle. Just the half dozen, only a month? Small beer! Reserve midfielder Archie Styles recalled the bruising nature of the era. *"When they went into the tackle, I could hear the bones crunching. It was not for me. I got out."*

As the fifties became the sixties, Joe continued his majestic form, with a posse of national and local journalists seeking weekly alternatives to their stock phrases. Still he looked international class, and frequent were the suggestions that he deserved a cap – even at the age of 34, and with 350 games behind him. Tom Finney, Manchester United's Dennis Violett, nor any of the big name forwards of the day for that matter, could defeat him. So positive was the feedback on his contribution to a FA Cup fourth round victory over Bolton, it could have glowed in the dark. A rare goal followed in the fifth round at Leicester, Joe's first for over four years. What turned out to be his final goal was a scrambled effort very late in the game from a corner. It came too late to save the Baggies from unexpected elimination. The match referee, Husband, didn't live to see the defeat as he collapsed and died at half-time.

Every month or so, there was speculation that Player A or Player B *"was to be Kennedy's successor"*. Most notable of these was defender Stan Jones, who signed in the summer of 1960 from Walsall.

Albion started the next term in dreadful style, and after three straight defeats, changes were deemed necessary. So in came Stan, fresh out of the Fourth Division. Although he did well enough, the defeats continued and so Joe returned. But 'Spring-heeled Joe' had lost his bounce and was distinctly human. (Say it ain't so!) There were still fixtures, mainly at home, where he stood as an unbeatable rock, Bolton's Nat Lofthouse among the frustrated centre-forwards who simply weren't permitted to do anything with the ball. Too often, though, by his immense standards, Joe was caught out of position, and an own goal at Everton (the fourth of his career) didn't help either. To compound his thoroughly miserable afternoon, he was knocked out in a collision. Fortunately, he recovered, and played on.

IN A HUGELY embarrassing episode, the Baggies were beaten 3-1 in the third round of the FA Cup by Lincoln City, bottom of the Second Division. City hadn't previously won a cup match for seven years. By sharp contrast, this was the first time in 29 years that West Brom had played just one FA Cup match in a season. Kennedy was moved to protest: *"Their first goal was well offside. We have had far too many like this given against us this season."* Or was it just that Joe's powers were on the wane? He was now 35. After a run of four defeats with 12 goals conceded, Joe was taken out of the firing line. Manager Gordon Clark explained: *"Joe tells me that he has been feeling the strain in the last few games. He agrees that every injury he has now takes twice as long to heal than it used to, and that he needs a rest. So I told him to go away and forget all about football. I believe he has gone to stay with his parents for a few days."*

With a new centre-half, the Baggies won seven matches in a row, their best run for 30 years. Joe would not be adding to his 397 games. In May 1961, he was given a free transfer. So too was Ronnie Allen. The last two remaining members of the '54 cup-winning side remembered to shut the door behind them.

Supporter, DJ Hill, penned a tribute in the local press. *"It is hard to believe that we shall not see Joe grace the Albion colours again. His value to the team can hardly be measured and he deserved more honours than he got."*

Joe was to demonstrate that the Midlands, or more specifically the Black Country, really was his home. He played one season as a professional for Chester before returning to a "proper job". Previously, he'd always refused all offers of going into business while playing but his £700 benefit cheque to mark his service to the club wouldn't last long. In the early sixties, he joined Brockhouse Works in West Bromwich. He worked on the shop floor on a big machine within their transmission division. There he worked for the rest of his days, sadly he collapsed and died at the side of his machine in September 1986.

Derek Kevan

1953-1963: 291 games, 173 goals

JUST AFTER WORLD War Two, an eleven-year-old called Derek Kevan discovered he was really rather good at heading a football. Once his sports teacher spotted said talent, young Derek found himself in the school team. He was a big lad for his age – he needed to be as the average age of the team was 13.

Unlike our other cult heroes, the Beautiful Game was warmly embraced by the whole family so there was no brake on Derek's progression. Brothers Joe and Jim both played for local side Ripon City while father Albert Kevan refereed games at junior level.

Eventually, Derek found his natural position up front. His first big break came when a Bradford Park Avenue scout saw him score twice for Harrogate and District in the West Riding County Cup. Three weeks later, he had his first PA outing in a local derby against Bradford City's juniors. He scored five in a 6-5 victory.

Such formidable form inevitably led to his signing professional forms for Park Avenue. Manager Vic Buckingham gave him his debut against Mansfield in October 1952. Buckingham departed for pastures new in January, but by then Derek had done enough to be an automatic choice. In his 15 League games for PA, he found the net eight times – an excellent ratio for a complete novice. Within a year, his name was being mentioned in some very high circles. On 29 July 1953, this 6ft, aggressive but raw 18-year-old forward moved from his local Fourth Division side to one of the biggest clubs in the country – WBA.

ALBION GAVE PARK Avenue £3,000 for his signature, safe in the knowledge that few knew more about Kevan than their new gaffer Buckingham. At less than one sixth of the fee paid for Ronnie Allen, Albion weren't taking that much of a risk though young Kevan disagreed. "*I think Vic was taking a bit of a gamble with me, for I was a big awkward devil. He told me I would have to work hard if I wanted to make the grade ...and that is just what I did.*" At the time, Kevan did what every teenager did in that era. He sought parental guidance. "*I asked my Dad if he thought I should sign for them and my Dad said, 'You get yourself down there. Listen to the advice and act on it. And remember do your best. ALWAYS do your best.'*"

Dutifully, Kevan followed his Dad's advice and that of the Albion management. Not that he had much choice in the matter. "*W.G. [Richardson, club trainer] would give you the biggest bawling out you could imagine, and that were only during practice! I never had a bad word for him because he pushed you to the limit.*" Derek's learning curve was flattened by the interference of National Service. During his square-bashing days he quickly learnt that permission to play for his unit was difficult enough, never mind for his club.

Anyway, there was no chance of forcing a way into Albion's first team. The country's best club – so close to achieving the mythical cup and league double in 1954 – already had the country's best strike force in Ronnie Allen and Johnny Nicholls. There was no room for novice raw-boned teenagers. So went the theory. Problem was, the first team strikers lacked experienced cover. The normal stand-in was half-back Ray Barlow, but moving him forward would be at the expense of his midfield talents. Furthermore Ray wasn't keen on playing up front. So when Ronnie Allen picked up an injury, big Kevan got his chance, making his top Division debut against Everton on 24 August 1955. The Baggies won 2-0 in blazing heat and the debutant scored both of them.

Such a start sounded remarkable and yet somehow it wasn't. Derek Kevan didn't look the part. He was clumsy, awkward, lacked finesse and of course being compared to uber smooth Ronnie Allen didn't help. The *Birmingham Mail* reporter was cautious. "*A story-book debut for the well-built Kevan inasmuch as he weighed in with both goals, but as usual, too much publicity from the national press for a quite ordinary performance. I hope Derek is wise enough not to let it go to his head. Strange to see a six-footer leading the Albion line, but this lad will no doubt learn that only 100 per cent ball control is good enough for the First Division. Let that ball wander too far from your foot and it's a 'gonner' against these quick-tackling defenders. Still he showed promise and I shall look forward to seeing what he can do when the weather has really broken."*

The following week, Kevan played at Old Trafford and scored again. A fortnight later, his fourth goal flew into Sheffield United's net. He was club top scorer – but after six games in the big time, Ronnie Allen regained his fitness and the newcomer was relegated to the stiffs.

Kevan was to play only one more game that season (a 4-0 defeat by Manchester City in March) as, when Allen was absent, Ray Barlow was reluctantly pressed into service again. In public at least, the teenager was philosophical, *"All I could do was carry on and wait for another chance."*

THE FOLLOWING SEASON (1956/57) spawned his 'marauding' reputation. A solitary win from the first five matches persuaded Buckingham to give the Ripon-born forward a second chance against Portsmouth. Scoring in a 2–1 win gave the manager the confidence to keep the big man in the team and once in, he was there to stay, missing only twenty games over the next seven years. But criticism was never far away.

Albion supporters had notoriously little patience in the mid-fifties. With classic big club arrogance, they expected the 1954 all-conquering side to continue ad infinitum, but football wasn't like that then.

There have been only three true dynasties in post-war British football history. Spurs' early sixties double winners collected silverware by the bucketful throughout the next 10 years. Liverpool won almost everything in sight from the mid-1970s for 15 years and then Alex Ferguson's Manchester United swept all before them in the 1990s. The introduction of the Premiership has changed all that, of course, with the cash concentrated in so few clubs that there are now concurrent dynasties which seem to the modern fan to be destined to share nearly all the silverware between them for ever more amen.

Back in the mid-fifties, most of Albion's players of what now must be recognised as the greatest era in the club's history, incredibly became targets. Even walk-on-water Ronnie Allen was jeered once against Bolton for a series of poor passes. In early 1957, Bobby Robson was being booed every week. Derek Kevan got the most stick of all because of his inelegant style of play. The difficulty lay in maximising his strengths and minimising his weak areas. Kevan needed the ball in front of him. That's how he worried the opposition. Playing with his back to goal was not his game because frankly, he didn't have the ball skills or the vision.

Provided he was finding the net, Kevan could ride the criticism. But between the Portsmouth game in September and late January 1957, he had just eight goals to his name. At that time, such a total was considered paltry. Far worse was the manager playing Ronnie Allen on the wing so he could accommodate the big man in the No. 9 shirt. Even those who were pro-Kevan expressed their concern at his lack of goals. Derek himself ruefully admitted, *"It seems incredible I can't turn out the sort of shots in a match that I hit in practice games."*

As ever, the local press reporters were stuck in the middle, trying to keep everybody happy. The *Birmingham Mail* again: *"Particularly on the receiving end is 22-year-old Derek Kevan, the up and at 'em Ripon man who stepped into Albion's centre-forward spot. The fans want a Ronnie Allen replica. Who doesn't? They should be satisfied with one Allen in the line-up and give more encouragement to the lad who has the unenviable job of stepping into their idol's shoes. In all fairness, of course, big Derek has not been an outstanding success. There has been room for criticism. But for him alone, I don't think so. Particularly when the service was anything but generous."*

Even the normally mild Ray Barlow had a strong view: *"It made a big difference to Derek Kevan's career when he moved to number 10, he was bloody awful at centre-forward."* And yet in September 1955, the *Argus* reporter wrote, *"Kevan is just not First Division class as inside-forward."* They particularly noted his inability to trap a ball. These opposite viewpoints from knowledgeable people say much about the mixed reception that The Tank endured in his leaner times.

After a run of poor results at the turn of the year, Ronnie Allen was restored to his preferred centre-forward role while Derek Kevan was switched permanently to inside-forward – a close supporting position for Allen. In his new role, he had slightly more room and space and as a result found the net more often. Gradually opinions on The Tank's capabilities softened. He still had his critics, but others were now appreciating his strengths such as tabloid journalist, Bob Morley, describing a 4-2 victory at Stamford Bridge: *"In inside-left Derek Kevan, they had the game's finest forward. Kevan had the ability to open an opposing defence with a well-judged pass and is a dangerous marksman. Certainly an England prospect"*

To force his way into the national side, he'd have to displace the then current favourites – Newcastle's 'Wor' Jackie Milburn, Middlesbrough's Brian Clough, and Bolton's Nat Lofthouse. All were similar in style, particularly Lofthouse, who had no qualms when it came to putting himself about at the expense of opposing defenders. But the England selectors picked the Albion man over them all for the side to play Scotland in March 1957. England's latest international was unaware of his call-up. Having spent the afternoon in the Tower cinema, he was astonished to be surrounded by a bevy of eager reporters when the film finished. *"I thought they were taking the mickey,"* he told me in 2006 from the comfort of his own armchair. When prompted for his memories of his international debut, his eyes twinkled, *"I could feel the hair rising on the back of the neck. When they played the National Anthem, it was a wonderful feeling. I wanted to prove my worth. It was a marvellous day."*

England won 2-1. Argus reporter Eric Woodward noted Kevan's contribution. *"Albion's 22-year-old blond giant, playing his first representative game, scored England's equalising goal before Duncan Edwards roared through to hit a great winner a few minutes from the end. ... On this show Derek is well worth his place. Not that Derek gave a five star display and was competent in everything he did. He must surely get another chance. The crying shame was the poor use his colleagues made of him. He ran into the open spaces intelligently, was ever ready to have a crack at goal, yet hardly had a pass worth sprinting for. So he looked little better than the rest. It was a wrong impression. Kevan in fact looked the only England man likely to score."* Maybe the most significant words of all were those that made up the headlines. "KUDOS FOR KEVAN – AND HIS CRITICS". The great dilemma – could Kevan play or not? – was yet to be fully resolved.

Albion's domestic season that had promised so much petered out. But the FA Cup was looking highly promising. Doncaster Rovers, Sunderland, Blackpool and Arsenal had all bitten the dust with Big Kev scoring four times. Aston Villa were the semi-final opponents. The first match was drawn with the Birmingham side scraping a fortunate equaliser near the end. That frustration was minor compared to the replay.

Even though the Baggies had ten men for most of the game after an injury to Allen, they hammered Villa all over the pitch. Except where it mattered. Villa scored once and grimly hung on to reach Wembley.

Like the shattered Albion support, Derek was inconsolable. *"I don't mind admitting tears came at the end. I missed several chances and I think I hit the woodwork twice. Once I was clean through and hit the ball quite hard. It beat Nigel Sims in goal, but it then struck Stan Lynn on his heel and flicked over the bar. I can't think of many printable comments aimed in my direction after the game. Most were in jest, but some people still haven't forgiven me."* It was perhaps fortunate that he didn't know then that he would never come that close to a domestic honour again. *"No player likes losing a game and if the other team is better than yours, you just have to accept it. But that match no matter what we did, the ball simply wouldn't go into the net. All teams have 'lucky' games and that day Villa had all the luck going."*

OVER THE NINE months of the 1956/57 season, the big forward had amassed 20 league and cup goals, including a purple patch of seven goals in seven league games. The total made him club top goalscorer, five ahead of Ronnie Allen. Clearly, the international had something about him and there was more, much more to come. But first, there was a tour of Russia, awkwardly timed exactly a month after the season finished.

If not all his own supporters appreciated the Tank, the Russians certainly did. Kevan's all-out, aggressive style earned him five of the Baggies eight goals in their trio of games. The Soviet press gave him a new name, 'Lion of Moscow'. Almost a half century later Derek wistfully reminisced, *"I really enjoyed the Russian tour. It was very noticeable how they treated their people. Mind, there were soldiers all over Moscow. We thought it would be very wise to be on our best behaviour."*

Buoyed by his success on foreign soil, the big man steamed into opponents in the new First Division season. In a 50/50 challenge, there would invariably be one winner. Shay Dunne recalled coming up against The Tank at the Hawthorns at a time when there was a running track around the pitch. Derek hit him so hard that he flew through the air, landing on the cinder track. That tackle, and the landing, really hurt and it took Shay about five minutes to get back on to the field of play with his shorts and legs covered in cinders from the running track. *"Only a tap,"* scoffed Derek, when the Luton man challenged him later. *"I'll get you back,"* threatened the sore opponent. Indeed he did in the return match, completely flattening The Tank when the referee wasn't looking. *"I thought you were kidding!"* lamented Derek.

The Tank regularly received knocks – in fact he became as legendary for them as for his goals. After one particular assault, he retired hurt to the dentist to have 11 teeth removed. Despite acute discomfort, he still kept his promise to attend Maurice Setters' wedding. The following year, he had another kick in the mouth at Newcastle, forcing his dentist to take his top front teeth out. His team-mates called him *"Gummy"*, fully utilising the sadistic humour of footballers. When fellow forward Johnny Nicholls heard The Tank was doing a TV interview, he hid his false teeth and only confessed to their whereabouts after much panicking by Derek.

Kevan was regularly on the receiving end. After a match at Goodison Park, in which he was booed throughout following an accidental collision, the Albion team found themselves surrounded by several hundred teenagers as they attempted to reach their coach. Blows and kicks were aimed at several Albion men. Derek recalled: *"As I tried to get into the coach, some of the fans tried to close the sliding door with me outside. I managed to get in, but as I was doing so, someone kicked me on my right leg."* Even when they were safely on board, the mob repeatedly spat at the windows and as at least one Albion player admitted later, they thought all the windows would be smashed.

When the Russian Army team made a return visit, the first name the Russian coach asked about *was* "Kev'van". As Desmond Hackett of the *Daily Express* reported after Albion had run out 6-5 winners, *"The crowd thrilled to the England-class positioning of big Derek Kevan, the man most feared by the Russians, the man who was hauled, pushed, and pulled down more than a dozen times. He scored a hat-trick. If he could only play like this for England."* Predictably Kevan was then overlooked for selection.

ADDING TO KEVAN'S natural power and strength was his determination to improve by working harder as reporter Charles Harrold observed: *"Albion's big, cheerful Derek Kevan has set a new fashion at the Hawthorns – voluntary afternoon practice and training. One by one he is getting all the players at it, even some of the older men, who are not always the most eager of trainers. But when you know Kevan it is understandable because his enthusiasm and keenness are infectious. Even when things are not going well for him, Kevan is still one of the most cheerful footballers I know. Ask him why he comes back most afternoons and he will tell you, 'I want to improve. I want to learn, and I want to get on in the game, and practice seems the way to do it.'"*

The additional work, particularly on his ball skills, paid off. Albion opened 1957/58 in fine style, promising to be even better than the 1954 Cup winning crew. Robson, Allen and Kevan were all scoring freely and Albion boasted star names right through the team. As journalist Alan Durrant wrote: *"Looking for a weakness in this West Bromwich side is like looking for a flaw in the koh-i-noor diamond."* Alan was perhaps not taking a wide enough view for, although they remained unbeaten away from home until mid-December, too many draws at the Hawthorns saw them lagging behind eventual champions Wolves.

Impatient supporters were considered at least partly to blame. At least their venom was no longer directed at Derek Kevan. His exploits in front of goal and his one-man battering ram act won over all the doubters. Despite his style, Derek was only 6ft tall and weighing just over 12st (virtually identical to Zoltan Gera). Derek again: *"You really have to be fit to play my type of game. It's hard work keeping down to that weight, that's why I train as hard as I do."*

Instead of Allen and Nicholls, Albion supporters revelled in the new partnership of Allen and Kevan. Through his *Sports Final* column, Ronnie Allen sought to sum up his main strike partner: *"'Churchill' as we call him. No 'tanks' for guessing why. The No. 1 target for our little japes. Takes some catching when he scores. Drives my barber crackers with precise instructions on how to harvest his mop. Would train all day if he was asked and he loves his football. Promises to buy me a set of golf clubs if we win the cup. That makes us all the more determined."*

Ah yes, the FA Cup. Manchester City were demolished 5-1. So, too, Forest in a replay despite the Baggies having ten men. Big Kev scored one of the five and then went one better in round five with a pair of goals in another demolition – 4-1 over Sheffield United, before an excited 57,000 crowd at the Hawthorns. With 18 FA Cup goals, the Albion team looked able to take on the world – which is exactly what they had to do. In the quarter-final, they drew the immediate post-Munich Manchester United. Albion couldn't overcome such raw emotion and a highly sympathetic referee, losing 1-0 in a replay.

THE TANK WAS in excellent form that term with 23 league and cup goals in 38 matches, though sufficient only to finish third in the Albion goalscoring list. Two of his goals came in a 5-3 win over Birmingham, two more against Forest, but it was the impressive 4-0 demolition of Everton which put a smile on everyone's face. As reporter Bill Davies claimed: *"Derek Kevan, the hell-bound goal snatcher is as good any other in British football for a decade or more."* But more importantly for Derek, this was World Cup year and the Ripon-born forward was now an England regular.

The Scots were his victims once again. Derek scored a hat-trick for the Football League against their Scottish counterparts and then added two more against their national side in a 4-0 thrashing at Hampden Park. The national press remained unimpressed and after England had lost 5-0 to Yugoslavia, it was again Kevan who took most of the flak. But if the cynical hacks weren't impressed, The Tank's fellow internationals certainly were. Tom Finney and Billy Wright advised the selectors they should retain Kevan up front as manager Walter Winterbottom explained, *"I understand the players are convinced he is still the best man for the job. They consider he's been a victim of the sleek short passing game that has been used in the last few months."* Kevan's big rival for the England shirt was Brian Clough, with 50 goals to his name for Middlesbrough. But as Big Kev pointed out: *"He'd been scoring in the Second Division. I'd scored all of mine in the First Division. Anyone can score goals in the Second Division."*

The endorsement from his colleagues persuaded the selectors to award several further caps in friendly matches, before the ultimate prize, representing England in the first ever televised World Cup, was announced. Kevan, together with fellow Albion man Bobby Robson, were the first Baggies chosen to represent their country in the 1958 Finals tournament in Sweden. Derek had a familiar face for company and apparently someone to share the stick from scribes such as Brian Glanville. *"There was no one to compensate for the staleness of Robson or the crudities of the huge centre-forward Derek Kevan."* The complaint that Kevan was only a crude journeyman was a familiar, if tedious, litany. Years later, author Bob Ferrier added his own perspective. *"All along, the newspaper critics obviously felt that Bobby Charlton's brilliant goalscoring was a ready made answer to England's problem. The simplicity of this argument proved irresistible to them."*

That huge centre-forward was to score half of his country's four goals in their Group Three matches in Sweden. *"Playing for England was probably the highlight of my career,"* explained Derek. *"But it was never easy. Johnny Haynes was the man alongside me in most of my games and he and I never really hit it off."*

Opening with a 2-2 draw against Russia, Kevan's goal prompted less hostile prose from Glanville. *"Kevan's fair head rose above the defence, even Yashin, and down into goal."* (Subsequently Kevan and Yashin forged a lifelong friendship and Derek is the proud owner of a pennant given to him by the goalkeeper). The game against Brazil finished goalless. The last group game another 2-2, this time against Austria, gave England joint second place with the Soviets. Unusually, a play-off was deemed necessary and it proved to be England's end as they were defeated by a single Soviet goal.

ANOTHER LEAGUE SEASON and the big striker lifted the bar a little higher with a mightily impressive 28 goals from 41 games plus another hat-trick for the Football League against the now increasingly fearful Scots and more goals for his country. Some journeyman! Derek could play.

During the fabulous 4-3 win over League Champions Manchester United, described by reporter Alan Durrant *"as some of the most breathtaking soccer it has been my privilege to see"*, Kevan demonstrated the full width of his repertoire, some of his cross-field passes *"had the United in some awful tangles"*, belaying his image as just *"a bustler and trier"*. There was no better example of this than a 6-0 romp over

Birmingham City. Kevan danced past three defenders for his goal. His team mates gaped.

More evidence was plentiful such as a hat-trick at Arsenal (though he still finished on the losing side) and a winner at Old Trafford. Writer David Jack still couldn't resist a dig: *"My old pal Derek Kevan (I criticise him, he calls me names, and we stay the best of friends) won this match for West Brom with the perfect winning goal a quarter of an hour before the end. Big Derek, who doesn't do such things when he wears an England shirt, hit his shot hard and true along the ground giving Harry Gregg no chance."*

Had the England selectors considered better utilising Kevan's strengths, perhaps the big striker's scoring ratio for his country might have been higher.

Ray Barlow regularly fed Kevan the through passes he so thrived on so logically why not call up Barlow? But the selectors weren't listening and so the much-maligned forward carried on taking the stick. *"I am fighting my hardest to show the critics just what Derek Kevan can do. All the criticism of my centre-forward performance was very embarrassing but I have shrugged it off and am concentrating on my football."*

IN APRIL, ALBION were 2-0 down at home to Newcastle when Joe Kennedy was carried off the pitch, head pouring with blood. The defender pleaded with the club doctor to return to the action but the official refused. Fortunately, Derek Kevan was in unstoppable mood and his two goals secured the Baggies a point. *"Gee, how they fought,"* said Joe admiringly. *"Perhaps it was just as well I didn't come back on."* All that effort and 26 League goals proved insufficient. Kevan was overlooked for the Scotland match and subsequently only won one more cap.

THERE'S SOMETHING about goalscoring forwards at the Albion. Think W.G., Ronnie Allen, Bomber Brown, The King, SuperBob, even Lee Hughes in his own way. All those big hitters were outgoing people, suggesting one goes with the other. Rather like a lead singer in a band, their personality is as important as the end result. Big Derek was also the life and soul of the party, gregarious and loved a drink as supporter Peter Whitehouse recalled: *"I met him at the Adelphi Dance Hall in West Bromwich and found him very pleasant. One Saturday night I was at a party in Garratt Street when he turned up along with Jock Wallace. Derek proceeded to help himself to our beer until the smallest one of our group told him he was being unfair to us working lads who had collected hard-earned money to buy the beer. He apologised and left only to return half an hour later with two crates of beer procured from the Waggon & Horses in West Bromwich and told us we were welcome to help ourselves."*

On another occasion, Derek Kevan and Alec Jackson hired a canoe in Stratford. The boat rocked so much that Kevan dived for the bank five feet away – he missed and ended up in three feet of water. Jackson continued to paddle valiantly as the canoe sank under him, watched by thousands of amused tourists.

Like many footballers, The Tank found other sports easy. After the Baggies hierarchy boldly installed a table tennis table in the players' recreation room, the Yorkshire-born forward proved to be the best exponent. He was, as Ray Barlow put it, *"the King of Ping"*. Similarly, he was the most competent darts player in the Albion squad.

KEVAN OPENED 1959-60 in much the same style as before with four goals in the first six games. He was now attempting to impress new manager Gordon Clark as Buckingham had resigned. The new man was often brutally frank with his players in an effort to bring out what he considered to be the best of their strengths. Clark was credited for changing Kevan's style. Sam Leitch, following a 3-2 first game victory against Manchester United, commented, *"Kevan was unrecognisable from last season. He positioned brilliantly. And from his devastating, side-flicks many a snap Albion raid was set in motion. And he prodded, paraded with a new certainty and confidence. He looked a fine footballer."*

Derek hit a bad patch with only three goals in the next 15 matches. *"Going through a wretched time,"* pronounced Eric Woodward in the *Birmingham Mail*. Curiously Clark didn't take the credit for that. 'The Tank', normally a light-hearted character, confessed: *"I know because of the way I play that I've got to get goals. That's the reason I'm in the team. But I couldn't get goals. Even worse, I couldn't get into positions to miss them. I reached the point when I asked the Boss to drop me because I felt I wasn't giving the team a fair deal. But he refused to leave me out explaining I wasn't the type of player who could get my form back in the second team. It was the Boxing Day fixture against Forest that put me right and confirmed it in my mind."*

Before 28,000 supporters, the striker scored twice, though it wasn't enough to prevent defeat. Reporter Dick Knight: *"Derek Kevan the man who reached the dizzy heights of England fame but has been a shadow of himself this season, knew the way. Here was something of the old Kevan; the big roaring spearhead whose flashes through the middle will be one of my memories of the decade now dying."*

Once he'd remembered where the net was, there was no stopping the big fella. His hat-trick knocked Plymouth out of the FA Cup in January, only his second in an Albion shirt, (an admirable feat at any time but not according to the *News Chronicle* who chose to highlight the chances he missed). Only handball by a West Ham defender on the goal line prevented another hat-trick against the Hammers just weeks later. Not that Derek had to wait long. Remarkably he topped all his previous scoring feats with five against Everton in March. His hat-trick goal was one of his classic, corkscrew headers. With just 20 minutes remaining, Albion trailed 2-1.

Small wonder then as correspondent Rod Davies noted, *"Kevan was immediately restored to his position of darling at the Hawthorns."* Only a few weeks earlier, supporters had clamoured for him to be dropped. Without the goals, the ridicule of his style quickly returned. Clearly some followers of the Baggies had very short memories.

SUPPORTER ROBERT PLANT summed up just how maligned he was. *"Surely no player in recent years has had to withstand such an avalanche of criticism, ranging from the cruel jeers of so-called Albion supporters who found the crudity of his play in his early days so highly amusing to the more refined snubs of our internal selectors who made him the scapegoat for the pathetic displays of the England team."* When The Tank was unable to lead the line, the team missed his strength, such as in a 3-0 defeat at Maine Road, where their forwards were described as *"lightweight in every sense of the word."*

A HOME MATCH against Blackburn produced his 100th Albion goal and just three matches later; there was another hat-trick to celebrate against Birmingham City. Not to be outdone, Ronnie Allen also found the net three times in a 7-1 win with the pair putting away almost every chance they had.

Derek beat his personal best again; finishing with 29 goals, virtually double that of the next highest Albion scorer. His club finished fourth, a slight improvement on fifth the previous season.

EXPECTATIONS OF A serious crack at the championship next time around were completely dashed by seven defeats in the first eight games. These were difficult times. Stalwart Ray Barlow had left while Ronnie Allen and Joe Kennedy were not to be far behind him. Kevan started the season not having fully recovered from an operation to straighten four toes. Even Clark admitted, *"This sort of operation takes time to heal."* The Baggies rallied briefly but then only secured two points from seven games in October and November.

From a fan's perspective, Albion's roller coaster form was indescribably frustrating. Covering a single goal defeat at Highbury, Bryon Butler concluded: *"Albion were a geometrician's delight. They pushed the ball around all the sides of the triangles in the book. Their patterns included squares, oblongs, and diamonds. They made me dizzy. They have in Derek Kevan one of the finest bulldozers in the business. He is also intelligent. Why, therefore he spent the game pushing and prodding I cannot understand. Albion's loss was Arsenal's gain."*

With Albion hovering just above the relegation zone and suffering an embarrassing 1-0 FA Cup exit at Lincoln, the board came under heavy fire via a welter of letters to the local press. The players also received abusive correspondence. The main target was hapless Kevan, both at the Hawthorns and at his accommodation. The striker had managed 10 goals in 24 matches, not outstanding, but far more effective than any of his team mates. *"All I could do was to do my best and wait for things to change,"* said Derek, resignedly.

Despite a mixed season, Albion eventually climbed to tenth in the table, Kevan's 18 League goals (in just 32 games as mumps ruled him out for four weeks) leaving him club top scorer for the third straight season.

IT WASN'T LONG before Kevan was the centre of attention once more. During a victory over Everton at the Hawthorns in August 1961, Bobby Collins was injured following a hefty challenge from The Tank. The Everton manager accused Albion of employing roughhouse tactics, hardly a diplomatic comment with the return match a week later.

These were very hard times for Kevan as he admitted himself: *"I must say I've never been as surprised or hurt as in the last few days. I was booed as soon as I set foot on Goodison Park and barracked every time I got near the ball. Their manager Harry Catterick had accused us of rough play the previous week and they seemed dead set on picking on me and I was a marked man. Then I come back to the Hawthorns and the crowd were on to me almost as cruelly."*

The home match was against Ipswich, in what was the Baggies fourth defeat in their opening five games. Journalist Alan Williams was shocked by the crowd's reaction: *"England's most jeered and criticised centre-forward shamed the fickle fans that have made his life a misery this season. Kevan was hooted mercilessly and the Hawthorns crowd kept up a slow handclapping symphony which lasted throughout the last 15 minutes."*

Quite why a side with a reputation for attractive football and including three England players in Don Howe, Bobby Robson and the Tank himself were playing so badly was indeed a cause for vexation but selecting the club top goalscorer as a scapegoat made little sense. Albion were now an unhappy ship. Burnside, Graham Williams and Chippy Clark all asked for transfers. Rumours circulated that Gordon Clark was unhappy due to a personality clash with the board of directors, intimating they refused to buy the players he recommended. Inevitably he resigned.

Enter Archie Mcaulay from Norwich City confirming, *"I have all the control I want."* In his second game in charge there was a Kevan hat-trick against Sheffield United. Despite this start, form continued to be patchy. Only a run of five wins in the last five games pushed the Baggies into the top half.

Big Kev's contribution was massive in those run-in games, with two each against a trio of London clubs and a remarkable four in a last-day 7-1 slaughter of Blackpool. What Kevan didn't realise at the time was that he'd spurned the chance to become an Albion record holder. Don Howe: *"He'd got four but the record demanded five. When a penalty cropped up, I offered to stand back and let him take the kick. He declined as he'd done before on the principle that the penalty kicker is the penalty kicker, no matter how badly anyone wants a hat-trick or a record."* Modest Kevan finished with an extraordinary 34 goals after playing in every match that season and missing a club record by just one goal. Albion were heavily dependent on him. Only one other player managed double figures.

The club's cause was not helped by Archie Macaulay's summer decision to transfer one of England's finest players, Bobby Robson, back to Fulham, for £5,000 less than they paid for him. *"I don't want to leave the Albion. I have had six happy years here and have made lots of friends. I wanted to stay. I am bitterly disappointed at the way Albion are letting me go,"* lamented the outgoing star. There was worse to come.

In the meantime, Kevan was still doing what he did best. There were four goals in Fulham's net with their manager Bedford Jezzard exclaiming, *"Kevan must be the most dangerous player in the First Division around the goal area. He takes an awful lot of stopping."* Three weeks later, Bolton certainly couldn't stop him as Derek netted three times in a 5-4 classic. Although results were improving, the team badly needed strengthening. However, the club continued to behave as if the recently abolished maximum wage was still in place and so big names looked the other way. After 13 months in charge, Macaulay made his first signing – forward Max Murray. The Scot was a complete and utter disaster. He joined the club already facing suspension and left after making just two senior appearances.

SPECULATION MOUNTED THAT The Tank would follow Robson out of the Hawthorns. Stoke City, Manchester City, Fulham, Sheffield Wednesday, and Chelsea had all made bids. Each was refused and the Chairman's regular *"no amount of money could buy Kevan"* quote became a cliché. Albion's top man wasn't at his best but 16 goals from 28 starts told its own story. Just days after the Baggies had been beaten by Nottingham Forest in an FA Cup replay, the 173-goal man was suddenly leaving the Hawthorns.

"I didn't feel Derek had done enough this season to justify keeping him in relation to the terrific offer we had. I think it will turn out to be a wise move," said Macaulay, who was himself to depart the Hawthorns just a month later. Albion received £45,000 from Chelsea for Kevan's signature – an Albion club record figure for a departing player.

Kevan's views were rather different. *"Macaulay accused me of not trying and I never let anyone say that about me, at any club. If my best wasn't good enough, I had a poor game. He accused me of not trying! He made some awful decisions. Generally, I never took it badly if a manager had a go at me but he went too far. I had to go because of his attitude. Macaulay felt I was one of the oldest players (although several were even older). When I went to see the directors and they said, 'We've had a bid come in for you.' I was struck rigid and I didn't know what to say, or what to think, and they said, 'Would you like to talk to Chelsea?' It came out of the blue, as there hadn't been any rumours, but I went. It was the worst mistake I ever made."*

Success was to elude both club and player for several years...

Tony Brown

1963-1981: 720 games, 279 goals

COMPARED WITH MANY other Hawthorns worthies featured within these pages, Tony 'Bomber' Brown is something of an enigma. Not because of his first-class goalscoring record, which features abundantly throughout this chapter, I hasten to add – more because back then, outwardly, at least, Oldham's finest footballing export presented – and still does – a personality totally in contrast to that of many others featured within this book. The strange thing about Bomber is that when you ask older supporters for anecdotes about Tony, most will scratch their (mostly balding!) heads a little, hum and haw a bit, then, following many awe-struck testimonials as to his prodigious goalscoring abilities – never once in doubt, of course – sheepishly confess they simply don't know of any!

IN SHORT, BOMBER Brown appears to be that footballing rarity, someone supremely good at what he did, but also possessive of a remarkable ability to blend into the background when not playing for the club. In theory, not the stuff of which cult heroes are made – and yet, when you ask those same supporters for their own list of Albion all-time greats, Tony Brown is always mentioned.

Quite a contradiction, that, but how come? Football isn't exactly the career of choice for those exhibiting all the hallmarks of a shrinking violet, now, is it? Self-effacement, and the Beautiful Game are when played at top-level, personality traits as incompatible, seemingly, as oil and water itself. Elsewhere in these pages, you'll find 'characters' in abundance: *'Good in the dressing room'*, managers constantly opined when waxing lyrical on the likes of, say, Jeff Astle, John Osborne, or serial disciplinary offender Willie Johnston, even. Turning the dog-eared pages of *Time* even further backward, there's the likes of W.G. Richardson, or little Tommy Magee, both most unremarkable people when briefly glimpsed strolling around town, say, but in total contrast to their 'public image', actually the very life and soul of the party, both on the field of play and off it. Even the highly talented but ultimately doomed Harold Bache would stand out in any crowd of footballers, if only for his undoubted academic ability, coupled with a remarkable natural talent for any other sport you'd care to name and a rather unique claim – as an amateur, Albion did not pay him for his services.

So, why was it Bomber was regarded with such high affection by Albion supporters when all common sense and logic would dictate that their admiration for him would always remain a little bare in comparison with his more outgoing peers and predecessors?

TO UNDERSTAND BETTER the dynamics that exist between Bomber and most Baggies supporters, it's necessary to understand just that little bit more about the Black Country and its chequered history.

Prior to the early 1980s, when much of its manufacturing industry closed down for good, go to pretty much any British shipyard, or factory churning out widgets in quantity, and it was a pretty safe bet that you'd find there at least some components emanating straight from the Black Country.

Even the massive anchor and chains for the ill-fated Titanic were forged in nearby Netherton: go to the museum dedicated to the region's history, in Dudley, and you'll find there a classic photograph of all those workmen, hordes of them, rendered Lilliputian by the sheer size of their cargo, of course, hauling the thing straight from Noah Hingley's foundry to the nearby railway station – and working themselves into a colossal sweat in the process, one largely assuaged by the ingestion of vast quantities of beer. Not because every labouring man in the region was on the verge of alcoholism, mind – we're actually talking fluid replacement, pure and simple. These people drank bucketfuls, sure – but they also sweated bucketfuls, too, and it was a wise employer around these parts that incorporated the provision of beer on a daily basis into terms and conditions of employment for such men.

This astonishing toughness of both mind and body was also reflected in their choice of pets. Staffordshire Bull Terriers might well sweep all the prizes at Crufts these days, but back then, they were kept with a serious purpose indeed, as fighting dogs. Despite the best efforts of both constabulary and RSPCA to suppress such illegalities at the time, clandestine events like these were very much considered part and parcel of the local scene, and the wise person left such matters well alone. As in industry by day, so it was in the fighting ring by night: relatively-small, powerfully-built, but muscular with it, hard as nails, and blessed with jaws of vice-like grip, these canines were very much forged in their owners' image. Not only could they take it, they could dish it out as well, and with 'knobs on', too. So devoted were they to these enduring little animals, it wasn't at all unusual for their owners to bring them to their place of work on a daily basis; again, it was a wise employer that 'turned a deaf 'un' to such practices.

And that, if you like, is the 'missing link'. If there's one thing Black Country folk really admired back then – and still do, to a great extent – it's a 'grafter'. In other words, someone blessed with the ability to work extremely hard, irrespective of how hard the task, obnoxious the gaffer, or disgusting the working conditions, just getting their heads down and seeing the job through, no matter what. Tough work for tough people, indeed – and around the time Bomber Brown emerged from comparative youth team anonymity and into the ranks of the first team, very much of the region's industrial base was still going full-blast, remember, and with it, an awful lot of the horny-handed workforce Hawthorns regulars, still drudging without (much) complaint five and a half days out of the stipulated seven per week.

Remember the old saying: 'It takes one to know one?' When you've spent a fair proportion of your precious half-day Saturday afternoons watching a raw-featured 18-year-old kid on the park, one seemingly blessed with talents far in advance of his chronological age, and mixing it with the very best both the Baggies and their opponents could offer, including more than a mere smattering of folk who'd represented their country at top-level, then it's only natural you end up taking a shine to the lad, isn't it? Think 'heavy manufacturing industry and the men who toiled in it', think 'hard graft', think 'Staffordshire Bull Terrier', even, and that's Bomber Brown, in a nutshell for you. No wonder his footballing skills were regarded with near-reverence by a generation with vivid memories, still, of both the Hungry Thirties and the destructive world war that followed shortly afterwards.

A convenient point, that, to make yet another comparison between Bomber and the tough world he entered as a spotty little kid some 40 or so years ago: since his retirement from the game, the ravages of Time have been unkind to the former Albion man, a situation that largely stems from the somewhat unreasonable demands that playing the game at top level constantly makes upon the human body. It didn't help, either, that largely through ignorance, the overwhelming inclination on the part of both managers and trainers was, back then, to instruct players to rise above the pain of injury and just get back out there, no matter what. Pain being the human body's way of letting you know something's not right, and by doing so giving the sufferer the clearest indication possible it's high time they took a break, should someone regularly ignore such warnings, then they invariably end up with a massive price to pay in later life. In Tony's case, the constant twisting and turning demands of professional football (not to mention some more-than-unwelcome attention from defenders with DNA and general outlook on life both bordering upon the Neanderthal) placed an excessive strain upon those sorely-overworked hips and knees, resulting in the need for some extensive joint-replacement surgery.

Pain killing cortisone injections were routinely administered in the sixties for short-term gains at the expense of long-term problems. Tony received dozens. Players endured them to maintain their first team place as half their wages were based on appearances. Manager Jimmy Hagan made his own decisions as to whether players were fit, regardless of medical advice. But there was a price to pay in later life.

It wasn't at all unusual to see Bomber with mobility aids such as crutches or sticks. He wasn't alone. The coroner infamously noted the impact of a heavy football upon Jeff Astle's brain. In addition, John Talbot has a replacement left knee and endured a heart attack. Ian Collard has an artificial hip while Tony has now had three. At the tail-end of 2011, his latest replacement meant he was confined to bed for six weeks. Yet the Bomber considered himself fortunate to have new hips – he'd seen at first hand what happened to the previous generation of players, such as Teddy Sandford. The only medical aids Teddy could use for his deteriorating hips were crutches. *"They more or less ordered you to play and right throughout my career – not just me but every player – a lot of the time you'd be playing when nowhere near fit"* declared Tony to the *Albion News*.

Again, it's a problem most Black Country blokes – well, those above and beyond what might be called a 'certain age', at least – can readily identify with. Amidst today's relative prosperity and advances in medical science, there's a nasty little flip-side to be encountered, and you don't have to look too far off the beaten track to see it, either. Just hang around any 'old-fashioned' boozer in the area and some pretty debilitating and disgusting occupational conditions – pneumonocosis, silicosis, asbestosis, to name just a few – will swiftly manifest themselves, breathlessly, in the main, for your general delight and delectation.

Watch Bomber performing on the park during the sixties and seventies, and you were more or less seeing Black Country Man in all his various incarnations, good, bad and (eventually) crippled: sociability or strength of personality didn't come into it. If there's one thing we in the region love – and still do – it's a grafter, a scrapper, one willing to put his future health on the line in order to get the job done that much quicker. No wonder the Hawthorns faithful took such a shine to him when they did. No wonder Bomber still suffers because of games played back when transistors, and not silicon chips, ruled the earth. No wonder we all love him to death for it now.

First and foremost, it was goals which bought Tony into the spotlight and held him there – even decades later. His popularity stems as much from the quality of his goals as their quantity. The power of his shot rivalled that of Ronnie Allen. In his salad days, Jimmy Hagan described his new first teamer as *"the lad with the thunderbolt shot."* His most celebrated effort was his poetry-in-motion ball-over-his-shoulder volley at Hillsborough in the 1970 FA Cup. *"It was the best goal I have ever scored,"* agrees Tony. *"It must be. It could have gone anywhere, but I happened to catch it just right. As the ball came down from Dennis Martin, I thought it was best to hit it first time rather than try to bring it under control, so I swivelled and hit it. If I live to be 100, I'll never score another goal like that."* Defender John Kaye's observation summed up the moment. *"There should be museums for goals like that."*

Bomber's other best-known spectacular followed later the same year. His 25-yard free kick swerved in a most banana-like fashion past Gordon Banks, with the England man not even seeing the ball. In 1970, balls just did not swerve in mid-air. Well, unless you were Jairzinho playing in that summer's World Cup at altitude in the Azteca Stadium.

Bomber went on to score again in a highly satisfying 5-2 victory over Stoke. But there were so many other fine goals to applaud. Take Oxford in February 1976. From a loose ball after a free kick in his own half (a free kick that he'd conceded himself), Bomber ran half the length of the pitch, holding off two determined opponents before powering the ball past Oxford keeper, Burton.

Brown had the remarkable instinct given to few players of running into the right spot at exactly the right time. *"Taking up position is one of those things that come naturally to me,"* he explained to the *Albion News* *"I have to play by coming from deep because I could never play with my back to goal, because I needed to see the game in front of me. I wasn't an out–and–out striker, I did a midfield job as well."*

Back in 1962, Albion's Manchester scout John Shore persuaded a young but talented Oldham teenager to move to the Hawthorns. Just as with Joe Kennedy, Manchester United thought they had him lined up (Tony was a regular Reds watcher), but his father told him United already had too many good youthful players. Young Brown agreed. *"I never really wanted to sign for them. They always struck me as having too much talent."*

The youngster needed to grow up quickly. As he recalled *"I used to walk to the ground with Bobby Robson, who lived just down the road from my digs. Very often, I didn't know what to say to him because he was an England international, and I was just starting out in the game."* To further widen the gap, it was "Mr Robson" to the apprentices.

Tony quickly won a spot in the reserves with his performance against Newcastle reserves early in the 1963-64 season turned significant heads with the *Mail* correspondent declaring, *"Young Albion inside-right Tony Brown gave one of his most determined ever displays since he arrived at the Hawthorns. In the 75th minute, Brown – who had worked so hard throughout – was justly rewarded when he ran on to the through ball, sidestepped the keeper and then held off right back Craig to pop the ball into the net."*

REMARKABLY YOUNG BROWN was to make his first team debut later that month, at Ipswich, just a few days shy of his 18th birthday. Hastily, he signed professional forms before the game. Although his inclusion was as a result of John Kaye failing a fitness test, manager Jimmy Hagan said of his young charge *"he has improved tremendously since last year. He deserves his chance."* The debutant added timorously, *"I am very thrilled."* At Portman Road, Albion came from behind to win 2-1, but it was Tony Brown's equaliser that stole all the headlines. The youngster received a pass from Doug Fraser, beat off two tackles and swung a rising left footer into the roof of the net. Journalist Geoffrey Beane considered that *"properly handled – and that means not rushed – he could make the grade."*

Tony was not being rushed. After being rested for two games, he returned for a home match against Aston Villa. This was a barnstorming encounter in which the Baggies fought back from a two-goal deficit to win 4-3. Tony, who later confessed to *"quaking in my boots"*, scored again, a tap-in from six yards, after a glorious run by Simpson. Even venerable Jesse Pennington was impressed with the action. *"Just about the most exciting, highest scoring and cleanest derby I can remember"* he enthused. By May, he had five goals to his name in only 13 appearances, sufficient to make him fourth top scorer. Manager Hagan was positive. *"This lad works himself into so many scoring positions that if goals come from only a small percentage of them, he must finish well up the charts."*

TONY WAS SELECTED for the club's first fixture of 1965-66 – back "home" at Old Trafford. This was the United of Charlton, Law and Best in front of a full house … but the first scorer that day was young Brown, finishing smartly a cross from Kenny Foggo. Albion, watched by Tony's parents, were happy to take a 2-2 draw. Tony followed this with his first-ever hat-trick in the next match against Sunderland. *"I don't feel like a hero,"* he protested afterwards, after his style had been compared to goal poacher extraordinaire Jimmy Greaves. *"Just relieved that the ball has started going for me at last."* Apparently missed chances in Holland and at Old Trafford were preying on his mind. *"I worry about things like that for days."* Tony was on a roll, fortunately for both himself and the club, as the main goalscorers 'Yorky' Kaye and Chipper Clark wanted out. As well as netting against United, Bomber also scored against neighbours City, prompting an intriguing *Argus* headline *"Brown hits No. 2 for Gay Albion."*

But after a run of defeats, Tony was dropped in October. Even so, "Boy Brown's" statistics looked impressive, with nine goals in 17 matches. Top scorer Jeff Astle had 10, but in 32 matches.

But the season did produce a trophy for the cabinet. Talking to the club programme, Tony claimed the team was always confident about winning the League Cup at the first time of asking. *"We fancied our chances because we had started the season so well."* Brown first troubled Albion statisticians by becoming WBA's first scorer in the League Cup – against Walsall. Then he added another for good measure, explaining, *"You know that Clive Clark will get crosses in so you just have to gamble and get in the box because something would come your way."* Bomber also scored in round three, round four, and every other round too. His hat-trick against Peterborough in the semi-final second leg finally squashed the determined Third Division side.

The first leg of the final against West Ham was tightly fought, finishing 2-1 to the home side, but the second leg was anything but tight. As Tony explains *"the game at the Hawthorns was the best performance I've ever been involved in. Nobody could have stood up to us in the first half hour. They didn't know what day it was."* Journalist Bryon Butler *"Albion played football of a sort that one always hopes, but rarely expects, to see in these days of safety-first thinking."* Bomber contributed the third in a four-goal 35-minute blitz when he headed in Clark's lob, his tenth goal in the League Cup.

The idea of a floating forward behind a target man is standard now yet it was relatively unusual in the 1960s. The big difference in that decade was that every club played with wingers, thus maintaining a far greater emphasis on attack. *"Tony used to float everywhere,"* agrees skipper Graham Williams. *"He wouldn't play in today's game."*

Tony added a new element to his game when regular spot kick man Bobby Cram wasn't selected for the club's first foray into Europe. When the home side won an early penalty for handball against DOS Utrecht, Tony's shooting power made him an obvious choice. Tony, who was on the right wing that night, was just grateful to be playing after missing 11 games through injury. He considered his second half header and carefully placed shot to complete his hat-trick, as a bonus. No other Albion man has ever scored three goals in a European game.

Fortunately, the season improved partly thanks to a new goalkeeper in Osborne, and the Bomber being switched to right-half (midfield).

Albion suffered only four defeats in the rest of the season, and seven wins in the last eight secured the club's position. Tony approved of the change. *"I am thoroughly enjoying my football there. As a wing-half, I am constantly in the game and can see all of the play. There are also chances to go forward and have a crack at goal when you spot an opportunity. When I am well upfield, John Kaye drops back to cover me."* As part of a 6-1 demolition of the Geordies on the last day of the season, Brown concluded his hat-trick of hat-tricks.

ALBION RESUMED PROCEEDINGS in August 1967 in much the same way as the previous campaign. Too many games were lost and their first point was a fortunate one – the infamous 3-3 at Molineux with Bomber's very own prequel to the "Hand of God". With only minutes left and Albion a goal behind, Tony punched a cross into the Wolves net – the only part of his anatomy with which he could reach the ball. He was as startled as anyone else when the referee gave the goal. Even the away supporters were more gob-smacked than goal hungry. The Wolves goalkeeper, Phil Parkes, was so enraged that he was sent off. His manager supported him. *"No wonder Parkes went mad. The ball was handled into the net."* The referee required a police escort to leave the pitch and the enraged home crowd gathered outside the main entrance to protest and who could blame them? In a quieter, less high profile team, such an occurrence would hugely uplift the profile of the individual. But in this Albion side with such an array of larger-than-life players like The King, Ossie and Bobby Hope, Tony merely continued his gentle ascent up the popularity ladder.

1968 was to be a special year. A life-changing goal scored by Jeff Astle with his wrong foot, secured Albion the FA Cup. As Tony recalls *"I was almost in tears as I congratulated Jeff after his goal. Wow, we didn't half have a party that night."*

Tony regularly tells his tale about the closing minutes of the Cup Final, when both he and Graham Lovett were put clear of all bar one of Everton's defenders. *"I was thinking 'we're through here'… and then I heard a voice saying, 'don't give it to me…'"* Feeling disturbed by his colleague's lack of enthusiasm, Tony was obliged to pass to him anyway as the Everton defender was upon him. Lovett skied the ball wildly amid universal groans. He turned to Tony and said: *"Told you not to give it to me."*

Tony, by his own admission, didn't make much impact on the Cup Final. His key contribution came earlier in the cup run, such as in the third round at Colchester when the Baggies were in grave danger of going out. Tony scored from a penalty, which he later confessed was his most nervous spot kick of his career. The goal was just enough to escape from Layer Road with a draw. The U's were flattened in the replay.

As journalist Tom Duckworth observed, *"The Manchester lad has developed into a brilliant midfield player with an invaluable capacity to score goals. Not since Bobby Robson has England had a really constructive wing-half with genuine attacking skills."* Rarely was that capacity more invaluable in the following round when once again the opposition was on top. That's until the Bomber levelled from fully 40 yards, with the aid of a divot. Albion beat Southampton in the replay, then their neighbours Portsmouth before defeating Liverpool in a three-match slog. And once again in the semi-final with Albion on the receiving end of a Birmingham City onslaught, it was Bomber's low shot off the post, which ensured that Albion were going to Wembley.

WEST BROMWICH ALBION, FA Cup holders, were in for a busy time. In addition to defending their trophy, playing league matches and the League Cup, there was also the Cup Winners Cup demanding their attention. Bomber Brown was the star turn of the first round, as RFC Bruges attempted to intimidate the Midlanders into submission. Reporter Gron Williams was quite clear. *"The man of the match for me was Brown, who hit the first goal and came through with great verve whenever he got the chance."* The midfielder scored twice in the next round against Dynamo Bucharest before the Baggies were beaten by Dunfermline in the quarter-final. By then, defending the FA Cup had become a priority. Goals by Tony Brown in the fifth and sixth rounds of the cup were the key to overcoming Arsenal and Chelsea respectively, though he did have a penalty saved at Stamford Bridge. A potentially Wembley passage against struggling Leicester awaited them, but not for the first time, the Baggies struggled with their favourites tag. Allan Clarke snatched the cup away three minutes from time. It was a horrible ending to a very long season. Of Albion's 55 matches, Tony only missed one, scoring 23 times.

THE LATE SIXTIES followed a familiar pattern. A mixed league picture balanced by success in the cups. This year, the League Cup offered excitement and glory. Home form carried them through after some sticky away matches with the semi-final against Carlisle proving particularly tricky. Only in the second half of the second leg did the game turn in the Baggies favour. Bomber's powerful free kick provided the key third goal in a 4-2 aggregate victory. Albion were back at Wembley! But Manchester City were too strong and the cup went north.

LEGEND SAYS DON Howe was appointed in the summer of 1971 because chairman Gaunt had wearied of Wembley trips and wanted his side to become league champions. Previous incumbent Ashman was never likely to do this as his side always lacked consistency. As 1970 slid into 1971, however, Ashman's side found some consistency – they were consistently bad! The Baggies were most unfortunate with injuries that denigrated their already indifferent back division to a distinctly dodgy level. *"The excuse that Albion are a very talented side who have just not clicked, is wearing a little thin,"* wrote exasperated reporter Tony Nash. Everyone was relying on the Bomber to maintain the club's First Division status. He did his very best.

During the close season, Tony was offered at 66/1 to finish First Division top scorer. *"It seemed a long shot, but I had a quid on it for fun,"* he admitted. The odds had shrunk to 11-4 by December and 1-2 in March. The division's top goalscorer claimed hat-tricks against both Manchester United and Spurs, scoring twice five times and even found the net on his 25th birthday, appropriately at Portman Road, the ground where he'd netted on his debut. Tony's last league goal of the season, which created a personal best (28), came in a 2-2 draw with soon-to-be double winners Arsenal.

HIS SKILLS WERE finally recognised with an appearance for the Football League against the Scottish League in March 1971 (only his second selection for the League side), followed by a full cap against Wales two months later. *"I was thrilled to bits when I learned I was playing,"* said Albion's top scorer, whose excitement would have tempered if he had known then that he would never get another cap.

THERE WERE PRECIOUS few wins to celebrate in Howe's first three months in charge. Bomber scored in each of the first four games, but after that, the entire team went on a goal fast, scoring just once (Tony again) in seven games. During several games, notably Manchester City (lost 0-2, third straight home defeat) at home, play was once again accompanied by slow handclapping.

Albion just weren't scoring enough goals. Prior to playing Newcastle, some Geordie friends ventured a cheeky question as to whether Tony could baby-sit their lad on Saturday afternoon. *"How can I do that if I'm playing?"* exclaimed Tony, setting himself up perfectly again as the comedic straight man. *"Just put him in the Newcastle net. He'll be perfectly safe there."*

Fortunes started to turn after beating Liverpool on Boxing Day, in front of 44,000 relieved spectators. This was followed with a recovery from going two down at Ipswich to win 3-2. Bomber scored the crucial opening goal and, according to newcomer John Wile, *"then things started to happen."* More goals against Sheffield United followed for Tony and by mid-January, he had 12 to his name, 60 per cent of the club total. Bomber was quoted as saying *"since I have moved up front again and got rid of the midfield responsibility, I have been more successful."* But this was the loyal clubman speaking. Brown considered himself to be an attacking midfielder, a Sneekes who could tackle, if you like. Still, the Bomber was flying again. As John Kaye pointed out: *"you can always tell when Tony is in with it. You notice it during training. In one practice session during the week, almost every shot he hit was a screamer into the net."*

Not everything went to plan, with an immediate exit from the FA Cup against Coventry. Tony scored once, but was blatantly denied another when defender Bobby Parker punched his shot off the line. One supporter was so disgusted that he famously threw his pipe and apple at the myopic linesman.

A decent run of half a dozen games in March was enough to keep Albion clear of relegation danger; form sufficient for Don Howe to win Manager of the Month. Instead of keeping the whisky in house, the fiery spirit was divided up into dozens of small glass miniatures and given out to the crowd by the players ... by the somewhat risky method of throwing them.

Something was clearly not right in the house of Hawthorns. A new striker, Ally Brown, arrived in March 1972, but moribund Albion needed far more strengthening. They didn't get it and the following season was even worse. The Baggies managed only nine wins in 42 games and were relegated in miserable fashion. *"This is my club,"* Tony insisted *"and going down really hurt.* "The Bomber found the net a dozen times, a modest total, yet considering the next highest scorer had six and his contribution was almost a third of the club total, he'd more than done his share. He didn't deserve to lose his First Division footballer status.

So just three years after a League Cup Final, Albion were more concerned with travelling to Bristol Rovers, Cardiff and Orient than Wembley. In the Second Division, Tony continued to earn "brownie points" from the Hawthorns exasperated faithful, a human beacon of hope in a depressing period. Bomber realised that as the senior professional in a struggling side. *"I have to set an example to the rest of the lads".* His 23 goals in Division Two, the only team member to break double figures gave hope, ultimately a false one, of a speedy return to the top league. Seven of his tally came in just a week, in a pair of matches against the Nottingham clubs. His hat-trick destroyed County's ambition of a FA Cup run and the following Saturday, his four goals at the City Ground did for their City rivals. *"A scintillating solo performance"* according to the *Argus* correspondent. *"He's so fast, you can't stop him,"* lamented the Forest manager.

BUT ALL WAS far from well behind the Albion scenes as Howe's promise of global domination seemed a long way off the mark. *"It was drills and sessions and a lot of the time you were just standing around getting cold. I'm sure it was all clever stuff, but it just didn't work at the Albion and things went from bad to worse"* said the Bomber of the former Arsenal coach, in a very rare outburst. *"Without doubt, the era was the worst I had played in 20 years at the Albion. The whole place had lost its spirit. The players just didn't enjoy playing."* John Osborne agreed: *"many of the older players found his intense, regimented approach very difficult to cope with. Tony Brown had to play the "numbers" game and went through probably the worst spell in his career."*

Bomber Brown's testimonial provided some light relief in May 1974. This was a curious affair of a combined Albion and Villa eleven taking on a composite Blues/Wolves XI. The idea was Don Howe's, with the two sides pre-selected by the readers of the *Sports Argus*.

Twelve thousand supporters rolled up to see Tony predictably score the winner. His gross profit was said to be around the £10,000 mark.

Few would have blamed the testimonial man for wishing to leave the club after his benefit. At the age of 29 and with an impressive CV, he could have easily secured a berth with any First Division side. By not doing so, Tony was putting club before self and in the philosophical moments between the tedium of matches, his lack of selfishness brilliantly underlined his crowd favourite status.

There was virtually another full season of Howe to endure. Tony was losing heart in the Hawthorns Gulag. *"I don't like playing in Division Two. It was a big come down after so many years at the top."* By November, he had only three goals to his name and sections of the crowd were openly showing their frustrations with his meagre tally. Home games had attendances only half of the required break-even figure. The directors finally got the message.

Willie Johnston described how they heard about the dismissal of Don Howe. *"Tony and I were driving down West Brom High Street when we heard the news. Tony stopped the car and shouted 'Yessss!' That's what Tony Brown thought of Don Howe."* His reaction was a common one.

The next incumbent at the Hawthorns was former Leeds midfielder Johnny Giles, who beat off strong competition from Ronnie Allen for the job. Giles knew an attacking midfielder when he saw one, and the Bomber was restored to his preferred position. *"I had to form a team and do it within the context of the style we play"* explained the Irishman *"and Tony in left midfield is part of that plan. He's a real pro. He has worked hard at his game and fitted in well. I know that I will always get 100 per cent from him."* Bomber was back to his best, uplifted by the new spirit of belief at the club. *"Some of his shooting has been tremendous,"* wrote John Wile, in his Argus column. Giles went on to fashion a promotion side for a cost of just £40,000.

Tony guaranteed his place in Albion history by scoring the goal in his birth town which secured promotion back to the First Division. *"On our way to Oldham all we saw were cars and buses decked out in Albion colours. There were so many Albion fans going to the game we couldn't get off the motorway and had to have a police escort to Boundary Park. In the dressing room before the game everyone was incredibly nervous, and then I'll always remember walking out to the pitch and seeing a mass of blue and white. It just hit you. All the players looked at each other as if to say*

'We've got to do it for them today.'" And they did, with Bomber at his best for the all-important goal – cushioning the ball with his right and volleying it into the net with his left. Cue pitch invasion with the scorer besieged by well-wishers, but that was a mere bagatelle compared to the celebrations after Ray Tinkler blew his whistle for the last time. The Bomber and the Baggies were back!

THE MAN WHO had tried single-handedly to keep the Baggies in the top flight three years earlier had appropriately scored the crucial goal to take them back to Division One. A hugely appreciative support would never forget that moment and his loyalty to stick with Albion in difficult times. Fact-by-fact, the now-revered-like-never-before post-Oldham Bomber was making an awful mess of the club record books. First to go was Jesse Pennington's league appearances record, equalled against Coventry in September 1976 and then raised over 100 times to an impressive 561 starts. Giles' possession-orientated game worked surprisingly well for Albion in the top flight and relegation was never a concern. Tony was often overshadowed by emerging talent like Bryan "Luigi" Robson (a dressing room reference to his dark hair), Derek Statham and paid-for talent like David Cross, Laurie Cunningham and later Cyrille Regis. With so many other names to worry the opposition, Tony now had a little more time and space to make an impact.

He made the most of this during 1977/78, when his ability to anticipate knockdowns and half clearance gave him 15 goals in open play. Throw in a further ten penalties in those nine months to make a remarkable total of 25 goals at the age of 33. Bomber was club top scorer for the seventh time. According to fellow veteran John Osborne, his contribution to a 3-1 early season win over Birmingham City was outstanding. *"I reckon Tony gave about his best all-round performance. Not only did he score a vintage goal and slam in a penalty, but he covered every inch of the pitch as if he was playing his fifth game and not his 500th or whatever."*

Expectations arose that ten years after his last FA Cup Final, Bomber might be heading for another. Albion had overcome big name opposition to reach the semi-final, but it was not to be. On a day when little went right against Ipswich Town, Bomber's spot-kick was one of the few highlights. The Baggies did recover from that stomach churning afternoon to grab the consolation of the UEFA Cup, then a prestigious straight knockout competition.

WITH SUCH A magnificent tally from the previous season, Tony was now not far short of the club's league goals record. *'I've never been one to keep an eye out for records,'* he claimed, but the publicity was overpowering. The record fell in October 1978 at Elland Road with Bomber's 25-yard effort crashing home off the post. West Brom presented him with the match ball to mark his feat. Tony immediately broke the record again by scoring against the Sky Blues – though admittedly most of his team were finding the net that day in a 7-1 demolition.

By now, a new generation of supporters were hearing the tales of the legendary 'Bomber' Brown, but unlike most legends, he was still playing. Supporters like Richard Scarlet: *"I saw my first ever match at the age of ten in February 1979, Albion v Leeds United at the Hawthorns. Scorer of my first ever live goal was the hero that is Tony Brown, edge of the box, caught on the chest and volleyed into the back of the Leeds net. I can remember it like it was yesterday. I jumped up and had my hat nicked because we were in the middle of a bunch of Leeds fans in the Rainbow Stand. For being responsible for the first goal I ever saw live, Tony Brown remains God like!"*

The midfielder had just set a new marker for FA Cup appearances. In March, he broke his own record for appearances in European competition. He'd already scored more goals against continental opposition than any other Albion man, but ten years on, he was able to add to the tally. Still to come was the mark for most FA Cup goals while the record for League goals was regularly re-set. Then there was 'most appearances in all competitions'. And by making a substitute appearance in a 3-1 defeat at Nottingham Forest on 12 January 1980, Albion's record breaker broke into his third decade as an Albion player.

In these later years, Bomber became the club's corner taker – preferred even to such fine crossers of the ball like Willie Johnston or Laurie Cunningham. Tony's talents even extended to donning the goalkeeper's shirt. Once, a very brave or very stupid John Osborne was injured in a mid-air collision with the rather large Mike Doyle of Manchester City. Despite a full five minutes of treatment, he was unable to carry on, so in between the sticks went Bomber. He stoutly kept out a fierce drive from Neil Young, but was otherwise protected by his fellow Baggies until Ossie's painkilling injection took effect and he could return. Only seven months later, Tony had another chance to literally get his hand in. Once again, 'Aunt Sally' Osborne was on the receiving end and came off worst. Tony replaced him for the last 25 minutes and once again kept the opposition out. More by luck than judgement, though, having dropped the ball on the goal line, he was grateful that an alert Ally Robertson was on hand to hack it away.

ONCE RON ATKINSON had departed for Old Trafford in the summer of 1981, the Bomber found himself on skid row. In a shabby stunt, second time around manager Ronnie Allen wanted Brown out immediately, even refusing him leave to train with his team-mates until he found a new club. Tony subsequently turned out for Torquay, New England Tea Men and Stafford Rangers, but there was no keeping him away for long. Bomber returned to the Hawthorns first as a coach and more recently as a radio commentator and programme contributor.

Jeff Astle always felt mightily aggrieved that Tony had not received the second testimonial that Ron Atkinson promised him. He began a one-man campaign to win hearts and minds, never missing a chance to make his point to supporters or club officials. Eventually, he wore them down and the Bomber got his match against the old enemy Aston Villa.

Tony "Bomber" Brown is the Baggies final clubman par excellence. No other Albion player in these transitory times will ever enjoy two testimonials. He commands huge admiration from both supporters and his fellow professionals, never complaining in public, always using the appropriate words and would never ever embarrass the club. Even on his 21st birthday (then a significant milestone), he refused to celebrate with his fellow players lest he further aggravate a back injury. Even now, the accolades continue to flow. He was given the Freedom of Sandwell and was the clear winner to be the WBA star on Birmingham's Broad Street's "Walk of Stars". Far more recently, his enduring cult hero status was underlined when he was chosen to be the supporters theme for the last away trip to Newcastle in May 2011. In the modern era, there is no greater supporter tribute.

Jeff Astle

1964-1974: 361 games, 174 goals

DURING THE OFFICIAL opening by Laraine and her grandchildren in 2003, the Astle Gates mysteriously parted, accompanied by a blast of cold air. Was that Jeff? That big, gregarious man appearing at the Hawthorns one more time, insisting, "*They're my gates. I'm going through them first.*" I really hope so.

The dignified Astle Gates dominate the black ironwork entrance to the Hawthorns' East Stand, as a tribute to King Jeff. Uniquely, a broad base of Albion fans worked together to achieve this ambitious goal. Supporters chose the form of the memorial (the Shankly Gates provided my inspiration), raised half of the cost, drew up designs and channelled grant aid towards the club. Fund-raising was never easier – the urge to give was overpowering. A fund-raising fanzine special edition broke sale records and was reprinted. Over 600 packets of Astle mintoe sweets also sold out an hour before kick-off, meaning another plea to the factory. Jeff Astle, who played his last game nearly four decades ago, still touches every generation of the Albion family.

Fan Tim Joyner can still remember the King's last Albion goal in February 1974. "*We were losing 2-1 to Bristol City and on came the King to rescue us with a classic header. The Brummie Roaders bellowed over and over again 'Astle is our King'. Some even invaded the pitch to congratulate him personally. I remember waiting anxiously for my Dad to return home from work on Monday evening, desperate to read the back page of the Post.*

There he was, in the centre of a big picture filling the sports page. Even though the memory is hazy, I'd still put it in my top 10 Albion moments." This final entry on his tally was Jeff's 171st goal for the club. Only three men will ever score more.

THE £22,400 SIGNING from Notts County made his home debut against Wolves, almost a decade earlier, in October 1964. *'Jeffrey"*, according to the *Albion News*, *"led the forwards brilliantly"*, scoring twice as Wolverhampton were hammered 5-1 (only the crossbar's width prevented his hat-trick). That was the sort of start of which cult heroes are made, but far better was to follow.

Astle's first ever Albion goal was a header from John Kaye's chip. *"It's good to be in First Division football and with the Albion"* exclaimed one very happy striker afterwards. Photographers captured that first celebration – big grin, arms above his head, fingers outstretched – the first of many. It was one of those seminal afternoons. A new signing entered the field, but a new crowd favourite left it. Wins over Villa and champions Liverpool (3-0) cemented his status. *'A.S.T.L.E.'* bellowed the Brummie Road faithful. *"To think I had to be asked twice to come here. I must be mad,"* admitted Jeff (a reference to manager Jimmy Hagan refusing his request for an under-the-counter payment, illegal but commonplace at the time).

Although Wolves was Jeff's first match at the Hawthorns, his debut had come ten days earlier at Leicester, a 'thrown-in-the-deep-end' introduction for a man who'd signed a contract barely three hours earlier. *"I was so nervous, I found myself biting my nails during the match"* admitted the striker later. Fortunately, his nerves were not visible off the pitch. Then *Mail* reporter Jeff Farmer wrote: *"Big, strong, good in the air and forceful on the ground, the 22 year-old had a highly satisfactory debut."*

In the next six years, Jeff would contribute enormously to his side reaching four Cup Finals and represent his country in the World Cup. But ever since those opening games, there was something different about Astle. Something far more significant than his hat-tricks, bravery and body strength, although all were essential. Jeff stood apart as a man.

JEFF ROLLED UP at Filbert Street wearing a green jacket and trousers. He'd not been previously introduced to his new colleagues, so they just assumed he was the bus driver. A decade of banter and jokes, with Jeff generally leading the way, was underway. The Eastwood-born striker was a supreme joke teller. As Tony Brown lamented, they were always the same jokes – even so Jeff was such an eloquent, convincing teller that the amusement factor never deserted him. John Osborne agreed. *"I've been hearing the same jokes for 30 years and they don't get any better. He did have a new joke once. He told it on the coach five times before we got to the motorway. And another 20 times before we got to Nottingham. I'll never forget that game. Ian Storey-Moore was about to take a corner and Jeff Astle came charging back into our half. I knew something was wrong because Jeff never did any defending. "Hang on, stories" said Jeff.* And he started to tell this joke in the penalty box to six Forest players. Best of all, he told 'stories' to *"hang on while he got back to the halfway line."*

Francis Lee: *"On my first England session, I met Jeff for the first time and he did nothing but tell jokes. He tells them in a voice something like Wilfred Pickles, and he has a gift of telling bad jokes with such a good delivery that you still have to laugh. The more you laugh, the more jokes he tells. I'm sure he has run out of material now, and that he is on the second time round but with a good scriptwriter he could certainly make a living out of it."*

IF JEFF'S JOKES were being recycled in the mid-sixties, it's a testament to England's No. 9 that he hadn't worn them out decades later. I can still reel them off – Steve Perryman and 'Peanuts' Astle, Graham Lovett and the bidet, the Irishman on the Golden Shot, Ossie's trousers, on tour in Blackpool – and the King reciting every one gleefully in his Eastwood accent. The delight came with the exuberant teller, not the words.

Inspired by a chance remark by John Osborne, *Grorty Dick* fanzine launched its *"Find Jeff a new Joke"* appeal, on the basis that every Astle joke was known to every living soul. Jeff never used any of the submissions, but that was secondary to his old team mates having Astle on the receiving end for once.

Jimmy Cumbes was a fast bowler with Surrey, in addition to his goalkeeping skills. Upon his arrival from Tranmere Rovers, Jeff just couldn't wait to take the mickey. *"£25,000 for a fast bowler!"* he scoffed. Cumbes had been around the circuit and had his reply ready. *"Aye and you could have got John Snow* [England fast bowler] *for £20,000."* It was so like Jeff to store this exchange away for future reference. His financially amended version became a famous much used one-liner *"That's typical of this club. For an extra £10,000, they could have got John Snow."*

As with every joker, there's always a danger of overstepping the mark or choosing the wrong person to be on the receiving end. John Osborne again *"Jeff came into the dressing room one day, kicked the door open and bawled 'Good morning, world. If you're not ready for me – tough luck!' Just what you wanted after a night out."*

The very large John Kaye didn't take kindly to being the butt of Jeff's humour. So he grabbed Jeff, picked him up (no mean feat) and pinned him to the wall while telling him exactly what he thought of his sense of humour. Nobody messed with Big John.

Inevitably, Jeff was suspected as being behind every wind-up, whether responsible or not. Tony Brown once took a phone call from an aristocratic sounding lady who claimed to be from the telephone exchange (this in the days when operators were needed to connect calls). According to the caller, there had been complaints in Tony's area from callers unable to get through. Although Tony protested there were no problems with his phone, the operator asked him to whistle down the line. This he did, but was then asked to repeat the whistle but louder. Tony obliged. *"In the next few days, you will get a packet of bird seed"* was the response and the line went dead. *"Astle!"* bawled Brown.

A few days later, Jeff did give him a packet of bird seed, but before any accusations could be levelled, the King was quick with his explanation. *"Somebody pulled the same trick on me and I had to get my own back on somebody."*

The big striker was at the centre of the coterie of Baggie players who did the rounds of social evenings at local pubs and clubs. Snooker, darts, bingo calling for old people, clothes shop modelling, pub singsongs, acting as the team's bookie, reading a lesson at a Methodist church – Jeff would have a go at anything. He even accepted an invite to visit a sports forum for a prominent Wolves player, despite the event being organised by Wolves supporter and held in a big Wolverhampton pub. The room was huge, with a stage at one end and as Jeff entered, row upon row of a Wolves supporters hissed at him. The King had an instant response, bursting into a rendition of *"What you makin' those eyes at me for?"* There were three Wolves players on the top table, plus one from Blues, one from Walsall and Jeff. Within a quarter of an hour, it was clear that the only person willing to provide honest and comprehensive responses was Jeff – he had them eating out of his hands, telling jokes and fully engaging with his audience. One Wolves supporter rose to his feet and said *"I've got to be honest now. You're the only Albion man I'd love to have seen wearing a gold and black shirt."* At the end, it was Jeff holding court, giving autographs, posing for photographs, shaking hands.

JEFF FINISHED HIS first season with ten goals. That this modest figure made him second top goalscorer (behind Clark with 11) said much for the Albion's need to bring in a finisher. Astle scored in the opening match of 1965/66 against West Ham, following that with another in the third game against Forest before notching his first ever hat-trick against Sheffield Wednesday. Jeff and Laraine had spent the morning in the unglamourous surroundings of Bilston market seeking a rocking horse for their daughter Dorice.

On the way home, Laraine felt ravenous, so they stopped at a chippy near West Bromwich town centre. Jeff purchased fish and chips for his missus; the trouble was, so good smelt those chips, temptation reared and Jeff succumbed, adding a fish to his purchases. Once home, not able to resist, he then nicked some chips from Laraine's plate to make the pre-match feast complete. Jeff scoffed the lot. Less than three hours later, he was lining up at the Hawthorns. Five hours later, after two deft headers and a third goal with his foot, all the press wanted to talk to him.

Clearly enjoying the attention, the striker then found the net at Everton and followed that with another hat-trick the following week against Northampton.

Jeff was now the First Division's top goalscorer and was treated as such by opposing defenders. During one hard game, he picked up a knee injury and although he soldiered on for a while (managing his third hat-trick, this time against Coventry in the League Cup), a cartilage operation was required. During that era, such an operation was tricky. Jeff was out of action for two months. But even then, he was still getting noticed.

Cyril Randle worked in a radio/TV shop in West Bromwich. *"Late in 1965, I was asked to put a couple of electrical sockets in a house in Springfield Crescent. When I arrived, I asked the lady her name, 'Mrs Astle', she replied. Blimey! Sure enough, it was Jeff's wife with small baby. I was full of questions while I worked, which she answered, but she was more*

interested in knowing what the supporters thought of Jeff. We thought he
was great, I said and, I added, if he learns that we also have to play away
matches as if we could win, then he could become an England player. Just
as I'd said those words, the door opened and in bounced Jeff himself. I was
challenged to repeat all the comments I'd just made. So I did. Meanwhile,
he'd grabbed the baby, and was lifting it high and laughing.

"I considered I was a bundle of energy. But compared to him, I was a
candle and Jeff was a tungsten-halogen spotlight. He heard everything I was
saying, but he was everywhere at the same time. I finished, they thanked me
and I left delighted!"

FORTUNATELY, ASTLE WAS fit to take his place in the two-
legged League Cup Final against West Ham. In the first leg in London,
Jeff went close to scoring twice before 'Chipper' Clark set him up to
despatch a low shot past Hammers' keeper Standen.

Even though the home side fought back to take a narrow 2-1 lead
into the second leg, it was never going to be enough. Four Albion goals
in 35 first half minutes at the Hawthorns flattened the Londoners.
West Ham couldn't cope with the power and pace of Astle, Kaye, Clark
and Brown. Jeff set up the final goal with a trademark header, which
made life very easy in the second half. *"Easy, easy, easy"* bellowed Albion
supporters, as they savoured each precious moment of the Baggies
winning a trophy on their own ground.

Despite his Cup Final goal, Jeff hadn't properly recovered from his
operation; he suffered the indignity of being dropped. Fred Bennett
of the *Sports Argus* noted during the Blackpool match how *"long*
suffering home fans showed their exasperation by chanting 'Astle, Astle' –
bewailing the absence of their hero, languishing in the reserves." Jeff was
immediately recalled against Leicester, claiming one goal and four
assists in a 5-1 victory. After City, Jeff found the net four times in the
next three matches. His season stats were impressive – 18 goals in just
27 matches.

ALBION'S CUP SUCCESS continued into the following season.
Fifteen goals in just four League Cup matches left a series of opponents
dazed (not least Villa, thrashed 6-1). Jeff found the net against both
Manchester City and Swindon, but his crowning glory was reserved for
the semi-final. West Ham were the déjà vu victims with four more goals

conceded, three of them from Astle. Two more efforts were disallowed. The Londoners probably realised it wasn't their night when Jeff scored his first – a header from Collard's cross – after just 50 seconds. A 4-0 lead made the second leg academic.

From that high point, the season nosedived. On 1st March, the Baggies were embarrassingly beaten 3-2 by Third Division QPR in the first ever League Cup Final at Wembley, despite being 2-0 ahead at the interval. Three days later, their initial foray into Europe was also over as Bologna completed a third round comfortable home and away double over the distraught Albion side.

Up to then, poor league results had been alleviated by progress in cup competitions. Jeff and his fellow forwards 'Chipper' Clark and 'Bomber' Brown scored 49 League goals between them, Jeff's contribution of 16 showed he had an eye for making something out of nothing, notably when he harassed Sheffield Wednesday's Ron Springett into dropping the ball. Astle was in swiftly, steering the ball around the keeper and into the net. And yet, despite the best efforts of the front men, the defence were conceding even more. Only a fine run of late season victories spared the Baggies from the embarrassment of relegation.

A week later, Jimmy Hagan was sacked, despite his five-year contract. Jeff shared his thoughts on his first Albion manager with me years later. *"Jimmy Hagan told me to stay in the opposition half of the field all the time. He came in the dressing room one Monday, with a sheet pasted with all the local press. 'Yer on that one, that one, an' that an' that one. Well yer should, yer the leading goalscorer, aren't yer?' And then he told John Kaye off because he wasn't! But I'll nivva say anything against Jimmy Hagan because he made me a First Division footballer. He was funny in certain ways. He were the type of bloke who wouldn't speak to you one minute and worship you the next."*

THE KING'S WORDS on his ex-manager to the press were typically guarded and suffered much from translation into BBC English. *"I can't help thinking that, if he'd relaxed just a little and revealed just a few human touches in his dealing, he could have been a great manager."* Often with Jeff's public utterances and also in his biography *Striker*, there was normally a stiffness, precision and formality about his words, functional phrases that concealed the real Jeff, the grinning, warm, endlessly gregarious Jeff who everyone loved.

Albion's new manager was Alan Ashman, a quiet, thoughtful man whom the players took to immediately. Team spirit was instantly enhanced, with Graham Williams an imposing and popular captain. *"Most of us were there for 16–17 years,"* he explained. *"We were all part of one family. If somebody kicked one of us, they'd kicked all of us."*

Jeff found the net even more regularly than before, notably in consecutive early season league matches. In the absence of regular expert Tony Brown, Jeff even managed one from the penalty spot against Stoke City. Under Ashman, the King was often the solitary forward, with supporting players backing him up. This system benefited the team, but Jeff of course had a very tough job.

Any hopes of a third straight League Cup final fell at the first hurdle in another embarrassing defeat by lower division opposition, this time a 3-1 humbling by Reading. But there was always the FA Cup. After a desperately close affair at Colchester, the Essex side was comfortably sorted out 4-0 in a replay, Jeff scoring twice. Another brace followed in a fourth round replay against Southampton and his crucial strike at Portsmouth helped to put the Baggies into the last eight, their first appearance in the quarter-finals for a decade. And then Albion pulled out... mighty Liverpool.

The Reds had a FA Cup system – blanket defence to earn a draw on the road and then beat the opposition at Anfield. They got their 0-0 at the Hawthorns, so probably considered the job was done. But they'd reckoned without Jeff Astle. Albion's main man was dominant in the air and when he got on the end of a cross from Bomber Brown in the 69th minute... well that just wasn't in the script. As John Kaye eloquently put it: *"Have you ever heard silence? Silence is the Kop after Jeff Astle nodded that great equaliser at Anfield."* The deadlock could not be broken, so the tie went to a third match at Maine Road.

This was a rough, tough, emotional encounter, watched by 56,000 people, the majority of which came from Merseyside. Goals from the King and Clive Clark were only just enough to keep the Reds at bay, who laid a late siege to the Albion goal. But this Liverpool team were big on effort, but short of class.

The semi-final against Second Division Birmingham was very different. City had nearly all the chances and missed them, whereas Albion had far fewer, but found the net. Astle, his name chanted before, during and after the game, grabbed the all-important first, pouncing on a rebound in the thirteenth minute. The goal was his 28th of the season, including at least one in every round of the Cup. When Bomber Brown added the second, Albion knew exactly where they were going.

JEFF WAS RAPIDLY becoming a national figure, as John Kaye explained, just a few days before the semi-final. *"Whenever Albion are on the TV, the standing joke in the dressing room is 'watch the Jeff Astle show.' Now it has come true. The 'Nottingham Flash' went through his paces at the Spring Road training ground for the television cameramen. His epic is due for showing on the commercial channel."* The timing was excellent, for the King scored two hat-tricks in three days. On the Monday, just two days after the semi-final triumph, 43,000 squeezed into the Hawthorns as Albion demolished Manchester United 6-3, with Jeff getting three of them and still finding time to brawl with Nobby Stiles. Journalist Colin Malam described the evening. *"Albion took Manchester United by the scruff of the neck and shook them so hard they tumbled from the top of the First Division."*

Two days later, the King found the net three more times, including two splendid headers, against West Ham. The chants of *"Astle for England"* had new belief about them. Tom Duckworth of the *Argus* was supportive. *"There is a new urgency and fire in Astle's play and there is no better header of a ball. But he is not just an in-the-air player. He is fast, runs into space splendidly and combines deft footwork with a splendid shot."*

The King and he was definitely the King by now, was a national phenomenon. *"How do you spell goal?"* was a standard Black Country schoolboy line followed by the punchline. *"A S T L E"*.

Jeff duly received his England call-up, which prompted a predictable response from 'Yorky' Kaye. *"We wouldn't object to Jeff being selected for England parties regularly so we can get some peace and quiet around the place."* However, Jeff's first cap was still a year away (v Wales at Wembley in April 1969) and only four more would follow. Five was perhaps a reasonable tally by Albion player standards, for which tradition dictates they will never earn the number of international appearances their form deserves.

But perhaps there was more to the King being passed over than the usual anti-Midlands bias as Tony Brown explained. *"Alan Ball told me Jeff was the only man who used to get Sir Alf wound up. Jeff was always so lively in the dressing room and he made such a row, he'd get Sir Alf steaming. The one time, it ended up with Sir Alf shouting 'Astle! Why don't you just piss orf?' Perhaps that's why he didn't get many caps?"*

Peace was the last thing on the minds of Albion players as they prepared for their FA Cup Final appearance against Everton. At their training base in Southport, everyone wanted to talk to the King, the First Division's top scorer with 35 goals. Jeff just carried on being Jeff, with 'Bomber' Brown regularly the Ernie Wise to Jeff's Eric Morecambe. Once, the pair staged a ventriloquist act for the rest of the squad with Jeff playing the part of the dummy.

If modern day supporters thought the play-off final v Derby was grim, the 1968 FA Cup Final was far worse. Play was constantly interrupted for free kicks as the two sides tore into each other. Despite loud and endlessly repeated plaintive chants of *"Jeff Astle"* from half of Wembley, the striker saw very little of the ball. The few chances that were created all fell to Everton, including a glorious opportunity that Husband missed minutes from the end. Albion looked like pardoned men in extra time, being far more enterprising in their play.

But such occasions are made for gods to rise above mere mortals. And, sure enough, within just a few minutes, the King made himself immortal. Astle's right foot shot rebounded back into his path off Everton central defender Brian Labone. Jeff hit it again with his far weaker left foot and the ball hit the net before Gordon West could react. *"Goals like that come once in a lifetime,"* admitted Jeff later.

The photograph of his celebrations (silent shout, both arms above his head, fingers outstretched to the skies) remains the most iconic of all Albion illustrations. The image was later immortalised in the Astle Gates. Naturally, Jeff was repeatedly asked how he felt after his goal; the endless chants of *"Astle, Astle"*, the lap of honour. He was quite candid. *"I didn't feel anything. I was just numb, physically and mentally drained."*

He continued *"Laraine and I never went to bed that night. I couldn't sleep if we had. We sat up all night talking to Kenneth Wolstenholme and when it got light we went for a walk around Hyde Park. "*

He quickly recovered to take a lead role in bringing the cup home to West Bromwich. It was a major operation, with 500 police failing to hold back a 250,000-strong crowd. The open top bus was almost an hour late reaching the town hall. Supporter Bryn Jones recalled: *"On the balcony outside West Bromwich Town Hall all the players were presented one by one as the Cup stood on a table at the front. Only one name remained to be announced. With perfect timing as his name came over the PA, Jeff bounded from the back of the balcony, plucked up the trophy and brandished it to a roaring cheer from the tens of thousands packed in the High Street below him."*

FEW OF THE Albion players fully appreciated just what glamour was attached to the FA Cup and the team that held it. They were invited to function after function and gradually became used to people simply standing and staring at the cup.

That this period is more laid back than today was underlined when Albion played their annual cricket match with Dartmouth Cricket club. Supporter Brian Maydew was asked to look after the FA Cup, purely on the basis that he was a regular attendee at the Merrivale pub, run by one of the umpires. Brian didn't know any of the players up to that point but after a day of carousing and eating in their company, he felt he knew them all.

THE NEXT SEASON started much as the previous one ended, with the King scoring against Manchester United, though a mere brace this time in a 3-1 win. Jeff was far more than just a fine header of the ball. He could shoot powerfully and his ball control was excellent. His long time chum 'Bomber' Brown reminded everyone that *"he was a terrific person, great to be around, a real man's man, but we shouldn't forget just what a top class striker he was."* Jeff wasn't as prolific as previously because he was now literally a marked man.

In November 1969, Jeff was carried from the field at Molineux after a sickening collision with John Holsgrove. Ambulancemen had to support his head. In the same month, he suffered double vision at Spurs. At Burnley later in the same season he was punched on the lip, elbowed in the eye and cracked on the nose. Neither were the first instant he'd taken a battering. In his first season with the club, he was carried off unconscious against Arsenal. The following season at Southampton, their defenders, particularly McGrath seemed out to get him. O'Neill finally succeeded with a wild tackle on the touchline. Jeff was carried off on a stretcher with an injured right leg. O'Neill was merely booked.

Jeff was brutally honest in his biography *"Striker"*: *"I rarely enjoy playing football. Enjoyment is something you experience when you are relaxed. In professional football, you cannot relax. You're subject to continuous pressure, mental as well as physical, from the kick-off right through to the final whistle. Sincere as my gratitude is to everyone who has helped and supported my career; the basic fact is that I play football because I'm paid to do so."*

After overcoming the physical presence of two foreign sides, the Baggies were eliminated from Europe by Dunfermline. The Scots grabbed an early goal in the second leg and defended it on a sand covered pitch in sub-artic conditions.

Worse was to follow in the FA Cup semi-final. Having overcome Chelsea in the quarter-final with the winner coming from Jeff, the Baggies were strong favourites to beat struggling Leicester in the last four. In the event, City sneaked a 1-0 win.

On the plus side, Jeff was the club's top scorer once more with 26 goals. But that wasn't enough for the King. He told everyone he'd get 30 during the 1969-70 season. And he did! As John Kaye wearily admitted, *"For some time, Jeff Astle bent our ears with his repeated vows that he would get 30 goals this season."* Jeff reached his target in the last league game of the season against Ipswich.

Along the way, he was presented with the match ball after scoring his 100th Baggies goal against Sheffield Wednesday in December. As ever, 'Yorky' Kaye got his retaliation in first. *"100 goals? You should have had 200 from the chances we've been making for you this season."*

INCREASINGLY, THERE WAS a price to pay for every achievement. Albion had battled their way to Wembley again in the League Cup. Goals had been shared around, but Jeff's own efforts played a main part in defeating Aston Villa, Ipswich and Leicester. The final opponents were the formidable Manchester City. Just to play at Wembley, Jeff had intensive treatment all week for his shin and ankle injuries. The desperate state of the pitch with mud on top of frozen soil could not have helped his limbs. Nevertheless, he scored after just five minutes. But City remained strong and won 2-1 in extra time.

In the same month as the Cup Final, Jeff was selected for the Football League versus the Scottish League in the rather mundane surroundings of Highfield Road. Most of the Albion team went along to see him score twice. This was widely perceived as a great boost to his chances of playing in the World Cup in Mexico and shortly afterwards, he was indeed named in Alf Ramsey's squad. Albion supporters now had a new chant: *"We all agree...Astle is better than Pelé."* Jeff was at the peak of his career, scoring regularly despite heavy legal or illegal marking.

AND SO TO MEXICO. And that miss. Brazilian goalkeeper Felix, who claims his performance in the England game was improved after two half-time cigarettes, was convinced that Jeff was not going to score, *"because when I saw Everaldo miss it. I moved to close him down. He tried to place the ball away from me and shot it out of play."* Alan Ashman put the King's contribution into perspective. *"Astle's fortunes in Mexico were rather mixed. When he came on against Brazil, everything started to happen. He made two chances for Ball and missed one himself. Against Czechoslovakia, he did not receive the right service."*

England lost to the eventual champions and so finished second in their group and advanced to play West Germany in the quarter-finals, where Franz Beckenbauer and his men would gain revenge for defeat in the final of '66. Astle did not feature in this game and so was able to do nothing more than watch as the Germans turned a two-goal deficit into a 3-2 win in extra time.

UNDERSTANDABLY WHEN HE returned, Jeff wasn't quite the same man who had left for South America will such high hopes. He was to receive much abuse from opposition supporters for that miss and shamefully from some of his own too. The stick was largely unjustified because England still qualified comfortably for the last eight.

He got off the mark in the second game of the season and added five more in the next four encounters, but overall struggled to find the net. Even being made captain made little difference to his luck. Tony Brown stuck by him loyally: *"So much depends on Jeff Astle. He's my best mate off the field and we have a good understanding. He may not be scoring so many but he's making some for me."* The King eventually managed 16 goals that term, barely half that of Tony Brown. But once again the real problem was the defence, not the attack. The Baggies finished 17th, an unacceptably low position in those days and Alan Ashman paid the price.

The new man at the helm was Don Howe, who promised much but delivered little. He told Jeff to stop heading the ball and to become a better defensive player. Jeff's response was plain speaking at its best. *"If you don't want me to head the ball, you might as well get rid of me."*

After a bright start, Albion won only one game in 20. Towards the end of the season, Howe dropped Astle for *"not trying."* The King's response, via the local press, was unusually frank. *"I think I am just as well out of the side the way we are playing. I need a supply from the wing but we are not using wingers."* Jeff considered he'd been rushed back to play only five weeks after an appendix operation. After a month with the stiffs, including one fixture at Bury where he reckoned, *"The attendance was 28, and 23 of those came to see me"*, he was selected against Manchester United, and scored the winner. But there were to be no more goals that season.

One cartilage injury followed by another kept the King away from the first team until February 1973. With Albion heading for relegation, Baggies supporters craved the return of their hero. Surely Jeff could save them. When word got around that Astle would play in a third team game at Spring Road, 500 supporters turned up to cheer him on. Jeff scored twice in a 5-1 win. As team mate Joe Mayo recalled, *"I used to play alongside Jeff in reserve games in the early seventies. Jeff hadn't got a cartilage left in his knees, but he was still the best player on the pitch."*

Astle's messianic return to the first team in February helped his side revive to a couple of wins, but defeat in the final four matches meant relegation. The writing was on the wall for both Jeff and the Albion. He was rarely fit and the club was not the one he joined. In July 1974, Barry Fry persuaded him to join Dunstable after no offers were forthcoming from other league clubs. Jeff didn't forget his supporters. *"The crowd were wonderful to me at Albion. I had my bad times, they happen to all strikers, but the fans stuck with me through thick and thin and if there is one thing I will never forget it is their complete loyalty."*

Jeff returned home later for his testimonial game – the '68 team against the current team. It was a fine opportunity for one final love-in. One supporter paid his own tribute by running on to the pitch with a bottle of champagne. And, as befitting a king, he was carried around the pitch shoulder-high after the game. Jeff tried to get one over Jimmy Cumbes again. Handing him a box of cut-glass tankards, he added, *"Don't drop them!"*

"Then why pick me?" was Cumbes' instant response.

FROM DUNSTABLE, THE King moved to the south coast. Jeff himself takes up the story. "*Weymouth? It were a fantastic place, but in the end the money weren't right so we come to the Midlands, to Atherstone. I had a season at Atherstone, but me knees were gerrin' worse, the injuries were cripplin', so I jacked it all in and started me own cleanin' business.*

"*There used to be winder cleaners in the Weymouth team, their full time job, see, and once somebody said to me, Jeff, for a bit of extra money, why don't ye do a bit of winder-cleaning, with us two at dinnertime. My missus said it was a good idea… so I did. I picked up the knack of window cleanin' – not using rags, using blades and so on, and so when I moved up ter Atherstone, I'd got nothing to do in the daytime, so I thought I'd start up me own winder cleanin' round. In them days, there weren't many winder cleaners about. I put advert in the papers an' I had no end o' people on phone, so I built it up from there! I don't do just winder cleaning narh. I do carpets and suites.*" The tale continues thanks to a more formal interview with a PFA journalist. "*I've got arthritis in both knees, now, although it doesn't affect me too badly at work. The knees couldn't stand up to football, though. It's got to the stage where I could hardly walk after a match. And I work quite a wide area. – about a 20 mile radius around where I live in Netherseal, just outside Burton.*"

West Bromwich-based Kevin Nolan needed a carpet cleaner so hired Jeff and was agape at the vista of "*an England international on his hands and knees scrubbing my carpet.*" Feeling a tad guilty and wanting more of the Astle charisma, Kevin dangled an invite for a post-clean drink at his local. The King was happy to accept. "*Just surreal*" Kevin was heard to mutter. A week later, Kevin's wife spotted that their Mexican footstool had been overlooked. Kevin couldn't resist, "*Now look here, Astle, that's twice you've missed a Mexican sitter.*"

Supporter Dan Fellows has only fond memories of the King. "*As well as my Uncle, I'd list Jeff as one of the reasons why I love football today. I remember him as a kind, decent man who always had time for everybody who wanted to speak to him. When I was about eight or nine, I remember having a kick about with him in our pub's beer garden. He didn't have to do that; he was there to clean windows. He also had a laugh when people would joke with him about his singing on Fantasy Football!*

A one-off *Fantasy Football* session, a handy excuse for Frank Skinner to meet his old Albion idol, had snowballed rapidly into Friday night post-pub TV gold. Jeff was game for anything – wearing outrageous costumes and trying to sing songs he'd never heard before on live TV 150 miles from home didn't bother him. *"No, it isn't degrading. It's a laugh and a joke, isn't it? You could be serious and say: 'No, I'm not going to do that,' but it's just a funny show."*

Out of *Fantasy Football* sprung the *Jeff Astle Roadshow*. Supporter Tim Joyner recalled one Roadshow in the Throstle Club in the late 1990s. *"It was an absolutely fantastic evening, during a period when Albion were absolutely dire on the pitch. Jeff's relationship with the fans in the club that evening, with all the funny stories and group singing, was a reminder that while the team, at that time, were serving up turgid dross week after week, the Albion "family" was and always will be a class act. I actually got to speak to the King that evening, in the gents toilets of all places, I'd had a few beers and was probably slurring my words but could only agree with Jeff's view that it had been a "bloody good night."*

The Astle family always had time for supporters, for instance Jeff and Laraine spent their 31st wedding anniversary in the company of Kidderminster Branch of the Supporters Club. Where else would they want to be? It was always a pleasure to listen to Jeff at supporters' club meetings. He had the rare quality, through sheer warmth and strength of personality, to be quite cocky and bigheaded about his own and Albion's ability during the "golden era" without a hint of arrogance.

Jeff's health declined rapidly in 1997 and didn't recover. Bravely, Laraine soldiered on as his carer while maintaining the cleaning business. She concealed Jeff's rapid decline from all but family and a few trusted friends. Even though I knew his time was limited, the midnight phone call in January 2002 was simply devastating. Supporters were overwhelmed. Flowers, scarves, shirts, photographs and other items were left at makeshift shrines all around the Hawthorns and from this public outpouring of grief came the genesis of the Albion Gates.

The Astle's home village of Netherseal was swamped with fans, players and TV cameras for the King's funeral. It was a desperately painful occasion. With the church full, many hundreds listened to the service from the churchyard.

He was cremated (his express wish) in Burton crematorium away from the madding crowd with only family and friends present.

The post-mortem made public family fears that repeatedly heading the heavy, sodden leather football of the 1960's and 1970's had *'traumatised the front of Jeff's brain'*. So not only was the King being injured externally by others during his playing days, he was injuring himself internally by heading the ball... Frank Skinner neatly captured supporters thoughts with his observation in the *Times*: *"God knows how many times I stood on the terraces as a kid, willing one of the players to whip in a cross so Jeff could climb above the centre half and thud another bullet-header towards the goal. I didn't know it was killing him."*

LARAINE ASTLE IS adamant that she doesn't *"want Albion supporters to have sad memories of Jeff, and I certainly don't want them to be sad about all the fine goals he scored with his head, even though it eventually contributed towards his illness and death. I want Albion supporters to have lovely memories of Jeff as he was."* And so it will be. The King will never be forgotten. The club marked the tenth anniversary of his death in January 2012 with a video tribute and lowering their flags to half mast. Days later, supporters repeatedly chorused "Astle is the King" at the Britannia Stadium as we finally ended 30 years of hurt. The majority of had never seen him play while the younger ones hadn't even seen him on *Fantasy Football*.

THE FINAL WORDS go to the originator of the "30 years of hurt" phrase Frank Skinner. *"It's often scary to meet your heroes but Jeff was everything I'd hoped he'd be. He was such a laugh, up for anything and a larger-than-life character. Jeff was always a performer. He really played the crowd on the pitch and off it. He was a proper old-fashioned showman."*

John Osborne

1962-1972 & 1973-1978: 312 games, 0 goals

"I once read a book by Lev Yashin. He said you could wait until the penalty is actually struck because you should be fast enough to block the shot. So I thought if it's good enough for Yashin, then I'll try it. It didn't help very much. I only saved three penalties in ten." In one self-deprecating paragraph, John Osborne unwittingly said so much about himself. These were the words of the man marked out by newspapers as the first of a new breed – an intelligent footballer. This insight was the usual tabloid nonsense, of course. John's much heralded six 'O' levels were not by themselves outstanding qualifications, and undoubtedly many other professionals had similar natural intelligence. But as the *Football League Review* pointed out in 1968, *"people who know little about the game seem surprised that footballers can be intelligent."*

What really made John stand out from the rest was his performance on a TV football-themed game show – *Quizball*.

A very youthful David Vine hosted the BBC series. The contestants were mainly from top flight football clubs, plus a guest from another sport. Osborne's team consisted of himself, manager Alan Ashman, team-mate Ray Wilson plus motor-cyclist Jeff Smith. The general knowledge questions were deliberately none-too-taxing, partly because most of the contestants were perceived to have limited recall, and because of its duration, the shows were very tiring to record. Lacking sophisticated equipment, filming a half hour quiz show needed several hours of patience in a pressurised environment – on one occasion, eleven hours of patience. The Albion quartet beat Sheffield United (Ossie scored all Albion's goals), Fulham and Forest to win the first series in March 1968. The trophy they triumphantly brought back to West Bromwich still resides in a club cabinet today. John's national fame was established.

JOHN OSBORNE WAS born on 1 December 1940 in the Derbyshire village of Barlborough, the proud son of a fitter. In his younger days, the village was short on organised activities, and so young John amused himself roaming around the local countryside identifying local birds and animals. The twin interests of bird spotting and a thirst for knowledge remained lifelong passions. In his Albion days, he endured tedious epithets such as "*The Birdman*" with his usual wry smile. A different kind of bird attracted his attention as a teenager when he started dating Jenny from the age of 15.

Although young John always played the Beautiful Game, in his early days he'd play either wing-half (midfield) or centre-half. His two England schoolboy caps were earned as an outfield player, one of them with a young Johnny Giles lining up in the opposition team. Playing left-half for the Chesterfield Boys side, progression to the last eight in the English Schools Shield competition in 1956 brought welcome attention both for himself and the team's goalkeeper, a young lad called Bob Wilson.

Making use of his 'O' levels, John found work as a clerk with a local firm, his football itch being scratched in a tough Miners' League. As the months passed, he became resigned to office life. Fortunately at the age of 18, his local club, Chesterfield, approached Osborne and signed him for their third team. Quickly, fate presented the youngster with an opportunity. The Spireites' regular keeper failed to turn up for a match against Sheffield United's thirds at the Ball Inn ground in Sheffield. Ossie volunteered and although the ball flew past him four times, he enjoyed the new position, and continued to wear a green shirt.

At that time, the youthful Gordon Banks was Chesterfield's main keeper. When he inevitably left for Leicester, Osborne became second choice behind Ron Powell, turning out regularly for the stiffs. Even then, John's status rose only marginally from amateur to part-time professional, not becoming full-time until September 1960.

OSSIE'S FIRST TEAM debut came against Shrewsbury three months later. Patience was important though, for additional appearances were limited over the next four years. In December 1964, a dreadful car accident injured Ron Powell so badly he never played again. Ossie became his replacement as first choice keeper. Chesterfield supporters praised him for his clever positioning, and his apparent near-suicidal determination to win the ball at all costs. He was also involved in some fairly comical moments (comical, at least, from the opposing fans' point of view) that led to the club conceding bizarre goals, such as a 50-yarder from Sammy Chapman against Mansfield in September, 1962.

John found nothing glamorous about his job. *"I thought Chesterfield was it – all football's like this. It was hard. The lads working in the steelworks next door got paid more. If ever I were asked what I did for a living, I'd say Chesterfield Corporation! I wasn't going to admit I played for the football club."*

The realities of lower division football were never far away. Such was the shortage of strikers, Osborne reluctantly played up front against Crewe in a home league match. Chesterfield won 3-1, though John didn't score – probably to his quiet relief. The club coach was Oliver Thompson, an old pro himself, who always smoked while applying the rubbing oils. Occasionally, ash would drop from his fag and mix in with the oils. John often joked that most of his team-mates thought that fag ash was part of the healing process.

ONE OF JOHN'S favourite tales was his account of an away fixture on the South Coast.

"I remember travelling to Brighton on the train. It was such a big treat for us to go on the train. When we got to Brighton, there was a big Women's Institute conference on and there weren't any taxis. So we had to go by bus. We got off by the ground and sauntered up to the players entrance. The doorman stepped out in front of us.

"Where are you off to?"

"We're the Chesterfield players."

"Yes, course you are. I've just seen you lot getting off the bus."

Anyway, Bobby Smith, the old Spurs forward was playing for Brighton, and we were 5-0 down. I was having a nightmare. Bobby was giving me hell and they got a corner with five minutes left. 'Right' I thought 'I'll sort him out" and hit him right on the side of the face. The first thing I noticed was that he didn't flinch. The second thing was that my hand was shaking. The referee came over, booked me and gave Brighton a penalty that they missed. You know those marks out of ten they give you in the Sunday People? Well, they gave me a nine. All the other players rang the paper up to complain, but that was the only time I hit anybody."

John's booking was one of only two he received during his entire career. The latter came two decades later in a brief return to European football with Shamrock Rovers against Banik Ostrava. *"I was ever so proud of that one,"* he later explained. *"I was booked for time wasting after 90 seconds in Czechoslovakia."*

JOHN WAS AN ever-present for over two seasons. His efforts attracted the attention of Jimmy Hagan, who had Osborne regularly watched. In January 1967, the Baggies made their move. When the Chesterfield manager inquired of him *"Would you like to go to West Brom?"* John's response apparently was a genuine *"Why, who are they playing?"*

The transfer was swiftly arranged. Ossie had a short conversation with Hagan, and quickly agreed to move, with Chesterfield receiving a £10,000 cheque in exchange. Plus, if self-effacing Ossie can be believed, *"double Green Shield stamps and three bags of coal"*. The increased salary at the Hawthorns was most welcome. John no longer needed to work part-time in the summer to make ends meet. Not only was he married to Jenny by then, he had also become a dad to little Suzanne Denise in mid-1966.

Albion, intent on enhancing their cup reputation, had rather neglected their league form. Far too many goals were flying past either Rick Sheppard or Ray Potter in the Albion goal. The club had secured only 16 points in their first 25 games (admittedly in the two points for a win era). John was handed the No. 1 shirt immediately to make his debut in a 2-1 defeat at Forest on 7 January. Within a month, he made his European debut in the third round of the Fairs Cup at Bologna. The Italian side ran out comfortable 3-0 winners. Ossie wasn't eligible to play for the Baggies in either their FA Cup matches or their League Cup defence that was ended in such embarrassing fashion by QPR at Wembley. At the time, improved league form seemed small consolation for followers with loftier ambitions, still struggling with Albion's fall from fifties grace. Once in between the sticks, there was no shifting Osborne, and one of his rivals for the green shirt, Ray Potter, was quickly transferred. His popularity wasn't of the instant kind, though. There wasn't any single moment, not in his early days anyway, when John suddenly became a favourite. His impact was a gradual one, combining his footballing abilities with social charm.

Supporter Gary Brookes recalls being introduced to the team's new keeper in a nightclub at Southampton after Albion had secured a 2-2 draw at the Dell in March.

His response was immediate, if ill-considered.

"*What the bloody hell have we bought a playwright for?*" (John shared his name with a well-known author and playwright from the 1950s, whose best-known work was *Look Back in Anger*).

"*To see that this lot play right,*" responded John instantly.

"*Taken aback by this witty response, the best I could do in reply was to point out that 'he better be good, or he would get a lot of looking back in anger from his team-mates.'*"

THE NEW GOALKEEPER was now part of a very tight-knit squad. They trained, socialised and even lived close together. Meeting supporters was a perfectly natural and regular activity, and spotting groups of Albion's finest playing snooker in a local hall on a Thursday night was commonplace. During such regular intercourse, the natural charisma of "life and soul" Jeff Astle, combined with Ossie's ever-ready wit cemented bridges and created reputations.

Disciplinarian manager Hagan was quickly gone, replaced by the gentler, more player-friendly style of Alan Ashman. Of that squad, five – Astle, Brown, Williams, Colquhoun and Hope – eventually became full internationals (although, of course, being West Midlands based, the caps were predictably few in number).

Ossie was regularly the butt of jokes, most famously when Jeff Astle was so appalled by the state of the goalkeeper's trousers – John never quite understood fashion – he cut them up with scissors. As Ossie pointed out wearily later, a dressing room whip-round for new trousers enabled him to replace said garment and make a small profit.

The keeper was always an easy target for mickey-taking. He was notoriously reluctant to train, never seeing the point. Talking to reporter Ray Matts, trainer Stuart Williams observed, "*Osborne would often be miserable first thing. He definitely wasn't a morning person.*" It was indeed fortunate for John that mild-mannered Ashman was in charge for his peak years. There was always one weekly highlight, the Friday morning five-a-side *"England"* v *"the scum"* (Scots, Irish, Welsh etc) on the tennis courts. *"Never mind losing to Arsenal on Saturday, we had to beat the scum on Friday morning. Nothing held back – the blood used to flow,"* enthused Ossie.

Rarely has a career professional footballer publicly suffered so much from pre-match nerves. As John freely admitted, *"the hardest part isn't the 90 minutes – that's the easy bit. It's the mental rehearsals – playing it out 400 times in your mind. I liken it to taking a driving test each week before 10,000 people and the examiner. I go out on Saturdays knowing that not only my livelihood, but that of ten other men, depends upon how I perform."* Being physically sick in the dressing room toilets was common. Reporter Dennis Shaw recalls being awoken late at night in a Southport hotel room where the squad were enjoying a break before an important cup match. The reporter stuck his head outside his bedroom door to see Ossie sporting full training gear and with fag bouncing the ball in the corridor, claiming to be practising his handling skills.

Long-term fan Glynis Wright has clear memories of the Albion keeper. *"Just watching him in action between the sticks was a riveting experience, for Ossie was nothing but a giant bundle of nerves for the entire 90 minutes. I don't know what manner of mental torture he was going through, but just watching his act had my stomach churning fit to bust for several hours thereafter. Give the opposition time to attack, and there he would be, sweaty dark hair slicked in all directions, eyes darting everywhere, constantly checking proximity to both goal and six-yard lines, shoulders slightly hunched, knees slightly bent, slender body swaying this way and that, awaiting the latest assault upon his peace of mind. "*

THE NIGHT BEFORE the 1970 League Cup Final, the players, and reporter Ray Matts, were taken to the West End to see *Fiddler On The Roof.* At the end of the first act, Ossie decided he couldn't sit still a moment longer and had to get out of the theatre. The club couldn't let him get lost so near to a vital game, so Ray accompanied him on his trek around Piccadilly Circus and the naughty nightclubs of London. He just walked, and walked and walked with his attendant weary journalist probably muttering darkly.

As it transpired, the capital route march offered no balm. The next day Ossie proved unusually vulnerable in the air at Wembley, and got away with a couple of glaring errors. A Summerbee follow-through, kicking him in the head and the hand, which later needed five stitches, didn't help his cause either. Albion were beaten 2-1 by Manchester City.

Being on the receiving end was commonplace. The 1968 FA Cup winning route was far longer and more painful than *Quizball's* Route 1 (the most difficult questions, but a quicker way of scoring). The hapless custodian was regularly in the wars, bravely accepting batterings from opponents to preserve his goal. His FA Cup debut came at Southampton in a fourth round replay, and by way of welcome, he was knocked out after just ten minutes in a collision. The Southampton player Frank Saul caught him full on the chin. With only one substitute available from the bench in those days, for the rest of the first half, trainer Stuart Williams stood behind the goal, giving the dazed and blurred keeper a commentary *"ball's on the left, Channon's moving forward, close your left hand post…"* Ossie kept going until half-time on instinct, pure and simple; that, and the sheer determination and bravery under stress that renders ordinary people quite immune to pain. Albion remarkably won 3-2, with captain Graham Williams between the sticks for the second half. While his fellow players celebrated a triumph against the odds, the battered goalkeeper was en-route to hospital. Alan Ashman explained *"He didn't know where he was or what time it was, and getting him off to hospital seemed the sensible thing to do."*

AT PORTSMOUTH IN the next round, his head got in the way of Jennings' boot. In the quarter-final, he managed to get through three fixtures against Liverpool without damaging himself. But remaining unbattered and perfectly conscious for so long created new problems as Albion supporter Keith Cotter recalls: *"After the Anfield replay, there were four of us eating sandwiches as we waited in traffic on the East Lancs road. The Albion team coach pulled up alongside, John leaned out and asked if he could scrounge a sandwich, explaining they had left the ground straight after the game, and he was starving. Such were his powers of persuasion; everyone donated all their sandwiches, only to remember too late that they were hungry as well. We reminded him of this many times at the Smethwick end, and he always reckoned they were the best sandwiches he'd ever tasted."*

Birmingham City deserved to win the FA Cup semi-final, but Osborne's string of saves from Fred Pickering gave the Baggies a platform for their strikers to complete the job. In the second half, Ossie was kicked painfully, but recovered quickly to crucially tip another Pickering shot on to the post. *"I had a fair game that day, but I did have some good defenders around me, you know"* was the goalkeeper's modest post-match response. Jeff Astle had a different opinion: *"Finest game he ever played."* In typical Astle style, he couldn't resist adding, *"He didn't have many good ones, mind!"*

And so to Wembley for the first FA Cup final ever to be televised in colour. Ossie, who was so worked up beforehand that he repeatedly bounced and missed the ball in the dressing room, didn't have a great deal to do in this brutal stalemate. Almost inevitably, he received another whack for his bravery, this time across his fingers. *"Everything was OK"* he confided in a later interview with the club programme, *"until the Everton forwards came roaring in towards me. I kept goal for 107 minutes with one hand."* He also complained about the state of his left shoulder. Midway through the second half, Royle's header beat Osborne, but thankfully, John Kaye headed clear on the goal line. On such moments are cups won and lost. Perhaps in part because of his Aunt Sally characteristics, Ossie had no recollections afterwards of the big day. *"Thank heavens for video,"* he repeatedly said later. The photographers behind his goal were happy to remind him of his urgent and repeated questions about how much time remained as the Toffees chased the game.

FROM HIS COLLEAGUES' point of view, their last line of defence seemed to always have at least one injury. Ossie's regular pre-match routine was to bind two of his fingers together. Perhaps his wounds were a kind of self-protection, a boost to morale along the lines of 'I'm definitely doing my bit for the team, look at all the injuries I've got.' In fact John was a born worrier, often fretting about non-existent injuries. As he was preparing for one match, he went through the ritual. Taping up his arthritic finger – later, a plastic knuckle joint was inserted – strapping up a wrist, bandaging a bruised leg, moaning about an ache in his neck. *'Don't bother any more, Ossie,'* said Bobby Hope once. *'We'll call the ambulance now – and I'll go in goal!'*

One of Ossie's most famous and painful interventions came during an FA Cup quarter-final. The Baggies led 2-1, with Chelsea hunting an equaliser in the last minute. Bodies were being thrown forward and when a high ball landed in the six-yard box, somehow the keeper ended up apparently sitting on the ball, though he later claimed, *"99 per cent of the pace of the ball was absorbed by a much more sensitive part of my anatomy."* Chelsea's Boyle tried to kick both Ossie and ball into the net, and players from both sides piled in, turning the confined area into a passable imitation of the Eton Wall game. Hard men Doug Fraser and John Kaye traded punches with Osgood and his team-mates.

In John's own words: *"In came the rushing Chelsea players kicking and hacking away. John Boyle was one – he lunged in and caught me somewhere. Biff, bang, wallop, and all of a sudden players were pushing and shoving each other, arms and legs were flying all over the place. As for me, I was still sitting on that darn ball and no way was I going to let go. The referee blew for full-time, although according to most people, there were still a couple of minutes left to play. The only other thing I remember from that day was that I took the soprano lead in the sing-song on the coach on the way home."*

Fans' views on John's batterings were mixed. Some were indifferent; others were concerned about whether the team would be hindered. Chris Flanagan was in no doubt. *"Ossie's back-from-the-dead heroics after injury were his greatest legacy. So often you'd see John stumbling around in anguish after being trampled on by a couple of cloggers only to scramble the ball away with a floundering lunge. Even when Ossie was down, he was never out. When courage was all that he'd got left, then that was what you got. John Osborne was the business."*

Steve Gregory was mindful of his reaction to being hurt. *"John wouldn't get shirty or downright aggressive with the perpetrator of the kick, knock or blow. You would be more than likely to see him sitting in the mud, blowing his cheeks out and shaking his crushed fingers or rubbing the bruised part of his body. After receiving a dose of the magic sponge, he would dust himself down and get ready to receive whatever else was to come his way. No whingeing, moaning or play-acting. He was honest."*

Manager Johnny Giles needed to take a wider view. *"At the end of every pre-match talk, I made a point of asking Ossie how he was feeling. Nine times out of ten, he would reply: 'Lousy, terrible, tired, aching or fed up'. I knew then that things were going to be OK."* In between mickey-taking, the rest of the squad quickly learnt that to get the best out of John, they'd need to gee him up as best they could in the dressing room. The results could be startling. Occasionally, Ossie declared to all that *"the opposition won't score today"*. Once in that frame of mind, he was nearly impossible to beat.

Corners would have him jumping around in true 'ants in the pants' fashion, all the while clinging on to one or other of the posts.

'Hyperactive' wasn't the half of it. Then would come the cross, and with it, an instantaneous transformation. Up Ossie would soar above the muck and blood of the goalmouth, attacker and defender alike, slender body breaking every law of gravity in sight to do so, skinny arms thrust skywards above his rapidly-ascending form, and, more often than not, with perfect timing. No fumbles, no indecision; once Ossie had made up his mind that ball was going to be his, that was it. 'Command of his area' they call it now, and in his own fiefdom, Ossie was Field Marshal Montgomery reincarnated. Keepers were afforded relatively little protection in those days, but no matter how desperate (or illegal!) the scramble for the ball, there weren't all that many top-flight attackers around with sufficient brute strength to either bundle the lad out of it, or force him into making an error.

He might have looked outwardly frail, did Ossie, but appearances were deceptive. Having won the battle for aerial supremacy, you'd then see both upper limbs curl protectively around his newly-won prize, all the while clutching it to his chest in similar fashion to that of a baby monkey with its mother. Then those darting eyes, once more machine-gunning the opposition. During one fixture, Albion were endlessly under the cosh. Corner after corner went sailing over our goalmouth, and Ossie snuffed them all out, first time, every time. Before too long, it got to the point where you didn't need to be blessed with the gift of telepathy to realise the opposition were all mentally wondering just what they had to do to beat him. As one Black Country wag put it at the time: *"It's no good yow doin' that, mate – 'ee 'as them fer cowin' breakfuss!"*

And then there were John's goal-kicks – not so much a mundane duty to be performed, more a hallowed ritual. Once the ball had been placed on the correct spot, Ossie would then engage reverse gear. Slowly backing on to one or other of the posts, he'd first give the mud-encrusted studs of one boot an almighty clout on the upright, then the other. That done to his satisfaction, he'd then spit into his gloved hands, rub both together – as neither ever came into contact with the ball at those times, this could only be his eccentricity shining forth – then the run-up, after which boot would swiftly be applied to leather, said ball sent speedily on its way upstream.

ALBION SUPPORTERS HAVE traditionally desired a rapport between themselves and the club goalkeeper. When the club's first ever custodian represents England, a feat followed by at least four more, despite the ever present bias against Midlands footballers, there's a certain standard to be maintained.

John Osborne took supporter interaction to a height never seen before or since. He set the gold standard that creates expectations to this day, a mark so high as to draw disbelief from recent Baggies keeper Russell Hoult. Russell simply refused to believe descriptions of Ossie's antics.

Turning to the crowd to ask about Villa's score, or to enquire how many minutes remained was quite low-key. Famously he'd regularly cadge fags ("No. 6" were most commonly offered) from Albion supporters, occasionally the opposition. Josie Garbett was regularly on hand to assist Albion's No.1 ease his nerves. *"I'd light up a Park Drive for him, and he'd generally managed to puff through half of it before he had to dash off back to the goal."* Photographers were a gentler bunch in those days, and there is only limited photographic evidence of John's smoking habit. He was snapped puffing away at Loftus Road in the mid-70s.

On other occasions, John would munch happily on Dairy Milk during the game. Other fans claim to have seen him lunching on a sandwich that he'd hidden in his cap, or even supping from a bottle of beer (widely available without restriction on the terraces until the end of the 60s). During a very one-sided game, Ossie perched himself on the wall behind the Smethwick End goal and talked to fans during the game.

Long-time Baggie follower Tim Joyner recalled: *"On two occasions I remember him asking the group I was standing with how the Villa were getting on. This as he took up position for the second half, and pulling a face if they were winning. It probably seems insignificant now, but in the eyes of youngsters in their early or pre-teens, for an Albion player to actually speak to you was a major event in itself."*

John didn't just charm his own supporters. In April 1970, the Baggies lost heavily, 7-0, at Old Trafford. The home following were trying to wind up the crestfallen keeper, but, game as ever, Ossie was happy to respond in like fashion. After making one save in the second half, he turned and chalked a mark on his post. The United fans loved the gesture, and chanted his name for the rest of the game. At the end of the match, he received as much applause as the home players.

Ossie impressed both sides of Manchester. During Albion's visit to Maine Road in the early 70s, a rather disturbing message was broadcast over the tannoy that the club had received a warning about a bomb in the ground. Albion's goalkeeper theatrically picked up the ball, placed it against his ear, and then shook it.

It's impossible to confirm the veracity of some alleged incidents. Such as for instance, the unlikely exchange recounted by Everton supporter Glenn King. An Evertonian at Goodison bellowed at Ossie, "*Hey Osborne, you've got a face like a pan of fried arseholes.*" To which the ever-jovial Osborne dropped his shorts as if to prove a similarity between his face and his posterior. This is the kind of anecdote that everyone would want to be true and would now be punishable by fine and suspension. Thankfully there were times when the sheer comedy of such moments was what mattered and this incident has become as much part of the Osborne folklore as those known to be true – another fine example of cult hero status, only applicable to the truly great characters.

AFTER THE REMARKABLE high of the 1968 FA Cup Final victory came a series of lows. A long-standing injury was made worse through badly damaging his middle finger during the FA Charity Shield game. Osborne was off the pitch early again as his side were battered 6-1 by Manchester City. Arthritis in a knuckle joint led to a plastic strip being inserted into one of his fingers. The only alternative, and a brutal one, was amputation. John now had another nickname – the *"bionic goalkeeper"*.

The Baggies' attempt to defend their cup came to an abrupt end in the last few minutes of the 1969 semi-final against Leicester City as a mis-hit shot left him clutching thin air. *"I think that was the goalkeeper's mistake"* carefully pronounced the TV commentator. "I *saw Clarkie's shot, much, much too late,*" confessed Ossie. *"The ball flew past me, and I knew we were out."* On such mistakes can careers be made or dashed. For someone so horribly aware of the responsibility for a full team of players, to make a fatal mistake in a semi-final presumably led to weeks of private self-recrimination. Yet in public, he maintained his affable persona. Nothing, as far as supporters could tell, seemed to depress him for long.

Managers have all the power over players that Roman emperors possessed over christians. Don Howe, appointed to the hot-seat in 1971, did not rate Ossie at all. Equally, nobody rated Don Howe, but he got to make the decisions until even the directors couldn't take any more. The Don Howe era simply wasn't the same club Ossie joined. Star men had either left, or were struggling with long-term injuries. Ossie wasn't enjoying participating any longer. "*When you get up in the morning thinking, 'Oh, I've got to go down to that bloody place again .. When you get to that stage, it's pointless carrying on.*"

A brief three-match spell on loan at Walsall was a sharp reminder of the hardships of the lower leagues. John bailed out, and in partnership with former green shirt rival Jimmy Cumbes, they ran a sports goods shop near Walsall. It seemed as if an era of fun, taciturn humour and no little achievement was over.

AND YET, OSSIE continued to turn out occasionally for the Baggies Midlands Intermediate side. After six months out of the game, he decided to have another go. He did so initially on a part-time basis.

During his semi-pro period, he was quoted as saying, regarding his terms of reference, "*Oh, I was being paid all right. In fact, for the time I was putting in, I was better paid then Pelé. I literally just turned up on Saturdays. I enjoyed it, though – by heck, I did. We won the Intermediate League and the Cup, and the Cup Final was one of the most fantastic matches I've ever known. We were level after extra time, and there was a right old barney about whether it should be decided on penalties. In the end, most people agreed, and we won it with the 20th penalty. It didn't matter to the other players, because they weren't old enough to drink. But I remember, by the time we'd finished, the blasted pubs were shut.*"

Howe would only pick Osborne for the first team games no one could be bothered with – such as the Anglo-Italian tournament. During one game in Italy, John literally had a rude awakening. Asleep in his sixth floor room, he was abruptly awoken by a knock on the door at 2am. The balcony door. "*Let me in,*" bellowed team-mate Asa Hartford. "*Quick! Don Howe's after me.*" For a serial disturber of other people's rest, the biter was being bit.

THE ARRIVAL OF Johnny Giles in the summer of 1975 gave the boy from Barlborough another go in the limelight at the unlikely age of 35. Osborne was grateful for the second chance. "*Johnny Giles was the best player I ever played with or against,*" wrote an unusually serious Ossie, reflecting on his career in the *Albion News* prior to his testimonial. "*I shall remember him for picking me up when I was almost ready to pack the game in, and giving me the opportunity to enjoy the two happiest seasons I've had in my career.*"

Those limelight moments almost didn't happen. Someone had whispered in the new manager's ear that Ossie *"could be a bit troublesome"*, an impression reinforced when the veteran goalkeeper didn't report at the agreed time for pre-season training. As Giles explained in his biography *A Football Man*, he offered Ossie the choice between sitting out the rest of his contract and training as normal. Osborne opted for the latter and a mutually respectful partnership was underway.

GILES INTRODUCED DISCIPLINED possession football to the Hawthorns, and, as if to boost Osborne's confidence, he sold fellow keeper Latchford. After an uncertain start on his return to first team action, the Baggies just stopped conceding goals. The veteran keeper played in every match of the 1976 season, setting a new club record for clean sheets.

Albion had to win their last match at Oldham to pip Bolton to promotion. The Baggies' blueprint was to work furiously, concede very few goals, score just enough and be consistent. This was the same blueprint subsequently used by Gary Megson and on both occasions, a faltering Wanderers side enabled them to sprint ahead at the finish line. Twelve thousand supporters marched on Boundary Park, outnumbering the home support. Tony 'Bomber' Brown poached a vital second half goal, and a late save from the resolute keeper had the Baggies heading for the top division after three seasons away. 'Bomber' Brown and John Osborne both became members of an elite group of Albion men who'd won both promotion and the FA Cup in the process.

AND IT WAS this time, even more than the preceding involvement in FA Cup triumph and regular top-flight competition, which sealed Ossie's place in Albion fans' hearts.

Tim Joyner again: *"in the eyes of my friends and I, starry-eyed 14 year-olds, the first impression of John Osborne was of how old he looked, he was tall and gangly and never gave the impression of being particularly quick-moving, or even match-fit which made him an unusual candidate for such a popular player, one who never seemed to fit the 1970s footballer caricature of being flash, brash and confident. I think it would be fair to say that in his mid-30s, Ossie actually could have passed for a 45-year-old."*

Ossie happily admitted that he was born old, and fashion had nothing to do with him. In addition, the lack of teeth and general scruffy demeanour created some kind of empathy with supporters. If this tatty-looking individual could play football in his middle age, maybe they could as well. Of course, few could equal Ossie's deftness in plucking awkward crosses from the air and fewer still were willing to hurl themselves bodily at a striker's boot to grab a football. He might have been an absolute bundle of nerves in the dressing room beforehand, but out there on the pitch, with the opposition chucking everything they could, legal or otherwise, in the direction of our goalmouth, and all the while gaining the upper hand, you'd see in Ossie an instantaneous transformation. Then, he was ice-cold calm itself, all pin-sharp reaction times, constantly swooping and diving for goalbound balls in similar fashion to that of the tiny feathered creatures he came to know and love, back in those familiar Derbyshire hills of his childhood.

Former fanzine editor Glynis Wright had her own thoughts: "*Think of Ossie now, and immediately, a mental image of Star Trek's Mr. Spock comes charging into my head. Why? One reason springs readily to mind; around the time John first assumed his Albion custodial duties, BBC1 were giving the first episodes of Gene Rodenberry's sci-fi masterpiece an early-evening airing – but that's not the whole story. The thing was, take away the pointy ears, the deadpan logic, and in Leonard Nimoy, you had a dead-ringer for our keeper. I'm not sure whether it was the lined, hollow cheeks, and toothless matchday grin that did it, or the pointy facial features, but the resemblance was distinctly uncanny, to say the least. Or was it his horribly gaunt and dishevelled appearance, I wonder? Certainly, the moment my mother first clapped eyes upon him, her immediate reaction was, "Bloody 'ell, that Ossie Wossie bloke, 'ee looks 'arf clammed to jeth – needs a cowin' good feed in 'is bally, 'ee does… An a decent suit ter wear." Always had a way with words, did my mum, bless her. Spot on, first time.*"

JOHN RETAINED HIS place for much of the first season in the top flight, despite his advancing years. Early on, league leaders Manchester United came to The Hawthorns. Giles put Albion ahead, but United were awarded a penalty and a chance to equalise. Ossie, who rarely saved penalties, was up against Irish international Gerry Daly, who was reputed never to have missed one. Daly placed his shot low to the keeper's left, but Ossie, remembering the thoughts of Lev Yashin, guessed correctly and saved. Albion went on to win 4-0.

THE BAGGIES WERE on the receiving end of the occasional hammering that term. Worst of these was a 7-0 mauling at Portman Road. In his later years, Ossie confessed that because he had yet another injury (a bruised shoulder) and was so fed up, he didn't even try to block the home side's final goal.

Towards the end of the season, Albion dropped only two points in nine games, prompting hopes of a UEFA Cup spot. They went to White Hart Lane with both Osborne, and understudy Bob Ward injured. Manager Giles gave a debut to a youngster called Tony Godden. Godden made an instant impact, conceding only five goals in six matches. Yet on 9 April for the visit of Arsenal, Giles dropped Godden, giving Ossie the green shirt instead.

It was said that Godden needed to be rested due to his inexperience, but it resulted in something rarely seen at the Shrine, as the Brummie Road End split into two factions, one favouring Godden, the other Osborne. *"Tony, Tony Godden"* bellowed one faction. *"John Osborne, John Osborne"* responded the other. There was some variation as *"Godden – Osborne", "Godden – Osborne"* echoed across the ground. And so it continued through the game until Ossie boobed, and the Gunners took the lead. *"Ossie is shit, Ossie is shit"* roared the Godden faction, and the atmosphere became quite hostile. Osborne looked rather bemused by this, but a few minutes later, he pulled off a flying save and a unanimous chorus of *"John Osborne, John Osborne"* echoed around the Hawthorns. John took a bow and the hostility melted away instantly. He'd won the crowd over again, as arguably only he could, and kept his place for the rest of the season, despite Arsenal winning 2-0.

Godden's elevation was inevitable. Talking to Dave Horridge of the *Daily Mirror*, John was philosophical. *"I have known for some time that Albion were looking for a good, reliable goalkeeper to do a job in the reserves. Now they have got one – ME!"* Ossie decided to retire at the age of 38.

His testimonial against a Johnny Giles Select XI raised £32,000, a record up to that time for a Midlands player. Over 12,000 Baggie people were keen to show their appreciation in what was the third biggest turn out for an Albion player testimonial since the war, behind only Norman Heath and Bobby Hope. Twelve thousand people plus a horse… Red Rum was paraded around the running track. The famous racehorse had a song in his honour. The Brummie Road End, in their own version of a popular chant of the time "Referee, referee, your old lady is a whore", offered: *"Red Rum, Red Rum, Your old lady is a horse, Your old lady is a horse."*

John was at his most adventurous that night. During one Albion attack, Ossie retrieved a toilet roll that had been thrown on to the pitch, placed it on the penalty spot and promptly "scored". At the end of the game, there was a mass pitch invasion. Hundreds of Albion supporters performed the *Dying Fly* (a feature of the cult TV programme *TISWAS*) in the Brummie Road penalty area. It was a fitting end to Ossie's Baggies career.

JOHN CONTINUED TO play football for anyone who would have him. He turned out for the Albion Old Stars and the *Birmingham Post and Mail* Rangers. Indeed, he was up for a game anywhere.

Albion supporter John Clegg recalls: *"He played for us once in the Warley Press team, after he'd retired, against the Warley Parks department (sorry, Sandwell Recreation and Amenities Division). We snuck him in because he was working for the Sandwell Mail, in the circulation department. He got through about ten tabs during the game, and blagged a Player's Number Six (plain, of course, brown packet) off me at half-time. It was men against boys. Those cheating council workers even had Dale Best from Watford in midfield. But we had Ossie, and we won 3-0."*

John then moved on to Worcestershire Country Cricket Club as their commercial manager. He stayed there for nine years and his popularity remained undimmed. A walk around the boundary would inevitably mean stopping every few yards for an autograph or a chat.

Ossie briefly managed a non-League outfit called Colinthians 83. *"My idea of management was to get 11 lads at the same ground at the same time. I was sub 18 times because we only had the 11 players. We entered the Midland Combination, but had to come out because we couldn't afford the fines. We got fined for everything. One time we kicked off with just four players and got fined £15 per player short. They were good times. Do you know that one year after I left 'em, they won the league?"* Delightfully chaotic, but it worked, and it was fun. Perhaps that's a fair epithet to describe John's footballing career.

Willie Johnston

1972-1979: 261 games, 28 goals

'HEART-WARMING PLEASURE' comes at a price, as Albion full-back Ray Wilson admitted: *"Willie was a great entertainer, but he wasn't easy to play behind. I'd try overlapping when Willie had the ball. I had 30, 40 yards to cover while he was beating a couple of players, and when I'd got level with him, I'd say, 'Willie... Now... Now... NOW!' But Willie was beating the opposition, and then sometimes he'd lose it, with me in front of him."* Team-mate Joe Mayo was also in the queue for Willie's attention. *"I'd be up front waiting for him to cross ... and waiting, and waiting. He didn't know himself what he was going to do most of the time, so what chance did the rest of us have?"* But Ray and Joe, and no doubt the rest of the side, were unable to vent frustration at length. How can any larger-than-life character or loveable rogue be resisted for long? Willie was life.

Willie's explanation was simple. *"People want entertainment. A man taking his wife and family to the match on Saturdays pay big money, they want to be entertained – it was so easy. The manager would say, 'get the ball over' and I thought I'd get it over when I'm good and ready. Besides, there were so many players in the team who would never, ever release the ball – Tony Brown, Len Cantello – if Tony Brown got the ball, he would shoot rather than pass it – and Len Cantello was the same. If I got the ball, I'd hang on to it, because I knew it would be ages before I would get it again."*

Another Albion stalwart, and fellow Scot Ally Robertson did his best to support his fellow countryman. *"People loved him because he was a one-off. You'll never see someone in the game like that now. Willie was a hero for me because he was a Glasgow Rangers supporter who played. I couldn't believe he was coming to West Brom. The first day he was in our dressing room, I was saying to him 'You're my hero', and he was just looking at me. And I was still so excited I even offered to polish his boots... It probably took me three months to realise he was Willie Johnston, one of our players. I'd put him on a pedestal up there somewhere."*

Fellow cult hero John Osborne's initial memories came from a different perspective. *"When we heard about the signing – it was big money for the Albion in those days – the first thing we thought of was his reputation. He'd been sent off more times than anybody else, and all that. I expected to see this huge raving lunatic at training. The following morning, there were just the normal faces. "I thought Willie Johnston was starting today?" "He is, he's right over there." And sitting right in the corner was this little lost lad."* Ossie had summed up the two sides of Willie – the public perception that he's loud and aggressive and the reality that the Scotsman is quiet and shy off the pitch.

Meanwhile on the terraces, supporter Steve Sant also had doubts. Big ones. *"I was dumbstruck with the Willie Johnston signing. He had the kind of reputation that Joey Barton or Craig Bellamy have today. He was trouble. He got sent off so many times that his accumulative bans saw him sitting out huge chunks of the Scottish season. Word was he was a clever player who would rather sit in the pub than train, and had a vicious temper that got him into trouble both on and off the pitch. That strict disciplinarian Don Howe had signed him made the whole thing a bit bizarre"*

The Scot came with a CV both impressive and alarming. Although born in Glasgow, Willie spent his childhood days in Fife (on the East coast of Scotland, next to Edinburgh). His father was a miner, and Willie did endure the pit for two months before offers of an easier working life came his way. His nearest club, Raith Rovers, wanted to sign him. So too did Manchester United, who took him and his dad to Old Trafford for a fortnight. But once the mighty Rangers indicated their interest, nothing else would do. Willie joined Rangers in February 1964.

Although the winger was something of a late starter, he was mightily quick in making up ground. Barely five months later, he had a

League Cup winners' medal to his name and this before he was legally old enough to drink. His status continued to rise, and by the following year, he was playing for his country against Poland.

"Bud", as he quickly became known after his purchase of a large overcoat similar to the one worn by veteran comedian Bud Flanagan on stage, was a big hit. He played initially as a central striker, including being paired with one Alex Ferguson (a partnership which spawned lifetime mutual respect, before moving later into a wider position). His goal scoring record was highly impressive, averaging almost a goal in every three of his 200 games. Topping the list of his many achievements was scoring two goals in the 1972 European Cup Winners Cup Final, when his side just held off Moscow Dynamo 3-2.

On the down side, Willie received his first dismissal in January 1969, with two more following within six months. His fourth early bath merited a three-week ban; his fifth six weeks: and then swinging a right hook at Alex Forsyth of Partick Thistle, in September 1972, earning him that infamous near ten-week final cooling off period immediately prior to his move to Albion.

THE HAWTHORNS WAS a culture shock for the winger. On his first day, Willie travelled down in the morning, and then trained in the afternoon. Don's first command was to insist upon 20 *"quick"* laps of the ground over hurdles with the rest of the players. *"Anyone who finishes behind Brian Whitehouse (the trainer) will have to come back tonight."* Willie had just completed another suspension, so *"I'd nae trained, so I wasnae fit."* Willie finished five laps behind Whitehouse, with several other first teamers also trailing in after the trainer. Protestations that this was his first day, and he'd only just arrived from Scotland, fell on deaf ears. Welcome to West Bromwich!

The transfer was a protracted one. *"Probably one of the longest transfer deals on record,"* claimed the *Albion News*. That Albion wanted the winger was clear: manager Don Howe travelled North four times to clinch the deal, although, according to the player himself, during none of those trips did Howe actually see him play. The fee agreed with Rangers was £135,000, a new club record.

Instinctively, Johnston didn't want to leave Rangers or Scotland. His reluctance to join a relegation struggle in a foreign country was understandable, but there were several very clear pointers that it was time to move. Any more sendings-off, and the Scottish Football Association would be likely to re-introduce hanging and flogging, just for him. In addition, Rangers' manager Jock Wallace had made it abundantly clear that he was no longer wanted at Ibrox. Willie had a long-standing grievance that the 'Gers were not paying him the same as other squad members. The Albion offer doubled his current salary, so with much reluctance, he signed for the English club on 1 December 1972. As he admitted in a recent interview *"at the end of the day, it's what you're in football for, isn't it: the money?' You can't eat medals."*

Rarely has one player's house evoked so many memories for so many people. The property, in Dunchurch Crescent, Sutton Coldfield, was always likely to stand apart from the rest, primarily because Willie bought it from the universally-detested Bobby Gould. One wonders quite what state the house was in when the Johnston family (wife Margaret, plus five year-old Stephanie, and three year-old Dean) moved in. Local supporter and scout Alan Sherwood recalls calling on Gould Towers during 'Bob A Job Week', a then-annual event when scouts would do menial jobs for anyone in exchange for a shilling (5p). Gould had the young scout washing his orange and black Ford Capri – which, Alan noted, was exactly the same colour scheme as the house. Gould departed to Bristol City within a couple of weeks of the Scot's arrival, so the Johnston family's Vauxhall Viva replaced Gould's Capri, although Margaret Johnston was to do all the driving.

Albion regular Andy Jenkins recalled how he and his dad would pass the time of day with Willie, whose major concern was that the local golf courses didn't match up to the ones he'd used in Scotland, Willie having played Troon, St Andrews, Gleneagles, and all the other top Scottish courses. The Johnston's neighbour was great uncle to another young West Bromwich enthusiast, Mark Hitcox. *"I remember going over there in 1973, ten-years-old, totally in awe of this man, who came out, knew my name, and then played 'shots-in' (with Willie as the goalie) with me and my oldest sister!"*

Willie made his debut at home to Liverpool. Sometimes, there's a collective decision made by Albion supporters that a player will be popular before he even takes the pitch, and Willie fell into that category. The Baggies were at the wrong end of the table, the "King" was out injured, and so the new winger was hailed as a messiah. His debut was a quiet one. A week later, his cross set up a late consolation goal for

Bomber in his second game at Highbury. And then... not much really. Supporter Steve Sant again *"I recall his first few games as being something of an anti-climax; he just played, and not all that well as a conventional winger. He had a few tricks, but they seldom came off, and he appeared a bit bored with the whole thing."*

STRUGGLING ALBION MANAGED only two wins in Johnston's first 16 League games. These were difficult moments for both club and homesick Scot. *"There were times,"* says Willie, *"when I felt like the man who had never tasted Tartan special."* The winger needed more involvement, more goals. He'd scored 60 for Rangers, and was used to roaming freely across the front line. At WBA, the wide man played 22 times without any goals at all, always wide and in a set pattern, as strictly prescribed by the manager. The one man who could really benefit from his crosses, the King – Jeff Astle – had cartilage problems, and couldn't play for three months. Even then, this wasn't the real King, and the newcomer had difficulty in building a relationship on or off the field, as the Scot explains: *"When I first arrived, Jeff Astle and I used to greet one another every morning before training – but for the first month or so, I never knew exactly what Jeff said – and he never knew what I had said either."*

But the real Willie surfaced occasionally. *"He was warming up on the pitch a few weeks after joining Albion from Rangers,"* recalled Brummie Road regular Tim Joyner, then 12-years-old. *"He noticed my friends and me watching, and kicked the ball high into the air towards the front of the terrace where we were standing. I can still see him laughing as we all ran for cover with expressions of terror on our faces."*

With only 38 goals to their name, and an endless litany of defeats, including the crucial last four matches, Albion finished bottom of Division One. Relegation came as a terrible blow for West Bromwich supporters. The Baggies had been in the top division since 1949, and success, admittedly more in cup competitions, was thought of as the norm.

Life started well in the Second Division, with wins in the first two games and then errr... another victory in the 13th game. West Bromwich were simply too inconsistent to truly threaten the leaders, finishing three wins behind promoted Luton Town. Albion's Scottish winger was, however, finally making his mark. Willie added to his total of dismissals by being sent off against Swindon in September. *"One defender persisted in trying to perform open surgery on my legs with his studs, and I eventually reacted by lifting my hands,"* wrote Willie in his first biography *Willie Johnston on the Wing*. Predictably, he was banned for three matches.

The season had few other highlights. Johnston's first Cup goal came against Exeter in October, glancing home John Wile's pass, but Albion lost in embarrassing fashion in the League Cup to their Fourth Division opposition. Two more months were to pass before Willie finally found the net in the league, one of only two that term. There was a double over Villa to celebrate, and a 1-0 victory, in a replay, over Everton in the FA Cup. Nearly all the healthy 27,000 crowd at the Hawthorns enjoyed the tense closing stages, even though both sides were down to ten men. Willie had been sent off again – for retaliation on Archie Styles, who also walked for the original foul. Supporters forgave him because he was, by then, firmly seated upon an untouchable pedestal, beyond criticism. Not so Don Howe.

WILLIE WAS FAST, reckless, a showman – and when he wanted to be, quite brilliant. In short, everything that Don Howe was not as a manager. With Jeff Astle forced to hang up his boots after just five more appearances, it was Willie upon whom the dreams of the Birmingham Road End rested, and they egged him on. The King is dead – Long Live the King!

Supporters like John Goddard loved his performances, and just wanted more. *"Willie loved to take on the opposing full-back. He was a real left-winger, fast over short distances, with a tremendous left foot to put pinpoint crosses into the box. He loved getting to the goal-line before putting in a cross, or trying to beat the full-back again with close possession and dribbling."* One of the winger's party pieces was trying to control the goalkeeper's drop kicks on the half-volley with his backside. It was always entertaining, but rarely successful, and guaranteed to irritate the hell out of Howe –not to mention Cloughie.

At least some of his team-mates tacitly encouraged Willie the Showman. Ally Robertson again: *"Being a West Brom player, we were always brought up to play football. For me, Willie was that type – he wanted to please the crowd. We would be getting beaten 7-0, and Willie would still be Willie. He'd be doing his tricks, anything to please the crowd. That's what fans wanted to see. Pity you couldn't have ten Willies in your side. You might not win a lot, and you'd have a few sent off, but…"*

As Willie said himself, *"We had a great dressing room, the lads were always daring one another to do things – I was the one who was always agreeing to do the dares!"* Such as the infamous mask. Prior to the last home match of the 1973/74 season, Willie accepted a £25 bet (equivalent then to two terrace season tickets) that he wouldn't wear a bank robber's mask during the referee's inspection and kick-about. During said inspection, he cunningly had a shirt over his head – and this being a 'nothing-on-it' end-of-season fixture against Luton, the bemasked Johnston dramatically lifted the mood on the terraces. Photographer Laurie Rampling was fortunately on hand to capture one of the iconic moments of recent Albion social history. The upbeat frame of mind also infected the players. Only Don Howe, not for the first time, didn't get it. He was furious with his record signing. *"This is the sort of standard we've got at this club…"* he bellowed, not for the first time totally misjudging where the hearts of supporters lay.

More money exchanged hands when the Scotsman accepted a bet to streak after training, along the old wooden Halfords Lane stand, and on to the pitch. Like many of Willie's tales, there's an alternative version. (For Willie, facts can be interchangeable as clothes). In this more lavish account, the players were inspired by the comic record 'The Streak' then at the top of the charts and sought one among their number to try it out – predictably Willie volunteered. The challenge was to run naked out of the dressing room, across Halfords Lane across the Halfords pub to the far side and then back again. With everything hanging loose, Willie had no problem completing the run only to find the players had locked the entrance into the dressing room. It took Willie 15 minutes to find another way in … and during this period, there was a photographer on hand to preserve one naked male body for eternity.

THESE WERE GRIM times to be a Baggie, the grimmest for several decades. Supporters generally disliked the dour Howe, with his emphasis on careful defence; they yearned instead for the Baggies' traditional game of attacking football and excitement. Willie was their only hope. *"Willie, Willie Johnston, Willie Johnston on the wing…"* was a song of praise, but also of hope. Even occasionally today, in dull times, the anthem is occasionally aired, and instantly recognised by all. There can be no greater measure of a hero's longevity at a football club than if people who were not even born when a player was in his pomp exalt his name as their saviour in times of woe.

The players had no more regard for Howe than the supporters did, but they were obliged to both listen and respond to him. The credibility of the former England international was damaged by some particularly offbeat training exercises, including the notorious episode of tying three senior midfielders together with a length of rope in order to boost co-ordination. Not surprisingly, maverick Johnston was one of his biggest critics. *"If games were won on a blackboard, Don Howe would have won the World Cup,"* he sniffs. Asking Fife's finest about Howe's man-management would guarantee a lurid reply.

The new 1974/75 season meandered along much like the previous one, with Albion rarely able to keep pace with the front-runners. Defeat at Villa Park in March was the final straw: apathy was setting in, with gates of only 10,000 or 11,000 commonplace. There were more goals for the winger this time, seven in all, sufficient to make him third top scorer behind Tony Brown (12), and Joe Mayo (8). And to no one's great surprise, there was another early bath, at home to Bristol City, in November. Willie maintained a robust defence. *"Before the match, you've got a 6ft Neanderthal telling you they're going to kill you on the pitch, and when you get on there, the first tackle is just below the knee, then in comes the second – just above the knee – it's very hard not to react."*

The winger was often 'quick to react', such as another red card in an away match at Ninian Park. But there was a curious tale behind this loss of temper. The side had travelled on Friday afternoon, and were encouraged to spend the evening in a local cinema. A new film, *Emmanuelle*, was showing, so naturally, the all-male party had to go in. Their fellow watchers within the auditorium seemed to have trouble finding something in their pockets. By coincidence, Willie's opponent the following day was called Emmanuel. A photographer got a picture of the incident (again!), and there was Emmanuel, down on all fours, with Willie standing over him, and it looked ever so sexual…

Albion's extrovert wide man was always up for enlivening proceedings. Supporter Peter Smith recalled a match at Craven Cottage. *"The ball went into a sparsely populated area of the terrace, but no one seemed willing to retrieve it, so Willie jumped over the fence himself. A few young kids ran over to him, so he dribbled the ball in and out of them for 20 seconds or so – they just couldn't get it off him. He then chipped the ball on to the pitch, and took the throw-in. The crowd went mad!"*

With gates now down to 8,000, the Albion board finally made a decision. They refused to extend the manager's contract, and suitably piqued, Howe resigned immediately, with four games remaining. His reign wasn't all bad. He introduced a modern physiotherapist, George Wright, who was quietly responsible for extending several players' careers. Howe also put together a squad not lacking in talent or discipline: furthermore, under his tutelage, Albion's youth set-up had blossomed. Indeed, in those four remaining games, caretaker manager Brian Whitehouse blooded an unknown youngster called Bryan Robson.

THE NEXT MANAGER, Johnny Giles, was to smoothly take the club back to where they felt they truly belonged. Giles had been there, done it, and was prepared to lead from the front. Despite his vast knowledge, Giles freely admitted in his biography *A Football Man* that he *"assumed Willie Johnston to be a lad who liked a drink and a bit of argy-bargy off the pitch. Turned out, he was a fitness fanatic who loved to train, was well-liked by the other players and a constructive influence in the dressing room. He liked a drink, too, it's just that he couldn't hold it. "*

Every player responded to the player-manager Irishman, and, after a shaky start, an 11-game unbeaten run provided the initial momentum for a real promotion challenge. Goalscoring remained a problem for Albion (Ally Brown top scored with a paltry ten), but, significantly, it was far more of a problem for the opposition, because Albion rarely permitted them to score.

Willie contributed six goals, including one at Blackpool that *Star Soccer* (ITV's response to *Match of the Day*) chose as Goal of the Season – it was the only goal of the match, a typical darting run before beating the goalkeeper from 25 yards. *"We worked with the ball nearly all the time,"* said Willie, many years later. *"Johnny was an intelligent manager, a majestic and graceful player, and a great guy. The man was a tonic."* Giles was also sent off at Luton for a hatchet job on Futcher, a former opponent, with whom he wanted to settle a score. You might say Willie and Johnny understood each other better after that, despite their different religions. Some elements of the press attempted to make capital upon the fact that one was an Irish Catholic and the other a Scottish Protestant, but neither man considered their differing faith a barrier. Willie was still Willie. His more famous antics that term included trapping the ball by sitting on it (a not unfamiliar move at Ibrox where it became known as *"Doing a Bud")*, and picking a fight with a linesman over a throw in.

Every Albion supporter has a favourite Willie story. Mark Pumphrey's tale occurred at home to Notts County, *"who were sporting a yellow kit with a green penguin stripe down the front and back. It was an autumnal midweek match, and my Dad and I sat in the old Halfords Lane stand – wooden benches, pipe smoke, I can see it as plain as day. Willie Johnston was giving Brian Stubbs the run around all game. We were right on the touchline, and able to hear his "frustration". Inevitably, Stubbs scythed Willie down, and I remember my Dad and I looking at each other and expecting Johnston to be sent off any second for retaliating. Instead, our premier Scottish entertainer jumped on to the back of his assailant, and Stubbs gave him a piggy-back up and down the touchline, with Willie pretending to whip him like a horse. I remember the crowd roaring them on, and my old man's face was a picture. He's in his 70s now, and may forget a few things... but he never forgets that moment."*

Years of poor gates had taken their toll on the Hawthorns coffers. The club were encouraging supporters to enter a sponsored walk in October 1975, so as to raise money for them, claiming they required 22,000 gates to break even. Until mid-November, they were marooned around the 10,000 mark, and although attendances picked up steadily after this point, Giles had to boost his ranks with either homegrown youngsters or old, cheap players, inevitably Irish. Nevertheless, cut-price Albion determinedly made the most of wobbling Wanderers, of the Bolton variety, who were struggling to maintain their promotion spot. West Bromwich reeled them in game by game, amid mounting tension. In the end, it came down to a genuine 'must-win' last game at Oldham.

In a tight, tense match, with visiting hordes making up the majority of the 22,000 crowd, a second-half Tony Brown goal was just enough. A predictable pitch invasion followed, with thousands of jubilant Baggies demanding their team should re-appear. Of course they did!

Yet more extraordinary scenes followed on the way home, with the team bus royally escorted all the way along the M6 by a phalanx of 120 supporters' coaches. An obviously tired and emotional Willie gave the royal wave to all and sundry, wearing the most devilish ear splitting grin as he did it. As his wise old team-mate, John Osborne, pronounced: *"Willie was the softest little bugger I've met – until he had four pints of lager inside him."*

BACK IN THE big time, Albion's favourite would have a far more realistic chance of playing for his country once more. He'd been ignored since November 1970, but top flight football, combined with his best form, and not being sent off since 1974, proved a powerful trio. Willie, being Willie, just had to press the self-destruct button in the League Cup. After a marvellous display against Liverpool, instrumental in defeating the Merseysiders 1-0 (some supporters swear to this day that he'd terrorised full-back Phil Neal so much that Neal was reduced to tears), the winger was spectacularly sent off against Brighton in the next round, because he aimed a kick at the referee's bottom. West Bromwich supporters didn't know whether to laugh or cry – so did both. Willie had varying explanations. *"He had me in such a rage with his cowardice..."*, "wouldn't protect the players" or the far more Willy-ish, *"He just wouldn't get out of the way..."* Johnston picked up a £100 fine and a five-match ban from the League, with a club punishment on top. His fourth dismissal with WBA set new club records, both numerically and for variety of competition.

Other than suspensions, Willie rarely missed games for any other reason. Remarkable, considering the treatment he regularly received from opponents he so often frustrated and teased. Even so, a break from the routine of training and playing was very welcome, which was why, come January, Albion would often treat the players to a few days in Torquay. They were encouraged to relax with the odd beer, but life was never straightforward with a certain Scottish winger around. He carried copious quantities of farting powder, and everybody's drinks were fair game. Senior players also learned to watch out for near-empty beer glasses that mysteriously filled themselves with a liquid that was warm to the touch. ...

One night, the players dressed up for an evening out. Willie, predictably different, wore a kilt. He told his colleagues to watch him carefully and soon enough, two bold girls asked, *"What's under your kilt?"*

"Why don't you have a look?" teased Willie.

So one of them did... only to find a large plastic extension to Willie's willy. The girls retired giggling, and soon there was a procession, all wishing to peer under his kilt. Pure Willie.

Many years later, I asked him, if he had his Albion time over again, would he have done things differently? Willie was quite clear. *"If I was playing today, I'd still have done the same things. Whether I would have got away with them is another matter! Being at the Albion was always more than just a job. My times there were the best years of my life. I was never interested in taking big cash offers from elsewhere, because West Brom were such a great club."*

The Baggies adapted surprisingly well to the pressures of the top league. Their goalscoring problem was eased considerably by the arrival of Ray Treacy, David Cross, and latterly, Laurie Cunningham. Although no one realised it at the time, the club had just signed Willie's replacement. Cunningham, in the absence of anyone else being fit, started his Albion career as a central striker, his six goals playing a significant part in Albion striving for – and only just missing out on – a UEFA Cup spot.

Willie only managed a single goal himself, but his all-round contribution was mighty. Having a target man (Cross) to aim at made a difference, and his consistency was such that he received a call to join his country against Sweden, in 1977, his first call-up for nearly seven years. Once back in the fold, Willie retained his place, playing in all the Home Internationals (a then popular round-robin tournament between the four home nations), and Scotland's summer tour of South America in preparation for the 1978 World Cup in Argentina.

These were exciting times for both Willie and his favourite English club. Johnny Giles had sadly departed wearied by the manager's lot, but led by Ronnie Allen, the Baggies carried on right from where they'd left off. Allen then introduced Cyrille Regis to the first team – and now, they were not afraid of anybody. Regis's power, allied to the trickery of Cunningham and Johnston, the emerging Bryan Robson, and the solid defence made for a powerful team. Albion lost only two of their first 12 matches.

Fan Lloyd Fletcher was among the hordes thrilled by the attacking splendours on offer. Cunningham and Johnston both featured against Manchester United in October 1977. Lloyd takes up the story: *"Cunningham hadn't had that great a game, but with the score at 3-0,*

Johnston and Mulligan overlapped in classic fashion on the right. Paddy Mulligan put in a fierce cross from the goal line, and Laurie Cunningham volleyed it in at the near post. I have several fond and vivid memories of this. Thrashing United 4-0 for the second season in a row was a thrill in itself, but I also remember Laurie being enveloped by his colleagues (physically) and the crowd (emotionally), both for putting the icing on that cake, and redeeming his performance in great style.

"And best of all, Willie celebrating near the side-line, standing still with arms aloft, was suddenly bear-hugged from behind by an old guy in a flat cap and trench coat! There was that moment of connection between the crowd, and two of our heroes; the fan on the pitch was like an emissary for those of us in the stands who just wanted to join in the jubilation of hugging those on the pitch. I think it was essential that this was an "ordinary" fan, not a youngster in baggy trousers and denim jacket- it seemed to make the moment even more poignant."

The Scot was now at his swaying, speedy best, buoyed by international recognition, having played in all the crucial qualifying matches as Scotland reached the finals of the 1978 World Cup. Willie had another new Albion record – the Baggies' most-capped Scottish player – and now he felt like he could take on the world, or even Middlesbrough defenders, as another Brummie Road Ender, John Goddard, recalls. *"I will never forget the time he terrorised a Middlesbrough full-back all match, beating him repeatedly. Willie reached the goal line at the Brummie Rd. End / Halfords Lane, and just stopped the ball. He put his foot on it, and gestured to the full-back with both hands to come and take it off him. It was typical Willie; he loved playing to the crowd. The full-back stood only a yard away, but refused to move, as he knew the winger would beat him again. Great theatre."*

For every winner in football, there's a loser. When Willie was on form, there was some poor sap on the receiving end, a full-back having a rotten afternoon and knowing they'd be no relief in the dressing room. In his autobiography, former Blues defender Mick Rathbone was blunt in his honesty. *"Willie Johnston was fast, aggressive, cocky and skilful. I was dreading marking him. I had been having nightmares all week. The team coach left St Andrew's for the short ride to the Hawthorns. I was close to being comatose with fear."* Very fortunately for the defender, a downpour led to a very late postponement.

WILLIE ENJOYED THE gallery but not the attention of journalists. He was distrustful, even before the dark days of 1978, so his responses were normally brief and to the point. He excelled himself during one "interview" with the universally disliked Gary Newbon (the reasons behind the dislike of Newbon are hard to define, he just *was*). In what Newbon admitted was his worst ever interviewing experience, he posed 37 open questions to Bud in a three minute live TV interview but the winger contrived to answer "yes" or "no" to each one. This was so extreme I suspect a dressing room dare.

WILLIE JOHNSTON WAS off the Newbon Christmas card list but making Newbon look foolish only increased his popularity. Thousands of Albion supporters were by now wearing tartan in homage to their favourite. Willie loved the attention, and played up to the crowd whenever he could, such as signing autographs in the Rainbow Stand paddock (the forerunner to the East Stand) during play or negotiating to buy a greenhouse while taking a corner.

There was a coterie of smokers in the first team squad that season. Other than Willie himself, Cyrille Regis, Ally Robertson, John Osborne, Derek Statham and Len Cantello all enjoyed the dreaded weed, but one day, chairman Bert Millichip made a decision to ban smoking on the coach. *"An' the boss said if the Chairman don't like it, we can't do it."*

The players wondered what they could do. They tried placing the smokers at the front, and leaving the door open. That didn't work because the bus was going too fast, so the smoke just blew back again. Eventually, a compromise was reached: the players could have a smoke in the dressing room prior to the match, and at half-time. The result, according to the winger, was a stream of players *"at quarter to three going intae the toilet for a quick drag. I even used to see players stubbin' 'em oot in the tunnel."*

DESPITE CARELESSLY LOSING another manager by not offering him a contract, Albion still managed to combine their UEFA Cup place chase with an FA Cup run. An away fourth round draw at Old Trafford against the cup holders was a big ask, and yet the Baggies so nearly won at the first time of asking. United couldn't cope with their visitors' lightning counter-attacking game. It was Willie who scored, although he was quick to admit afterwards, *"It was a bit of an accident. I went to nip it under Roche, but I hit it a bit too hard, and it rolled across the line. We'll murder them in the replay though – they were lucky today."* (United equalised in the last minute when the ball crossed the line via the back of goalkeeper Godden's head).

United weren't murdered in the re-match but the Baggies did triumph 3-2 after extra time in a remarkable encounter. Twice crosses from Willie set up Albion goals, and twice United retaliated, Regis scoring the crucial overtime goal. After overcoming Derby 3-2, including another goal from Willie, West Bromwich were in unchartered waters. They hadn't reached the last eight for nine years. To their horror, they pulled out domestic treble-chasers Nottingham Forest in the draw. Still, there was always Willie. He took to the field sporting a tartan bonnet. Tension, what tension? The Baggies won 2-0, with the winger showing his style by using his bottom once more to try to trap the ball. Not to mention a booking after an altercation with Archie Gemmill and a running verbal battle with Brian Clough.

After such triumphs, surely West Bromwich Albion were Wembley-bound? New manager Ron Atkinson thought so, allowing the BBC to film him lifting the FA Cup. Predictably peeved, semi-final opponents Ipswich girded their loins, and hit Albion like a tornado. Nothing went right that afternoon, as their Suffolk opponents just would not let them play. Worse, Willie received a bad shoulder injury that left him little more than a passenger. Albion, 2-1 down, were chasing the game when Mick Martin was sent off for two bookable offences. Town scored a third and the FA Cup was over for the Baggies.

So, too, was the season for Willie, hampered by his shoulder complaint. He sat out the last seven games with Laurie Cunningham ominously standing in for him on the wing. Four games were won, and two drawn, sufficient for sixth spot, and a place in Europe.

AND SO TO Argentina. Famously, after their first match in the tournament (lost 3-1 to Peru), Johnston, along with Kenny Dalglish, were selected for the random drugs test. To this day, Willie maintains that the Albion club doctor, Dr Rimmer, had given him two reactivan pills to treat a cold. Because he'd been given them before, he saw no need to declare their use, but reactivan includes a stimulant called fencamsamin; it was this stimulant that would make Willie headline news all around the world. The winger was sent home in disgrace. In that era, the concept of professional sportsmen taking stimulants, either knowingly or inadvertently was still a relatively new one. The Scottish FA banned him for life, while hostile tabloids made hay. Privately, his fellow professionals were hugely sympathetic; at least two of his team-mates admitting later that they'd also popped the same type of pills. Ally Robertson summed up the professionals' response *"reactivan wasn't a drug to us, it was just a cold cure, and was blown up out of all proportion"*

Willie was mentally shattered. Scorn and opprobrium poured on his head. *'Junkie'*, and much worse were hurled at him, both on the field and off it while his family were also considered fair game. It was all too much for the unsophisticated Willie. Albion tried their best by offering him a new four-year deal, which would give him security until he was 36, Albion supporters giving their best shot too, cheering his every move, even when he was on the bench. But it wasn't enough. Laurie Cunningham had his shirt, and Willie's heart just wasn't in it any more. By Christmas, the Scot had made only eight appearances.

He requested a transfer. It was turned down. Willie asked again and again. It was refused once more, but in the long term, there was little value in keeping an unsettled out-of-form reserve player. Willie made one last hurrah, coming off the bench to replace Regis in a 1-0 victory over Chelsea in March, his 261st and last appearance in an Albion shirt.

Although other English clubs had expressed an interest, it was the £100,000 offer from Vancouver Whitecaps that appealed, offering a fresh start in a different country. Playing in the North American Soccer League (NASL) did wonders for the winger, who responded favourably to admiration from supporters. With "World Cup Willie" (as he became known) featuring prominently, the Whitecaps went on to win the Soccerbowl (the NASL equivalent of the league and cup rolled into one).

In between NASL seasons, he was permitted a five-month loan spell back in the West Midlands, not at the Hawthorns (although he was asked) but at impoverished neighbours Birmingham City. Although nearly all their fixtures clashed with those of the Baggies, numerous Albion supporters took in the odd game at St Andrew's for nostalgic reasons, just to see Willie once more in full flight. Frank

Worthington was in the same side, so not surprisingly – he and Willie were an entertaining double act on and off the pitch.

Among the Black Country spectating contingent was former team-mate Joe Mayo. *"My mother loved Willie. I took her to see the Blues play once. Willie didn't do anything all night other than one nutmeg. After the game, we went into the players' lounge and my mother asked if I could introduce her to Willie. So I did, knowing that Willie's always polite in these situations, particularly to older people. The first thing my mother said was, "Well, that was a load of rubbish, Willie!" And Willie replied, "You're just like your son..."*

Another season in Canada and short spells at numerous clubs followed before retirement as a player in 1985. There then followed coaching jobs at Raith Rovers and Falkirk. Willie was now back home, with his *"ain folk"*, in the all-embracing, insular community of the Kingdom of Fife. In 1987, he took over the Port Brae pub on the Esplanade (sea front) at Kirkcaldy and there he stayed for over two decades, living above the shop. The 'Brae' was a traditional old boozer of modest appearance but it became a place of pilgrimage to Black Country folk. It's often been said, with varying degrees of seriousness, that you're not a proper Albion supporter unless you've visited the Brae. But no more. Willie handed over the reins to his son Dean in 2000 but in August 2010, Dean was held to be in breach of their agreement and the Belhaven brewery took possession of the pub and tried to sell it. Many months later, the premises remain unsold but worse Willie's memorabilia was locked inside with the brewery unwilling to release them.

THE WINGER RETURNED to West Bromwich in late 1997. He filled the Throstles Club on both Saturday and Sunday night. The evenings were full-on celebrations of the return (albeit briefly) of the great man, a whirl of noise, humour, and endless choruses of *"Willie Johnston on the wing."* The star guest was drinking spirits for Dutch courage (normally, he stuck to lager), and was rather mellow.

A decade later he returned once more, in the full gaze of the nation's press, with his second biography, *Sent Off at Gunpoint*. His first biography in 1983 was feeble, not capturing the Scotsman's spirit at all – even Willie himself described it as *"a load of sh**e"*. Willie, understandably after Argentina, had a problem with all journalists, and so asked one of his bar staff, Tam Bullimore, to be the author. Tam is a children's book illustrator who had never written a book in his life. He also had to contend with Willie regularly remembering anecdotes differently and having no interest in proofreading. It is to Tam's credit that his debut book contains so much of merit.

THE 2008 WILLIE Johnston was more laid back and confident than in his youth. He was nearly a pensioner and is a Grandad several times over. He was comfortable with a large enthusiastic crowd in the East Stand, including a few noisy Rangers followers who wanted to pay homage. He still has an aura and my little group were the last to leave his side that night.

Six years on from their original inclusion in cult heroes, the words of supporter Steve Sant remain unbeatable as an end piece: *"Willie was a decent player, but much more than that, he was a real bloke who lived a real life in the pubs and clubs of the area. He had weaknesses. He was too quick-tempered, and he drank too much, but in the mid-to-late 1970s, Willie was your average young bloke with a wad in his pocket. People identified with him. He was, perhaps, the last cult hero of that ilk. Everyone since has been more aloof, harder to engage with. Willie earned perhaps three times what the blokes watching him earned: by the time of Super Bob it was 10 times. The players just didn't and don't mix with fans any more. You won't find Odenwingie in the Handsworth Social Club downing mild and whisky chasers, and playing snooker. Willie was the last real star who led that sort of life. I loved him."*

Cyrille Regis

1977-1984: 302 games, 112 goals

THE REGIS FAMILY are very sporty. Younger brother Dave works in the Charlton academy after a long football career. Cousin John was a damn good Olympic athlete. Half-brother Otis Robert was a Grenadian football international, niece Yasmine Regis is an exciting international class triple jumper and, of course, nephew Jason Roberts MBE is a Premier League striker. Having been dumped by Chelsea, Uncle Cyrille got Jason back on the bandwagon with a trial at Hayes, to rekindle his football career, and since then, he is both agent and advisor.

To this day, Cyrille digs out the famous 5-3 win at Old Trafford for *"his nephew's benefit,"* as Jason explained wearily. *"He keeps stopping it, and saying: 'That's me!' He's great for me though, a really big influence."* He too has grown as a person, from the shy individual who joined the Albion from Bristol Rovers, just as his uncle developed his own personality. Jason, Cyrille, Otis and Dave are all trustees of the children's charity Jason Roberts Foundation, operating in both the UK and Grenada.

EVEN WITH A biased eye, Cyrille is the most acceptable face of modern football agents. He commands respect, knows his subject intimately, and oozes honesty, charisma and charm. His eloquence is highly pervasive. His paper credentials are impressive, with his MEBSM sports diploma; UEFA Grade A coaching licence and

FA Players' Agent Licence accreditation. In 2008, he had a MBE to add to the list for his services to football and the voluntary sector.

Cyrille remains a highly popular and regular visitor to both the Hawthorns and Supporters' Club functions. He is always surrounded by people of every age seeking his autograph, testimony to the compelling nature of his celebrity amongst Baggies fans. Even the late Vic Stirrup, an uber supporter not always easy to impress was voluble in his praise *"He was brilliant, the fans loved him at the time and they still do, he's brilliant to watch and an absolute gentleman."*

AS CYRILLE WILL himself tell you, respect has to be earned. His came the hard way. In 1963, young Cyrille was only five years-old when his parents brought him to London from French Guyana. The harshness of his younger days are captured with style in Cyrille's biography – *My Story* (August 2010 – co-writer Chris Green).

Football was unknown to young Regis then, an interest to be kindled initially at school. But once started, it was hard to stop in more ways than one. As his mother cheerfully observed: *"If it was in front of him, he'd kick it."* The enthusiastic late starter then progressed, through a series of minor clubs, to Hayes, in the Isthmian League. Cyrille was an apprentice electrician working on building sites all over London, thus he both worked and played in tough environments. Merely making training sessions on time was difficult and tiring, never mind fitting in the 60 home or away matches that comprised a single season for Hayes.

Despite his comparative youth, Cyrille competed so well that he quickly attracted interest from professional sides. Numbers vary from account to account. All were London-based, and one reputedly didn't make a move because *they "didn't sign black players."* It was the oft-recalled arrival of Ronnie Allen within Hayes' modest little stand at their Church Road ground near Heathrow airport that would change Cyrille's life. Albion's chief scout watched in astonishment as the young Regis went up for a ball at a corner, despite the attention of four Ilford defenders, then put both ball and all four defenders in the net. As the then chief scout explained, *"I went down on a cold, wintry night. In ten minutes, I was convinced."* This was one of 24 Regis goals that season, following 25 with his previous side Molesey.

Allen set to work to persuade the Baggies this youthful attacker was an essential buy. It wasn't easy. Famously, Allen threatened to buy Regis with his own money though Cyrille doubts the veracity of the story. Allen did get his way, finally, in May 1977; one of the last acts of the Giles regime. According to *My Story*, Willie Johnston almost scuppered the transfer by trying to get him to go to Manchester City instead in Willie's typical perverse way.

Hayes received £1,500 immediately, and later, a further £3,500, sufficient to pay for their floodlight bulbs. Cyrille didn't arrive at the Hawthorns until July 1977, by which time Ronnie Allen had become club manager.

In the short term, Cyrille didn't even consider rapid upward mobility. As he readily admitted, *"my only ambition at the start of the season was to work my way gradually into the Central League side."* Albion's training regime, sometimes twice daily in pre-season, was a shock to his system, both in its intensity and frequency. Endurance was never one of his strong points. He'd never been taught anything professionally, so relied on enthusiasm and raw power to get him through. In the short term, this offered something of an advantage, as professionals are routinely taught by their clubs how to respond to moves from their fellow professionals. But Cyrille had never been given an opportunity of reading the handbook, so defenders couldn't anticipate his intentions. A decade later, Lee Hughes was to enjoy the same short-term benefit.

CYRILLE STOOD 6ft tall, but somehow seemed bigger. His build was a major part of the overall picture, appearing almost as wide as he was tall, not unlike Darren Moore, incredibly strong and swift for such a big barrel-chested man. Team-mate Martyn Bennett, no midget himself, gaped, *"I remember the bloody size of him when he first arrived at the club. When he took his shirt off in the dressing room, he'd got muscles on muscles. Nobody would stand next to him in the shower."* Much to his consternation, Albion captain John Wile found that Cyrille could beat him comfortably in the air during training. Not just once, by luck, but repeatedly.

The new arrival was called up for Albion's third reserve match of the season against Sheffield Wednesday on 27 August 1977. Writing in the *Albion News*, Clive Leighton was impressed, *"He has good ball control for a big man, shields the ball remarkably well, and can turn defenders almost at will."* Cyrille scored after 22 minutes, running on to a through ball from Ally Brown, but the Baggies' second goal had far more significance. Cyrille neatly turned two markers before setting up his fellow striker. Only splendid saves from Wednesday keeper Peter Fox prevented more goals from the new boy, including tipping over a fierce drive after the striker had shaken off the attentions of no less than three Wednesday men. Other than making an early exit due to cramp, Cyrille had treated a professional side no differently than a London semi-pro outfit.

Four days after his reserve team debut, Cyrille turned out for the first team. With first choice David Cross injured, Ronnie Allen was happy to give his protégé a go against Rotherham in the League Cup.

He was fortunate to join a settled and assured side currently lacking only a regular goalscorer to move them up another level. Albion already possessed defensive solidity, exciting attacking players in Johnston and Cunningham, while a youthful Bryan Robson was key to a solid midfield also featuring Tony Brown and Len Cantello. Allen's suggestion that Cyrille should: *"just go out and enjoy yourself"* fell on nervous ears. *"I was scared,"* admitted the soon-to-be crowd favourite, who actually walked to the ground from his digs. *"The biggest gate I'd ever appeared in front of was about 500, and there must have been 20,000 there at the Hawthorns."* The real attendance was 14,000, but the newcomer's confusion was wholly understandable.

IMAGINE, IF YOU will, a youthful muscleman, oozing pace and enthusiasm, getting by on natural instinct. The Yorkshire club's defenders were completely bamboozled by the debutant, who clearly had no clue whatsoever about the professionals' way of doing things. It was love at first sight for the Albion faithful.

The Baggies, already two goals to the good, then won a penalty. With spot-kick expert 'Bomber' Brown injured, Willie Johnston somewhat reluctantly stepped up. *"Give it to Cyrille"* was the cry, a single voice at first from the terraces, but picked up immediately, a demand that quickly became universal. After signals between Cantello and the bench, the crowd (for once) had their way. Cyrille stepped up and gently despatched his first ever (and last) penalty. He was regaled with choruses of *"Nice one, Cyrille"*, duly responding to requests for *"another one"* by scoring again before the end. The debutant and four of his team-mates walked across the road to the Hawthorns Hotel to drink themselves silly in the company of supporters until the early hours in finest cult hero traditions.

FIRST CHOICE DAVID Cross was fit again for the next fixture against Middlesbrough, but Allen stuck with the youngster. He knew momentum when he saw it. *"He wasn't fit to play, but he created such an instant success, I didn't dare leave him out because the crowd will have my head."* Supporter Lloyd Fletcher was among the 19,000 crowd. *"There was already great expectation and excitement in his potential raw talent, you sensed a burning power waiting to be activated – and then he turned it on, beat three defenders (or five, depending on the version of the legend!) from the halfway line. The rejoicing, like the incident above, was just that notch higher, as you thrilled in something extraordinary, so exciting, that it was impossible to express it in any articulate form at all (howling, arms to the rafters). There began Regis's journey down the hero road."*

The now-adoring crowd rose as one to their new striker's first league goal. The shot was scuffed past Platt in the Boro goal: perhaps it's not surprising that the debutant couldn't get a clean shot in, as he had the rather large Stuart Boam hanging on to his back at the time. Chants of *"Astle is back, Astle is back..."* said much about the impact of both young Cyrille and Baggies supporters' collective need for a new focal point. Actually – erm – not quite the whole crowd, as former fanzine editor Glynis Wright remembered... *"In those days, I had a seat in the Rainbow Stand, the one opposite the players' tunnel. Sitting behind me was a chap whom I already knew had taken a very dim view of coloured players turning out in the sacred stripes – racist to the core and rumoured to be something to do with the National Front. Which wouldn't have mattered, really, that's the way he was, and you couldn't change bitter prejudices built up over the course of 60 years or so. And he rarely tried to impose his particular brand of poison upon others. But, that day, when Cyrille scored that wonderful goal, one of the best I've ever seen any Baggies player put away for the club, Astle included, the entire stand erupted with sheer joy. They, at least, knew raw talent bordering upon genius when they saw it. Chummy? As both sets of combatants returned to the centre-circle once more, and I was about to sit down, something made me turn around – that's when I caught a brief glimpse of him. Scowling fit to turn the entire contents of a milk-float sour, he was – and, more tellingly, amongst a stand containing thousands of people, not all of them Baggies by any means, some Boro, too, he was the only one still remaining in his seat. How sad."*

He was not alone. The new recruit was aware of the disquiet from a minority of Albion people. *"I think they were rebelling against me 'cause I'd taken a white guy's place."*

For the sensible majority, it was one of those out-of-this-world moments when anyone can justify being a supporter; *"That's why I support my team."* Sadly no recording exists of this extraordinary goal. It was, after all, Middlesbrough. Who wanted to watch them? As Ronnie Allen boldly claimed: *"It was worth the entrance fee alone, a goal ten times better than any I scored."* Cyrille himself modestly responded that he didn't think it was anything special, claiming to have scored better goals in non-league football.

IN THEORY, CYRILLE didn't fit Albion's possession style, drilled into them by the recently departed Johnny Giles. But the new boy simply didn't know how to hold the ball up, so Allen cutely decided that the team would be set up around Regis. As if to support his decision, Cyrille scored again the following week, at St James' Park, in an impressive 3-0 demolition.

In all, he scored ten league goals that season, playing a significant part in helping the club qualify for Europe via a high league placing for the first time in their history. A dramatic chested-down and volleyed strike against Everton in April 1978 is still regarded by a number of supporters as Cyrille's best ever. The man himself prefers his effort at Maine Road: *"I scored one against Manchester City where I was even further out than for 'Boro. I took the ball from ten yards inside my own half, took it all the way, and blasted it past Joe Corrigan. But the game wasn't televised, so nobody can see it now!"*

There was an FA Cup run too, under, technically, Cyrille's third manager. Ron Atkinson had replaced Ronnie Allen, who'd upped sticks abruptly to Saudi Arabia. Here again, the big man's goals were crucial. Two strikes and Manchester United were knocked out in a mud-bespattered replay. Two more at Derby and another rocket past Peter Shilton in the mighty Forest goal in the quarter-final propelled the Baggies to semi-final destiny against Ipswich. And a painful, painful exit, as Cyrille recalls: *"We just froze. After 15 minutes, we were losing 2-0: you looked around, we hadn't played our strongest side, Laurie was substitute, John Wile was injured. It was chaos."* Ipswich eventually won 3-1.

But there was a special price for those goals that, virtually, only Cyrille had to pay. Wolves' supporters were the most noticeable, but there were many others such as Newcastle and West Ham. In their book *Samba in the Smethwick End*, Dave Bowler and Jas Bains described the *Apocalypse Now* scene. *"At the back of the Smethwick End are corrugated iron sheets. Throughout the game, the Wolves supporters drum on these in a jungle rhythm, and thousands of voices chant, 'Nigger, nigger, lick my boots...'"*

These were the opening bars of a disturbing symphony. Racist comments abounded from the opposition. In public, Cyrille's response was to try harder, to put a little more oomph into his shooting, to quieten the bigots by defeating their side. He didn't have to endure this alone, for team-mate Laurie Cunningham had already been there, and endured much. Only those who've truly suffered can genuinely appreciate the negative impact of such treatment. Privately, away from the need to offer the 'correct' response, what psychological effect did this insidious campaign really have upon him? I imagine we'll never know.

Shamefully, there were even racists within the club staff, as Ronnie Allen admitted, *"Tony Brown had a sprained ankle, that's why I took him off at Bury (League Cup), to bring Cyrille Regis on. There was a big row on the coach on the way back from that match. One of the staff – not a player – said, 'How dare you put Cyrille Regis on for Tony Brown – we don't have black players.' Cyrille was just around the corner, and he came round in such a temper – it took four of us to stop him. It's hard to rouse Cyrille, but when he's mad, he's really mad. He shouldn't have said it, and he wouldn't apologise."*

Off the field, he already had to combat his painful shyness and missing all the people he knew from London. For a time, he lived in digs near Oldbury and was a regular visitor to the Blue Ball pub, known locally as 'Alice's Palace'. The formidable Alice ran this traditional old boozer. Remarkably, despite her normal antipathy towards all people she considered not to be British (i.e. white), she took a shine to Cyrille, even maintaining a stock of Mars bars behind the bar just for his consumption. His shyness would persist. As late as 1982, the striker attended a Supporters Club function in Halesowen, but felt completely unable to say anything to the assembled few dozen faithful. A surprised, but diplomatic branch chairman hastily came to his rescue. Decades later, Cyrille is an accomplished after dinner speaker.

Gradually over the years, Regis found ways to overcome his somewhat reticent nature. The premature demise of a friend had a dramatic impact, as Cyrille himself explains: *"I became a Christian after the death of Laurie Cunningham in a road accident in 1989. We were good friends, very close. We'd had a few beers in Madrid one day… we had a crash. The car rolled over two or three times, but we managed to get out. Two years later, it was the same circumstances, but Laurie's dead. His life was like mine, he had everything as far as material wealth, and when he died, it made me realise that wealth isn't everything, and I needed answers."* His new faith had a profound impact on the striker. His whole persona changed, and for a time, he resembled an American evangelical speaker, his presence a little overwhelming. Perhaps fortunately, his psychological metamorphosis continued further.

ALBION COULD HAVE lost Regis almost as quickly as they found him. St. Etienne were dangling £750,000 in the summer of 1978. He could have taken the 800 per cent pay increase and broken away from the abuse, but he saw a football club on a roll, and decided to stay. In addition, France still had conscription and there was a real danger that if he moved, Cyrille might end up in the Army. This was the first of several temptations put in front of "Big C", some official approaches, others definitely not.

Cyrille started the 1978/79 season as the leader of the attack, yet it was all too easily forgotten that he'd played barely 30 league games at the age of 20. He was a year younger than Bryan Robson, and two years behind Laurie Cunningham: indeed Albion's No. 9 was the youngest member of that delightful side. Alistair Brown was a clever foil for the youngster, scoring 18 times, but the weight of expectation was always with Cyrille. He was our leader, our figurehead, and our inspiration. The big goalscoring centre-forward thing is always a factor with Baggie people.

Laurie Cunningham was hugely respected, but the thought constantly persisted that he came across as somewhat aloof, and a bit of a 'loner'. Not true for those who really knew him, but that was an opportunity denied to nearly all supporters. The feeling was commonplace that Cyrille could do anything, that his solid frame was unstoppable: the only thing perceived to be holding him back was Cyrille himself. Even his great chum, Cunningham, used to call him "Pussyfoot".

It was always 'Cyrille', never 'Regis'. The media freely used both names and certain other artificial nicknames, too, but for the supporters; 'Cyrille' was identification enough and remains so to this day. That season, nearly all the senior players had their own chant. It was a pre-match ritual to go through the card. *"Laurie, Laurie Cunningham"*. *"One Bryan Robson"*, *"Wile, Wile, Wile"* and so on, but the most familiar refrain *was "Cee-rul, Cee-rul"* or the slightly-less-often: *"We'll drink a drink a drink to Cyrille the King, the King..."*

The trouble with great teams like the 1978/79 side is that they're not appreciated fully until their demise. At the time, supporters simply took high quality for granted, and asked for more. With three wins and two draws in the first five games, the pace was set. Drawing 1-1 with the then mighty Liverpool was a disappointment, and so too was a single goal defeat by Spurs. Supporters wanted more. A remarkable 19-match unbeaten run followed, including back-to-back wins at Highbury, and Old Trafford; *"The 5-3"*, as awestruck contemporary Baggies supporters refer to it. Every subsequent generation has seen and admired the recording of the 5-3, including commentator Gerald Sinstadt's adulatory shriek of *"Oh, what a goal!"* as Cyrille buried the Baggies' final strike, courtesy of his chum Laurie Cunningham, who was at his very best on that brass-monkey December afternoon.

Cyrille wasn't a terribly regular scorer – but he didn't need to be. Most of the 16 first-teamers (and of those, three only managed five games between them) knew where the net was, so the big striker was just as invaluable creating holes for others to run into.

On New Year's Day, the Baggies beat Bristol City 3-1 on a distinctly icebound Hawthorns pitch. A week later, a draw at Norwich was sufficient to give them top spot. Having got to the top of the mountain, they then proceeded to slide, very gently at first, down again. A big freeze concertinaed their fixtures, and painful defeats by main rivals Liverpool, and then Leeds, knocked them back. Even losing only one of their next 16 league matches wasn't quite sufficient to keep them in contention with The Reds. A weary WBA team often scored once, and were then obliged to hang on to their advantage like grim death. Still, a 1-0 defeat of Everton in April seemed significant insofar as at least this ensured second spot. The Scousers' top striker was regaled throughout with chants of *"Bobby Latchford, Cyrille wants your England shirt."* But even that consolation was removed by a goal from Nottingham Forest's

Trevor Francis in the 81st minute of the last game. Albion finished third, not second. The frustration was intense.

Cyrille was then badly injured in a pre-season friendly against China, and without him, plus the now-departed Cunningham and Cantello; the following season was mightily frustrating. By the time he returned in November, the priority was pulling away from the bottom end of the division. As a measure of their paucity of attacking ideas, Albion had no less than ten goalless league draws, and 19 draws in all, in 42 league games. Twelve more followed in 1980-81, with half of those without goals. Albion qualified for Europe, but it seemed such small beer, compared to Aston Villa winning the Championship.

ALBION MANAGER RON Atkinson's oft-repeated comment: *"To see the best of Cyrille, it's necessary to give him a sharp kick up the backside..."* was accepted as common wisdom. The manager would thump his charge in the stomach, or rub Vicks (an over-the-counter embrocation) all over him, anything to give the striker *"motivation."* On another occasion, the forward was summoned into Atkinson's office to be told, *"I want more aggression and more goals from you."*

It's undoubtedly true that Big C often looked languid, lacked sufficient belligerence, even, but a more productive approach for such a shrinking violet may have been an arm around the shoulder. As Coventry manager John Sillett so pertinently commented much later: *"He couldn't stand a rollicking that well."*

Cyrille claimed, *"I don't get angry. I don't need to."* Everybody loses it sometimes, Albion's No. 9 included. He was sent off against Aston Villa in May 1982, after an incident with Ken McNaught. *"Just a niggling thing,"* Cyrille explained. Some niggle, with the defender receiving a retaliatory punch. There's something primeval buried inside most Albion supporters, quietly whispering: *"Punched a Villa player? Good for him!"* But more sensible counsel prevails. Not only did his dismissal play a part in giving the Birmingham side a late winner, his subsequent suspension damaged Albion's chances of staying up. Regis tried to excuse his actions: *"I can take all the kickings, and all the elbows. I always have. But when someone does you off the ball, that's beyond the mark."* Big C didn't have a distinguished record against the neighbours. As he said himself, the following season: *"I have never scored against Aston Villa"*, adding: *"Derby games against Villa are always more like a war."*

His first goal against the Brummies from B6 finally came on the opening day of the 1983/84 season, in a 4-3 spectacular, sadly at Albion's expense. In the return game, the claret and blue side had their noses in front with only six minutes left. Dramatically, Garry Thompson scored twice in three minutes, and while the alleged fish-lovers were still reeling, big Cyrille took the ball off Des Bremner on the halfway line, and ran half the length of the pitch to defeat Nigel Spink. The only pity was that the goal blitz came so late; it was hard to take in, let alone savour reminding the visitors of the score.

Cyrille scored more goals under the returned Ronnie Allen in the1981/82 season than in any of the Atkinson years, and this despite a random rotation of five different partners that term. Allen had the advantage of being the man who gave Cyrille his chance but, more importantly, being a great forward himself, he had a better understanding of the job requirements. He listened. He encouraged. As Ronnie put it: "*I was disappointed he hasn't got any better during my absence. He needs help and understanding, and then you'll see something really special.*" More prosaically, he told Cyrille not to defend. Said the striker:"*Ronnie said I was an explosive player. He wanted me to do all my work in one half of the pitch.*" Mutual respect was the key, for few of Cyrille's team-mates enjoyed the same rapport, or even understanding, with Ronnie Allen.

Ah yes, respect. As much as goals, skills and endeavour matter on the football field, it's often positive human contact that elevates a footballer to new levels of respect and admiration. 'Crumbs from the rich man's table' syndrome creates a dining out experience for many, but sometimes, there's more to be had. Take, for example, the experience of long-time Baggie Steve Sant: "*I walked back from a training session at the Albion School in Halfords Lane with a very muddied Cyrille and Laurie Cunningham. They asked me if I shouldn't be at school. That brassed me off no end, as I was 19, actually on strike at the time, and told them so. They joked around, throwing snowballs at the other players. Len Cantello responded by chucking a bucket of icy water over them (and me!) They disappeared into the changing rooms in the Halfords Lane stand, and that was that.*

I went into the Woodman pub, more to dry out and get warm than anything else, and ten minutes later Cyrille came in, wearing just a shirt and jeans. He asked the barmaid if somebody was about, the answer was negative and he made to walk out when he spotted me. He then banged some change down on the counter, then nodded at me, saying to the barmaid:

'His next one's on me'. He smiled a huge smile, and disappeared. I sat up, and saw a sports car speed off toward Handsworth. I didn't get the chance to say anything, but in magical days of my life that's up there, top ten no question!"

Long-time supporter Keith Cotter witnessed another 'Cyrille meets the public' incident, albeit one with a less positive outcome. *"Half a dozen building workers entered the West Bromwich Conservative Club, and spotted Len Cantello and Cyrille were playing snooker. The workmen loudly questioned the footballers' fitness, claiming that their proper job made them fitter and stronger. They were persistent, refusing to be ignored.*

"Finally Len grew weary of the taunts, and set a challenge to one of the workers, asking him to do one press-up, and then jump and touch a mark he set on the wall, repeating the exercise with an extra press-up each time. The local tittered, saying he could do press-ups all night. Unfortunately for him, Len was astute. The jump in between the press-ups is a killer, and he only managed six before collapsing breathlessly, completing 21 in total. Len did 55 without breathing hard. Cyrille's competitor was asked to lift one of the heavy easy chairs upright by one leg. He couldn't get it off the ground. Cyrille simply grasped the leg of the chair and raised it to waist height before replacing it. Len and Cyrille returned to their snooker, as their red-faced challengers exited stage right."

RONNIE ALLEN'S ALBION was in transition that term, using 28 players. After England international Bryan Robson had been lured away by medals, fame and fortune at Old Trafford, the Baggies needed at least a month to recover. Another third of the regular midfield, Remi Moses, went with him. The previous season's top scorer, Peter Barnes, had already departed. Mills, Deehan, Owen, Batson, Cowdrill and Godden all indicated they would rather like to follow them out. The ship was not a terribly happy one.

Albion relied heavily on the attacking impetus of two men – the overlapping talents of Derek Statham, and the goals and acceleration of Cyrille. Initially, his form varied from hat-tricks against Swansea (his power with the gas pedal the catalyst for all three), and Blues (City manager Jim Smith: *"The lad is incredible. When he wants to play, he can be terrifying")* to rather lethargic showings. In November, everything clicked for Cyrille, and his 13 goals in the next eleven games made him the First Division's top goalscorer. He'd never previously been this consistent, nor would he be so again. *"I've never scored so well for so long in one season."* The manager readily offered his explanation. *"The problem was to find ways to use Cyrille's power. All the good players I've ever known have gone to meet the ball, always attacked the ball. Cyrille would come so far, and then stop, so that he was getting clobbered by the centre-back and losing control."*

Regis particularly got up West Ham's nose, scoring in all three of Albion's League Cup matches against the Londoners, ignoring abuse from the supporters he'd identified as being the most racist. As reporter Ray Matts wrote: *"As an exercise in perception, pace and powerful running it was sheer perfection."*

Two goals from the striker saw off Wolverhampton Wanderers, though his marker, Joe Gallagher, remained unimpressed. *"Cyrille Regis for England? Don't make me laugh. Cyrille is a very good pal of mine, and we have a drink together, but I have never rated him as a centre-forward."* With friends like these…

Fortunately, Gallagher wasn't picking the national side. Ron Greenwood chose him for the bench against Northern Ireland, and so it came to be that with 20 minutes left, Cyrille Regis became a full England international. He didn't find the net but enjoyed the experience. *"The crowd singing "Nice One, Cyrille" gave me a little more confidence."* Bit-part roles followed against Wales and Iceland, as Big C nurtured hopes of joining the World Cup squad for Spain that year, but a thigh muscle injury then made the question academic.

SIX GOALS FROM Cyrille made the difference in a hard fought League Cup campaign. However, the two legged semi-final tie against Spurs, who were to finish fourth in the league that season, was always a big ask. The Londoners' defence paid special attention to Albion's only real goalscorer (the next highest scorer that season, midfielder Steve Mackenzie, managed just five), and they pinched the tie 1-0 on aggregate.

A trio of lower division clubs were uncomfortably overcome in the FA Cup, including Norwich in the fifth round. The Canaries' defence could only look helpless as Cyrille famously controlled the ball, steamed forward and beat the goalkeeper with an archetypal shot. *Match of the Day's* Alan Parry's memorable commentary ran thus: *"Regis takes it well on the chest, and that's a lovely piece of control by Regis, and – OH WHAT A SHOT, OH WHAT A GOAL OF THE SEASON! CYRILLE REGIS!"* The quarter-final draw was kind, with perennially-wet Coventry rolling up at the Hawthorns for a comfortable 2-0 defeat, with goals by Owen and Cyrille again, who hit the ball with such force that the goalkeeper, only a yard distant as it entered the net, could only watch.

After losing against Spurs, everyone connected with Albion was frantic to win the FA Cup semi-final to get to Wembley. Second Division QPR were their opponents, which didn't sound daunting, however the Baggies' form was wretched, with only one win in the previous nine league games. Rangers knew exactly what to do. Man-mark Regis with big Bob Hazell, make sure that full-back Statham couldn't get forward, and then just wait for a chance. The plan worked perfectly. QPR won 1-0, leaving the Black Country's finest bereft. As the Rangers defender explained, *"I was told to follow him everywhere. I just knew he wouldn't score, man, I just knew it. I had so much adrenalin pumping inside me."*

Morale wrecked, the league slump continued, with even Coventry managing to beat the Baggies. Albion lost seven in a row. During the last of these, a solitary supporter staged a sit-down protest on the centre-circle at half-time. His efforts were warmly appreciated.

Perhaps buoyed by his second international appearance (ten minutes against Wales), Cyrille's first goal in almost two months, and his late assist for Monaghan, helped immensely in defeating Wolves 2-1. It was a horribly tense affair. Surely sufficient to relegate Wanderers, and keep Albion up? But three more defeats followed, and in the end, the Baggies had to win two of their three remaining games to stay up. In another sweat-filled encounter, goals from Regis *"the most important one I've scored all season"* and Owen were enough to beat Notts County 2-1, leaving WBA to beat either Leeds or Stoke to send one of them down in their place. The Leeds game will be forever remembered for the actions of the United supporters pulling down the Smethwick End fencing, thereby incurring the wrath of the police. In an evil atmosphere, the Baggies were the better of two nervous sides. Big Cyrille came to the rescue again with a goal in a 2-0 win. The Baggies were safe, which is more than could be said of both the ground and its Black Country occupants after the game.

HAVING COME SO close to relegation, Ronnie Allen stood aside as manager. A replacement was urgently required to get WBA back to the right end of the table. With home matches often drawing only eleven or twelve thousand, somebody with bags of both presence and charisma was needed to bring back the crowds.

Ron Wylie was a mighty curious choice being a former Villa man, possessing no Albion link, and no great pedigree for the position either. With four preferred candidates having declined the job, there was an element of desperation, of having to get anybody as manager. Cyrille scored his first goal at the Victoria Ground, Stoke, in a 3-0 win, in only The Baggies' fourth game of the season (an incredibly fortuitous result, for which, ever since, West Brom have had to pay with endless defeats in the Potteries). The Baggies were briefly second in the league table, but this was not to last. Form came and went, but patience for poor results was in short supply. Two 6-1 defeats in the space of a month didn't help the mood either. As did being 3-0 up at home to Swansea, where the *"defence were out of their wits with worry every time Cyrille Regis charged at them"*, only to concede three in 16 minutes. In an attempt to steady the ship, Wylie opted for three central defenders, thereby grinding out a series of goalless draws – but now he was being accused of boring football. Dissatisfaction continued, with gates at only half the number required to meet the club's 23,000 break-even target as poor football conspired with the recession, and the ever-present fear of hooliganism, to keep supporters away.

There were some highlights. Beating Ipswich at Portman Road 4-3, after being 3-2 behind, with three minutes to play, was remarkable in itself. Even more unusual was the fact that all the goalscorers – Regis, Thompson, Perry and Zondervan – had all previously endured abuse in their careers because of the colour of their skin. And beating Villa 3-1 in a snowstorm is always worth savouring.

To be fair, Wylie's team suffered a horrendous run of injuries just at the time he was under orders to cut the wage bill. His downfall, though, was his loyalty: his No. 2, Mike Kelly, was deeply unpopular. With the league position deteriorating, patience ran out at home to Nottingham Forest. When the manager can hear supporters of his own club urging the opposition to score more, it's time to go. Within a week he had done precisely that, resigning in protest after the directors asked searching questions about the future of Mike Kelly.

Johnny Giles was brought back – and the excitement was tangible, almost. As Cyrille said himself, *"There's a real buzz about the place, and a new challenge for all the players. I never had the chance to work with Mr Giles because he left so soon, but I can't wait to work with him now."*

But he had to wait because yet another injury put him out for five weeks. His presence was missed. Giles had a rocky start, including losing a FA Cup fifth round match to Third Division Plymouth. Thankfully, the arrival of two new midfielders, Hunt and Grealish, produced three superb results on the bounce – a 1-0 win at Spurs (Cyrille's header won the day against the club he supported as a boy), a 3-0 slaughter of Stoke City (a purists' treat, including one sequence of 38 passes) and, best of all, beating Manchester United 2-0, Atkinson, Robson and all. Cyrille notched the clinching second goal. After that, a series of hard luck stories and missed opportunities meant the Baggies weren't safe until the last but one game. These were uncomfortable times all round.

Regis found the net in a 4-0 defeat of Luton in September 1984, with what turned out to be his final Albion goal. The following month, Cyrille signed for Coventry for £300,000, with the Baggies basically taking the first offer that came along. Perhaps the absence of an agent to advise caution was significant. After all, local media had implied interest from a series of big name clubs over the previous six months. But Coventry, the only local-ish club that Albion supporters cannot take too seriously? Regis freely admitted to being off his game and furthermore thought that the manager didn't rate him alongside Thompson. Giles, in effect, agreed, saying, *"I did not feel Cyrille and Thompson complemented each other."*

At the time the big striker's departure was not greatly mourned. Loss of form over an extended period, including endless missed chances, regular injuries (playing only 26 and 30 league games in the previous two seasons), and the presence of the even bigger and never-shirked-a-challenge Garry Thompson, who scored a hat-trick against Forest just a week later, all provided reasons to look the other way. His cult-hero light bulb had dimmed slowly, albeit perceptibly, over two exasperating years.

BUT CYRILLE ALWAYS maintained a semi-presence at the Hawthorns and in Baggies fans' hearts while he was away.

For a long time, the Highfield Road move looked a hasty, ill-thought-out one. City manager Gould was sacked within two months, thus maintaining the pattern that whenever an Albion icon moved in, Gould moved out (quite literally, in the case of Willie Johnston).

City struggled badly for two years, until a fortunate coming-together of John Sillett and George Curtis gradually created a marvellous dressing room. Cyrille had a new role. He held the ball, and his team-mates played off him. As he explained later, *"It made me a better person to go through those tough times."* The Sky Blues then had an unlikely FA Cup run, beating one fancied opponent after another. Coventry did battle with then-Second Division Leeds United in a semi-final at the same time WBA played a league game at St Andrews. Respect now restored, *"Cyrille's going to Wembley"* was chant of the day in Small Heath. Coventry duly overcame Leeds, and went on to beat Spurs in the Cup Final. Many Albion supporters had eyes only for Cyrille, and were so pleased that a member of the excellent 78/79 side had won a medal – something, anything! This feeling extended to all of the team, with some fans even willing to accept Wolves lifting the Freight Rover trophy, purely because of the benefits it bestowed on Ally Robertson.

Cyrille's form not only won him an FA Cup winners medal, but, some five years after winning a previous one against West Germany, he also managed to earn another England cap by making a cameo appearance in England's 8-0 shoot of Turkey in October 1987.

Some two years later, when City manager Sillett left in 1990, his replacement Terry Butcher gave Cyrille a free. Ron Atkinson, now running Aston Villa, was quick to recruit him as his first signing, even though the former Albion man was 32. Cyrille was heading home, but in easy stages. *"I know Cyrille has found God. Now I want him to find the devil,"* said Ron Atkinson. It was a typical Atkinson one-liner, showing his knowledge of how to make friends in the press, but perhaps not really understanding those people whose careers were in his hands.

Two years later, the striker wasn't quite ready to return to his favourite football ground, so made do by signing for Wolverhampton instead. During his time with Villa, Albion were enduring a dismal time in the lower divisions, so their paths did not cross. Not so with Wolves, who found themselves quickly up against a revitalised Albion team back in the old Second Division, and quite desperate to get one over the old-gold gang. The clubs literally clashed at the Hawthorns. With the home side 3-2 up and all fingernails gone, the visitors made a substitution. Baggies man Stew Jeens remembered the moment. *"When*

Cyrille stepped out to replace an injured Bully in the 3-2 game, the ovation he received from both sets of supporters that day is still a cherished memory. If he'd scored an equaliser, I can't imagine what my reaction would have been."
It was a big dilemma, fortunately not one to be faced.

After Wolves, Cyrille played for Wycombe Wanderers and then Chester City before being forced into hanging up his boots after 740 appearances, suffering from calcification of his leg muscles. After trying for managerial posts elsewhere, Cyrille was welcomed back to the Hawthorns in a coaching capacity in February 1997. In his autobiography *My Story*, Cyrille wrote: *"Albion have always been my club, Football-wise they were my first love. I had a special relationship with the Albion fans too, and always will have."*

But Cyrille discovered that he didn't have a love for coaching. After four managers used his skills on the margins of the club rather than the first team, he resigned to embark on a new career.

BUT BEFORE THEN, there was one final appearance in an Albion shirt. In August 1999, a 41-year-old Cyrille made a four-minute cameo appearance in the Bass Charity Vase. A scratch Albion side beat Gresley Rovers to finally win the ancient trophy after twelve years of trying. To the 100 or so spectators present, the moment of a cult hero entering the field one final time felt special.

Don Goodman

1987-1991: 181 games, 63 goals

ODSAL WAS A harsh reality check of how the once proud had fallen. A Friday evening in December 1986 saw an attendance of 4,500 in a huge, but uncovered and rutted rugby ground. Welcome to the Second Division, Albion! The only shelter for visitors were in the toilets and the only 'food' in a hot-dog van. Stair-rod rain descended all evening. Modest and cheap though the Albion side appeared that night, they were far too fluent for City. The Baggies won 3-1.

City played at the vast desolate stadium at the other end of Bradford due to the Valley Parade fire. Most of their players from that horrific day were still with the club and each endured searing memories, none more so than their young forward Don Goodman. His ex-girlfriend had been among the victims. As he explained many years later: *"It's not something I like to dwell on... but you can imagine. Every time there's a disaster around the world, whether it's an earthquake, crash or whatever, it all brings it all back to you."* He wasn't alone. City favourite Stuart McCall dashed to hospital to see his badly burned father while skipper Peter Jackson broke a window in the players' lounge to get his family clear.

Despite their defeat by the Albion, Ron Saunders was impressed by two of the younger City players. He immediately approached Bradford to buy Martin Singleton, who duly made his Albion debut the following week. And there was another he fancied, who wasn't immediately available – 20-year-old Don Goodman, a striker who boasted oodles of pace, but only a 1 in 4 strike rate. Three months later, the deal was done.

Don explained to me how the transfer had come about: *"I was training on transfer deadline day on 26th March 1987, thinking, 'That's me stuck here to the end of the season,' when all of a sudden these cameras from BBC Nationwide turned up. They seemed to be zooming in on me. I thought 'great'. Somebody said it must be a big club, but then I heard it was to do with Elland Road racial taunts.*

"So I went back after training and a couple of players had heard whispers about plastic. Somebody with a plastic pitch is in for you, they said. City had got Ron Futcher from Oldham, who wanted to swap him for me. Bradford wanted Futcher plus £10,000 and Oldham didn't have the money. Then I got a call, so I thought, 'There's no harm in having a chat with Oldham.' I went into the office and the manager asked if I still wanted to go and I said, 'Yes.' He said, 'Well, it's West Brom.' Funnily enough, as a young lad, I'd supported West Brom. Heroes such as Cyrille for no reason other than I liked the way they played when Atkinson was in charge the first time. It was mainly my Dad. He's a big West Brom fan. He follows attractive football."

His official version for the press and Albion supporters struck a different tone, though it's to his credit that he didn't overplay his tenuous Albion links.

"I was out training at 11 o'clock on the Thursday morning. By 4 o'clock, I'd signed the transfer forms after a car dash down the M6." Don added, hopefully, for the benefit of his new employers: *"I needed to get away and I couldn't have landed at a better set-up. It's like a different planet here. The club are geared to First Division football, they belong there and I want to help them to promotion."*

Don's £50,000 recruitment was just part of a busy day for the Baggies. They'd sold two forwards that day – Garth Crooks and Stewart Evans – and bought in Steve Lynex and Don, at a small profit, naturally. Deals could only be done that way because those were the orders Saunders operated under. It's undeniable that the former Villa manager took on this role with enthusiasm, mercilessly rooting out all the big earners/ names at the club since he'd taken over Albion's sinking top Division ship. Having spent limited time in his company, it was easy to argue that he simply disliked all big name players. But as the talent went out of the door, the positive results went with them.

Goodman arrived at a severely depressed club, with sagging gates and, after only one win in twelve matches, one nervously eying relegation places only three points distant. The previous Saturday had seen a 1-0 defeat by Blackburn Rovers, with the 8,500 supporters bellowing "*Saunders out*" and "*what a load of rubbish.*"

DONALD RALPH GOODMAN was to become the main reason to stick with the Albion in these desperate times. He was born in Leeds in May 1966. At an early age, football was his passion. He joined a boys' team. One of his team-mates Peter Swan (yes, that one) revealed in his biography Swanny "*Don was quick but he wasn't the best player in the world. In fact, even if we only had ten players, we'd make him sub.*" Master Goodman was a better paper boy, according to Peter Swan's Dad who ran the local newsagents. "*He was the quickest of the lot. He was given the first bag and went flying out of the shop on his round. He'd sometimes be back before Swan senior had finished packing the fourth bag.*"

Young Don needed some extra assistance: "*When I was a youngster, I was quite a puny kid and my Dad decided I needed building up quite a bit. He was a champion weightlifter on his island over in the West Indies before coming to this country, so he knew what he was doing. He kitted me out with a set of weights up in the bedroom and put me through a series of weight-training exercises that did the trick. Without that little bit of extra strength and power, I doubt whether I would have ever got into the pro game in the first place.*"

His chance came after a recommendation by Ken Parkin, manager of his Leeds-based junior club Collingham FC. City were impressed and agreed a flexible arrangement whereby Don signed non-contract terms for them in July 1983, but continued his apprenticeship as an electrician. Don passed both part 1 and part 2 of his City and Guilds qualifications, but then put any idea of becoming a sparks to one side by signing professional forms on his 18th birthday. His debut came against Newport County. He later went on to score five times as part of the powerful City side that won the Third Division Championship in 1985. His biggest impact on a single game to date was a seven-minute FA Cup hat-trick against Tow Law Town.

Goodman went straight into the Albion side to face rampant Oldham Athletic at Boundary Park. His contribution is best described as "low-key", though he did set up one opportunity for striking partner

Bobby Williamson. The visitors led for most of the game, but two Athletic goals in the last three minutes flattened them.

The reality of West Brom's situation sunk in a week later for Don when barely 6,000 turned out for Sunderland at the Hawthorns. When the Mackems took a two-goal lead, *"Saunders out"* again did the rounds. Every mistake by an Albion player was booed, and, possibly affected by the situation Goodman could never quite reach the passes directed at him. Unexpectedly, Albion recovered to draw 2-2.

Results improved slightly – they simply had to. Don notched his first goal at Selhurst Park on 18 April, sufficient to earn the Black Country outfit a vital point. A slick four-man move led to Hopkins crossing to Goodman who mercifully was completely unmarked and gleefully thumped in his debut goal. There was nearly a second goal as Don made use of his best asset – his pace – to steam past three Palace men. Keeper George Wood was equal to his shot. Unfortunately for Don, the *Sports Argus* waxed lyrical about Albion's new goal scorer – *John* Goodman!

Albion ground out a couple of functional 1-0 wins to ensure their safety. Thus there was nothing riding on the last day of the season when Goodman lined up against his old side Bradford City at the Hawthorns – and on his 21st birthday too. The birthday boy scored when he finished off Anderson's cross with a comfortable header. The Baggies went 2-0 up while City proceeded to have two players sent off. Don was embarrassed, *"sending someone off a quarter of an hour before the end of the season? There's no need for it, I told the ref. One of them – Evans – just caught me, no big deal. The funny thing is that Evans' father and father-in-law are a couple of my biggest fans. His own father was saying after the game 'deserved to go for that.'"* With the aid of a dubious late penalty and an overhead kick, the nine-men Yorkshiremen scrambled a draw. The outcome somehow summed up the frustrations of the gritted teeth season.

RON SAUNDERS CONTINUED his remoulding of the squad in the close season. England B cap Steve Mackenzie left for Charlton and full international Derek Statham followed him out shortly afterwards to Southampton. Saunders signed Tony *"the Belly"* Kelly from Stoke for £60,000, so there was no need for alarm. *"He's a tremendous player,"* insisted Ron. *"Some West Brom supporters always seem to have something to moan about. They are only interested in knocking us."* Presumably the few remaining loyal contributors to the club coffers were cheered by those kind words. *"Kelly is twenty light years ahead of McKenzie,"* insisted the manager, clearly by now inhabiting his own planet.

By the end of August, Albion sat on the bottom of Division Two, also hurting from a two-legged defeat in the League Cup by Walsall. These were simply desperate times. Supporters made a big effort to have Saunders sacked at Elland Road including some who discreetly entered the home end to cheer on Leeds. The board finally agreed and Saunders was out of a job. Goodman was generous in his praise of the outgoing gaffer at the time. *"I liked him. I owe him a lot; he brought me here. He taught me a few tricks. I'm 21 and I've got a lot to learn. He liked the odd joke, and he was a joker, it's just that occasionally we didn't know whether he was joking or not."*

Much to everyone's relief, Ron Atkinson was chosen as the new manager. The Hawthorns badly needed a lift and Ron, on his second coming, talked a great job. One of Mr Bojangles' numerous early proclamations was, *"I have a feeling that Don Goodman has a lot going for him."*

Don scored in his first game for the new incumbent, a route one effort in a vital 2-1 win over Shrewsbury. Subsequently he played second fiddle to new signing Andy Gray. Goodman looked more enthusiastic under Atkinson, but his co-ordination remained a problem. Put simply, he fell over at key moments. Were it ever thus. City supporters described their former striker as *"spending more time on his arse than his feet."* Don, as ever, was candid in response to my obvious question. *"Yeah, It's weird. I think I've got flat feet, but I do think I'm getting over it now. You couldn't have believed it at one time."*

Prince, as he was sometimes known due to his resemblance to the pop star of the same name, next found the net in Portugal. Atkinson had used his contacts to set up a relaxing break on the Algarve, with a token match against a Portuguese Second Division side. The relaxing break turned out to be anything but as Goodman played a bit part in Tony Kelly punching a local fireman through a plate glass window. Both players were fined two weeks' wages and *"twenty light years"* Kelly was transfer-listed.

Prince Goodman featured only rarely as a goalscorer during these times – certainly not enough to bring him any kind of hero status. He'd certainly contributed to the team, setting up Andy Gray for his debut goal at Plymouth and winning a penalty at Middlesbrough. Don was a genuinely nice guy with a ready grin, but seven goals in 34 starts plus six more from the bench wasn't what Albion needed. A hat-trick in a testimonial match in February against Spurs raised everyone's hopes, producing a supportive quote from Andy Gray.

"Don gets into good positions, but he has missed a few chances this season and to knock three past Tottenham will have done his confidence no harm at all." Sadly, this was a false dawn.

Every match report included variants of '*Goodman glaring misses*' or '*had Goodman's finishing matched his tenacity…*' "*I'm not a natural goalscorer,*" admitted Don. "*I like to think I cause a lot of problems and take a lot of weight off other people – maybe I wear their defence out a bit. Mind, it got to the point against Bournemouth where I'm through for the third time and I thought 'Bloody hell, here I am again.'*" Don wasn't alone in his thoughts and with top scorer Andy Gray only managing ten, the Baggies had to work desperately hard to retain their Second Division status, which they eventually did with only one game to spare.

FORTUNATELY HELP WAS on the way in the shape of one-to-one tuition with new coach Stuart Pearson. "*Stuart transformed my game – he made me unrecognisable to the player I was. He had tremendous knowledge of how strikers should play. I learned, for example, to be more relaxed in front of goal, not to panic or snatch at chances and also to be a bit greedier than I was. Ninety nine per cent of the credit for my game goes to Stuart.* "

Naturally such an improvement needed time. Fortunately careful (and cheap) teambuilding by Atkinson gave the Baggies new confidence. Centre-half Chris Whyte's arrival gave the defence a new solidity and a new striker, South African John Paskin, made an early positive impact. Carlton Palmer's influence was increasing and so too was that of midfield anchor Brian Talbot. Results were much improved.

"*Donno*" was finding the net once more, though being sent off at Home Park, Plymouth didn't help his cause. He retaliated after Plymouth keeper Cherry barged into him. The referee missed the incident, but the linesman didn't and so the striker walked. Team-mate Brian Talbot was not impressed, "*I didn't see exactly what happened myself, but listening to Don, it seems he did retaliate with his elbow. There can be no excuse, and speaking as chairman of the PFA as well as a player, this type of incident, which has been creeping more and more into the game, does concern me."*

Unwisely, in the very next game, Goodman again reacted angrily to a challenge from Ipswich's Forrest. Fortunately, the referee let the incident go. Had the official reached a different conclusion to make a pair of dismissals, Goodman's career path may have been different.

Ron Atkinson's career path was definitely different – he was lured away to Spain. Brian Talbot was given temporary charge and under him the Baggies blossomed, winning five straight league games. This was manna from heaven for success-starved supporters who told the board very loudly and repeatedly *"Talbot is our man"*. The board were obliged to agree. Because of his suspension, the Leeds-born man only appeared in the fifth of those wins, an exciting come-from-behind triumph over Oxford. The feel good factor was everywhere, except possibly from Albion's underscoring striker. The new manager expected more effort and more goals from him.

Suddenly he got them.

At the end of November, Albion lined up against Palace in their most exciting league position for years. In a terrific 5-3 spectacular, Don hit his first league hat-trick. The *Argus* described his final goal thus: *"Palmer released Anderson down the left. The winger measured his centre to perfection enabling Goodman to complete his hat-trick with a downward header at the far post."* He also found time and space to set up Hopkins for the killer fifth, a tap-in, which the ex-Blues man seemingly did his best to miss… and failed.

Brian Talbot was a relieved man – though cautious, *"He knows that one performance doesn't suddenly make him a good player. I will be expecting many more goals from him this season."* Talbot had a limited amount of money to spend to improve the team and if Goodman could find the net more regularly, the money could be better invested elsewhere.

"I wouldn't call myself a natural goalscorer like Tommy Tynan at Plymouth," bizarrely confessed the hat-trick man. *"Or even my own hero, Mark Hughes at Man United. I like to get involved in all aspects of the game and to make opportunities for other players. In the Palace game I had three chances and put them all away. Before that, I could have six in a match and miss the lot."* He added, in best football speak *"hopefully, this is the turning point."* It was.

Albion defeated Hull City 2-0 in their next home game. Goodman scored both, one of them set up by his manager. Eight days on, the Baggies slaughtered Stoke City 6-0 in one of the most comprehensive stuffings anyone might wish for. This was personal as Talbot felt that Stoke's manager had pushed him out unfairly. The whole side responded to the gaffer's frenzied urgings and Don added two more to his personal tally.

Prince had seven goals to his name in just three home matches – previously that would have been equivalent to a whole season's worth. He was elevated from his 'just another forward' status, his name was repeatedly chanted "*Donno, Donno*". Goodman was now the main man, a source of hope and inspiration in these difficult times. He knew where the net was – at last. He was Albion supporters much needed response to the up-the-road running sore that was Steve Bull –well en route to 37 goals and a second straight promotion. Wolves' fans never missed an opportunity to remind their neighbours just how cheaply Albion had sold the Tipton born striker to them. Now there could be a retort, genuine ammunition to hurl back. With his Charlie George-esque long hair, Don looked the part, a freewheeling, quick turning, imaginative, youthful and good-looking striker. Then regular attendee Ian Thomas remembered Don. "*He gave us hope. In a team of old men and plodders, he was young, dynamic and fast. Don deserves recognition for single handledly trying to re-introduce moustaches to the football scene.*" Goodman had far more hair than most – at times enough for three men. His 'tache was broad and lavish.

RON SAUNDERS, ROUNDLY blamed for selling Bull so cheaply, was quick to chip in. "*People thought I'd made a mistake, but I always reckoned he would go up in value. All that is happening now is that his potential is coming to fruition. With Don, it's very much a matter of confidence.*" The reborn striker went to to find the net against Oldham and Shrewsbury as Albion overtook Chelsea to go top of the division in the New Year.

HIS MENTOR STUART Pearson also pitched into the Goodman vocal love-in. "*He is a good learner and listener, and prepared to work hard at his game to get still better. What impresses me is his close control and the effectiveness of the runs he now makes. He has always been as quick as any striker in the league, but now he puts that to better use. He has got self-belief now and bags of confidence. The world is his oyster."* In yet another of those curious links that always seem to tie one Albion cult hero with another, Clare Astle, youngest daughter of the King called her new rabbit Goodman.

BUT SUCH ELEVATED status brings with it plenty of attention of all kinds – much of it of the unwanted variety. In an act both ruthless and cynical, FA Cup opponents Everton singled out Goodman and Colin Anderson as the Baggies main men. Anderson was taken out in the first match with a quite appalling lunge. Goodman followed in the replay. As the *Argus* had it: *"A team who underlined their fear of Goodman by dragging him down whenever he threatened them."* Everton eventually secured their fourth round place 1-0 in extra time, despite all the backing that 5,000 travelling supporters could offer. *"It's all very well having a mean defence,"* said Martin Lewis, one of the travelling throng *"but without Donno, it was only going to be a matter of time before they scored."* Gary Robson agreed. *"Losing Don was the worst thing that could have happened to us. I'm convinced we would have beaten Everton if Don had stayed on the pitch."* It was a victory for brute force over footballing skill.

THE BAGGIES' SEASON was wrecked. Their squad, already painfully thin on numbers, couldn't cope without their key men. Goodman was out for a month and invaluable wide man "Diego" Anderson never fully recovered. The one-time league leaders went seven games without a victory.

As Goodman himself pondered: *"I wonder how many goals I might have scored but for that injury? That completely threw me. I was never the same again – never 100 per cent when I returned."* Goodman's brace sparked a 2-1 win over Leeds in March (the first one volleyed in after 21 seconds). Following that win, his team collected a further 11 points out of the next 15. The play-off dream was back on. But those were the last goals from the club's top striker.

BRIAN TALBOT HAD one more chance to turn the season around. Club bad boys Hopkins and Palmer were sent off at Bradford City. Both had previously caused the club embarrassment off the field and so Talbot acted – transferring them. The sale of Palmer to Sheffield Wednesday for £850,000 funded the purchase of new forwards Colin West and Gary Bannister plus Ian Banks, Paul Raven and Ronnie Robinson. West scored reasonably frequently and "Raves" stayed for ten years. However the perception remained that Talbot had not bought well and the side were poorer for it.

The arrival of target man West changed Albion's game to a more predictable physical pattern. April came and went without any league victories. *"It is a fact that Don Goodman's goals, so important to us at one stage, have dried up for seven games"* admitted the once more stressed Brian Talbot. *"Of course, all strikers go through lean periods like this, but maybe Don will have to give way to the challenge of others if he can't get it back."* Empty words for Albion didn't have a replacement for a fit and scoring Goodman.

A 0-0 draw against Sunderland in the last but one game in early May finally killed off any promotion hopes. The Baggies finished 9th, four points short of a play-off place. After so many years of struggling at the wrong end of the table, Albion supporters regarded ninth spot as highly positive. Many hundreds, dressed in beachware and carrying surfboards, refused to leave Boothferry Park, Hull until the team returned to take a bow at the end of a generally positive campaign, sparked by top scorer Goodman's goals.

SEASON 1989-90, THEN, was obviously going to build on the achievement of the previous one. Classy Bernard McNally was added to the team's engine room, while the now fully fit Don had a new partner in Kevin Bartlett, a young Goodman Mark II – incredibly fast, but with only a limited knowledge of where he was going and why. Albion supporters expected... and in classic Albion style were let down. Sheffield United in dayglo yellow were the Baggies first opponents and dazzled their hosts in a comfortable 3-0 victory. Neither Brian Talbot nor Albion ever fully recovered from this shock. Goodman was in decent form, though, with three goals in the next four games and in addition forced Greenall of Oxford United into conceding an own goal. Reporter Dennis Sunley summed up the resurgence after a victory at Filbert Street in September. *"Goodman's goal was his third in four games and on this sort of form, he is going to cause defences up and down the country quite a few headaches."*

Three straight away wins followed at West Ham, Bradford City in the League Cup (6-6 on away goals after being 3-1 down from the home leg) and Watford. Kevin Bartlett was quick to praise his striking partner. *"Don holds things up and wins a lot in the air"*, not realising just how new these attributes really were, the results of so many hours training with "Pancho" Pearson.

The hat-trick of wins on the road boosted everyone's morale. A boost was necessary as the arrival of Wolves in the division and the resumption of local derby hostilities had upped the stakes. It was so typical of Albion that there were no victories in any of the next six league matches. These were grim afternoons for their brittle defence – particularly a painful home defeat by Wolves not to mention the shocking 5-1 defeat at home to Newcastle, in which Sam Allardyce made his only appearance in an Albion shirt. Goodman's 50th senior goal was no comfort at all.

THERE WAS SOME consolation in the cups when the team showed something of their best form. After the remarkable comeback against Bradford City, WBA travelled to Newcastle in the next round and pulled off a backs-to-the-wall 1-0 victory. The run ended at Derby in round four. In the FA Cup, Albion beat two First Division sides at home before pulling out the plum – home to Aston Villa. The Villains were too strong in the end, but had to work very hard and notably adjusted their rearguard line-up to stop Goodman running at them. The cup victories were sufficient to ward off some criticism of Brian Talbot, despite his side slipping down the table.

Blameless too was Goodman, enjoying his most prolific season ever. His final tally was 21 league goals, easily sufficient to top the club goalscoring charts for the second time (no one else could muster double figures), indeed it was the highest league tally since Bomber Brown in 1970. Most noticeably, there was a hat-trick against Barnsley in a 7-0 slaughter, through a header and by twice breaking the Tykes' offside trap and yet he remains overshadowed by the return from injury of the hugely popular Martyn Bennett. There was also Don's one and only successful penalty conversion to note, against Swindon Town, which was born out of desperation. Regular penalty taker Bernie McNally had already missed one. So had Graham Harbey. When the Baggies remarkably secured a third spot-kick, it was the striker who stepped up. Despite such largesse from the referee, the Baggies still contrived to lose 2-1.

Goodman managed to score both home and away against Leeds United, helping Albion to take four points from the eventual champions. At Elland Road, Leeds were 2-0 up after 54 minutes. The hometown boy takes up the tale: *"they must have caught us offside 20 times, but we beat the trap three times and scored twice."* Goodman was rugby-tackled by Chris Fairclough the first time he broke free. *"I think he would have done it the second time – but he knew he would have been sent off."* Set free by Hodson, Don sped off to score Albion's first ... and later he teamed up with Bartlett for an unexpected equaliser. *"I now approach every game believing I can score,"* exulted Don afterwards. And Baggies' fans felt likewise. Not since the advent of Cyrille Regis had they imbued so much confidence in a regular supply of goals from one source.

DON FREQUENTED BARS in and around Broad Street, Birmingham and all who who met him were struck by his charm and ready wit. He was frank too, perhaps dangerously so for an off-duty footballer. Such was his new found respect that all his confidences appeared to be respected. Perversely these attributes only properly came to the fore after his departure. With Albion's manager imposing a ban on players attending fans' functions, supporters of other age groups didn't have an opportunity to meet Don socially. The easy-going sixties with regular supporter-player interaction as the norm was long gone.

Subsequent extended interviews allowed his perception and easy going style to show through, a style which later would give him a new media career. Such was his positive influence that when he returned to the Hawthorns wearing a Wolves shirt, barracking was at best half-hearted and largely confined to his increasing rampant hair which frankly did invite ridicule. The style, if that's the word, resembled a black sprouting bush. Albion supporters did stop short of applauding him as they did with Cyrille. After all, there are pecking orders to observe, even with cult heroes. Supporter Ian Thomas remembers seeing Don with his family: *"His two lads had wild afros – just like their Dad."*

THE BAGGIES ONLY secured their 1990 league safety in the 45th match with a nervous 2-2 draw at Oakwell. Albion's main striker came close to securing a stress-relieving win when his shot was kicked off the line. Relegation fears hampered his morale during the run-in with much poor ball control and according to one correspondent to the *Argus* *"needing a field to turn around in."* With only six home wins all season, the faithful following were despondent once more. The manager was asked for explanations and his observations included, *"We didn't have anybody alongside Don Goodman to score goals."* Bartlett ultimately wasn't the answer. Neither were Thomas, West, Bannister, Foster nor Robson. Meanwhile Everton, Oldham and Nottingham Forest had all enquired about Prince's availability.

THE ANSWER WAS never found. The question was removed instead. In a particularly grim pre-season friendly at Swansea, Albion lost 5-0 with Goodman sent off for violent conduct. The referee claimed the Albion man headbutted his opponent. Don was adamant: *"I did not strike or even lay a finger on the Swansea player"* a view shared in the away end. Curiously, although the Football League indicated the referee had made a mistake, the official refused to confirm his error in writing so the three-match ban remained.

Don's post-ban return was brief – lasting only a couple of games, thanks to a torn hamstring at Hull City. *"It was as if a bullet had exploded in my leg,"* he lamented, through gritted teeth. *"I can't find the words to describe how depressed I feel."* His manager probably felt the same way. His top striker was out of action for a further seven weeks. As Andy Colquhoun of the *Birmingham Post* put it: *"Goodman has been a source of frustration as well as hope for Albion supporters."*

Even though West and Bannister had bought Talbot some credibility with eight goals each, a succession of goals conceded in the last ten minutes made the Hawthorns natives quite hostile. Six goals hit Albion's net inside the last seven minutes in just four games, four of them in the 89th minute. When this was followed by Wolves equalising in injury time, Albion supporters were incandescent. *"We've lost our best striker for half a season"* wailed the beleaguered manager.

As if to prove his talismanic status, Goodman returned with a big bang. As a substitute against Blackburn he set up a goal for Colin West. He won a penalty against Swindon and scored his first of the season on Boxing Day – but then he was out again, this time with a calf strain.

The Baggies – top striker out, leaking defence, only six wins all season, manager under pressure, supporters militant – were drawn against a hitherto unknown non-league side Woking in the FA Cup. Not even a Conference club yet, but a team on a roll and full of confidence. In Albion's often glorious history, they had never previously lost to non-league opposition, home or away. The fear was palpable that afternoon. Although Colin West scored first, by the time Darren Bradley had added Albion's second, Woking had four to their name – three of them notched by a man whose name still grates – Tim Buzaglo.

Such was the bitterness and depression that Bradley's goal was barracked. Goodman himself offered a fair summary of the club's most depressing cup exit. *"We were humiliated, embarrassed. A part-time side trounced us and even though I wasn't playing, it didn't make the weekend pass any easier. I was in a foul mood and never forgot the experience."*

Neither did Brian Talbot. Within days, he left the building, P45 in hand. With Stuart "Pancho" Pearson in temporary charge, the technical quality of the play improved greatly, but the results remained mixed. The highlight was a comprehensive and classy stuffing of Blackburn Rovers 3-0 at Ewood Park with Don trebling his contribution for the season.

The question of who should be the next manager divided supporters, but the nearest to any kind of consensus held that long ball merchant Bobby Gould was not welcome at the Hawthorns. There was plentiful evidence to support this, such as a fanzine survey and regular chants of *"We don't want you, Bobby Gould."* The directors chose Bobby Gould. Years later, certain directors privately admitted that Gould had sweet-talked them into giving him the job.

The new manager's first game finished 0-0 against eventually promoted West Ham, but six wretched defeats followed, destroying the club's safety margin.

The football was grim. The results were grim and so was the mood. But amidst all the grime there was still Don Goodman, who resumed his one man scoring spree. Hardly anyone else could find the net as Gould tinkered vainly with one useless signing after another. Draws were not really good enough, but that's all the team could manage. In the 44th game, they drew with Port Vale after missing two penalties – Goodman was the culprit for one of them. Infamously, much-maligned club chairman John Silk tried to defend his own position later with the words *"I didn't miss the penalties against Port Vale."* The 45th game was yet another 1-1 draw, this time against Newcastle United. The good news was, it was just enough if Albion could win their final match at Bristol Rovers' Twerton Park in Bath. The bad news was they'd have to do it without Goodman, who was injured once again. Certain club officials to this day hint that Goodman could have played at Bath, a claim denied to this day by the player.

Displaying the eccentricity which later became his trademark, Gould paired two forwards at Bristol Rovers who'd never previously played together, introduced a rookie forward in er... midfield while the top goalscorer (Bannister) sat on the bench. The result was yet another draw, even after Rovers had a man sent off. The Bristol side, urged on by fanatical support, fought tigerishly to relegate their former highly unpopular manager. Unbelievably the famous West Bromwich Albion were in the Third Division for the first time in their long history. No day since or probably before was quite this black for Albion supporters.

FOOTBALL LIFE MUST go on – even though the Baggies' next League fixture was against Exeter City. Albion swept the Devon side away 6-3 with Goodman twice outpacing his opponents. When Donno notched the winner in the next game at Darlington, everyone felt more confident.

But although results were OK, the performances were poor, not helped by another seven game absence from Goodman. He returned to score against Shrewsbury and league leaders Brentford, also achieving a personal milestone – finally scoring in a Cup match for Albion. With the exception of a solitary effort in the much-derided Simod Cup, Don had not found the net in either FA Cup or League Cup. His goal against Swindon in the League Cup was matched by another, during the indignity of a first round FA Cup match against Marlow. His presence during a 6-0 win was later to cost him dearly.

For he was clearly better than the Third Division and Albion were struggling to hold on to him. His Albion days were numbered. The player himself admitted he wanted out. Talking to the *Albion News* in October 1991, he admitted: *"Whether I'm still here in May remains to be seen. I am ambitious and I want to play in the First Division."* His comments were remarkably candid for an official publication.

Actually, Don had already privately agreed with Albion's board that if the right offer came in, he could go. The board anticipated £1m, possibly from West Ham and so rejected outright the initial £750,000 proferred by Sunderland, who needed a replacement for their hero, 'Magic' Marco Gabbiadini, recently departed for Crystal Palace. The North-East side were aware of the Baggies' financial difficulties, so let them sweat for six weeks before returning to offer £900,000. By December, Albion's overdraft was in excess of £1m, and their bank threatened to foreclose. They had to accept the Mackems' offer. Sunderland's manager Denis Smith was confident with his new purchase. *"He's quick, strong, brave, and above all, he scores goals."*

"I had no wish to play Third Division football for a second longer than was necessary" explained the Baggies top striker. Neither did Albion's supporters, but they were stuck with it. From their perspective, the players who'd got this famous old club into this sorry state should be busting a gut to retrieve the position. The prospect of their talisman jumping ship was not well received.

After what turned out to be his final game against Stoke in November 1991, supporters hurled abuse at Goodman, even though his 63rd Albion goal contributed to a 2-2 draw. As supporter David Norman concluded at the time, *"WBA are effluent rather than affluent following the sale of Don Goodman."*

Without Goodman, the already grey season took on all the attraction of Torquay in January. Albion even managed to lose there as well – 1-0.

Just who would score the goals? The answer was but another month away, though no one knew that at the time. Goodman offered a departing olive branch. *"Albion supporters put me on the pedestal, they were absolutely wonderful towards me and I'll never ever forget that nor be able to thank them enough for that. They were great, and they gave me confidence and they helped me become a better player."*

There was a silver lining in the cloud of their hero's sale. Goodman's departure presented a handy stick to beat Gould with (even though it wasn't his fault) and as the results worsened, even the board realised he just had to go. With his departure in May, the rebuilding could properly start.

SUNDERLAND WENT ALL the way to the FA Cup Final that season, but the Leeds-born striker remained a frustrated watcher, after his appearance against Marlow for Albion. Neither did he ever reach the Premiership, getting no nearer than defeat in the play-off semi-final. Meanwhile, proceeds from his sale enabled Bobby Gould to purchase one Bob Taylor.

Bob Taylor

1992-1998 & 2000-2003: 377 games, 131 goals

IN 1991 ALBION were slumped at their lowest point in their history in status terms, if not financially, though pennies were far from abundant. The highly unpopular Bobby Gould took over a club in disarray following the FA Cup defeat by Woking and arguably made the situation worse with his odd signings and even odder tactics. Albion were relegated to the old Third Division, on the last day of the season at Twerton Park, unable to beat a ten-man Bristol Rovers.

Albion's first ever third-tier season started brightly, but progress became staccato. With the club guaranteed to finish in their lowest position ever, nothing but full involvement in chasing automatic promotion would satisfy supporters.

Don "Donno" Goodman was the big hope to get us out of this mess, with nine goals to his name, but a combination of the club's financial shortcomings and Goodman's frustrations at operating at such a low level, meant a swift parting of the ways was inevitable. He left in December, and with him went the remaining hopes of the frustrated following. The remaining forwards were not frankly of the lineage of Bache, Richardson, Allen, Astle, Brown and Regis and it says much that the most effective attacker was the diminutive Gary Robson, normally a midfielder, but pressed into service up front. The football was poor, but the results were about acceptable until Donno's departure. Subsequently, there was only one win in five games in January, culminating in a 3-2 defeat at home to Swansea, after being two goals ahead. This was one poke in the eye too many for the remaining faithful, who staged a protest sit-in at the Brummie Road End.

Gould, ever the eccentric, volunteered to take a microphone into the fulminating masses to answer their questions. In response to one shouted enquiry, he promised that a new forward would be signed very soon. He kept his word. That forward was Bob Taylor.

BOB WAS BORN in Easington, County Durham on 3 February 1967, an addition to a mining family. His father went down the pit. So did his brother and his father before him. Inevitably, Bob was earmarked for the same job – what other work was there in Horden? The prospect didn't appeal. *"I didn't want to be stuck down a pit in the dark or have to do that kind of back-breaking work."* In the end, he didn't have the choice to make because the mine closed shortly before he left school. Horden was never the same again. His Dad and the rest of the workforce were all out of work.

But there was always sport, the traditional "out" for North East folk. Young Bob had talent and it wasn't long before it was recognised.

Leeds United was his first professional club. He played alongside David Batty in the juniors' team, but took better penalties. Known then as *Bobby Box* (after a TV character of the period), his first team debut arrived in April 1986. He played around 40 games for the Whites and was part of the Leeds squad that came so close to reaching the Premier League in a tense three-match play-off Final.

Then came a move to the West Country and a highly successful spell with Bristol City as fan Chris Smith recalls: *"The 1989/90 season was the most enjoyable that I can remember and SuperBob was largely responsible for that. There was a feeling of invincibility that season, that however many the opposition scored, we would score at least one more, with Bob at the heart of it. The partnership with Robbie Turner was fantastic, a strong target man, the perfect foil for Taylor, who made the most of Turner's flick-ons and hold up play. Not that Bob didn't create a fair few of his own goals, he was the all round striker with both tap-ins in the six-yard area or powerful shots from outside the box. The other memorable moments included his hat-tricks, the professionalism that he displayed on and off the pitch, the injury that caused him to miss four or five games at the end of the season, a massive factor in the Gas (Rovers) pipping us to the title, and his habit of wearing sweatbands and throwing them into the crowd at the end of the game. My mate still has one and treasures it to this day."*

Allegedly, *"Bob, Bob Super Bob"* (as he was serenaded at Ashton Gate) was once carried off in pain on a stretcher in a match against Crewe. He insisted on the bearers carrying him around three sides of the ground so he could sign autographs from his prone position. It's a great story but almost certainly a myth.

A change of management at Ashton Gate had the new manager, Jimmy Lumsden, in need of cash for new signings. Dangling was £300,000 on offer from Albion for Taylor. By then, City had a number of decent strikers and Bob was far from an automatic choice. They took the money. Bob was happy with the chance of a new start. He'd recently lost his mother and living in the West Country seemed just too far away from home.

ALBION'S NEW MAN started in fine style as author and supporter Richard Brentnall recalls: *"In his first 142 minutes, Taylor cut a dream coat figure. The touch, perception, elusiveness and finishing has been evident against Brentford, and against Blues, he displayed with his first goal, two other qualities that we've been sorely lacking; alertness and agility inside the box."*

Brentford were the league leaders and fancied their chances against the misfiring Albion side. However, Gary Robson's through ball gave the debutant a chance in the 11th minute. The new boy buried his chance, rebounding off the body of the charging goalkeeper. A second goal by Fereday completed a highly satisfactory win.

A week later came the local derby at St Andrew's and another win – this time by an impressive 3-0 margin – and Albion were top of the Division, thanks to SuperBob. Taylor scored two of the three, the first a diving header. There was new belief born that day. Albion supporters had a new focus, a new favourite. The slim, almost gangly figure with a mass of black hair and Dirk Bogarde thighs was quick to add reality to an unreal situation. *"It's not always going to be this good,"* he warned on Radio WM. He was correct. A narrow defeat four days later to perennial pests Stoke City saw Albion's bubble burst and the side went backwards rapidly.

Bob was originally labelled 'Trigger" Taylor, because of his resemblance to the dim character in *Only Fools and Horses*. This was a short-lived moniker. Prefixing suitable Christian names with "Super" was quite fashionable at that time; indeed the new signing was already SuperBob at Ashton Gate.

His arrival and early achievements gave everyone a reason to keep going, to stick with the under performing outfit rather than shrug the shoulders and take up needlepoint. That and the opportunity to tell Gould exactly what you thought of him. 'Back Bob, Barrack Gould,' if you will. Most did. At least, the referees were grateful that focus was elsewhere. With Gould's infamous player selection and his increasingly bizarre "motivation tactics", he simply had to go. The board didn't respond until the season was over at Shrewsbury. SuperBob had seven goals to his name in a limited number of matches, but they couldn't save Gould.

WITH THE BENEFIT of sepia-tinged and brightly-hued spectacles, the second season in the Third Division is the most enjoyable one for the post-1978 generation. New manager Osvaldo Ardiles had an attacking policy, aided by nervous opponents, who regularly felt an urge to defend and hardly anybody could stop the Baggies – or Bob in particular – from finding the net. *"They were such nail-biting games to play in,"* agreed Bob. *"Even if we were in front, you could never be sure we'd hold on to it because all we ever did was push further and further forwards."*

The memories of dreadful games, such as losing 1-0 at Springfield Park in heavy rain, on open terrace and a muddy grassy bank, are hard to retain. Albion's manager Ardiles wasn't terribly concerned about any setbacks, remaining typically laid-back. *"My players are human and have problems like everybody else. They may have rowed with their partners, not had much sleep or be feeling a little under the weather."* The frustrations of only finishing fourth, behind three other strong sides, also faded quickly after promotion was secured the hard way.

WHAT DOES LODGE in the memory about 1992/93 are matches when we strutted like kings on and off the pitch at places like Chester, Mansfield and Rotherham – taking over the ground (or even the town), while the players took over the pitch. These are powerful, positive memories. Bob Taylor found the net 37 times that season. This despite making do with an assortment of ill-fitting partners such as Garner, Speedie, Blissett and Robson. Not to mention the play-offs. It's completely impossible to describe the bubbling raw emotions of what going to Wembley means to supporters, after being deprived of visiting the Twin Towers for almost a quarter of a century.

The business end of that season saw the arrival of a young forward from Newcastle – Andy Hunt. The pair became an immediate success. *"Me and Hunty hit it off straight away. Andy was a bit like me, the fans liked him and he was level headed, but he never got above his status. If one of us wasn't scoring, then the other one was. We also read each other's games really well, which helped a lot. Andy was good in the air, won a few flick-ons for me, and I used to hold up the ball and bring Andy into the game. We never worked on it either, we just clicked, the only time I can remember us working on our game was when we used to do shooting practice in training."*

Although the Taylor and Hunt partnership blossomed, West Brom found progress hard to maintain in the higher division and struggled for several seasons. As a result, both Hunt and Taylor left the First Division for the Premiership. Bob genuinely didn't want to leave. *"There were a lot of issues within the club. The manager wanted me to go on loan and I didn't want to go at first. It was a major wrench to leave, but, in the end, I went out on loan to the Premiership to Bolton. I loved it; I scored against Manchester United at Old Trafford, and against the Villa at their place. I was living out my dreams."*

Albion's manager by this time was Denis Smith, who by coincidence, bought Goodman while at Sunderland and who, shortly after Bob left Bristol, took over the manager's hot seat at Ashton Gate. The striker always maintains he got on well with all Albion managers, even the irascible Alan Buckley. *"When I went in for training with Alan Buckley, I'd say "Morning, Gaffer" and he goes down on his knees to me, you know, and does the "I'm not worthy" thing – "I'm not worthy, SuperBob".* Bob would make an exception for Denis Smith. Bob privately seethed at the treatment meted out to him. He was adamant that Denis had it in for him from the day he started, claiming that Bob was overweight and liked a drink too often. After the spell on loan, Bob returned briefly to the Hawthorns before leaving permanently for Bolton.

Denis Smith assured everyone that SuperBob was offered a new deal. He *"implored him to stay"* prior to the final home game – yet according to him, Bob didn't give him the courtesy of responding to his offer. *"What more could I do – short of going down on my knees and licking his boots?"* It was true that a new deal was offered – a non-negotiable one-year deal. Bob wanted three years to take him to a testimonial. As the 12-month offer was non-negotiable, the response could be only 'yes' or 'no.'

Director John Wile backed his manager: *"The manager couldn't agree a contract with him at the level the player wanted and that was it. He was just another player that had come to the end of his contract and he was allowed to leave to Bolton, the same as anybody else."* But Super Bob was never just another player like everybody else, and such ill-judged management-speak did little for Wile's standing amongst supporters.

Smith left. Wile left. The chairman left. The resident rats left, weary of such thin pickings. A new manager arrived … and then left. Situation normal. In came another manager, a hungry one this time in Gary Megson, but Albion continued to flounder. Relegation back among the dead men of the newly rechristened Division Two beckoned. He needed inspiration, the kind that can only come from a goalscorer, a talisman, a legend. But Megson had to find a cheap one. Someone who lived locally and better still, knew at least some of the current players. There could only be one.

"I got a phone call asking me if I'd like to go back to West Brom," says Bob, *"and I jumped at the chance. I didn't even think about it, my heart ruled my head really!"* This time the deal was for two-and-half-years, plus a testimonial. Less money than at Bolton, but a longer deal and a welcome opportunity to spend more time at the family home in Lichfield.

Martin Lewis, plus daughters Carly and Bethany are Newcastle (Staffs) based Albion supporters. *"I'll never forget that day,"* explains Martin. *"When I picked up Carly from school, I said to her 'we're staying up.' 'How do you know?' asks my daughter. 'Because we've got Bob Taylor back.'"*

IT WAS A shrewd move. The return of the great man pumped raw excitement into mentally battered supporters, while his charisma boosted his team-mates, including Lee Hughes, who'd always looked up to the elder statesman. Lee was to play only two more games that season, due to injury and so goalscoring was down to Bob. His first came at promotion-chasing Barnsley in April, a looping header from a free kick. Relief and belief flowed in equal measure. Four more precious strikes that term did just enough to maintain First Division status. SuperBob was the saviour.

From this modest position, Albion moved forward rapidly, propelled by maximum velocity by Megson and a string of new, more talented arrivals. The signing of a cult hero's nephew, Jason Roberts, meant Bob was relegated to a bit-part role. He was on hand to score vital goals against Tranmere and Burnley, the latter effectively knocking the Lancastrians out of the play-off picture. That place went to the Baggies instead, who had their chances to beat Bolton, but didn't take them and were knocked out. The 2001/02 season explored exciting new ground, but the one after would far exceed it.

In the early matches, little went right. Losing at Bescot 4-1 in blazing opening day heat, was grim. In the first home game, came an infuriating 0-1 to bloody Grimsby, Bob not only missed a penalty, Jimmy Quinn replaced him. It's hard to say which was more embarrassing. Was the King dead?

Watford away, after two home wins, felt significant. *"Bobby on the spot"* followed up to tuck home a penalty rebound. The Baggies grabbed a two-goal lead, and hung on to the three points, despite being down to ten men and defending their penalty area in Alamo-like fashion. Goalkeeper Russell Hoult even saved an injury time penalty. The result lifted everybody, and the chase was on at the right end of the table.

The high at Watford contrasted with the low of Preston in February. Not only did Albion lose to a promotion rival, far worse was the season-ending injury to top striker Jason Roberts. This combination of defeat, combined with the loss of JR, felt like a turning point. Worse still, Wolves were disappearing over the horizon, believing they'd already secured the second automatic promotion spot. Just reaching the play-offs that night felt an impossible target. Gaining 28 points from the remaining 30 on offer sounded as likely as striking matches on soap. And yet…

ARISE SIR BOB. His instinctive positional sense found him right time, right place, to score a late winner at Nottingham Forest. In a Nuremberg rally atmosphere, Bob polished off an early corner at Highfield Road. Coventry, which was sufficient to push the Baggies alongside a now brown-shorted Wolverhampton. Despite a dislocated finger, the rejuvenated striker's volley then earned a point against Rotherham to put the Baggies clear in second place. Then came Bradford City.

Tales to tell your grandchildren No. 73. In a match that Albion *had* to win, there was no score as the game moved into injury time. Super Bob, on the left hand touchline of the penalty box, attempted to twist round Andy Myers, who made contact with his knee. Down went Bob. The referee gave a penalty and Igor Balis did the business. Those are the bare facts, but these do no justice to the occasion, don't reflect the finger-chewing tension or the screaming frustration of the 6,000-strong away support. Bradford City were saying goodbye to Stuart McCall and didn't want his farewell spoilt. Albion had pounded away in the later stages, with every forward possible on the field.

The penalty stretched the elastic band of tension further. The Baggies had missed penalties all season long and this was Igor's first for WBA. Life, as we knew it, stopped for several minutes. Myers protested about the decision. Bob needed treatment. Apparently McCall just had to be substituted, very slowly, at that moment. City's keeper Coombe dallied as long as he dared. Igor wasn't worried. Bang – top corner, no problem. Players and supporters rushed together in a mass hugging session. Others sat down sharply, legs suddenly wobbly. Others openly wept. Rarely has life as an Albion supporter felt so overwhelming.

After such drama, the final match of the season against Palace seemed quite tame really – even though it was truly shit or bust. The Londoners knew their place as "also rans" and only threatened the Albion goal once. Strikes from Darren "Big Dave" Moore and, inevitably, SuperBob lit the touch paper for the biggest celebrations in the town for a decade or more – all the bigger for having denied the Wolves.

BOB ONLY PLAYED parts of six games for the Baggies in the Premier League. *"I'd have liked to have played more. I've played in the Premiership before with Bolton, but to play there with West Brom was special. I'd worked hard for ten years of my life to get there and to come on in the first game against Man United was special for me. My only wish was if I could have got a goal for West Brom, which really would have been the icing on the cake for me."*

The end of Bob's Albion career was terribly sad and so unnecessary. For a reason that remains unclear to Bob and was never explained in public by the manager, he was completely frozen out for the last five months of his contract. Bob trained with the kids and played for the reserve side. This was no way to treat such a fine clubman. After the last reserve game of the season, he was told not to bother training any more, with the clear inference that his career was over.

THAT LEFT BOB ample time to work on his testimonial projects. Various fundraising activities had already taken place throughout the year, such as a casino night. Supporter John Groarke, in the mistaken belief that an evening with Bob as a drinking buddy was up for grabs rather than just his shirt, invested literally hundreds of pounds in casino chips. It was an inadvertent gesture that said much about the popularity of the man. On the day of Albion's final Premier League game against Newcastle, Bob was booked into the club shop for a pre-match autograph signing session of his tribute video/ DVD. Imagine his surprise when he discovered he was playing!

Having not trained for a week or having met his first team colleagues professionally that year was not great preparation. Bob was predictably out-of-sorts. He only lasted 15 minutes before limping off injured with tears in his eyes. Both sets of supporters gave him a standing ovation, many with moist eyes of their own.

Despite the rather bold £15 admission charge for what was a scratch match against an assortment of former team-mates plus add-ons, Bob's testimonial was attended by 12,000 people, which tells its own story. It was genuinely fun too. Despite his injury, Bob made a token appearance up front. He returned again in the second half in goal, playing to the crowd at every opportunity. Finally, he grabbed a microphone and gave an impromptu speech over the PA to tumultuous enthusiasm. Such poignancy. It felt to everyone present like the end of an era.

Why does he remain a crowd hero even now? Initially goals. Finding the net gets you noticed at the Hawthorns and regular scorers are always most popular. Bob boasts 131 Albion goals to his name, and only seven men in Albion's long and glorious history can claim more.

His goals were rarely spectacular – with a few exceptions. In the infamous "paddy field" match at Luton in May 1994, Bob took on and beat several defenders, who just couldn't keep their feet, before sliding the ball past the keeper. Also, in 1995, he dived between two Wolves defenders to reach a perfect centre from Lee Ashcroft to finish off the Staffordshire side. His qualities revolved more around timing, being in the right place at the right moment, and holding the ball up to bring others into play. He was all effort and never shrank from the physical side of the game.

Long-time fan Ian Thomson recalls another match at Kenilworth Road: *"There was the slightly comical sight of Bob Taylor squaring up to Luton's yellow-shirted giant Feuer. The keeper was chatting away to Bob and doing a lot of finger wagging. Bob pulled himself up to his greatest height in this standoff and put on a brave face. Try as he did, poor Bob was made to look like a small schoolkid being confronted by the school bully. The unfortunate ending to the incident was a booking for the striker."*

Similarly, in a much celebrated comeback at Exeter City (2-0 down to 3-2 up), Bob was undeterred by goalkeeper Kevin Miller charging out at him, hands at neck height and ran straight into a boot in his ribs. While Bob was off the field receiving treatment, team-mate Ian Hamilton put away the winner from the spot past the substitute keeper – Miller having been sent off.

Years later, Miller got his revenge. Albion had just scored at Barnsley to reduce a deficit to 3-2. Miller refused to release the ball to Bob for a quick kick-off. Worse, he acted as though the Albion man had punched him. Bob denied any wrongdoing, but was still dismissed, one of only two dismissals whilst with the Baggies. The other early bath came at Southend, for two tackles, neither of which was particularly vicious.

Bob was never quick, so asking him to chase long balls was rather futile. Because the North-Easterner became a favourite so quickly, Bob was never at fault for losing possession, but rather the passing player. *"Give him a ball"* was the more polite of comments, but indicates how supporters confer a certain elevated status to a favourite.

Typically as a striker, his confidence dipped when he wasn't scoring as the man himself explains: *"I hate going on a long spell without scoring. I'm a goalscorer, that's what I do. I know I can score goals, but the more games go on, the more frustrated you get and the more you suffer and the more your game suffers. Goals are what you're judged on."*

Suffering such as the Huddersfield home match in 1997/98 when Bob played 45 minutes where he couldn't win the ball, couldn't hold it, couldn't pass it. Each mistake drew another curse and another agonised expression from a man painfully at war with himself. The half-time substitution was a mercy.

Bob went from November 1994 to March 1995 without a goal, eventually finding the net at Fratton Park. Typically, the match had significance. The Baggies were slipping worryingly towards the bottom three with only one win in seven. The first was a gift from 25 yards that keeper Knight fumbled. Thus rejuvenated, and with the small midweek travelling crowd urging him on, Bob then hit the bar and had another cleared off the line before winning the game in the 87th minute, running on to a perfect Agnew cross. Bob was back. A week later, came his previously mentioned diving header to secure a win against Wolverhampton.

A measure of any Albion player's popularity is the supporter's reaction to them when they return with their new club. Comparatively few, if any, these days have their affections maintained once they depart for footballing pastures new. Bob Taylor was an exception, as author and supporter Ian Thomson recalled on a visit to the Reebok Stadium in February 1999. *"I can't imagine that any player can ever have received a more rousing ovation from the fans of a former club than that which we heard when the announcer read Bob's name out before the game. If Bolton fans didn't realise what an absolute diamond they have got their hands on before that wonderfully spontaneous show of appreciation, they should have been left in no doubt thereafter."*

Bob scored his 12th goal of his season that day – for Bolton. This was the game where, in an emotional and utterly genuine moment, he swapped shirts with Lee Hughes post-match and ran to the away supporters kissing the Baggies' badge. He explained later that his departure to Bolton was hasty and there was no time to say goodbye to Albion people. This was his belated thank-you.

Bob still remembers his first visit to the Hawthorns as a Bolton player. When he came on as a substitute, *"the whole ground stood up for me, a standing ovation all the way round. The press guys at Bolton said they'd never seen anything like it, I had the chairman come down to say he'd never seen such a response for a single player. People talk about the hair standing up on the back of your neck and it does, you get a tingle and that's what does it for me. I do love the club and the bond I have with the people, the fans and that's special for me."*

SuperBob is far more than the sum of his goals and the significance behind them. There's both gratitude and relief that for a decade, it was

Bob who was there when we needed him to keep us in the Division and propel us into the division above.

Despite all those goals in the 1992/93 play-off Season, he surprisingly didn't score in the play-offs. But he did set up Andy Hunt for the aggregate equaliser in the semi-final against Swansea and he was through on goal at Wembley before Swan brought him down and was sent off. A year later, he started the move for Ashcroft's goal at Fratton Park, which kept the Baggies up. In May 2000, Bob scored the key first goal against champions Charlton that again preserved our status. Two years after that came the goal of dreams – the clincher against Palace, which put Albion into the Premier League. Promotion and what it meant to players and supporters alike are captured in that iconic picture of Bob celebrating that goal. There are variants on the background, depending on the photographer, but all centre on the popular striker – mouth open in a bellow of triumph, eyes alight and arms seeking the skies in which it was written that the veteran striker would score that day. Captain Derek McInnes picked up on the vibe and dreamt the previous night that Bob would find the net. Bob was modest enough to laugh at that prophecy.

More recently, it was Taylor the Showman who did his best to push his team towards another promotion in 2007. In the first leg of the Wolves v Albion play-off, the Staffordshire mob had Steve Bull on the pitch to whip up their followers. Retaliation was necessary. Bob Taylor bounced on to the familiar Hawthorns turf and with effortless style, urged greater vocal effort from three and a half sides of the stadium. How could we possibly ignore SuperBob? Less than two hours later, Albion were Wembley bound, the team pushed forward by roars of encouragement.

One of Bob's major endearing qualities is that he doesn't seek to exploit his status, wage negotiations excepted. He's always got time for supporters. *"For me, the club is the fans. They welcomed me with open arms, they gave me a chance and still to this day, they give me a chance. I missed a penalty against Grimsby, a chance against Swindon and many others and still they support me and chant my name."* Fine words, almost a cliché for modern players, but Bob backs the words with deeds, attending supporters' functions, weddings, birthdays – often low key, refusing all expenses in a throwback to Jeff Astle's day. Presumably his modest background helps maintain his popularity and his 'man of the people' status – son of a miner, who endured a YTS scheme with Age Concern for a year, and later worked as a bin man. Bob understands hard times and those in need of a hand.

SuperBob was one of a tiny handful of Albion people who visited Ronnie Allen in his care home. When Lee Hughes needed a friend, Taylor was there for him, offering what support he could. Once the press lost interest, he visited the prison. In addition; he was a one-man human booster for sick children in Sandwell Hospital.

HE DOES FIND being a supporter quite difficult. To repeat him literally, *"I dunnoor how yees stond it"*. Bob was at the famous 'Great Escape" fixture against Portsmouth in May 2005. During the second half, it all became too much for him and, stricken with nervous tension, our hero had to retreat to the bar downstairs instead. *"I was up and down like a yo-yo!"* After the tension was over, he was spotted capering around on the turf with several thousand others.

The Bob Taylor sense of humour is never far away. In May 2003, the end of season theme at Blackburn was 'Referees at Rovers' to reflect the influence the men in black had had on our season. Although technically still on Albion's books, Bob travelled on the supporters' coaches and wore referee's gear.

There's a legendary Albion supporter known universally as *"long-haired Mick"* for obvious reasons. Mick Hamblett was one of 14 Baggies followers who travelled to Cosenza for a pointless Anglo-Italian League fixture (neither side could qualify) just before one Christmas. As the numbers were so small, fans and players mixed freely the previous night. Mick had just bought a round of drinks and was carrying them on a tray across the bar, when he was seized around the waist from behind. Before he could protest too much, his belt was swiftly undone and his trousers sank to his ankles. The contents of the tray capsized in all directions. Mick swivelled angrily to meet his assailant only to find a grinning Bob Taylor. And yes, Bob did get another round in.

Albion supporter Simon Cotter has only embarrassing memories of his contact with the Great Man. He confessed, *"I crashed into the back of Super Bob's car at the Scott Arms* (a road junction in Great Barr, Birmingham). *This was during his first spell with us and just after an operation on his ankle, so his wife was driving. I didn't care that I'd dented my own car. I was thinking about his, but thankfully it was fine."*

TAYLOR'S FOOTBALL ODYSSEY continued elsewhere post-Albion – firstly at Cheltenham, where he scored a few goals though recurring injuries proved his downfall. Followers of the Robins became accustomed to the regular presence of Albion supporters at their games as Bob admitted. *"I don't want to sound wrong but at Cheltenham, the number of Albion supporters turning up was embarrassing. They'd come in cars, minibuses, coaches sometimes, all be wearing the blue and white stripes and the Cheltenham people got used to having them about – like part of the scenery."* It was this author's misfortune that when he went to Whaddon Road for a league match with Hull City, Bob was on the subs' bench. He left the bench in the second half, only to return to it a minute later after a sickening but accidental collision with the opposition goalkeeper. Another injury and several more games missed. Cheltenham didn't renew his deal and so, as no more full-time offers came his way, he settled for the less stressful life of a part-time professional with Tamworth in the Conference.

"PLAYING FOOTBALL IS the only thing I know... I've always said I'm as thick as two short planks" are familiar sentiments from the North-Easterner over the years. Bob is anything but thick. As an orator, he's erudite, passionate and eminently believable. He was both fortunate and unfortunate to realise at a very early age that all he wanted to do was play football. Fortunate that his schoolboy realisation gave him complete focus to chase his dream. He was fortunate to have the talent to back his imagination but unfortunate that his dream affected his schooling. *"I sometimes wish I'd put more into other things at school."* In the meantime, he continued to pull on his boots right up until May 2006 at his final club Kidderminster Harriers, where manager Mark Yates was his admirer as well as his gaffer.

SINCE THEN, SUPERBOB has pursued various occupations without great success before finally settling on being a children's football coach, often working with Richard Sneekes. He's just a natural coach. If such an occupation existed, he could be a professional celebrity book signer. At least part of the success of "Cult Heroes" has been Bob's willingness to turn out repeatedly for book signing sessions and work a queue with his easy charm.

FINAL WORD, AS ever, from the man himself: *"I'd like to think I've always given value for money, whatever the results. I don't think I've ever gone on the pitch and not given 100 per cent for whichever club I've played for. I always try and work hard even when things are going well for me, and mebbe that's why the fans have always been behind me so much, even when things haven't been so good, because they can see how hard I'm trying."*

Lee Hughes

1997-2001 & 2002-2004: 237 games, 98 goals

LEE HUGHES HAD it all – fame, family, wealth, dream job and respect. He lost the lot.

It's not easy to pinpoint when exactly his career moved from upward mobility on to a slippery slope. Rumours about Lee's nocturnal activities (early morning revels, drink, drugs, women etc) were always part of his baggage, as were consequent tales of the football club's alleged level of 'smoothing'. In December 1998, for instance, Lee sported a fat lip. This was the result of a fall, a fight or even a slip on ice, depending on which account you believed. Clearly though, Lee's departure to Coventry was a watershed, the end of an era. His 'local boy made good' image was traded in for a bigger bank balance.

Lee had a contract clause that enabled him to go if Albion were offered over £5m; one agreed by then chairman Paul Thompson. Manager Gary Megson didn't want the "*best goalscorer outside the Premier League*" to leave. Certainly he fitted the manager's mould of an ideal footballer – enthusiastic with a maniacal work rate. The Smethwick striker played for Megson either as a central striker or occasionally wide and tackled back with gusto.

Coventry was a wretched choice but the Sky Blues were the only bidders. They were not a Premiership side, so the transfer was easy to perceive as greed rather than ambition. As an Albion man, Lee should have known that Coventry are never taken seriously, much to do with numerous stuffings over three decades. His insistence that *"Coventry were a more ambitious club"* or the even more unrealistic claim that Albion were trying to sell him to Wolves sounded simply pathetic.

No, he'd gone for the money, head turned by an agent. Lee's salary increased spectacularly – probably by 60 per cent. However, he wasn't exactly on the breadline at the Hawthorns. His numerous critics wondered just how much money he really needed. A five-figure weekly cheque seemed decent enough remuneration for someone in his or her dream job.

The Sky Blues' comparative nearness didn't help either because there were too many reminders via local newspapers and television. City frankly couldn't afford a £5,001,000 transfer. Few non-Premier League clubs can. And with City being in the same division as the Baggies, days of reckoning were in store.

While City struggled to come to terms with the in-your-face nature of the second tier of football, Albion managed very nicely without him. The meeting of the two clubs at the Hawthorns brought down much opprobrium upon the exile's head. *'One greedy roofer'* was a loud, popular, but not universal refrain. A goodly proportion of the home support refused to join in, silently preferring to remember the happier times. So-called 'big club' Coventry could only half-fill the away end and predictably lost to Albion again, 1-0. Lee salvaged some brownie points by applauding his former supporters after the game.

By the time of the return match in Easter, Lee Hughes was but a mere sideshow. *'Dingle Chasing'* was occupying all supporters' waking hours, including some when they'd rather be asleep. Albion sat in third spot, just behind a wilting Wolverhampton. The Staffordshire side were left wandering after a lunchtime defeat by Manchester City. An Albion win would leave the Baggies just a point short of second place. Could 16 years of hurt be at an end?

Urged by a frantic, bulging-eyed support, Albion acted like a threshing machine on their Coventry opponents. Hughes was left isolated, receiving only high balls from his harried colleagues. It was quickly clear anyway from his body language that he had no intention of hurting Albion that afternoon. He was subbed early in the second half to deafening choruses of *"you should have stayed with a big club"*. More magnanimously, later cries of *"Hughesie, Hughesie, give us a wave"* from the Albion following brought an enthusiastic if naive response.

After the match, which WBA won 1-0 to continue their march on the Premier League, prodigal Lee was spotted leaning out of a window in the main stand, punching the air in triumph at any passing Albion supporters. He later left Highfield Road in the company of his former team-mates.

THE SCENE WAS set for the prodigal's return to the Hawthorns in the summer, an inevitable one, given that Coventry were flat broke, while the Baggies needed more talent for the Premier League. Furthermore, Hughes goalscoring record for City was modest and twice he'd been sent off (despite his regular disputes with referees, he was never dismissed in Albion colours).

City tried for more cash, but Albion kept their nerve and agreed that the second half of the original transfer fee would not be paid. Lee bounced around the Hawthorns excitedly as if nothing had changed. *"It felt like I'd come back home,"* he said. *"It was just such a great feeling pulling the shirt on. Playing in the Premiership was always a dream for me."*

But the player-supporter relationship would never be the same again. He was now just another forward. Scoring goals changes moods, but Lee was to manage just one all season – and that in the League Cup against a Wigan Athletic side then two divisions lower. Lack of goals dogged the Baggies all season, as did ill luck and they were all-too soon relegated. A match report in the Albion fanzine *Grorty Dick* summed up the strikers' showing: *"All our best chances fell to the former roofer, (yes, it was a good match in that respect as we had more than one) and typically these days, the opposition keeper swallowed the lot. It was both heartening and disheartening at the same time. Heartening that he was in the right positions to shoot and disheartening because our Rooney prototype is a football jaffa."*

Ah yes, Rooney. The similarities between Wayne Rooney and Lee Hughes in their early days are obvious. Both were street footballers, angry, unpredictable, grateful young men, and so marvellous to watch. They were spontaneous. But Albion's Rooney was no more. The season at Highfield Road seemed to put more thought into Lee's life. His interviews were now at least semi-lucid, now that he was familiar with the footballers' lexicon of clichés. The thought process changed his game too. His ball control was tighter, but only at the expense of his instinct. That inner sixth sense, which lay behind his extraordinary goalscoring, was no more, replaced by traditional moves learnt on the training ground. His performance was poorer for it.

Post Coventry, the quiet whispers that surrounded his non-playing activities rose to a new shrillness. The delights of playing for the Baggies seemed to take second place to earthier pleasures as the striker hinted, when asked about the downside of playing on a Sunday. *"All yer mates gooing aert Sat'day night and yow cor goo aert."*

A FEW STORIES were just too far-fetched to have any credence, such as *"He's staying at Megson's house because it's the only way he can keep Hughes off drugs."* The rest were not so easily dismissed, such was their volume and impressive provenance. His driving record was far from good. After one earlier incident, he'd taken the option of a two-day driving improvement course at Oldbury, in a class with several Wolves supporters in it but had failed to benefit from the experience. A later potential drink-driving charge was headed off by means of a large cheque to the victim. He became even more notoriously unreliable, regularly failing to attend pre-arranged PR-type functions. While Albion were winning matches back in Division One and Hughes scoring reasonably regularly, the emperor's clothes syndrome prevailed. Nobody seriously wanted that boat rocked. There were management blind eyes. Lee was a natural athlete, and regardless of whatever he'd allegedly done or not done the previous night, full-on training was never a problem.

In October 2003, Lee scored a surprise winner in extra time at St James' Park to knock Premiership Newcastle out of the Carling Cup. He ran off to the left side of the stadium to celebrate, curious as the away support was in the opposite direction. Another winning goal followed just a few days later in a quite extraordinary victory at West Ham. Neil Clement recalled: *"I remember warming up with Lee Hughes, and he was getting a lot of stick from their fans. He just said to me he fancied himself to score if he came on."* Albion battled back from 3-0 down to win 4-3, with substitute Hughes taking advantage of a David James' error to find the net via a defender's leg. Off the back of such memorable moments are crowd favourites made. The former roofer was well on the way to rebuilding affections.

But barely a fortnight later on 22nd November, Lee Hughes was at the wheel of his Mercedes when it struck a Renault Megane driven by 56-year-old Douglas Graham. Graham was killed instantly, while his wife Maureen was badly injured. Lee panicked and left the scene, before turning himself in two days later.

Once processed and bailed, he was available again for selection. Because Hughes was on the receiving end from opposition supporters, the instinctive desire to defend your club and all who sailed in her took over. During Lee's return to first team football as a substitute at Bradford City, a mixed reception from the sparse away following was countered with overwhelming hostility from the Yorkshiremen. The instinct of *"My club – right or wrong"*, kicked in immediately. The striker, who looked well off the pace, looked grateful for any kind of support, and expansively showed his appreciation after the end of the game. Slowly, after a few matches, the opposition abuse faded away and with it the need to support the Smethwick striker. Hughes completed the season with a reasonable, if not outstanding goalscoring record.

But at the trial in August 2004, the bald facts were that an Albion player drove recklessly and killed Douglas Graham. Hughes had absconded, with the judge deciding that he had done so because he had exceeded the alcohol limit. What was quickly apparent was that Lee had no real defence. His hugely expensive legal team had nothing to work with. Hughes was sentenced to six years in prison. There was no doubt about his guilt, but the length of the sentence was surprisingly punitive.

LEE BRETT HUGHES was born on 22 May 1976 in Dudley Road Hospital in Birmingham. In line with his brothers, Clint and Brett, parents Bill and Gail chose his name from a cowboy film. Lee was what might be perceived as a traditional Black Country child. He was never considered to have any academic tendencies. When put on the spot, one of his primary school teachers diplomatically said, *"Put it this way, he wasn't in my top group."* Sport has always been his passion – football, cricket, golf (though all water obstacles continued to defeat him) – it all came so naturally. He was friendly and amiable, and only really knew Smethwick. He once described his favourite smell as 'curry'.

After turning out for a number of well-known boys football teams, he signed for Albion as a full-back aged 13. As Lee himself put it, *"the organisation wasn't very good."* There's a cute picture in *Grorty Dick* fanzine of a training session with guest Stanley Matthews next to a wide-eyed 14-year-old Lee Hughes, wearing full WBA gear. Eventually, coach Cyril Lea broke the news that the Baggies weren't going to offer him a YTS deal. *"That was horrible. It killed me really. I thought that was my chance at West Brom over and done with,"* admitted Lee, years later.

The Smethwick youngster tried out unsuccessfully for Walsall, where in his two games, he played once in goal and the other up front, where he scored a hat-trick. According to Hughes, Walsall reneged on a promise to offer him an apprenticeship. Then *"I played a few games for Swansea and things were going well, but I played the last game with flu and didn't do myself justice. I thought I'd blown my chance of ever becoming a footballer then."* Oldbury United were also similarly unimpressed before Kidderminster Harriers Youth gave him a go.

The young forward hoped to get a YTS place at the Harriers, but the Conference side cut their whole programme. Lee continued to play for the youth side until he was 18, in between working with his uncle in his long-established roofing business. Not always with the greatest of success. Wendy Maxfield observed Lee and two other workers re-roofing her neighbour's garage. One of the three subsequently put his foot through the roof, and the hole was "patched" with a refuse sack.

Lee made his Harriers' first team debut against Northwich Victoria in September 1994. His impact wasn't immediate, and there were numerous substitute appearances, but there was no doubt the youngster with bright red hair was both quick and direct.

Lee's Dad travelled to every game. Bill Hughes is a genuine Albion fan, but put his son first and followed the Harriers home and away. Lee always wanted to turn professional, and had trials with Sheffield Wednesday, *"I got injured on the second day there,"* and Wolves, *"I wouldn't have been that keen on signing for them."*

Hughes played at Wembley in the 1995 FA Trophy Final (lost 2-1 to Woking after extra time). *"I was nervous. When I was getting changed, I kept thinking about all the other people who'd got changed in that changing room. And the pitch was like a carpet."* The experience remained one of his all-time favourite football moments. The other came later – scoring from the penalty spot against Wolves.

With Lee driving them forward, Kidderminster improved. Their 11th place in the Conference in 1994/95 became seventh a year later and then, with Hughes leading the Conference scoring charts, they finished second, five points behind champions Macclesfield. The redhead was setting new records, becoming the youngest player to turn out for the England semi-pro team (v Ireland in 1996) and the youngest to score a hat-trick in the Conference (v Bath). It was obvious that even if Harriers weren't joining the Football League, their top goalscorer would be. Bristol City made the first pitch, offering £200,000. Harriers declined the offer.

Albion coach John Trewick first watched Lee Hughes, and recommended him to WBA in 1995. Albion manager Buckley always knew best and considered he didn't need any advice from anybody. Howard Martin was one of a number of supporters who gently tried to persuade irascible Bucko that a certain ginger-haired Albion-loving wide player at Kiddy Harriers was worth purchasing. Although Howard's enquiry was gently put using all of his experience as a business consultant, the response was not. *"I pick the team, not you."*

The departure of Buckley late in the 1996/97 season led to the arrival of Ray Harford, a progressive manager keen to embrace new ideas. Trewick's suggestion was well received. Albion approached Harriers in the summer and Kidderminster listened. The Baggies offered more than the £200,000 dangled by Bristol City, and could add the carrot of regular lucrative pre-season friendlies. Furthermore, Harriers knew that Hughes' dream was to play for 'his' club (*"I never wanted to play anywhere else."*) and to block his path would be counterproductive. A fee of £250,000 was agreed.

HUGHES' FIRST APPEARANCES in the famous blue and white came in pre-season friendlies in July 1997. Lee worked hard, even frantically. Sometimes a player is a cult hero before he kicks a ball, purely because of his reputation, such as Michael Owen's arrival at Newcastle. Lee was willed to succeed, 'our representative on the pitch', the ultimate player – *"lived local, supported local"* a kid who kissed the club badge and meant it.

The programme of warm-up games concluded with a Hawthorns match against Premier League Chelsea. The Londoners were strolling, with an experienced, albeit second-string defence, dominating the huffing lower division opposition. At half-time, on came a slim player with fiery red hair who didn't know or care about the conventions of the professional game. He was going to run at Chelsea, and they could try to stop him.

Within minutes, the Londoners back four were looking at each other anxiously. This unknown kid could embarrass them. They double-marked him, sometimes with a third man behind. Lee loved it. He just ran at them with the ball. Chelsea were just happy to get the ball away anywhere… for a corner, free-kick, whatever. *"Hughesey, Hughesey"* bellowed the Hawthorns faithful for the first time. Lee didn't manage to score that day, though he had nine shots.

His competitive debut followed in a brief showing as a substitute in the first league game against Tranmere. Albion's next fixture was at Gresty Road. Two late goals from Lee turned the 2-1 deficit into a late 3-2 win. His first, from a Kilbane pass, saw him arc the ball with his right foot past the keeper. The winner saw him twist free inside the box before lashing the ball into the roof of the net. As supporter Richard Brentnall put it, *"the 90th minute strike provoked the visitors' enclosure into a passable impression of Rampton hit by a mortar shell."*

The "Alex" had been outwitting Albion for years, so this victory was particularly sweet, not least because the Baggies were second in the table after three games. During those difficult times, desperate supporters would milk every positive dry. Lee was interviewed on national radio where he sounded every inch a naïve Black Country lad. Comparisons were quickly drawn with Cyrille Regis's dramatic debut against Rotherham. Even Sean Bean in *When Saturday Comes* would be impressed with such a start.

Hughes only played 30 minutes at Crewe. This was often the case under Harford, who wanted to *"introduce him gently."* From his perspective, there wasn't any hurry. His chosen formation was 4-5-1 with the clever Andy Hunt as the preferred front-runner. Should he need to chase the game or rest Hunt, he had Bob Taylor and Paul Peschisolido to call upon.

Only when Harford resigned, to be replaced by Denis Smith, could Lee remove the splinters from his bottom. Denis realised straightaway that he'd got a natural goalscorer in the squad, and made full use of his talents. He was wise enough not to impose rigid training methods on his protégé. Lee succeeded through pure instinct. Nature simply took over, and guided the youngster at high speed towards the net. His philosophy was simple. *"Other than one or two like Steve Bruce, I dunno their nairmes. Never bovva to look at the programme. I just stond on their shoulder and do 'em for pairce."*

LEE HUGHES WAS born to score goals. His natural speed was allied to an instinctive ability to defeat goalkeepers. Give him time to think about options, such as one-on-ones and he'd struggle, but try *"hit this ball"* and he'd hit it. Throw in aggression, a genuine love of a football club, and unpredictable play, and the combination made him mightily difficult to subdue.

"There's nothing to match playing for Albion at the Hawthorns. You run through the tunnel and look at where you used to stand as a lad. It's just the biggest buzz." Sounds as though a benevolent journalist added a little polish to the original expression, but the enthusiasm was genuine.

One prominent Albion supporter stopped outside Barclays Bank in Soho Road, Birmingham to use the cash point. Lee arrived shortly after and, as they knew each other slightly, easily fell into conversation. Albion's new signing was bubbling over with excitement, and couldn't help himself. The conversation became a monologue as the ginger-haired one rattled on like a busted flush about WBA, oblivious of subtle and not so subtle hints that the supporter wanted to move on. The fan finally resorted to direct action. *"Lee... f**** off!"*

Lee demonstrated his genuine passion for the club when he missed a match at Gigg Lane due to suspension. Being booked was an occupational hazard for Lee; nearly all were for kicking the ball away or dissent. He was invited to appear on cult Saturday morning Sky TV show *Soccer AM* to demonstrate his arm-swinging goal celebration. Afterwards, he chose to fly from London to Manchester, then onward to Bury to sit with the Albion supporters. He was famously received. By then, he even had an Albion tattoo to show off. Following a dismal team performance, he was ironically voted as *"Man of the Match"* by supporters, just for turning up.

Before he became a regular, Lee was happy to join his Dad on the terracing. The author witnessed the youngster being searched by a steward at Kenilworth Road and couldn't resist adding *"be careful what you're doing. That's a million pound striker you're handling."* The official looked suitably embarrassed: *"I'm sorry – I didn't know."* Months later at a fans' function, Lee admitted *"I still see myself as a supporter."*

Even in his later, more cynical days, he still remembered his roots. The Balti Kid attended Jeff Astle's funeral at Netherseal in Derbyshire. As a Coventry player, he could easily consider that the occasion was nothing to do with him. But the prodigal son made the effort, and

Laraine Astle was pleased to see him. Perhaps his appearance was not so much of a surprise. When Albion were at home and Coventry without a game, he could be spotted at the Hawthorns, celebrating goals as lustily as any supporter.

His obvious dislike of Wolves only added to his popularity. Through fair means or sometimes foul, as in Kevin Muscat's sly elbow, he was never permitted a goal in open play against the Wanderers, though he did once score from a penalty that he'd won himself. When Albion defeated their Staffordshire rivals 2-0 in November 1998, Lee celebrated as if he'd scored the Baggies second goal, rather than Shaun Murphy. He later admitted that he knew he hadn't scored, but just wanted to wind the Wolves fans up.

INTO HIS SECOND season in 1998/99, with a lucrative new four-year contract, there was an expectation that Lee would score in every game. Those expectations were close to being met with 28 goals by January (only one in cup competitions as Albion didn't really do cups then). Had he not missed six one-on-ones with the goalkeeper in the first three games, the tally would have been even higher. Still, as the *Sunday Mirror* put it, *"Hughes doesn't just score goals, he scores quality goals – the brace against Stockport were world class."*

Lee scored numerous pairs plus three hat-tricks, just one short of the club record tally for a single season. His first triple came in twenty second-half minutes at Port Vale, even if the linesman was the only person to spot the ball having crossed the line for his third. *"His fresh faced enthusiasm was positively anachronistic in today's cynical game,"* offered the *Stoke Sentinel*. After his third hat-trick, against Huddersfield Town in November, *"Hughesie for England"* was the chant of the day.

The Ginger Ninja achieved all this with intermittent support from a mediocre team. He was expected to win high balls and chase anything. As supporter Kevin Candon opined at the time, *"The obsession with belting the ball towards the bobbing red head of the pale goal-magician may be understandable, but it asks too much of Hughes, as it would any striker given accuracy on the scale of custard pie throwing."* Hughes was now the *"hottest striker in the country"* according to the *Birmingham Post*. Sister publication the *Sunday Mercury* produced a life-size poster of a young-looking Lee.

BUT SIGNS OF burn-out were quickly evident. While the team depended upon him for goals, Lee became a marked man – literally sometimes in the case of Oxford's goalkeeper Gerrard, who *"chased Hughes like a schoolboy in the playground, before knocking him to the floor."* Lee was substituted quickly, but still missed the next two games. Gerrard remained on the field.

As the festive season rolled round, the press concentrated on Lee's efforts to score 28 goals before Christmas, a feat that would win him a Mazda sports car. In the end, he needed a hat-trick against Tranmere and couldn't even manage one against very determined opposition. The striker found the extra pressure uncomfortable. *"I'm just glad it's all over now"* being his post-match comment. The car was later lent to him anyway, though it was probably rather pedestrian for Lee, who, toyshop-like, seemingly bought a new BMW or Mercedes every three months. But the high expectation of scoring goals, plus dealing with fans, agents, the press and so on was becoming generally too much of a burden for such a callow youth. As manager Denis Smith noted, *"He's constantly being pestered by people and he's too nice a lad to say 'no' and everybody wants him..."*

Lee bought his first house, literally around the corner from his parents' home, in modest Smethwick. The advantages of staying close to both his family, and his favourite local Balti restaurants were obvious, but this was not a wise move. Apart from being a BMW insurer's nightmare location (Lee's annual insurance bill was thought to be £8,000), over-enthusiastic Albion supporters, the local drunks and Wolves followers all considered Chez Hughes fair game. Newspaper speculation that he was moving to Middlesbrough didn't help either...or a written transfer request, code for an agent-inspired *"I want more money"*.

After so long in the lower division footballing wilderness, the need for a prophet for supporters to pin their hopes upon became increasingly important to them. In the end, an abrasive, yet eloquent Mancunian, who lived in Yorkshire but worked in the Black Country took that role. But years before the arrival of Megson, Lee was discovering just how hard it was to please everybody all of the time. His very naiveté at first was his protection. But as he grew used to the lucrative football life and paradise became a workplace, his attitude slowly hardened. So did his moods. He learnt to say 'no'. He learnt rudeness quite easily in his quest for self.

Another season meant another pay rise for Lee, and another manager. Mogadon man Brian Little dampened everyone's enthusiasm, including his own. His insistence of regularly playing Lee as a sole striker, a role he was ill-equipped to carry out, had a major impact on the forward's goal tally being cut by half.

This was a dreadful, couldn't-care-less time, with the manager so wrapped up in his own personal problems the team were able to do what they wished. Dwindling supporter interest increased the pressure at the bank, which insisted on the sale of Kevin Kilbane to Sunderland in December, or they would foreclose on the overdraft. For the bare 200 supporters who travelled to sub-zero Grimsby the same day, the club had rarely hit such a low. For months, chairman Tony Hale insisted there was money to spend, when clearly there was not. The gallant few were more interested in inquests than action that night, though Lee did find the net as Albion secured a 1-1 draw. After a further three months of awful performances, Brian Little invited the board to sack him. They took him up on his kind offer. In came the whirling hurricane Gary Megson to retain the club's second tier status – just. A Lee Hughes hat-trick against Tranmere helped so did his brave effort against Ipswich but it came at a price. He damaged his knee so badly in a full-on collision with visiting 'keeper Richard Wright that he missed Albion's last six games. There was arguably a long-term impact as to this day; his family are convinced that he never regained his top speed after the injury. In the short term however, his re-focused team-mates did enough without him. The Throstles, and Lee, were about to fly again.

BUT BEFORE THAT, the Smethwick striker made a major commitment. He'd previously had a very public and embarrassing relationship with a lap dancer, but this was the real deal. He travelled to Croatia to marry air stewardess Anna Kuzmanic in June 2000. When baby Mia followed at the end of the year, fervent hopes were widely expressed that the former roofer would change his ways. He was a husband, a father, his mentor and inspiration Bob Taylor was back at the Hawthorns, and he had a dream lucrative job… what more could anybody want?

But still the accusations and tittle-tattle persisted. Now they had a harder edge, with drugs mentioned most often.

Buoyed by a better team, including costly strike partner Jason Roberts, and the urgings of manager Megson, Lee returned to form in season 2000/01. In a brilliant purple patch, he scored back-to-back hat-tricks against Gillingham and Preston in November. Neither opposition played poorly, it was just their misfortune to come up against a marksman who was in devastating form.

Chance, goal. Chance, goal – metronome like. The sense of inevitability was palpable, with the roar of triumph seeming to start before he made contact with the ball. The striker was also in remarkable form in training.

Said his manager: *"Lee has had a marvellous few days and he deserves all his success. His three goals against Gillingham all came from inside the box. This week, they were all long-range efforts. His all-round game at the moment is magnificent and he has a real appetite for goals. He is working his socks off."* Or even his boots, because the pair of threes were both scored in borrowed boots, those of injured skipper Derek McInnes.

The consecutive hat-tricks coincided with the birth of his first child. Everything seemed to be going right for Lee – almost too much happiness in one go. At the time, questions were asked that if Lee was in such good form without having sex, just what was own-goal king centre-half Tony Butler doing off the field? By the end of the season, Lee had an impressive 23 goals in all competitions. Albion reached the play-offs, the club's highest finishing position for 15 years. This was real excitement for Baggies everywhere. And then Lee sent himself to Coventry.

AFTER THE COURT pronounced sentence, most Albion supporters were quick to condemn. They felt betrayed, and took the words of the tabloid press as their opinion. Only a minority, such as long-time fan Stuart Russell, tried to understand or look beyond the superficial facts: *"How the old adages 'Judge not lest ye be judged' and 'There but for the grace of God...' apply! Us older members of the community remember a time before breathalysers and the like when we frequently got behind the wheel knowing ourselves to be well over any sensible limit. In Africa, party after party saw cars roar off after the driver had to be virtually carried to his vehicle. A small percentage didn't get away with it, killing themselves or someone else and in the process ruining several lives. I and many others were the lucky ones – Lee Hughes was part of that unlucky 'small percentage'.*

"None of this is to excuse him or to try to reduce the impact his behaviour has had on the Graham family, or the passenger who now has to spend the rest of their life in a wheelchair. For her, there is no reprieve. Lee has lost his income and his reputation. Mr Graham has lost his life. But Lee has to live with something worse than loss. It is the fact that he himself caused the loss. How he must wish he could go back to the moment just before the crash and phoned for a taxi. Even worse than loss is the corrosive effect of guilt and irreversibility. Lee is now suffering far more than a six-year gaol sentence; every day he has to live with the guilt that is surely eating into his soul – and so he should. But then, so should a lot of the rest of us – and we've got off scot free."

In some small technical way, all Albion supporters have a cameo role in Lee Hughes' downfall. Accidentally of course, but to hero-worship Lee was a burden for him in many ways. (To develop the analogy to even more uncomfortable heights, there were terrace encouragements for The King to head the ball more often and supporters offering John Osborne cigarettes. Both were detrimental to the individuals' health. Neither the players nor their families would ever point fingers, more likely the opposite. The risks in that era were not always obvious.)

Many of the current England squad came from modest, inner-city council estate backgrounds. They've all had the benefit of media training and lifestyle guidance from Premier League clubs anxious to protect their investment. Lee didn't even have the benefit of an apprenticeship. The Albion were not strong financially or, arguably, even in common sense terms, when the Ginger One arrived in exchange for a big cheque. New arrivals, irrespective of cost or country of origin, had to fend for themselves as best they could. One bank official of the author's acquaintance, who remains anonymous, told me a sad tale of one of the club's foreign players who barely spoke a word of English, trying vainly to open an account with a West Bromwich bank. Had my acquaintance not been an Albion supporter who went out of his way to resolve the issue, the outcome for said player might have been a frustrating one.

But that doesn't matter. This lad was local, lived with his family, and was scoring goals, so everything must be OK. 'He'll be fine,' such was the club view.

LEE HUGHES ONCE had much in common with Robbie Fowler. Both lived near to their club. Both came from a close family of football lovers. Both were natural goalscorers and hit the big-time at an unprepared age. In his frank autobiography, Fowler readily admitted to a "*lot of mistakes*". He wised up quickly through his own efforts with the full support of a huge club. Fowler became the richest sportsman in the country, while Lee Hughes was At Her Majesty's Pleasure.

Lee became a different person inside. He was tougher physically with hour after hour spent in the gymnasium. Tougher mentally – after several years inside, Lee has heard and seen it all. He's well beyond responding to any barb which opposition supporters may hurl at him.

He needed a football club to give him a chance. Not just for his benefit but to enable him to support his children. Rather surprisingly it was Oldham Athletic who came to the rescue. After the predictable media storm, Lee Hughes was allowed to get on with playing football. He had a decent 18-month spell leading the line before an incident during a players' night had him packed off to Blackpool. The Seasiders didn't want him permanently and his future looked bleak. Fortunately, briefly *nouveau-riche* Notts County stepped in.

Lee quietly re-built some of his reputation at Meadow Lane. He's a senior pro, comfortable with the media and a wily old campaigner on the pitch. He's popular with supporters too, who bellow "*let's all do the Hughesie*". Lee was part of County's promotion team and the following season led the team to an FA Cup victory at Sunderland. They very nearly defeated Wolves in the League Cup, a near upset which won him Black Country brownie points.

TIME IS A healer for some Albion supporters. Lee's appearance among the travelling fans at Leicester in the League Cup was surprisingly well received. Many hugged him and wanted their picture taken with the former striker. Others chanted his name. *You Tube* footage show him lustily joining in with anti-Wolves chants, with a big grin and an illegal fag between his fingers. You can't take the Black Country out of the man...

Not everyone in the near 5,000 following that night was pleased to see him. Some resented his appearance at all; others were critical that some Albion fans "*were treating him like a hero*". The prodigal son took the difficult first step back into the Albion "family".

WE CAN NEVER forget that Lee's been incredibly stupid, and the Graham family will have to live with the tragic consequences. The hurt he's inflicted on his family cannot easily be dismissed either. Lee had too much too soon and didn't have the education or the right support to deal with it. Had he been born ten years later and cocooned by Albion's Premier League machine, his life may have been very different.

Richard Sneekes

1996-2001: 253 games, 34 goals

THE LEICESTER GOALKEEPER pulled a face at the ball wedged in the supportive metal triangle between post and bar. He'd barely seen it whiz past him from 30 yards out. A visiting Albion player with spectacularly long hair was accepting congratulations from team-mates while hundreds of exuberant supporters in the visitors' accommodation at Filbert Street bellowed his name. *"Sneekes... Sneekes"*. There were other cries too from a smug group waving their betting slips: *"That's my gas bill paid"*. Midfielder Richard Sneekes, the Black Country's answer to *Rapunzel*, was in the middle of an extraordinary purple patch for the Baggies. The news clearly hadn't reached the bookmakers of Leicester who offered highly generous 12/1 odds on the visitors new signing scoring the first goal. The betting kiosk had never seen such a long queue... No other cult hero can fairly claim their brilliance has subsidised supporters' household costs.

RICHARD SNEEKES' FIRST club was his local side Ajax of Amsterdam, a pedigree both unhelpful and helpful. He'd joined their famous academy straight from school, learning what he wanted to learn. Even at that early age, he was showing signs of being his own person, to make up his own mind – difficult in the essentially dictatorial world of football. Initially, his talent took centre stage and he made his first team debut at the age of 16 in 1985 against Haarlem, playing with Marco van Basten and Frank Rijkaard. He became the club's youngest ever debutant (even though the record was subsequently beaten by Clarence Seedorf, Richard's picture still hangs in the club museum).

A combination of his ego and stiff competition meant that, although he was playing regular Dutch schoolboy internationals, even a couple of under-21 matches, his club appearances were limited to just three. Shouting something very uncomplimentary at the Ajax reserve manager during a game was not a great career move, particularly as club boss Cruyff was in earshot.

He was transferred to FC Volendam for the 1988/89 season, where he scored his first senior goals, seven in 31 matches. From there, he moved on to play 127 games for Fortuna Sittard where he took on a surprisingly defensive role. After three seasons' experience, he took the chance of a season-long loan to Lugano in Switzerland. Richard found the football easy, a lower standard than he was used to. Most players spoke German, so he could communicate well enough until he learned Italian. Languages have never been a problem for the midfielder – he's fluent in four and can get by in several others. Richard had a scoring ratio of one in two, which attracted attention elsewhere which was fortunate because there was no contract on offer with hard-up Lugano.

Bolton Wanderers offered him a trial and Richard was tempted by the passion of English football. *"In England, the dressing room is noisy with lots of nice music. In Holland, it is very different, very tactical, the dressing room is very quiet and you must concentrate all the time."* The trialist was made part of Bruce Rioch's summer tour of Scotland in 1994. He had a stinker in the first game at Dunfermline, startled by the speed and physical presence of the British style. *"Thankfully, I played well and scored four goals in the next two games (at Ross County and Caledonian Thistle) and everything took off from there."* Bolton gave Fortuna Sittard £160,000 for his services in August 1994. It was a bold move all round as there were at that time few foreign players in the English game.

"I knew a lot of people back home thought that I wouldn't stay at Bolton very long, that I wouldn't last six months," admitted Richard. Fortunately Wanderers were a passing side, which helped his style. He regularly played alongside Jason McAteer in central midfield, though it was generally Jason who had the license to roam forward. There were other plus points as the man himself explained, *"It was a family club, something*

I didn't find at other clubs and Bruce Rioch was a fantastic manager. He could be firm, but he was a lovely man." Even today, Rioch remains Richard's favourite gaffer, in what is a very short list including the late Ray Harford and (surprisingly) Brian Little. Off the pitch, the Dutchman lived in a hotel only for a month, thanks to the Bolton chairman, who used his property business interests to find the newcomer a house.

RICHARD WAS LATER to follow in the chairman's footsteps and invest significantly in local property himself. In his time with Bolton, Richard was part of the side that reached the League Cup Final and also won the play-offs (mainly thanks to two goals from Fabian de Freitas) to enter the Premiership. *"Playing at Wembley for Bolton was the pinnacle of my career,"* said Sneekes a decade later. Promotion brought with it new players and Richard was increasingly overlooked. Rioch had left and his replacement Colin Todd gave him only 14 games (one goal). With Bolton lying bottom of the Premiership and more new players arriving, Richard couldn't see much future at Burnden Park.

MEANWHILE, BACK IN the real Second Division, West Bromwich Albion were once again struggling to retain their status. The previous year, manager Alan Buckley kept a floundering Albion side up, but a record-breaking dismal run of one point in 14 matches saw them in grave danger once again. Through dint of much shouting and punishment training, the diminutive gaffer steadied the ship to a degree, but linkage between deafened midfield and punch-drunk forwards was poor in an essentially rigid defensive line-up.

Richard sat in the directors' box for the Albion versus Port Vale match in March 1996. As a selling tool, a grim 1-1 draw didn't overly help. *"A lack of cerebral function,"* wrote the *Birmingham Post* reporter of his would-be team mates. More positively, it was the fifth game unbeaten and there was clearly a first team place up for grabs. After almost a fortnight of agonising, consultation with former Albion man Romeo Zondervan and backroom negotiations, the Dutchman signed for his second English club on 11th March. The Bolton manager was clear there was no future for him and so the Dutchman ultimately chose Albion over Megson's Norwich and Grimsby who'd all expressed interest. Deciding factor was the club's potential and the quality of SuperBob and Andy Hunt. The fee was £400,000, so the Wanderers had more than doubled their money. Equally it was a big commitment for the Baggies, their biggest single outgoing for 15 years, a transaction only made possible by a cash injection by new director Paul Thompson. It was to be the biggest ever transfer in Alan Buckley's long managerial career.

Naturally Richard was pounced upon for his thoughts and, as was to become the norm, he was always willing to express them. *"Albion have the quality players and skill to keep us in this division,"* he offered as his token PR gesture, before adding: *"The manager is very enthusiastic and he likes to play passing football. That is my kind of game and the reason I finally decided to come here."*

As ever, the acid test came on the Hawthorns pitch. Sneekes' debut was against bottom of the table Watford. Although he barely knew the rest of the side, he just got on with his trademark runs through the middle. One such run earned him his debut goal, a feat overshadowed by Bob Taylor's solitary Albion hat-trick and the home side somehow conspiring to lose a 3-0 lead. The eventual 4-4 draw felt a big letdown, but manager Alan Buckley praised the debutant, *"he was brilliant on the ball and the movement leading up to the goal was something else."* But the old-school Boss couldn't resist adding a barb *"after spending two weeks talking to his agent, the least he could do was give us a goal or two."*

His new signing obliged, scoring the winner in his second game, a 2-1 defeat of Barnsley and followed that with another, a close-range effort in a morale-boosting 1-1 draw at St Andrew's. Local sports writer Leon Hickman was impressed: *"Sneekes has provided West Brom with definition, as well as three goals in three games, speeding through midfield into positions of such menace they were possibly even less appreciated by his team mates than by Blues defenders. He is exactly what Albion have been missing for years, a player of pace and accuracy around whom to make the passing patterns that are only pretty embroidery unless they also have needle."* Cyrille Regis in 1977 was the last Albion man to score in his first three games, but there was more at stake in 1996 as every point was precious.

RICHARD'S STYLE AND panache enlivened a functional team playing carefully to orders. Most supporters took to the new arrival immediately. Supporter David Norman wrote in the pages of *Grorty Dick* fanzine: *"On his first couple of performances, Sneekes looks a different class to the typical run of the mill players we have signed in the past. He made an immediate impact and he's the only player in the side who can make a one on one chance look so simple. That said, he tends to drift out of games in the later stages and he hasn't added a great deal of bulk to an already light midfield."* Sneekes himself explained, *"It's my natural game. In Holland, they call it the Bergkamp position, but I was playing that way for Ajax before Bergkamp ever played for the club."*

But not everyone was won over or indeed ever would be. In this more cynical age, more is expected in return for big salaries. Supporter and author Ian Thomson offered a different perspective: *"Everybody tried, even hardened shirkers like Richard Sneekes. He even arrived in time for some physical confrontations, though I don't know whether this was deliberate on his part. Richard does remind me of the battleground stretcher-bearer, forever arriving at the scene of the action just after it has moved off somewhere else."* Both comments retained a measure of validity throughout Sneekes' Albion days.

Scoring in four consecutive games (Watford away 1-1) was too much to ask, however Sneekes immediately made up for it by scoring both goals in a 2-0 win at Portsmouth. Both were trademark dashes, accompanied by absolute belief that he'd score. After another blank against Luton, Richard's last minute six-yard tap-in winner against Millwall gave him six from seven matches – from midfield. And it was with this exciting background that Albion supporters multiplied their money twelve fold by loaning it temporarily to a bookmaker in Leicester.

THE DUTCHMAN'S GOAL wasn't sufficient to win the Filbert Street encounter as the play-off hopefuls battered away frantically at Albion's defence. They equalised and threatened to win it until, in injury time, Sneekes' corner found Raven's head presenting Albion with an unlikely win. At the time, the victory felt massive for both clubs. The Baggies believed they could stay up while followers of Leicester thought they'd missed the promotion boat (they hadn't).

WITH SUCH A run of results, relegation for the Baggies was unthinkable. Richard scored his eighth in a 3-1 defeat of Grimsby. Local radio commentator Tom Ross tried to sum up the moment. *"The delightful Dutchman does it again. A saviour, a hero and the fans and stewards are bowing to this long haired man from Holland. Michael Bolton in shorts has done it again."* There was another goal to celebrate in a 2-2 draw at Norwich. So many Albion supporters were thrilled by the revival that 500 were locked out, despite City having 10,000 empty seats.

Albion could ease off a little. Sunderland needed a point for promotion so we let them have it. The last away game was a 1-1 jog at Barnsley before the Baggies finished with a flourish in a 3-2 defeat of promoted Derby. The three top scorers Hunt, Taylor and Sneekes all found the net to make a round 50 goals for the three of them in league and cup. The newcomer had chipped in with ten in just 13 games. The Baggies finished 11th, ahead of both Blues and Wolves.

SNEEKES SWEPT THE boards at the Player of the Year award, although it was difficult to spot him because everyone seemed to be wearing long blond Sneekes wigs. As supporters' club chairman Clive Stapleton pointed out during the presentations: *"He has to go down as one of the best bits of business this club has ever done."* The man himself was genuinely embarrassed, uncomfortable with the hero-worshipping rituals and trying to dampen down expectations in what was Molby-esque Scouse overtones (a Brummie twang was to quickly replace the Liverpudlian). Only a decade later could he bring himself to admit, *"I had a great time."*

Such form couldn't last and indeed it didn't. Opposition got the message about the running man from Holland. Although the side remained unbeaten away until November 1997, too many draws and home defeats left everyone frustrated. Each loss was followed by Buckley screaming at his charges for a minimum of 45 minutes. In addition, Buckley had returned yet again to former club Grimsby to buy another attacking midfielder, Paul Groves. Playing the two together didn't work. The hapless Groves received a lot of stick partly because he was from Grimsby and because there was a perception he was literally getting in Richard's way.

There were some glimpses of the Dutchman at his best, such as setting up all three goals against Tranmere in September. In his painfully honest self-penned column in the *Sports Argus*, he insisted, *"I want to be known as a team player. To me, assisting in a goal is just as important. It is the result that matters, not who scores."* His thoughts were always bold and brave, providing a fascinating read, but, by not towing the party line, there were so many recriminations that he eventually felt obliged to give it up. *"Playing football is a privilege and it also carries with it a responsibility,"* he sadly noted.

Alan Buckley was the first of several Albion gaffers who wanted Sneekes to play his part in defending. Richard didn't really do tackling. Neither did he respond well to Buckley's rants. Although in public, he tried albeit half heartedly to maintain the status quo, in private he considered his boss lacked constructive ideas. Defeats were punished by endless sessions of running.

Furthermore, Richard found his disciplinarian attitude stifling. When he and another midfielder Stacey Coldicott were told to cut their hair, Stacey immediately complied. Richard ignored the instruction. By November, he could contain his frustrations no longer and talked to the press, *"I've had no chance to run on to the ball. All I have been able to do is play the ball back that is negative. I am being asked to get back and cover."* His PR timing was spot on because disillusionment with Buckley was increasing all round the Hawthorns.

Richard had just four goals by Christmas, including one on his 28th birthday at Swindon Town. He ran with the ball from 35 yards out into the penalty box and volleyed home with aplomb. There was also a 25-yard spectacular against QPR in a 4-1 triumph. Reporter Leon Hickman: *"Sneekes set the tone of the game with a whiplash fifth minute shot of the kind he delivered with the dependability of the milkman last season. The Dutchman then proceeded to probe tellingly, now more like a dentist."*

A second defeat by Wolves in embarrassing fashion (the infamous Crichton "dodgy 'keeper" match) saw the wolves gathering outside Buckley's door. Restraining his true feelings, Richard's line to the local press was a party line cry. *"We need to show we are mentally tough and we can do that by getting harder into challenges."* He hastily felt obliged to add, *"I know that I am not the best in that area, but I will have to start working harder."* After a limp showing in the next home game against Oldham, Buckley was sacked.

HIS REPLACEMENT WAS Ray Harford, better known as a coach than a manager, but what a coach! Sneekes and the rest of the side took to him immediately. The team recorded a memorable 3-2 win at

St Andrew's before Harford's appointment was made official. Suitably encouraged, Richard scored against Norwich and Southend, the latter a spectacular effort when, with back to goal, he turned and volleyed home from 25 yards. The gallant few in Sneekes wigs in the Brummie End were suitably impressed.

The Dutchman now felt he could come clean on his Buckley frustrations. *"I reached the stage where I hated getting up in the morning to go training. I was played out of position and I was lucky if I got one chance every five games. I was frustrated, angry and very unhappy. I seriously thought of asking for a transfer. But the new manager has totally transformed the atmosphere in our dressing room and on the pitch. He doesn't need to shout at players or belittle them."*

Albion finished the season in 16th place, with Sneekes scoring eight times. But his goals weren't so important in a squad that now boasted Hunt, Taylor and Peschisolido. That summer, Harford added the attacking talents of Kevin Kilbane and the youthful Lee Hughes to his ranks. There was no shortage of goalscorers, but could Albion stop the goals going in? Harford's solution was to strengthen the midfield in a 4-5-1 formation. The tactically astute Hunt was the lone striker, with Sneekes given free rein in support. Two powerful ball winners sat behind him. Such an arrangement was perfect for the Dutchman. *"As long as I've got the freedom to express myself, to do what I do best, I'm happy."* His game was at an exuberant peak – passing with panache, running, jinking – even a bit of tackling. Richard was so impressed with Harford both as a coach and as an intelligent man. *"Brilliant coach: he kept players interested and involved, even when they weren't in the side, and he was a lovely guy to talk to. You might have thought by looking at him he was a grumpy sort of guy but he wasn't like that at all. He knew the game, and knew what he was talking about..."* The respect was mutual. *"Sneekes makes some great runs,"* said Harford. *"He allows others to get chances because he takes the eye of the defenders."*

West Bromwich began to string results together. The first three games were won, opponents caught unawares by the Baggies' new formation. But they learnt and results became harder to achieve. Oxford United were one of the beneficiaries and their manager Denis Smith later admitted that Sneekes was quite easy to mark. *"You could see him charging forward as soon as Albion had the ball. 'Here he comes again.' Our defenders at Oxford used to laugh at him."*

A week later, Portsmouth defenders weren't laughing as Richard showed the full width of his vision. His corner set up Mardon for the first goal, his free kick set up Hunt for the second while his deflected volley gave Hunt the third. Urged on by some inspirational coaching, Albion actually won four games in a row, to reach the startling heights of second place. The last victory came courtesy of a winning goal by Sneekes against a bewildered Birmingham City, bewildered because they'd dominated the entire game. Sneekes had one chance late in the game and took it. It was his fourth successive goal in this hotly contested local derby and showcased Sneekes at his imperial best. He picked up the ball ten yards outside his own box before laying it off, kept on running and received the return pass just inside the Blues' box and fired in Müller-like from a low angle. Cue fantastic scenes and a spontaneous chant of *"One chance, we only need one chance."* – a cry still remembered to this day.

Paul Franks on BBC Radio WM spoke of *"daylight robbery"*. He asked, *"Did you see anything? It happened between 1.00pm and 2.50pm in the Hawthorns area of West Bromwich. A wealthy former England international footballer* [Trevor Francis] *and his team were robbed. It was pleasant. The assailant had long blond hair and spoke with a foreign accent, believed to be Dutch. Do you know him? He left his victims with nothing. Battered, bruised and cursing their luck, were you in the area at the time. Did you see what happened?"*

Sadly, this was to be the pinnacle for Ray Harford and Sneekes too. The following week, promotion certainties Middlesbrough beat their visitors 1-0. The Dutchman missed a good chance and gave the ball away for their winner. And then... Harford announced he was leaving. His argument that his regular travelling from his London base was damaging his marriage sounded dubious, considering his previous club was Blackburn and that his Hawthorns training sessions were regularly only twice weekly, leaving the other days to his coach John Trewick. But, despite much begging and pleading, exit stage left Harford. He was to admit later it was the biggest mistake he'd ever made, but that was no consolation at the time.

THEIR CONFIDENCE DENTED, the Baggies managed only one win (a close run 3-2 victory over Stockport with Sneekes scoring) in the next nine games. In the tenth game, they travelled to Molineux.

The home side singled out the Dutchman for special treatment. After various wild hacks at his person, the infamous Kevin Muscat finished off the job in only the 14th minute with a lunge that Rob Bishop of the *Mail* described as *"crude beyond belief"*. Sneekes, understandably, was furious, complaining he was the *"victim of a hatchet job"*. He feared his leg was broken. Thankfully it wasn't.

Perversely the loss of their stretchered-off creative midfielder only aided Albion, who brought on hard running Stacey Coldicott to join the simply hard Butler in the middle. The pair of them steamed into Wolves and took over midfield. Once on top, Andy Hunt's 72nd minute goal completed a memorable double.

But only two more wins that season left the Baggies in tenth spot. There were no more league goals for the Dutchman, though, he did score twice in an enjoyable 3-1 FA Cup defeat of bogey side Stoke. This prompted the *Evening Mail* to comment *"there is a small piece of land, front right of the penalty area at the Brummie Road end of the Hawthorns that is forever Richard Sneekes."*

Through his column in the *Argus*, Richard dropped repeated heavy hints that the 1997/98 season was to be his last in England. *"I love the club, but I have been thinking about this for some time."* As befits a man who polarised opinions between fans who loved him one minute for scoring a wonderful goal and loathed him the next for not racing back 40 yards to tackle, some supporters were offended by his words, considering him to be selfish and greedy, sentiments that in reality made little sense. Ray Harford offered him a three-year contract and with just one forward, Sneekes' support runs were fundamental to the whole team plan. Any return to Holland would be to a poorer league and far poorer wages. Richard simply missed his extended family. His *Argus* notes also revealed his social conscience – rare even then; a genuine awareness of those less fortunate than himself. For instance in the last pain-wracked, confused months of Ronnie Allen's life, Richard did his best to comfort Ronnie's wife Cynthia. He understood much of the turmoil they endured because his own grandfather was also suffering from Alzheimer's.

But Richard didn't move his family from Sutton that summer or any other, though there were to be many more occasions when he spoke longingly of moving home. His problem was simple, as he explained years later. *"The kids have grown up here. Three of them were born in England and they've all lived as English kids. They like going to*

Holland to visit relatives, but we go back less and less." Richard and former Miss Holland contestant Shirley have five children aged between 11 and 28. In Richard's latter Albion days, his eldest daughter, later to be Miss Holland and a Miss World contender, dated his team-mate. The mickey-taking was no doubt unrelenting.

AFTER HARFORD, THE next Albion managers were Denis Smith and Brian Little. Rugged ex-defender Smith was passionate and honest, but couldn't stop Albion leaking goals whereas Little gave the worrying appearance of heading towards a breakdown. Neither could bring Albion any success and neither really got the best from Sneekes, though he responded far better to Little. As webmaster Sid Collins from wbaunofficial.com had it: *"Under Brian Little, Sneekes was a bit more like his old self, but started running around like a man possessed. His work rate seemed to double for many of the games, but only to the detriment of his attacking play."* One outcome of this manic behaviour was Sneekes rapidly picking up seven bookings for tackling the man rather than the ball. Comically for one so regularly criticised for not getting 'stuck in', he was briefly one of the most booked players in the division.

It was highly noticeable how Smith sung from a diplomatic team sheet about the Dutch midfielder, *"Richard's been a big part of us all season. I have more conversations with Richard than anybody else. He is tremendously intelligent, super as far as his football is concerned, he's first class, and he can play. What I want to do is blend it into a team pattern, at times he wants to do it his way, and I want him to do it my way, but you know, fair play to him, he's a good trainer, he might not always like it. It'd taken time for Richard to decide, whether we like one another off the field or about what we do on the field, we might agree to differ, but when he's comes in here, he's been super for me for the foreign players with the language."*

How carefully and finely tuned those words were and from a gaffer not really noted for sophiscated prose. One major coup for Smith was the signing of a young Italian player in Enzo Maresca (together with two other Italians) and Sneekes' fluency in their mother tongue was vital to prevent the young genius from being isolated. In theory, the pair competed for the *"centro campista"* position, but Richard was only going to put the man ahead of the football. His translation/ mentor duties became quite familiar as more and more foreign players joined the Hawthorns.

RICHARD WAS ALWAYS a bit different, as Glynis Wright recalled after one encounter: *"The strange thing about Richard is the fact that should you ever pass him in the street, it wouldn't immediately hit you that he was a former player. Most recently, I saw him wearing his trademark baseball cap, rounded off with hooded top, T-shirt, well-worn jeans and white trainers, he looked for all the world more like an off-duty brickie than someone who had graced both Premiership and First Division stages. Add to that those well-remembered long blond locks of his, and what you have left is an image far removed indeed from the normal media stereotype of a top-rank player."*

Richard befriended some rank and file supporters and met them regularly socially. He made the effort to learn the names of many others and always acknowledged their presence with unfailing politeness. On away trips, as Lee Hughes wrestled with the bigger words in the *Sun*, Sneekes was studying the *Financial Times*. He's a highly intelligent, articulate and independent man – all qualities that many managers regard as a threat.

Truthfully, it's quite easy to imagine the former Ajax man (in itself another source of division) would not be straightforward to manage. Being a complex character, there were so many people and policies he wasn't keen on. He often appeared moody. All shades of Cantona, though Richard would resent the comparison. Echoes of Ruud Gullit too, with his understated laid-back cool image. *"Who gives a shit?"* was his view on many minor football matters. Also *"There are more important things than football."* Such as his family. Always first for him to the degree that he resented overnight stays or foreign tours.

There were only a few highlights for Richard as the year 2000 approached. His comically elevated position in the bookings chart (which earned him a new sobriquet "Dick Van Clog"); a fine strike in an unexpected 2-0 win at play-off hopefuls Watford briefly (and falsely) raised everyone's hopes; and a rare headed goal in an otherwise awful 5-1 rout by Crewe. That rare bright spot had to last a long time as Richard suffered more than most during the torpor of Brian Little's reign. One win in 16 matches told its own story. Little was finally led away, but not before Albion's league status was again in danger. The team were horrible to watch, low on confidence and generally only playing one forward. As the end approached, gallows humour surfaced *"we'll score before I die"* was a popular refrain.

The turnstile entrance to the manager's office clicked again. Little was out replaced by the relative unknown Gary Megson. The newcomer was a man in a hurry – having been turfed out of Stoke City by an Icelandic consortium – to get more from the players, get disillusioned supporters back on board and make the most of his opportunity at a club with potential. His handpicked cavalry arrived in the shape of five new players, including the inspirational return of Bob Taylor. Bob is everybody's mate, but he is a particularly good friend of Richard's.

Seemingly, everybody was now pulling for the club in their hour of need. Results improved and 'King Dick' finally found the net at promotion-chasing Barnsley in April 2000, his first goal in 12 months. It was a penalty, Sneekes' first go from the spot, but the regular marksman was injured and he was a senior player who needed a goal... A week later he scored again from the same position, in an extraordinary 4-4 draw against his old club Bolton Wanderers. The great escape was now most definitely on.

Urged on by passionate supporters, the Albion side sweated through the last few games and did just enough to keep their fate in their own hands for the last match – home to champions Charlton. Fortunately Athletic weren't overly concerned, particularly one Andy Hunt who showed no inclination to inflict grief on his old team mates. Cometh the hour, cometh the man – Richard Sneekes tucked away the first goal, sweeping in a left-wing centre. Taylor added a second and the job was done. At the time, the overwhelming feeling of relief felt like promotion, probably because Albion supporters had forgotten what promotion felt like.

FROM THAT POSITION, Albion moved forward, buoyed by six more signings and driven forward by their manager. This was a novelty, an exciting one and nobody wanted to rock the boat. But independent Richard was hinting subtly, and then not so subtly, that the emperor wore no clothes. These were brave suggestions at a time when Gary Megson walked on water. Few wanted to hear that there was another side to the manager – a domineering bully, a Ferguson without the silverware, if you like. His observations were dismissed and Sneekes was derided as *"lazy"*, *"do him good"* etc. But Richard was used to walking alone. Years would pass before other players dared to come out of the cupboard with similar grievances. Only then did understanding and appreciation of the issue widen, even if it is a truth still not accepted universally. Some supporters consider poor man-management as being of no great consequence.

It's entirely appropriate that Sneekes' most spectacular contribution to the season came against the manager's wishes. Albion were drawing 1-1 at Premier League Derby County in the League Cup – a respectable situation given, at that time, the Baggies had been unable to beat a side from a higher division for at least a decade. When Sneekes received the ball 30 yards from goal, he ignored his manager's bawled command to pass and instead found the net in spectacular fashion. Albion had a hugely enjoyable first leg win to savour while Richard later secured 'Goal of the Season' from supporters.

As Richard said later: *"I played a certain way to stay in the team and be part of a team that looked as if it might get promoted, which every player wants to be associated with. You can either turn against it like some of my colleagues did only to rot in the reserves or you get on with it."* His manager demanded that all his midfielders had to play like he did in his playing days, ultra high tempo, endless tackling and running. So Richard ran... and ran and even tackled occasionally too – which always drew a half-ironic cheer. He kept his place in the team, in fact only three players made more starts that season.

But as Richard, the purveyor of the beautiful game, explained, *"I wasn't looking forward to games. I wasn't playing how I was brought up. That year with Megson destroyed my love for football."* Playing an unnatural game was only part of the problem, because after all he'd grafted immensely under Ray Harford. It was more carrying out the orders of a man he didn't respect, despised even. He was particularly critical that Megson bore a grudge for evermore, citing examples of players ten years down the line who were still suffering from negative references from Megson. His private opinion on his last Albion manager isn't printable.

Richard didn't score many goals, but then again finding the net was not really his job. In the Megson team, the forwards scored the goals and the central midfield provided the graft and some inspiration. Albion did have a strong team spirit and guts. After so many years of limp passionless showings, this was great news indeed. Being a goal down or even two goals down was no longer "game over" as Crystal Palace discovered in February. They were 2-0 up very quickly but found themselves under siege. It was the Dutchman who led the fightback. The BBC's Adrian Goldberg described the goal, *"His brilliant drive after 43 minutes brought Albion back into the match at 2-1. A free-kick 25 yards out was tapped short by Clement to Sneekes, who skipped past the lunging Ruddock (a very blunt razor) and his vicious shot skimmed all the way home."* Albion drew 2-2, yet had created so many chances they could easily have taken all three points. Sneekes' strike was his 30th Albion goal. It was also his last.

Amid huge excitement, the Baggies made the play-offs with a game to spare. This was heady stuff indeed that reached its zenith with a 2-0 lead over Bolton in the first leg. Sadly Wanderers took advantage of defensive nervousness to escape with a 2-2 draw, took the lead early in the second leg and there was no way back. To an extent, defeat almost didn't matter such was the pride in achieving something after so many years of struggle. The last few pointless minutes were played out amid a cacophony of noise from the away end. The victorious Bolton fans were embarrassingly drowned out. Few realised that the weary Sneekes saluting the now all-standing, saluting Albion support was the last glimpse we'd have of him in an Albion shirt after 200 plus starts.

He was released on a free transfer in June 2001 amid a bitter exchange of words. *"Everyone expected that I would be offered a new contract, but it just didn't happen. I was disappointed with that."* Such was the rancour between manager and player that a parting of the ways had become inevitable. Had Albion finished mid-table or skipper McInnes been fit; Richard may have left even sooner. The manager's view was that Sneekes hadn't worked hard enough and hadn't followed his instructions. There were moves behind the scenes to extend his stay but with neither manager nor player willing to compromise, the initiative broke down.

SNEEKES TOOK THE first local-ish offer that came along – from Stockport County. He'd had offers from clubs in other countries including a three-year deal in Holland, but now had no wish to move his family. He rejected a two week trial at Crewe, believing he had nothing to prove. As he later admitted, *"I made the wrong choice in going to Stockport. I was too impatient and made a bad decision. It was awful."* County had hung on grimly to their First Division place for so long through organisation and workrate. Now they were on the slippery slope from whence they came. It's hard to imagine a sharper contrast between Stockport's long ball game and Richard's free thinking subtlety and intelligence. *"They're a Conference side,"* he astutely told friends later.

Albion visited Stockport in October. Bottom placed County could do no more than hump long balls out of defence, a fatal tactic against Megson's Albion. The Dutchman ran around helplessly in the middle, harassed by Derek McInnes, craving the ball, but seeing none of it. His name was chanted repeatedly by the Albion support mostly filling two sides of the ground. Mercifully, Sneekes was substituted midway through the second half with County two down. The visiting contingent once again chanted his name and demanded *"Sneekes, Sneekes, give us a wave"* (a huge and rare honour for an opposition player). Richard obliged with a wave and a rueful grin in his swansong for Albion supporters.

SNEEKES GOT OUT of Stockport quickly and tried Fourth Division Hull City. This suited him more, but he decided to leave when a new manager insisted he move to the area. He then played briefly in Denmark, commuting each weekend, but his heart was no longer in it. He bailed out of the Beautiful Game completely and found other ways to make a living. As he outlined during an interview, *"You move on. I've got a restaurant, property interests and a family which means there are thousands of other things to think about."*

WITHOUT THE LIMITATIONS placed upon him by football, he mellowed and was a laid-back host in the Italian restaurant he once co-owned. He tried his hand in finance, green lighting and property but most appeared short-lived. Richard plays for fun in charity matches and annually stars in the Midland Masters tournament, a format for which his skills are ideally suited. He turned out for Dudley Town a few times as a favour to the team coach. But the Dutchman wanted to put something back and started up a children's coaching business and bought in several old team mates such as fellow cult hero Bob Taylor to help him.

TO HIS OWN surprise, Richard caught the coaching bug. This was more than satisfaction for him, it was pure enjoyment. He became involved in Tamworth's Academy and started on his coaching badges.

EVER THE SHREWD operator, he spotted that basement side Hereford United needed a coach and he'd recently been on a coaching course with a fellow professional who had the ear of United manager Jamie Pitman. Backed by a glowing reference from former Bulls coach Richard O'Kelly, Richard was appointed first team coach at Edgar Street and was back in the professional game. Albion's most individual cult hero had wrong-footed everybody again.

Why Hereford? Probably because the Bulls were willing to recruit a coach with virtually no adult coaching experience just at a time when his children were growing up (or even playing alongside him) and media reports of separation from his wife indicated he was looking for a new focus. But mainly he wanted back into the professional game. Quickly, he realised how much he had missed the day-to-day involvement.

Although Hereford had a wretched 2011/12, with too much long ball and a confusing plethora of coaching staff, the Dutchman took much satisfaction from using his UEFA B licence to work with younger players. He's convinced now that coaching will be his future. Maybe one day at the Hawthorns?

Darren Moore

2001-2006: 116 games, 6 goals

LITTLE CONSIDERATION OR appreciation is accorded to the lengthy apprenticeship undergone by would-be professional footballers. Nowadays, this starts at eight-years-old and although its billed as none-too-serious, there are expectations and even diet sheets to follow. There is an imperative to learn, to progress, and to catch the coach's eye. Commitments slowly build – more training, learning, sacrifices, more games and even impacts on a choice of schools. Parents are involved too, transporting their offspring at awkward times to awkward places. Teenage footballers have their social and school activities limited and cannot enjoy the monetary benefits of a weekend job. For those still hanging on grimly to their hopes and the programme at 16, there are mandatory college studies. Always, individuals must be better, quicker and fitter than their team-mates. A few, a tiny few, are destined for the very top. The rest have to slog on in the hope of a lucky break, catching someone's eye. This after what is arguably an eight-to-ten year learning programme, longer than that of a nurse, an engineer...

DARREN MOORE WAS a "slogger". As he told *Faith and Football* website: *"By the time I got to 9 or 10 years of age my head was full of football. A love of the game was instilled in me from a very early age, and all I wanted to be was a professional footballer. The teachers would laugh at me at school when I announced my intentions."* Yet at the ridiculously early age of 16, the Handsworth-born teenager was already in the last chance career saloon having been released by Walsall. He was reduced to being panned by lower division prospectors.

Torquay United were furiously prospecting in Birmingham, offering trials to anyone looking remotely likely. Young Darren already stood out as a big lad and being big at Torquay's level is literally half the battle. After a week, the Gulls offered him an apprenticeship and the teenager took it a little reluctantly. Leaving behind his close family at just 16 was tough.

Torquay programme contributor Jon Aroussi takes up the story. *"I was a regular at Torquay's reserve games in the early nineties. He was a raw (and very hefty!) talent at that stage, but you could see he'd go far – he was the clichéd defensive rock, and you could see he scared forwards. Thus it was quite a surprise to discover what a gentle soul he was off the pitch.*

"You get used to seeing Gulls players around the pubs and clubs, but I only once saw Darren out on the town. Otherwise, I used to live just around the corner from his future wife Angie in Paignton, and would often see them very traditionally 'courting', walking in the nearby gardens and the like. Never saw Lee Sharpe (another Torquay recruit from the West Midlands) doing that! There's no denying he was a very popular player at Torquay. He looked a bit iffy in his early first team appearances, and inevitably drew a few guffaws at his physique, but I think the fans warmed to him so much because he was such a trier.

"Once, when we were attacking the family stand, 'Bruno' (as he was inevitably nicknamed) went up for a corner and met the cross perfectly. From the edge of the area, he headed the ball right over the family stand and towards Ellacombe Baths. To this day, I can count on the fingers of one hand the other players who've managed to head the ball out of the ground.

"One of his most notable days was being sent off in the 1994 play-offs. Torquay were at Preston with a two-goal lead to defend. The second leg score was 1-1 and Wembley was in sight... but then the sending off of Bruno changed the game completely. Torquay's ten men eventually lost 4-1 after extra time. Bruno was on the ground, being held down by North End's Raynor who had hold of his shirt and in an effort to free himself, he put downward pressure on Raynor's forearm ... you could hardly call it a punch. However, Raynor immediately threw his hands up to his face and rolled around dramatically. The 17,000 strong PNE crowd bayed for Bruno to be sent off and the official duly obliged.

"Darren was also known for attempting the odd 'sprint' down the wing, most of which usually ended somewhere past the halfway line. I remember one particular end to end run which saw Bruno puffing like a steam train, thighs wobbling, ground shaking (possibly), evading tackle after tackle. Naturally, he got to the edge of the box and scuffed his shot miles wide, but he got a massive ovation and cheers." Exactly the stuff that Baggies heroes are made from.

AFTER JUST OVER 100 games for Torquay, Doncaster made an offer for Darren. Rovers were in a higher division, so this was a step up for the now 19-year-old. The fee of £62,500 was at the time a new club record for Rovers. Darren or Bruno, as he was still called, was as popular at Belle Vue as he was in Devon. He was chosen as Supporters' Club Player of the Year in each of the next two years.

IN THE SUMMER of 1997, First Division Bradford City made an approach. Rovers asked for £750,000 for his signature, over ten times the fee they'd paid Torquay. Manager Kerry Dixon defended the club position. *"Some people might think that figure is a little over the top for a Division Three player, but it is how highly we rate Darren. He is only a young man and we consider him to be the best centre-half in the lower divisions. He is unbeatable in the air and he is very quick for such a big man. I am sorry to see Darren go."* The final fee was £90,000.

At City, Darren quickly found a travelling companion in defender Wayne Jacobs. They both lived in Rotherham. Wayne was a born-again Christian, a source of great fascination for Darren, who'd been bought up in a strongly Christian family, but decided that faith and football weren't compatible. He'd put football first *"I didn't think I could serve God and serve football at the same time"* but always a nagging doubt remained. Jacobs bought the issue to the fore. Darren accompanied Wayne when he addressed 'Christians in Sport' meetings and felt both inspired and uplifted.

Within twelve months of his arrival, Bradford City had a serious go at promotion to the Premier League. That season, WBA were just play-off hopefuls, reliant on Lee Hughes' goals. They needed points from a February visit to Valley Parade, but never looked like getting any because Hughes was completely marked out of the game by one Darren Moore. In desperation, Hughes resorted to some pretty feeble diving. It was the first time that Albion supporters became aware of the existence of the huge defender, and his efforts earned some grudging respect, mainly along the lines of *"look at the size of him!"*

On the last day of the season, Bradford City had to win at Molineux for promotion and the home side had to win to get into the play-offs. Thus it was at Prenton Park that a huge away following gave up backing Albion's feeble, lifeless efforts and listened excitedly as City recorded a 3-2 victory.

Darren had his dream shot at the Premiership, but the dream didn't last long. He thought he was worth almost double the weekly wage City were offering him, but Bradford chairman Geoffrey Richmond disagreed strongly. The player remained a fixture in the reserve team with just three appearances on the first team bench, as the defender explained. *"I trained with the first team, but I was told I wouldn't be considered. It meant I was training all week, but there was nothing at the end of it."*

BUT SOMETHING ELSE was happening in Moore's life, something more significant than mere football. *"That autumn, Wayne was facing a potentially career-ending injury, but I witnessed him making a remarkable recovery after attending a prayer meeting. Wayne went along to a church where people prayed and prayed for him, and, that night, he felt things begin to happen in his knee. Within three or four weeks he was back playing again."* Darren knew what he must do next. *"I invited Him into my life to be my Lord and Saviour"*

When the chance to move to Portsmouth for £550,000 on a four-year deal came up in November, the Yorkshire side, fearful of a free transfer at the end of the season, were eager to take the money. Darren didn't share this sense of certainty. He didn't know anybody in Hampshire. He prayed for guidance and trusted his faith to lead him. His faith led him to the South Coast. Darren and his wife Angie joined a Baptist church in Portsmouth and quickly found themselves amongst friends.

Comically, a month after the big stopper had departed – City posted their annual Christmas card, featuring a team photograph from the start of the season. Somebody else's head was 'photoshopped' on to Darren's body. They might have got away with it, had it been another black player. A year later, Bradford were offering players twice as much money as Darren was seeking, even though they didn't have it. Financial ruin was imminent.

THE BIG DEFENDER'S indecision about moving to Portsmouth seemed inconsequential compared to his leaving the Hampshire club 66 games later. This was a drama, a long-winded, confusing and tedious soap opera with claims and counter claims. As Albion people saw it, Darren had an opportunity to move out of the reserves at Pompey to Albion's up-and-coming first team and return home to boot. Naturally, supporters assumed that money was at the root of the impasse. It was only later, much later that it slowly dawned that Darren's reasons were not financial, it was far more about leaving his chum Linvoy Primus and leaving behind his Faith and Football charity project work in which he was heavily involved.

The transfer saga began shortly after pre-season training started and wasn't finalised until several weeks into the season. Most managers would have moved on by then. But Megson was adamant that nobody else would do. It was only later that Albion supporters understood just why this man mountain was worth waiting for. Throughout the Great Wait for his services, the man at the centre was unfazed. He knew exactly what was to happen and when, as Darren explained to the Faith and Football website. *"One night a still voice told me that I would move to West Brom, but that there were still things which needed to be done at Portsmouth before it would be completed."* Things that needed to be done included supporting his chum Linvoy Primus through the process of becoming a Christian. Unfortunately, none of these secular needs were communicated through the press.

Darren finally put pen to paper in mid-September with Pompey receiving £750,000 in exchange. Then fanzine editor Glynis Wright, who happened to be inside the club offices the following day, was the first fan to meet the new signing. *"When I clapped eyes on him, I thought it was an eclipse walking down the stairs, such is the sheer size and bulk of the bloke."* With no one at the club apparently looking after the new boy, it was beholden on Glynis to direct Darren to the players' lounge.

THE MOORES BOUGHT a new house in Solihull, sensibly situated next to an Albion supporter. At first glance, it was all too easy to do a double take as Angie is as short and small as her husband is tall and wide.

Albion supporters seem to like their players large. If they've got a modicum of skill to go with their build, then they've a decent chance of becoming a crowd favourite. Other than the obvious successes like "The King", Cyrille and Derek "The Tank" Kevan, Garry Thompson was a mightily big lad who earned admiration for his suicidal approach to the game. Brian "the Beast" Jensen was another and so too John "Yorky" Kaye.

Megson, too, liked his men big, introducing Sean Gregan and Geoff Horsfield, both of whom were popular. Few appeared larger than Big Dave at 6ft 2in and 15st. His talents dovetailed perfectly with the job that Gary Megson had in mind – a bloody big stopper that nobody was going to get past.

Moore made his debut at Watford, an ideal substitute as Albion were hanging on to a slender lead with only ten men. A seriously big defender was just what the wagon-circled Baggies backline needed. The large away following cheered him on enthusiastically, while it was all too easy to imagine the Watford players muttering *"Oh shit, look at the size of him."* The Baggies managed to hold on to their 2-1 score. It felt significant, a big victory against the odds, not least because of Russell Hoult's penalty save in injury time. Previously stuttering West Bromwich now had an away win to their name.

Moore's first start was at home to Burnley in a trademark Albion 1-0 victory and he quickly became a regular. His height and power fitted Megson's workrate and effort ethos. As skipper Derek McInnes put it, *"You look at Darren and you feel like it's going to take something to get past him."*

AS ALL ALBION supporters know, Darren Moore's nickname stems from a character in a Pot Noodle advert. Not for us the obvious *"Mooro"* from his fellow players or *"Bruno"* from all his previous clubs. The new name just popped up spontaneously during an evening match at Stockport County. There are at least two supporters claiming to be the originator, so let's credit both Fab Tracanna and Mark Dixon for their inspiration. Here's Mark's version: *"It dawned on me that the increasingly impressive monster at the heart of our defence looked like the big haired invisible friend from the Pot Noodle advert. I relayed this information to the lads around me and they agreed the surprising similarity. Thereafter, every full-blooded defensive header was cheered with a 'Go on, Big Dave' and other similar shouts. It generated much mirth around us and soon after, the chant of 'Big Dave, there's only Big Dave' seemed to spread into general usage."*

In public at least, Darren was polite about his new monicker. This was fortunate, as "Big Dave" became his proper name as far as supporters were concerned. Children would regularly ask *"Dave, can I have your autograph?"* and all too many adults would similarly forget when encountering the big man. *"I like to think I'm approachable off the field, that I give time to help people when I can, and that takes strength. The 'Big Dave' shouts are great. It's nice to hear all that."*

Even though he'd only been at the club a few months and was unlikely to have ever met any of the family, Darren attended Jeff Astle's funeral, along with captain Derek McInnes, Gary Megson and Frank Burrows. His thoughts were so typical of the man. *"It was a real honour to be there and it was important for us all to do the right thing for him in his memory."*

Ian Thomson is an author and an Albion supporter of some vintage. *"Other than Matt Elliott, I haven't seen a First Division centre-half snuff out West Brom's attacking threat with such consummate command. He has this ability, scarcely attributable to Albion defenders of recent times, to position himself correctly for dealing with crosses and dispatching them upfield with some power. Curiously, he seems to struggle with what you would imagine is the easier skill of positioning himself on the end of goalkeeper's punts."*

HIS FIRST GOAL came in November 2001. Not from a set piece as you might imagine, but an unlikely shot from 40 yards. The goal came too late to salvage a point in an irritating 2-1 defeat by Rotherham United. No one was more irritated than Big Dave, who thought he was the victim of a racist slur that afternoon and complained. Rotherham duly investigated and discovered a simple misunderstanding. Exhortations from the crowd of *"Come on, Monkey"* were not racist, but words of encouragement for the Millers' wide player Andy Monkhouse.

A month later and the Baggies had some business to sort out at Molineux. Just like the previous season, Albion were competing for the play-offs. Yet their comparative success was being eclipsed by a Wolverhampton mob confident of automatic promotion. That lunchtime, numerous Black Country folks of (normally) sober habit and demeanour screamed like madmen and whirled like dervishes on acid.

WBA got their noses in front thanks to a Jordao goal and would not give it up. Tempers flared and players piled into a scrimmage. Shaun Newton was late for the party. He charged into the fray, straight into Big Dave and rebounded like a table-tennis ball. After that, he kept his distance. Wolves were trying to mix it, but mix it with a Megson team? They've never been very bright.

Sheffield United were the ultimate mixers in the infamous 'Battle of Bramall Lane'. The Blades' three dismissals are too fresh in the memory to need repeating though one counter accusation was that Big Dave punched a Sheffield player during a ruck. Frankly, it's impossible to imagine Darren hitting anybody. Ever.

After Sheffield, there were just seven games remaining. Manchester City were certain champions, but just behind them Wolves were wobbling. To have any hope of overhauling them, Albion needed nearly all of those 21 remaining points. They grabbed 19 and it would have been 21 had the referee joined the rest of the world in seeing the infamous shot over the line against Rotherham.

It's hard a decade on to fully do justice to how desperately, gut-wrenchingly tense those remaining games really were. Only three goals were conceded as Big Dave & Co formed an impenetrable barrier in front of Russell Hoult's deckchair (Hoult was unbeaten in 27 league and Cup games). But scoring themselves was hard without key forward Jason Roberts. Old warhorse Bob Taylor's ability to be in the right place at the right time proved crucial.

The Baggies 93rd minute penalty at Bradford in the 45th game, put away by a hitherto unknown spot-kick specialist, is one classic tale for the grandchildren. Wolves were so nearly back in pole position with one game left, black talons outstretched for the prize…and then one Igor Balis snatched it back. The celebration was primeval.

The final game at home to Palace was a moist-eyed one. I never ever thought I'd see the day that the Baggies would re-join the top Division of the English League. Did Frank Skinner really only have thoughts for England with his famous line *"so many years of hurt?"* And our man mountain was there at the right place at the right time at both ends of the field. Big Dave's first half close-in effort killed the growing tension dead. The Baggies were 1-0 up and even a Dingle knew what that meant.

Wolves' pre-match grasping at straw contention that Palace striker Morrison would score a hat-trick, merely demonstrated that their nerve (or another part of their anatomy), had gone. Morrison, barracked throughout, barely had a kick. Perhaps, just perhaps as scuttlebutt has it, Big Dave had "a word" in his ear. SuperBob Taylor (who else?) added Albion's second. Job done, it was party time. I doubt being an Albion supporter will ever feel so good again.

BIG DAVE HAD no time to rest that summer. His charity, Faith in Football, aims to break down myths about Christianity and help underprivileged children through football. He and Linvoy Primus, together with others, spent nine days in India in May, running football workshops and visiting churches and orphanages during the rest of the day. *"It hits you in the face wherever you go, the poverty is frightening, and yet the people out there are so warm, so welcoming, so generous with their time and with what little they have. It's very humbling, and it was one of the best things I've ever done in my life."* Though he's understandably reticent on the subject, stories abound that Darren donated his entire promotion bonus to the charity.

Just what constitutes a cult hero is an ever-evolving concept over the decades. Around the birth of our football club, they were invariably local lads who made good. Later, a goal-scoring centre-forward was always likely to be favourite. That the players lived in and were part of the community was taken as the norm, remaining true into the Sixties and slightly beyond. In the days of the King and the Bomber, supporters knew their team would regularly visit the Throstles Club en bloc and be genuinely pleased to do so, smoking, drinking, playing snooker, darts etc with fans were perfectly normal activities. To see Mrs Astle or Mrs 'Bomber' in the queue in the butcher's shop was routine. The local press were considered part of the Albion family, where the Baggies went so did they and if the players ended up having too many drinks so did Ray Matts etc.

In the modern era, supporters and players rarely, if ever, meet and so a modern equivalent of cult status is largely defined by hand signals and body language. An upraised thumb, acknowledgement of the support or just looking committed is normally as good as it gets at the top level. 'Big Dave's' charity and church work was possibly the last exception remaining to the current 'no fraternisation' rule, though even here, anecdotal evidence strongly indicates club officials 'had a word' to limit his interaction with outsiders.

The Baggies' first attempt at running up the Premier League mountain ultimately flopped. Everything conspired against them – a change of chairman, the introduction of a transfer window and a quite awful run of opening fixtures against all the best clubs. When myopic referees were added to the club's burden, the tipping point was reached and the club sank. After 38 matches, the total of victories had only risen to a miserable six. The seemingly endless succession of defeats took its toll on everybody, even though Albion supporters made a stupendous effort to back the team. That their efforts met with so little response on the field or off it, was at least a contributory factor in reducing vocal support at the Hawthorns for several years.

THE SWIFT FORWARDS of the top Division regularly showed up Big Dave's lack of pace yet his popularity remained undiminished. To his credit, two headed goals were instrumental in setting up two of Albion's six wins. On the debit side, his short backpass was directly responsible for Russell Hoult bringing down Michael Owen at Anfield. Hoult was sent off and another defeat was imminent. At Goodison Park, Wayne Rooney teased him by standing off the big defender with the ball and inviting him to come and get it. The subsequent backlash says much about the changing nature of the game. His peers deemed young Wayne's party trick *'unprofessional'*. Whither now Willie Johnston at his best?

Big Dave's season finished two months early with a cruciate knee problem. Even though the league position was hopeless, his reassuringly large presence and charisma was instantly missed. Missed for nine months before a joyful roar greeted his late appearance from the bench in Albion's 3-0 win at the City Ground, Nottingham in November 2003. Most footballers would be depressed by such a lengthy absence. Not so Big Dave who literally had faith. *"I believe that such experiences mould you as a person, and I turned this one into a positive. We are taught to count such a test and trial as a joy and my time in physiotherapy was a joyous period."*

Once relegated, Megson set out to secure a second straight promotion, using exactly same tactics as before. Spend big money on big physical players and squeeze the life out of the opposition. The tactics worked again, but with a different response from many supporters. Enthusiasm for grinding out 1-0 results with now ample resources had waned.

Of course, there were some highlights – such as a return visit to Bramall Lane. In a predictably bone-shuddering encounter, the Baggies pinched a 2-1 victory, with Big Dave managing to score at both ends. The visitors' crucial equaliser came from a corner. As Neil Clement lined up in his appointed attacking position, Darren told him *"to get out of the way"* and took his place. Seconds later, Big Dave's head was making Mr Warnock very cross indeed.

Those who had doubts about the inevitability of promotion were silenced in a genuinely thrilling 3-2 win at Ipswich, the first win at Portman Road since 1984. A Sunday evening victory at Sunderland, the last opposition still standing, effectively wrapped promotion up with four games remaining. Albion defended with 11 men for the full game and pinched a 1-0 win in the last minute.

IN AN ATTEMPT to stay in the Premier League the second time around, new players were brought in, including several expensive defenders. Big Dave was out of the picture as new boys like Purse and Albrechtsen were preferred. Big Dave was completely unabashed at being overlooked and kept his belief in himself and the team as Glynis Wright discovered. *"Let me pass on a helpful hint; when talking to our enormous defender, never, never let it slip that you lack faith in the ability of the lads to come up trumps, because if you do, you'll get not a bunch of fives, but a five or ten-minute lecture on the power of positive thought! And that's what I got in heaps and Darren being the charismatic guy that he is, I came away thinking we could conquer the Universe tomorrow, never mind bloody Man City the following day! If that's a small sample of his preaching style, I reckon the greater part of the population in these parts will be converted unto the ways of righteousness by the time Mr Moore hangs up his boots."*

After eight games without a win, Big Dave got his chance against Bolton. He was an ideal choice to deal with the Wanderers' muscle men and the Baggies finally got their first win. But it was too little, too late for the manager. His Premier League players rebelled against his abrasive manner and the dismal 3-0 defeat at Crystal Palace a fortnight later was Megson's last in charge. Big Dave kept his place for a few games under new manager Bryan Robson, but the former England international needed more than Darren could give and he was out of the first team once more. Full-back Neil Clement was converted to centre-half and performed so effectively that Big Dave's days as a Premier League player were numbered.

He played little direct part in the tense later stages of the so-called 'Great Escape'. Big Dave did his best to encourage from the bench or the sidelines as the Baggies famously became the first, and so far only, club who were bottom at Christmas to retain their Premier League place.

BIG DAVE HAD his own challenge – a five day sponsored walk of the Great Wall of China for his charity. This was no tourist stroll. The group of walkers were tackling uncultivated parts of the Wall as the man himself explained: *"I think we covered something like 80,000 steps up on the Wall according to the guys who had pedometers – I didn't need to go into pre-season after that! In the five days we covered about 50 miles, which doesn't sound that much, but when you think about the terrain, the fact that about 80 per cent of it was uphill, that was pretty fierce. The walk raised at least £50,000 to support orphanages in India."*

Why did he go? Because he cared. *"We want people to understand our vision of what we're trying to do and to buy into it. I've been very lucky in my life and it's important to me that I can help out people less fortunate than me, to give them a head start, or shed some light on their lives."*

Darren's Albion days ended abruptly and painfully at Wigan early in 2006 where a pair of challenges, the first possibly excusable, the second definitely not, forced the referee to send him off. His crude lunge at Jason Roberts in Wigan's half of the field took some swallowing. Running off the pitch prematurely amid a chorus of angry cries from the frustrated away support was a rotten curtain call. That Darren couldn't handle the pace of the Premiership had become more and more evident.

It was clear that, barring emergencies, Big Dave wasn't going to be playing any more for the first team. He was still under contract for a further 18 months. Indeed, the club's media department would wheel him out every time they had a difficult message to sell. But Darren just wanted to play and honourably accepted a bid from Derby for his services in the January 2006 transfer window, just days after Wigan.

As Jeremy Peace put it: *"Darren has been a tremendous ambassador for the club both on and off the pitch since he joined us four years ago. He has been unstinting in his support of the club in its dealings with the local community and on that front he leaves a big hole to fill."*

One regular fan, known universally as Des Baggie (nicknames are commonplace around the Hawthorns), had his own personal recollection. *"My best memory of Big Dave was at the famous 'it was in the 93rd minute' Bradford game. Hundreds of otherwise ticket-less Baggies bought corporate tickets in desperation. Such were their numbers, they swamped the posh seats and someone was even bold enough to take a flag. Naturally, they had to travel to the game in suits and ties, but there was compensation in the form of access to the club lounge after the game. The atmosphere resembled a drug high without any drugs after the last minute penalty winner. Big Dave was the only player to come into the lounge and meet the supporters to a roar of 'Big Dave. There's only one Big Dave'.*

"He stayed and signed autographs for everyone that wanted one, standing head and shoulders above all the Baggie supporters. I'm looking at his autograph on my Bradford programme and feeling very sad that he has left us. He was a giant amongst so many pygmies at the Albion and if only our hierarchy had a fraction of the honesty and passion for the club that he did we would be in so much better shape."

His departure was immediate, as the Rams needed new blood to prevent relegation. There wasn't much time to say goodbye to his playing colleagues, never mind supporters. Just like Bob Taylor, that wasn't sufficient. Big Dave cheered everyone up during a moribund home defeat by Middlesbrough by the simple act of stepping on to the pitch at half-time.

Boldly, he took the microphone. *"I'd like to thank everyone for their support. The amount of letters and emails I have received from fans since I left has been truly tremendous. That's why I wanted to come back and say my farewells properly."* The chorus of '*Big Dave, there's only one Big Dave*' was predictable, its volume and scale with all four sides of the ground joining in was not.

But this was not to be Darren's last involvement in Albion's fortunes. With Albion predictably relegated again, Derby were now among our opponents. For both league matches, there was the bizarre spectacle of "Mr T" (as he was known by the Pride Park regulars) being cheered to the heavens by the opposition support yet receiving only lukewarm enthusiasm from Rams supporters. Both Derby and Albion were fighting for promotion. Under Billy Davies, the Rams competed strongly for automatic promotion but just missed out and finished third. They avoided the Baggies in the play-off semi-finals but with both sides winning, Darren was in the uncomfortable position of playing against us at Wembley. It says much for the man himself that he voiced his unease. As he explained to author Nick Johnson: *"It was hard because all my old team-mates and all the staff I knew so well were there. West Brom is a fantastic club and I had five great years with them."*

Most footballers playing against their old side in a big match either wouldn't be bothered, would want to prove a point or be wary of concerted abuse. No one would be barracking big Darren Moore.

On paper, Albion had far better players than Derby – men such as Koumas, Kamara, and Phillips were all match winners. But a team – no, there were too many within the ranks who were overtly selfish. Billy Davies' spoiling tactics and his team's togetherness made for a horrible, horrible day at Wembley which infamously the Rams won 1-0. Big Dave didn't celebrate with his East Midland team-mates. His concern was for his former Hawthorns mates. He moved from man to man, offering words of consolation and a sympathetic handshake. Then he turned to applaud the departing Albion hordes. His was a magnificent gesture, worthy only of a cult hero. *"I spoke to a few of the Albion players at the end because I wanted to show my respect for them. I wanted to let them know that they'd taken part in a great final. I also showed my appreciation to the Albion fans that I still enjoy a good relationship with."*

DERBY WEREN'T READY for promotion. Billy Davies knew it and his reward was the sack in November. Derby were simply the worst ever team since the advent of the Premiership, amassing just 12 points. For their players, it came down to mental strength and there was no one stronger than the man from Handsworth. If anything, he was slower than his previous sojourn at the top level but the County managers kept sending him out because he could handle the pressure.

Darren's reward was another move – this time to unfashionable Barnsley, striving as usual to stay in the Championship. Of course, he remained unbeatable in the air but his increasing lack of mobility regularly drew criticism from the Oakwell faithful. In turn, they couldn't understand why Darren was so insanely popular with Albion supporters, especially as his keeping-things-simple at the back style gave the Tykes another win over our favourites.

It was somehow fate that the big defender's last game in a Barnsley shirt should be at the Hawthorns on 1 May 2010. We were already promoted and could afford to be magnanimous but even so the outpouring of affection for the big man was immense. Once again, Albion couldn't score past him so it was a relief as well as a noble gesture that Darren was substituted close to the end. Perhaps shamed into it, the Barnsley supporters joined the rest of the stadium in rising to their feet to cheer the old warrior, for the last time. "*Big Dave, there's only one Big Dave*" was roared lustily. Darren admitted later, "*I will never forget the reception I received. It was incredible.*" Albion finally found the net in injury time.

His full-on Hawthorns exit would have been a fitting end to a decent career but there was life in the veteran yet. His neighbour, one Paul Peschisolido, needed an experienced professional for his Burton Albion team. It was the basement division of course but the challenge, the opportunity to continue playing at a very local club was too much to resist. The manager wanted Darren for his influence in the dressing room (and a chauffeur too after his car was stolen) almost as much as his experience on the field. At the age of 37, Darren still enjoys playing so much, but his legs sometimes betray him. He played in around two-thirds of the Brewers' League matches and his motivational skills were vital as his club only just retained their league status in 2011. Despite his ageing limbs, Pesch retained Darren for another six months before a parting of the ways was agreed in January 2012.

THERE WAS FINALLY some recognition for his activities in the community when he won the PFA Player in the Community Award at the 2011 Football League Awards. In his acceptance speech, the big man confessed: "*I am almost lost for words to have won an award for something that I enjoy doing very much.*"

Darren's officially remembered with the newly built 'Darren Moore' Suite, next to the boardroom. People with £3,000 to spare each season can enjoy Premier League hospitality surrounded by photographs and memorabilia of Darren. For the rest of us, we have the memories of a down-to-earth Man of the People. A genuine cult hero.

Tony Mowbray

2006-2009: 140 games (as manager)

IN MAY 2009, relegation was imminent. West Bromwich Albion had to beat Liverpool to retain any chance of staying up. Given that the Baggies hadn't scored against the Reds since 1986, the cause seemed hopeless. Some supporters merely hoped for an Albion goal, regardless of the ultimate outcome, just to say, *"I was there when..."* Behind the scenes, Tony Mowbray was certain that he would be sacked after the match. Albion being bottom of the Premier League made him vulnerable and more significantly, his relations with the club owner were grim.

No hindsight was necessary to realise Mogga's men were in trouble before the opening fixture. Not for the first time before a Premier League season started, an Albion manager didn't have the tools to do the job. The champions needed strengthening, yet started without two of their main men, having lost Gera to Fulham, and Phillips to Birmingham City, both without a fee. A quarter of the club's goal output went with them. Given the financial strictures that Mowbray operated under, finding ready-made replacements was a near-impossible task. As he said himself: *"We have one of the lowest wage bills. But that is the challenge. I have to find diamonds among the pebbles."*

His policy options were to gamble on old lags (as Robson did), buy "damaged goods" or bring in potential for a long-term plan. Mainly Mowbray opted for the latter. His long-term successes would include

Olsson, Dorrans and Mulumbu although all were on a slow learning curve. He didn't – or couldn't – address the need for a goal scorer, which was predictably fatal.

THE FIRST WIN came in mid-September against West Ham. Two more quickly followed, which gave some hope but a horrible run of one point in eight games and goals pouring into our net was deflating. After a predictable outmuscling at Stoke in November, Mogga could only wearily say, *"Our players are making the wrong decisions at the moment and we're not scoring enough."* As the defeats continued, Albion's search for a striker revealed the reality of being their manager. *"Our club is scouring Europe trying to find somebody we think could come and help us. If we are going to buy, he's going to have to come from one of the minor leagues and that is a bit of a gamble. The best bet is to try and bring in two or three and hope one of them falls good, rather than get one who doesn't quite do it and you're stuck with that. We'll look to hedge our bets in January."* In February, the home match against fellow strugglers Newcastle was built up as a must-win. More defensive howlers gave the Geordies all three points. After that, hope ebbed away after another long run without a victory.

In April, Mogga admitted: *"We got the squad balance wrong but I knew that in August. It's about buying the right players. We are where we are on the money we've got with a football club that carries no debt whatsoever."* He drew a comparison with Portsmouth, who'd bought quality players with money they didn't have.

There was common belief in the stands that had the Baggies had more steel, or the manager varied his tactics a little, the season's outcome may have been different, a viewpoint given strength with hindsight by the later successes of Roy Hodgson's team. The view of DJ EmmJee of www.westbrom.com was typical. *"I think he focuses TOO much on ball retention and playing a 'pretty' game. This is good, but I think he needs to realise that we have to be more aggressive and get in these team's faces."*

Fellow cult hero Don Goodman disagreed. In his opinion *"Albion went down because too many players made silly individual errors at key moments in games."* Donno's conclusion was probably closer. Mowbray rotated his defensive options but the mistakes continued and the solution could only be better, more expensive purchases. There is another school of thought that the pain of relegation was necessary again as the only way to ensure that the Albion board had a re-think about their transfer policy. Experienced Premier League players expected a salary to match.

The Baggies' likely return to the second tier would be before a TV audience thus there was a collective determination among supporters for dignity in defeat. As if they were similarly minded, within their limitations, the team were having a real go at Liverpool. Team and supporters drew strength from each other and, at times, the Scousers were genuinely stretched. Not stretched enough, though, because the visitors scored against the run of play, thanks to another defensive gift.

Somehow, it didn't matter that much, after all, such an outcome was familiar. Relegation was near enough certain anyway, we just wanted that goal. Albion were really going for it, hammering away at the Reds' defence with some style, urged on by tumultuous vocal backing. *"Tony Mowbray's Barmy Army"* rang out again and again. The man himself was exhorted to wave to the crowd, which he did gratefully. Meanwhile, his team became so desperate to score that Liverpool exploited yawning gaps to net their second goal. Albion strikers hit the post, were denied a decent-looking penalty, and missed several other fine chances. Situation normal.

So the Baggies were relegated again, and still hadn't found the net against Liverpool. Albion's full-on effort that day received rapturous support, while there was a special acknowledgement of the manager and his philosophy. His name was chanted repeatedly. A full-on lap of honour was expected ... and delivered. Players and management walked all four sides of stadium to genuine applause. Such a response to relegation defied traditional logic, but it was all about supporting a cult hero – a man of decency, honesty and purveyor of football in the best Albion traditions – Tony Mowbray. The national media were taken aback. Ewan Murray of the *Guardian*: *"Only Hawthorns regulars could fully explain why Mowbray was still afforded a rousing reception..."* Pounced upon by the media for comment, our manager said: *"The overriding thought is one of disappointment for the supporters, because we have been relegated, frustration as well because I think today's game really epitomised our season."*

There was no "empty your desk" call from the club owner that night. Jeremy Peace is always sensitive to strong public opinion. Mowbray was still the "man".

There was one more Premier League game to play at Ewood Park. The theme was Tony Mowbray, with masks supplied by Maskarade. At that time, Tony was only the second individual considered worthy of a theme day (Tommy Gaardsoe was the first in 2004 and the incomparable Tony Brown would become the third in 2011). Thus it's an honour worthy only of cult heroes. Mogga sounded quite shocked when asked for his thoughts by Chris Lepkowski: *"Masks of me? That will be scary. I don't know why I was chosen. But, from a guy who didn't know anything about West Midlands' football before I came, the supporters have been amazing in their support of the team and backing. I'm not trying to be sycophantic but it's quite humbling to have a support that's so supportive of a team that's bottom of the league."*

The occasion (Tugay was playing his final game for Blackburn) was bigger than the match, which predictably ended goalless. The Baggies finished four points short of retaining their status, which, given how far the side fell short of previous survival targets might optimistically be deemed as a step forward. They conceded 77 goals (the Albion side that finished 11th in 2011 only let in six fewer goals) but the key was not scoring enough.

For Tony Mowbray, the root relationship problem remained. Peace held the purse strings, and had the final say on transfers. Trust and belief in a club manager is fundamental to the success of any football club, and the former 'Boro star was certain that he enjoyed neither.

Jeremy Peace has built a reputation of not getting on with managers. Megson obviously, but Di Matteo and Robson also saw red. Of course, we don't have Peace's version of events and truth is an inexact science. It is, however, difficult to see how many managers could be so wrong so often. Wily old Roy Hodgson has the huge advantage of having spent half his lifetime dealing with club owners' egos all around the world, but his frustrations were visible to astute observers.

Monetary restrictions and transfer blocks always have flashpoint potential, but according to Mogga, his relationship had reached such grim proportions that he loathed going to work, a difficult place for a self-confessed football nut. He dreaded seeing the chairman's car in his training ground car park. In his mind, the Liverpool show of affection could offer only a stay of execution. He noted Bryan Robson's early season exit and could envisage only the same fate for himself.

But like most talented people in the game, Tony had options. Media whispers of his taking the Celtic job had started a full year earlier. The Glasgow outfit were "special" to him (In a much earlier open letter to their supporters he wrote *"Celtic is more than a football club and all of us who support the team help to make it a special institution."*) Glasgow was also the home of his first wife's family, with whom he remains in daily contact. The decision was far from easy, despite soundbites suggesting otherwise. He liked and respected his Albion squad, who remained "work in progress." The feeling was largely mutual. During an interview with Simon Turnbull, Dean Kiely said: *"If somebody's honest, open and genuine you respond to it. That's what's refreshing about our manager, because in football there's a lot of political manoeuvring and people are not always straightforward, shall we say."*

Mowbray knew Scotland was no nirvana. In an interview with the *Scotsman* newspaper, Tony found Scottish football *"suffocating"*, with the *"same old faces, the same managers, players and media people, all the time"*. Far worse was the power of the Scottish media. Tony isn't terribly comfortable with journalists at any time, and the Celtic hacks were infamously intolerant. Put simply, would the frying pan be more comfortable than the fire? It was a hard choice, but Tony opted for Scotland. Peace's demand to reduce his first team squad by a third was probably decisive.

It's nothing new for a popular manager to feel obliged to leave a club, having fallen out with the chairman. Martin O'Neill splitting the blanket with Villa is a recent example. Our own Johnny Giles and Ronnie Allen both felt their positions were untenable, and bailed out. Even Brian Clough did it. So too did Don Revie, after years of wrangling with Leeds United directors.

The saga dragged on painfully for a few weeks, until the middle of June, before Celtic realised they had to pay top dollar to Albion to take Mowbray, or lose face. Peace was at his ruthless best, citing the supporters' reaction to Mogga after the Liverpool match, among the reasons why Albion weren't going to let him go cheaply.

The public thoughts of the ex-Albion manager were carefully understated. *"I think relationships are very crucial in the hierarchy of football clubs. As the Premier League season unfolded the true personalities of people come out. I've got to enjoy going in to work every day, it's what keeps me driven and that had become a little bit strained, so this opportunity is something that I have taken on with a very clear conscience."* He also added: *"If supporters feel let down, I can only apologise"*, though very few media sources included that phrase in their coverage.

Although he was understandably focusing on his own future, Mowbray's resignation was most helpful to his successor. Instead of having to take over mid-season with a budget further shrunk by having to pay off Mowbray, Di Matteo took over in pre-season with an extra £2m to spend (this sum being the compensation clause in Mowbray's contract). Had the scenario been the former rather than the latter, who knows whether Albion would still have achieved promotion?

Many Albion supporters revised their opinions on Mowbray after his summer exit, unaware or simply not caring about behind-the-scenes issues. There was a feeling of betrayal and letdown after buying into the manager's philosophy. What was most damaging was his public appeal to players to show the ancient culture of "loyalty". There were many variants on the theme of *"he asks for loyalty then pees off himself..."* Impossible to defend it, and our ex-manager was quick to apologise each time his attention was drawn to this dichotomy.

To maintain popularity as a manager is far more difficult than for a player, certainly in the higher levels of the game. His opinion is sought almost daily on a wide range of subjects and there are always difficult decisions to make around team selection, selling and buying. It's impossible to please all of the people all of the time especially when managers deal with the consequences of board-level decisions.

Among the baggage which Mowbray inherited was John Hartson, with a salary even more vulgar than his waistline. He was criticised for not dispensing with his services, but who'd have him? There were moans too about the infamously lazy-looking Luke Moore even though his arrival was not the manager's choice. There was bewilderment about the number of chances offered to "Shergar" McDonald, who was just enthusiastic at best. Mowbray's belief was later vindicated when the player was sold for several times his buying price.

It's unfortunate that more Albion supporters didn't take the chance to attend a supporters' meeting when Mowbray was the speaker. This was the real deal. Put aside the *Daily Mail* image of Mogga being *"Jack Dee without the jokes"*. It's only when talking directly to supporters that the decency and honesty of the man can emerge. The ever-persistent Amanda Hume invited him to guest at Sutton Branch WBASC during his extended gardening leave from Celtic. He didn't have to attend but was happy to do so. He was very warmly received by a large, enthusiastic attendance. But that's Mogga – to meet him is to be impressed by him, and that goes for every club on his CV – even Celtic.

A whole generation know exactly when Anthony Mark Mowbray was born, because 22 November 1963 is the same day on which President Kennedy was assassinated. Tony was born and raised in the modest surroundings of Saltburn-on-the-Sea in the North East. From a very early age, he decided football would be his life, much to the concern of his head teacher. Tony acquired his nickname Mog or Mogga in primary school because he loved to play in goal – Mog the Cat. One treasured memory from his youth was as captain of a tournament-winning team, collecting the trophy from one David Mills.

Tony watched Middlesbrough for several years from the terraces. It was always his ambition to play for his local club. Aston Villa came close to hijacking that plan by inviting the 15-year-old to Birmingham and introducing him to their big names. If meeting Andy Gray had turned the head of the Saltburn-born youngster a little bit more, the immersion into Seal culture would have changed his, and Albion's history. But it was 'Boro who secured his teenage signature, Tony felt his best position was as a goalscoring midfielder but his size meant that his coaches always wanted to play him at the back.

MOGGA MADE HIS first team debut in 1982, at fiercest rivals Newcastle before his 19th birthday. By the following campaign he was a fixture at left back before moving to central defence for the start of 1984-5. Thereafter he was the first name on the team sheet. The fans loved him because unlike so many of the expensive but uncaring superstars that came later, it was obvious Boro meant as much to Mogga as it did to all the supporters. Bruce Rioch soon made him captain and famously said: *"If I ever had to fly to the moon, I would want Tony alongside me."*

BUT THE NORTH-EAST club had just been relegated to the third tier (sensibly still called Division Three in those days). The crowd for the final League game was below 5,500. The financial wolves were baying and 'Boro slipped into administration. Rescue was the usual series of missed deadlines and delayed crunch points. The creditors were finally satisfied at 5pm on the day before the new season started. Ayresome Park had been locked since early May and was in no state to stage a fixture so 'Boro's opening game took place the following day at Hartlepool's Victoria Park.

The fact that there was a team ready to play is quite remarkable. Nobody had been paid since the end of the previous season so, their contracts having been breached, players and staff had been free to join other clubs. Almost all remained, loyal but unpaid. They took their cue from manager Bruce Rioch who turned down an offer from a top flight club saying *"I have unfinished business here."* It is widely rumoured many of the players were persuaded to stay by a 22-year-old defender – Tony Mowbray.

AFTER THE TRIALS and tribulations of the summer of 86, a lunar mission for Mogga and his gaffer seemed relatively straightforward but Rioch's remark became the title of the Boro Fanzine *Fly Me to the Moon*. Loyal supporter, defensive lynchpin, fanzine inspiration, captain and, eventually, (after the fans called for his appointment ever since the departure of Bryan Robson) manager. There will truly only ever be one Tony Mowbray.

Local newspaper columnist Anthony Vickers added: *"Mogga attained iconic demi-god status. He was a good player, a great leader and an industrious and committed defender who scored his share of goals but it goes beyond that. Mogga is the one who the crowd identified with: a worker, a battler, a gritty never-say-die, bleed-for-Boro supporter transported to the pitch as a cypher for us all."*

MOGGA PLAYED WELL over 400 games for Middlesbrough before asking for a move in November 1991. Celtic offered £1m, then an extraordinarily large sum, and Mogga was on the move. In July 1992, he returned to Ayresome Park for his testimonial match against his new side. Despite kick-off being an unlikely 11am on a Sunday, over half of the 20,000 plus attendance were Scottish visitors. It was an extraordinary show of support from two sets of supporters.

To truly understand Tony Mowbray, it's essential to read his co-written 1995 book *Kissed by an Angel*. This painfully poignant account outlines how he met his first wife in Glasgow, and then had her taken away with breast cancer at the ridiculously young age of 26. Contributors to the book detail the footballer's devotion and determination to be with her constantly right until the end. Lou Macari described his amazement how Tony nursed Bernadette all night and all morning, and then insisted on playing in the Old Firm match three hours later. Tony's own thoughts are matter-of-fact but heartfelt, and always grateful to his team-mates and Celtic fans for their support. The sum of the whole book is quite overwhelming.

Many could never recover from such a desperate experience. It is to Tony's immense credit that he's moved on to have a fine career, while maintaining his generosity of spirit. Celtic legend Andy Walker said: *"Everyone associated with Celtic remembers that awful, difficult time that Tony had. But there was this great dignity and humility about Tony. He went through the dreadful tragedy of losing his wife to cancer while he was a Celtic player, and anyone who knew Tony and saw the way he handled that situation will know what an impressive figure he is."* Tony is clear that his top priority in life is his family, and there are more important concerns than losing a football match. As he told the *Daily Mail* years later, *"It has given me a certain perspective. I don't get too uptight with my team."* The book includes the thought from Tony that one day he would return to Middlesbrough as their "gaffer." Fifteen years later, he got his wish.

Thanks to numerous injuries and supporting his wife's battle against cancer, Tony only managed 78 appearances for the Scottish side. But he did leave a lasting legacy – the Huddle. Years after that first Huddle on 23 July, 1995 before a friendly in Germany, he said: *"Every player likes to leave something that people can remember them by and maybe the Huddle is mine at Celtic. I'm delighted to see it's still going strong, because it's a brilliant way of uniting the players and the fans. It's in the fabric of Celtic now."* Celtic teams at every level do the Huddle, and since 2010, supporters have followed suit.

With so many painful memories, he needed to move on and literally did so, joining Ipswich for £300,000 in July 1995. In a letter to Celtic supporters, he remembered: *"At a time when my life was decimated, and I was as low as any human being can get, the love and warmth I will never forget. Words of support poured in from Celtic folk, from all over the world and at a time when my life was empty, they helped fill that void with their compassion. ..Celtic will always be 'my club'."* New signing John Hughes was sad to see him go. *"The class just oozed out of him, the way he conducted himself. There's only one word to describe him and that's a 'gent'. There was nothing false about Tony, he was a gent and you could see the respect everyone had for him."* Fourteen years later, Hughes was the manager of Hibernian battling against Mogga's Celtic team.

Tony Mowbray finished his career in the heart of the Ipswich defence. By playing as a sweeper and literally using his head while those around him (notably Mark Venus) did the running, Tony extended his playing career to the age of 37. His 661st and final game was a dramatic one, the 1990 Championship play-off Final against Barnsley. Captain Tony was a Wembley virgin, but he scored the crucial equaliser and led his team to promotion with a 4-2 victory. After 150 odd games for the farmers, his enthusiasm and know-how was vital to the club, and he was retained as first team coach. To mark his relationship with Ipswich fans, Mowbray remained as president of the Ipswich Town Supporters' Club, even though he was no longer a player.

Derek Davis of the *Green 'Un* remembered an incident, typical of the club coach. *"Mowbray was on a coaching course in Essex. A girl working in reception was going through a difficult time, and was depressed. She opened her heart to a sympathetic Mowbray, who offered not just words of wisdom and support but a simple gift. It was a pin of a guardian angel."*

In an extraordinary Premier League debut season, the self-styled 'Tractor Boys' finished fifth and qualified for Europe. But second season syndrome sunk Ipswich, and with it went the manager. Mowbray was in temporary charge for the last four games of the season as Town were relegated. More significantly as a long-term influencer, Tony travelled to London by train to see all of Arsenal's Champions League games to *"marvel at what they do".*

Happily Tony started a new relationship with his hairdresser, Amber. They eventually wed, having worked through the issue of the third person in the relationship. However, their marital home would be short-lived as Mogga was ambitious, and wanted to manage his own club. He made applications for posts at Hartlepool and Blackpool among others, but his lack of experience held him back. Fortunately, he persisted. At Hibernian, both directors and players alike were frustrated by the efforts of ex-Albion man Bobby Williamson, who once candidly said *"if you want entertainment on a Saturday afternoon, go to the cinema."* For a club in need of attractive football, Mogga struck a chord. Two directors flew down to interview Mowbray in his own home. By the time their plane landed in Edinburgh, they knew who they wanted as the next Hibs manager to replace Williamson. Their chief executive Lewandowski said: "*Everyone we have spoken to about Tony has given us glowing references on his abilities as a coach, about his philosophy on football, and about his character and integrity.*"

Mogga's philosophy meshed well with a group of hungry young players. In his two full seasons in charge, Hibs finished third and fourth with a stylish display of attacking football. Famously they won once at Celtic and three times at Ibrox. Hibs hadn't previously beaten the 'Gers on their own pitch for a decade. The manager won the Scottish Football Writers' Association Manager of the Year award in his first season. By strange coincidence, his Scottish Player of the Year counterpart that year was one John Hartson. There was never quite enough money for Hibs to make a full breakthrough, not least because Mowbray insisted on the club building their own training ground, rather than making a major signing.

His efforts got him noticed. Tony's easy-on-the-eye playing style, an ability to "grow his own" cheaply, and to compete comparatively well against bigger fish, were all key selling points. Ipswich were first to ask about his availability but Tony turned them down politely. There were also links with Middlesbrough.

In September, West Bromwich Albion made an enquiry. They'd just sacked Bryan Robson, despite the club being just a single point short of third spot in the Championship. There were no vehement protests, but the timing of the sacking was odd.

The Scottish side didn't seem to put up much resistance once the Baggies agreed £120,000 compensation with them. "*When the chance arose to speak to West Brom, a club steeped in great tradition, it was an opportunity I could not turn down,*" said our new recruit.

Mowbray joined the Baggies in mid-October 2006. He was a brave choice, and many watchers were unsure, including cult hero Don Goodman. "*I have to admit I raised my eyebrows when Mowbray was appointed. I didn't think he had the experience as a manager.*" With Mogga now more than an interested onlooker, the Baggies had won in some style at both Ipswich and Crystal Palace, moving up to third in the league.

There can be few better starts to achieving cult hero status than a joyful 3-0 demolition of the Wolves on your official debut. Greening's spectacular volley set the tone for a display of passing football that had the moribund neighbours looking second-rate. But the triumph was followed by five games without a win.

On paper, the Baggies squad was formidable – loaded with expensive-looking individuals like Kamara, Koumas, Ellington, Hartson, Curtis Davies, Robinson, Greening, Gera and recent arrival Kevin Phillips. But some were exactly that – individuals – and unwilling to embrace the team ethic consistently. Jason Koumas could be a match-winner on his day but could also be a liability. Diomansy Kamara had pace and knew where the net was, but was lazy and selfish. Hartson was a bad joke.

Tony quickly saw the squad needed a culture change. He explained to *The Scotsman* in 2008. *"I said to Jeremy Peace that he had to stick with me because there are going to be some choppy times to start with. I took over a team just relegated and some of the squad still looked at themselves as Premiership players. They saw this guy coming down from Scotland they didn't know and didn't want to buy into my work ethic; didn't want to work hard in the training ground to achieve the repetition that is the vital currency in my playing ethos. It was like oil and water. They had big cars, big houses, were on 25 times the money the players I had at Easter Road were on and thought that meant they could go their own way. With transfer windows I needed time to change the make-up of the squad because you can't let the lunatics run the asylum."*

In public, Tony was pointedly supportive of his players, even managing to be polite about Hartson. The dressing room divisions remained there. Most supporters could see that something was not quite right with the team, but exactly what wasn't clear until the season had ended.

In between the frustrating setbacks, such as the four defeats in five matches in November, there were numerous uplifting performances. We demonstrated our superiority against McCarthy's Staffordshire mob five times that season and were unlucky not to win all five. The delicious FA Cup slaughter of the not-so-innocents, and a play-off derby double are both worthy of boring future generations with. The pay-off for the FA Cup victory was a fifth round match against Mogga's hometown club Middlesbrough. Although the cup wasn't a priority for either side, there was an impressive 31,000 attendance, and Tony Mowbray received a rapturous reception from all four sides of the ground. Albion matched the Premiership side and the tie was only settled on penalties after a replay. The cup battles were part of an impressive run of one defeat in 19 matches.

But in the business end of the season, five home matches produced only one point for the cause. Certain players were going missing just when they were needed most. The last regular league game saw a stylish 7-0 demolition of Barnsley completing a season of 100 plus Albion goals.

The new manager insisted on an elegant passing style, and like Margaret Thatcher, was not for turning. *"I was told plenty of times you can't get out of this league unless you adopt a form of kick and rush,"* he admitted. *"But not being able to retain possession, master the football, attack on the flanks and in expansive fashion, has to hold you back at some point. I think I'm doing right for the long term."* In the short term, his unchanging tactics meant that Albion could be bullied or outmanoeuvred in games. Mogga himself understood the problems. *"It hasn't always been easy. There have been times I have been sitting in other managers' offices having a beer after games and they have been drooling about our style, telling me how great it is and what good footballers I have almost to a sycophantic extent… on the back of them beating us 2-0. That is hard to accept, but you don't change what you do, you just try to become better at it."*

Supporter Martyn Cotterill summed up the fans' perspective: *"He can be a little stubborn at times can our Mr Mowbray. He will not change the way we approach games, or how we play during them. When Mowbray is around, you buy into a way of life, a culture and a set of ethics rather than just a football manager."*

As the season reached its business end, Mowbray's men finally clinched a play-off berth in the last game. Following the often nervous play-off victory over the aggressive-as-ever Wolves, hopes soared that Mogga's formula was really working. Unfortunately, there was one big hurdle to overcome – Billy Davies and his Rams. The Derby manager had already countered Mogga's men effectively in both league games. At Wembley, his team's combination of blocking tactics or flying tackles hustled Albion out of their stride sufficiently for County to pinch the game 1-0. It was a horrible afternoon.

Paul McShane declared before Wembley that he wanted to move, irrespective of the result of the final. Others followed suit after the defeat. Peace ensured that he extracted 31 pieces of silver from the sale of Kamara, Koumas, Ellington, McShane and several more. It is noticeable that all those Premier League wannabes found themselves back in the Championship by 2010-2011. Mogga told the *Express and Star* with typical understatement: *"The vibes had been around a little bit of discontent within the dressing room. I don't think it was advisable, even during the week building up to the play-off final, that there were players' advisors talking about players leaving. There was a lack of focus from certain areas and it was pretty evident that needed to change and the chemistry had to improve."*

More positively, here was Mogga's opportunity to bring in new players who fitted his philosophy, more intelligent ball players to produce an even slicker, quicker footballing team, at a lower cost than in the previous season. The midfield was bolstered by new arrivals Chris Brunt, and James Morrison. Big money was also invested in Leon Barnett to improve the defence but this was not one of Mogga's better moves. The back four was to remain suspect throughout the entire campaign, partly because of the emphasis on attack to break down the massed opposition defences. Mogga was candid: *"This is a brutal division, no doubt. Half the teams will stick only one up front and have another nine outfield players behind the ball."*

The new season included several defensive lapses but once up and running, the Baggies were generally able to outscore the opposition. We were unbeaten at home in the league until December when a fired-up Coventry side wanted revenge for a 4-0 hammering we'd inflicted on them at the Ricoh on live TV. (Two months later, we returned to Coventry in the cup and beat them 5-0 to restore the status quo.) By the end of the month, after beating Bristol City 4-1 and Scunny 5-0, the Baggies went top of the table.

Of course, there would be painful setbacks along the route such as the mandatory defeats at Oakwell and at Stoke, plus an embarrassing 2-3 at ultimately-relegated Colchester. There was so much fatigue to overcome when chasing both league and cup success in the New Year. Yet Mogga continued to be brave, urging his charges forward, and his courage paid off.

Just days after a painful Wembley defeat, a lesser side may have caved in at cold, windswept Blackpool. The struggling Seasiders were a goal up and grimly determined to hang on to it. But this Albion fought back in the last ten minutes to win 3-1 to go top of the league.

The equaliser was Albion's 100th goal of the season. Just a few weeks later, Mowbray triumphantly led his team to their third victory at the Custard Bowl in eighteen months. This was a night for strong men to resist a long-ball assault, and a night to have pride in your team. Bouncing up and down after the final whistle, we all knew this Albion side was going up.

A nervous 2-1 victory at Carrow Road virtually guaranteed promotion. We really only needed one point from two games to be sure. A sellout crowd at the Hawthorns wanted to party, but Southampton kept us at bay magnificently until Chris Brunt gave us the late goal and the point required.

This was Mogga's moment, a chance to sell himself and his winning formula. But this modest manager was far more eager to say: "*I'm delighted for the players, the supporters and the staff.*" He went on to add: "*I am portrayed as this guy who is only interested in passing football; I am not. I'm genuinely interested in being successful and giving the supporters joy from the elation of winning football matches.*"

Six days later, the all-important Championship was bolted onto the bare promotion tag. For manager and supporters alike, it was our first League trophy since 1920 and oh my, it felt so good. Sodden in champagne, the guv'nor offered: "*This is a proud moment. When you think back to when we lost to Burnley on the opening day, we've come a long way and made a lot of progress.*" He was then obliged to field numerous questions about whether Albion would survive in the top flight. Perhaps the press were asking the wrong man. His captain, Jonathan Greening, is never noted for his keen insight, but his comment that "*it will be interesting to see if the chairman backs the gaffer to the full*" was perceptive.

TO WIN A trophy, and be crowned as league champions felt so special. This achievement alone elevates Tony Mowbray above other recent managers and was arguably the most significant trophy secured in the last three decades. To mark his achievement, the gaffer won the League Managers' Association Manager of The Year award, to add to his pair of manager of the month successes. For this most likeable of football men, it was significant that tributes quickly poured in from supporters of Hibernian, Celtic, Middlesbrough and Ipswich.

We'd done it playing football in a fiercely competitive division, outthinking rather than outmuscling our opponents. Scoring just one goal wasn't considered enough, Mogga's men always wanted more, albeit not necessarily Luke Moore. They were so often a delight to watch, and recovered from going a goal behind eight times.

We were genuinely close to winning the FA Cup too. After leaving the Posh, Coventry and Bristol Rovers trailing in our goal-strewn wake and swaggering home, we pressed morally-bankrupt Pompey all the way at Wembley.

Supporters wanted an open-top bus parade. So did the council. Runners-up Stoke had one, so too did play-off winners Hull City. But Albion didn't. Someone within the club decided they weren't going to play. Promotion celebrations post-Southampton was truncated due to the midweek lateness of the hour, and QPR was open only to the select few. It remains a curiosity that Mowbray received a more full-on appreciation from supporters for his team being relegated than for winning the Championship. A formal recognition of his and the club's achievements would only have strengthened his hand.

Post-Albion, the Scottish grass wasn't any greener for Tony Mowbray. His philosophy to always build for the future didn't sit comfortably with the pressure to win every game. Furthermore, he'd inherited an unbalanced squad from Gordon Strachan. His side lost 13 of the 45 games under his charge, and he was predictably slaughtered by the Glasgow press. Fighting back, as Mowbray tried to do, just made matters worse. He became the object of ridicule, and the butt of jokes for fans. One popular crack doing the rounds was: *"Mowbray's just been offered a coaching job with the British skiing team. Apparently they were impressed at just how quick he could make a team go downhill."* A particularly toe-curling 4-0 defeat by St Mirren with the accompanying image of Mogga with his head in his hands, forced the board's hand. He was sidelined on gardening leave until the end of his contract. There was regret on both sides. Chief Executive Peter Lawwell: *"This is a sad day for everyone. Tony will always maintain a strong affection for Celtic and I am sure he will always be highly thought of within the Celtic family. He is a man who demonstrates decency and integrity in everything he does."*

Similarly, the Celtic ETIMS website accused Mogga of *"naivety, an inability to find an alternative, poor decision-making and poorer performances"* yet felt compelled to add, *"We all wanted him to succeed. Tony Mowbray, despite all of the above, you leave the club with our best wishes. Whatever the future holds it'll be better than the last eight months for you, the Club and the fans. Good luck, whatever you do next, Tony."*

Mowbray was out of the game for six months. He had several managerial offers but was in no rush because Celtic were obliged to continue paying him until March 2011. Then he got THE call. His hometown club needed a rescue job after Strachan's efforts had the Smoggies in the relegation places.

In October 2010, Mogga turned his back on £350,000 still owed to him by Celtic, and went home with his wife and three young sons. For the second time, he set about untangling Strachan's legacy – an unbalanced squad, an impossibly high wage bill, no scouting system, or any sports scientist assistance. Somehow, under his tutelage, Middlesbrough rose up the table, and finished in the top half of the Championship.

The following season, despite all their limitations, his side made a real fist of going for promotion. Mogga had given his hometown club its pride back.

The last word should go to the man himself: *"I'm a manager with a belief really. I try and manage on a philosophy of playing, a philosophy of life and I try and expect the standards from my players that I try and bring myself to the party. I feel, however you live your life, whatever you do away from the training pitch, however you apply yourself, will bring the benefits... so I am a philosopher-coach. If you want to stick a label on something, I believe in a way of playing, I believe in a way of living your life and I try and bring those qualities to the job...integrity, honesty, humility. I want my footballers to be all those things as well if we can, so when we win I don't want us bleating about it and when we lose we just get back to hard work, take it on the chin and move on. Humility for me is one of the most important human traits and allied with hard work, you give yourself a chance."*